ARCHITECTURAL RESEARCH METHODS

SECOND EDITION

LINDA N. GROAT AND DAVID WANG

WILEY

For general information about our other products and services, please contact our Customer Care
Department within the United States at (800) 762-2974, outside the United States at (317) 572-3993
or fax (317) 572-4002.

Wiley publishes in a variety of print and electronic formats and by print-on-demand. Some material
included with standard print versions of this book may not be included in e-books or in print-
on-demand. If this book refers to media such as a CD or DVD that is not included in the version you
purchased, you may download this material at http://booksupport.wiley.com. For more information
about Wiley products, visit www.wiley.com.

Library of Congress Cataloging-in-Publication Data:

Groat, Linda N., 1946-
    Architectural research methods.–Second Edition / Linda N. Groat, David Wang.
        pages cm
    Includes index.
    ISBN 978-0-470-90855-6 (pbk.); ISBN 978-1-118-41851-2 (ebk);
    ISBN 978-1-118-43353-9 (ebk); ISBN 978-1-118-41547-4 (ebk)
    1. Architecture—Research.   2. Architecture—Study and teaching.   I. Wang, David. II. Title.
    NA2000.G76 2013
    720.072–dc23

                                                                                        2012031765

Printed in the United States of America

10 9 8 7 6 5 4 3

Contents

Acknowledgments

In the years since the initial publication of *Architectural Research Methods,* I've been immensely gratified by the interest of readers whose comments, suggestions, and questions have inspired this second edition. In this regard, I am indebted to many people: colleagues who took the time to answer my queries about what changes might best enhance the new edition, or recommended and/or contributed specific research exemplars; a host of unnamed readers who passed on suggestions through an informal grapevine of commentary; and most especially my students over the years whose insightful questions have challenged me to rethink and reframe the conceptual premises, analyses, and diagrammatic clarity of some of the material in the first edition.

David Wang, my co-author, has remained a steadfast partner whose insights have been absolutely essential to the fruitful pulls and tugs of this collaborative process. I am deeply appreciative of the encouragement and ongoing support from Wiley for this new edition, and especially the guidance of Paul Drougas and Mike New.

I am deeply grateful to the University of Michigan for its continuing institutional support for this project. Funding from the Horace Rackham School of Graduate Studies, Taubman College's Program in Architecture, and the Office of the Vice-President for Research has provided support for research assistants Kush Patel and Justin Ferguson. Kush and Justin have been invaluable in tracking down, organizing, and maintaining the myriad resources and files inherent in a project of this scope, not to mention keeping the inevitable glitches to a minimum.

LINDA GROAT

It is a privilege to issue this second edition of *Architectural Research Methods*. In writing it, I was struck by just how much has progressed in this arena even since the first issue of this book a decade ago. I am once again grateful to work with Linda Groat, from whom I continue to learn. Thanks also to Paul Drougas and Mike New at Wiley, who understood the time it takes to update a manuscript such as this one. Many new contributors made this second edition possible; I hope all their names and affiliations are noted in the pages of this book; a heartfelt thanks to them all.

DAVID WANG

ARCHITECTURAL
RESEARCH METHODS

Part I

The Domain of Architectural Research

Chapter 1

The Scope of This Book

1.1   INTRODUCTION: THE AUDIENCE FOR THIS BOOK

The aim of this book is to provide an introductory handbook for anyone wishing to conduct research—or more informally, inquiry—on an aspect of the built environment—from the scale of a building component, a room, a building, a neighborhood, to an urban center.

By this we mean to suggest that this book is intended to be both comprehensive and an entry point. Our intent is to be comprehensive by providing a single text that addresses the full range of research methods available and applicable to the diverse array of topics germane to architectural research. Our intent is also to offer an entry point by introducing readers to the major characteristics and applications of each research method, while simultaneously providing references to more specific books and articles on the methods of interest.

This overarching goal, as articulated in the introduction to the first edition of this book, remains a constant. However, both the nature and role of architectural research, as conducted in the academy and practice, have gradually shifted over the decade since the first edition was published in 2002. Some areas of inquiry—for example, the multiple dimensions and applications of sustainable design—have become relatively more prominent. Other research foci (e.g., the application of notable schools of thought such as critical theory or poststructuralism to design theory) have waned in some contexts, while the hands-on exploration of digital technologies and prototype fabrication has become a significant emphasis in many settings.

In the academic context specifically, the number of doctoral programs in architecture has increased and now figures at close to 30 programs in North America alone; many schools have likewise initiated or expanded research-based master's programs and/or research studio options.[1] Worldwide, countless other research-oriented programs in architectural and environmental design fields are available to students. Not surprisingly, given the expansion of doctoral programs, the proportion of faculty with PhDs has now risen to over 25% in U.S. architecture programs.[2]

In the realm of practice, the shifting tides of the economy as well as the competitive pressures among professional fields have led many firms to reshape the contours of their practices. Many have incorporated or expanded new realms of services (from distinct specialty niches to expansion into design/build) or sought to enhance collaborative relations with other professional specialists.[3] Many of these initiatives entail an enhanced role for research in professional practice.

Taken together, the recent evolution of the research enterprise in academic and professional settings has, at least from our vantage point, led to an increasing convergence among the constituent audiences for this book. So, although the various audiences are addressed separately in the following paragraphs, we see many overlaps and intersections among them. Certainly, over the course of a lifetime career in architecture or allied field, most people will find themselves in every audience category listed below.

1.1.1   *Students in Doctoral and MSc Programs*

Compared to many other disciplinary and professional fields, architectural research encompasses a relatively wider diversity of substantive foci and methodological choices. Even within academic research programs where there is a more narrowly defined research agenda, students will be well served by an appreciation of how their research specialty is situated within the full spectrum of architectural research, as well as within the entire multidisciplinary research enterprise. To this end, one of the aims of this book is to bring the most engaging and fruitful principles from the robust interdisciplinary discourse on methods to the architectural and design context.

1.1.2   *Faculty Scholars and Researchers*

For at least 40 years now, an increasing number of architectural faculty have chosen research and scholarship, rather than practice, as their academic mission. For faculty who are already well versed in research, this book may either provide a "refresher" text in methodological issues or perhaps expand their horizons beyond the research methods they are most familiar with. For faculty who are new to research, this book aims to serve as a broad introduction to the conceptual framework underlying the research design process.

1.1.3 *Master's and Upper-Level Bachelor's Students*

At some point(s) in their academic program, most, if not all, architecture students will be challenged to undertake some sort of research, whether it be a thesis project, research studio, or a subject area course. And as future professionals, students will need to develop the ability to critically review and understand the basic research foundation of all manner of architectural products and processes. Our intention is to provide a fundamental understanding about the multiplicity of research processes and standards that underlie research in architecture and allied fields.

1.1.4 *Architectural and Design Practitioners*

Although it may not yet be the norm, many firms have in recent years either developed or expanded their research capabilities, and some have established a distinct research arm or division. In some market areas, many client organizations now expect architects to be able to demonstrate capabilities in specific research-based practices, for example, "evidence-based design" (EBD) in the health care field.[4] Regardless of the scale or specialty niche of the practice, most designers will likely conduct some exploratory investigations or more focused inquiry—research, in other words—in the course of a design project. While certainly more limited than a typical research project in academia, the practitioner will still need to spend some time structuring and organizing the inquiry. This book provides the practitioner with a basic guide to thinking through how best to find the answers to the questions that arise throughout a design project.

1.1.5 *All Together Now*

Given the evolving convergence among the diverse readership outlined above, we have found the diagram in Figure 1.1 particularly useful. Overall, the diagram suggests the complementary nature of research and design. While we argue that design and research are relatively distinct domains of activity, they nevertheless share many comparable and similar qualities.

This particular diagram suggests the relative proportion of these two activities on the range of contexts in design and practice. The left-hand third of the diagram suggests that professional program students and practitioners are likely to emphasize design-related activities, while employing research less frequently and more episodically. The middle third of the diagram suggests that students in research master's programs, practitioners in consulting roles, and/or firms specializing in more focused areas of practice are likely to experience a more equal balance of activities. Finally, the right-hand segment of the diagram represents the context in

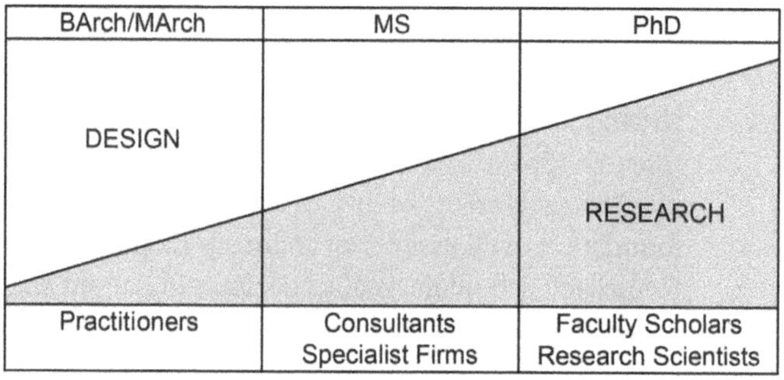

BArch/MArch	MS	PhD
DESIGN		RESEARCH
Practitioners	Consultants Specialist Firms	Faculty Scholars Research Scientists

Figure 1.1   The complementary nature of research and design.

which doctoral students, many research-oriented faculty, and research lab practitioners are more likely to find themselves. For them, the research activity is likely to dominate, even while the research questions may well flow directly from architectural design questions.

In sum, our goal is for each reader to find this book to be a valuable resource for whatever type and quantity of research activity she or he pursues. Our firm belief is that whatever our individual contributions to architectural research may be, ultimately these efforts will not only complement each other but will also substantially further the long-term vitality of the architectural field.

1.2   WHAT IS ARCHITECTURAL RESEARCH?

In one sense, architectural research has been conducted throughout the history of architecture. The development of particular structural forms or building materials over the centuries is the outcome of trial-and-error experimentation, systematic observation, and application of such building principles to other building projects. Take, for example, the development of the flying buttress, the first visible external examples of which are attributed to the nave of Notre Dame de Paris.[5] A combination of archaeological reconstruction and structural analysis conducted by authors William Clark and Robert Mark demonstrates the technical validity of what they conclude to be the original buttress design (see Figure 1.2). However, the authors argue that structural stress points resulting from that design, in conjunction with associated maintenance requirements, seem to have led to the major documented alterations to the buttress system early in the 13th century. More generally, continued modifications and systematic observations in subsequent cathedral projects led to further innovations, and so on. Parallel

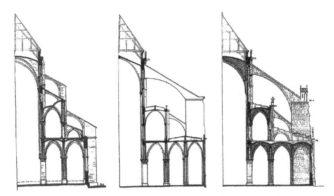

Figure 1.2　Flying buttress. (Left to right) After Sanders and Clark; Clark, after Leconte; Clark, after Chaine. Courtesy of William W. Clark.

developments in all manner of materials and structural innovation can be cited throughout the history of the field.

However, the conduct of architectural research outside the confines of specific building projects is a much more recent phenomenon. Although climate, product development, and building systems design seem to have been a focal point of research in the 1950s, the research enterprise in architecture emerged more broadly across a range of topic areas—including sociobehavioral issues, design methods, and energy conservation—in the 1960s and early 1970s.[6] It was during this period that funding from an array of federal agencies, from the National Science Foundation to the National Endowment for the Arts, became more widely available; university programs provided internal support for architecture faculty to pursue research topics; doctoral programs in architecture began to emerge in greater numbers; architecture-affiliated organizations such as the American Institute of Architects and the Association of Collegiate Schools of Architecture sponsored joint ventures to promote research; a few major architectural firms developed research-oriented divisions; and the professional journals began to publish evaluation studies and/or offer research award programs.

Over the past three decades, this great variety of research activity has continued, but often in a more varied way. Many areas of research have experienced an ebb and flow of funding and interest. Energy conservation, for example, was a dominant feature of much technical research in the 1970s due to the energy crisis, but received much less attention in the 1980s. From the 1990s onward, however, interest in and funding for research in sustainability has reintroduced many of the earlier issues, but now framed within a relatively new conceptual model.

Similar fluctuations in the scope of other substantive topics, the significance of particular theoretical influences, rapid advances in building technologies, innovations in design processes, and so on mean that architectural research will continue to encompass a breathtaking range of research endeavors. That is certainly all to the good, but it also means that mastering the range of research concepts and tools to address such a diversity of research questions is all the more challenging *and* rewarding.

One obvious starting point is simply to consider a basic definition of research. In one of the earliest compendiums on architectural research, author James Snyder provides a commonly accepted definition of research; it is "systematic inquiry directed toward the creation of knowledge."[7] Two elements of this definition are significant. First, the inquiry is systematic in some way. Although one might unconsciously acquire important information simply by strolling down the street observing the array of buildings in view, the notion of a systematic inquiry suggests that there is a conscious demarcation of how particular information is culled from the rest of our experience, how it is categorized, analyzed, and presented.

Most important, however, the term systematic is *not* conceived exclusively in terms of the classic notion of a "scientific experiment," a format of inquiry that is often appropriate to the task, but nevertheless regarded by critics in some fields as being too reductionist. While it is certainly true that structuring a study around precisely defined variables is reductionist, it is just as true that culling or coding key themes from an in-depth interview or historical archives is also reductionist. The truth is that *all* research is reductionist in some form or other. For research to be research, it necessarily involves reducing lived experience or observed phenomena to chunks of information that are noted and categorized in some way. The difference between a lab experiment, a qualitative study of a particular setting, or historical narrative is a consequence of choosing one strategy for reduction over another.

Second, the notion of knowledge creation is frequently cited as characteristic of the research endeavor. To many readers this may seem to imply something on the scale of grand theories of various sciences, akin to Einstein's theory of relativity or geological theories of plate tectonics. Although such theories certainly encapsulate new knowledge, we do not mean to suggest that such theories are the only model of knowledge creation. Rather, we would argue that new knowledge can also emerge through the relatively small increments of knowledge attained through a variety of means, including assessing the outcome of integrating two previously distinct functional building types; materials testing through a series of built projects; or evaluating the success of particular building forms in communicating intended meanings in the public realm.

Finally, though much architectural research may well focus on the physical outcomes of design—from the scale of building components to neighborhood and urban design—research on the processes of design and the practices of architectural firms is just as vital. This is all the more true as a consequence of the use of computer technology in multiple phases of the design process. Also, significant changes across a variety of professions in response to global economic trends make research on the structure and scope of architectural practice key to the future of the profession.

1.3   A CONCEPTUAL FRAMEWORK FOR SITUATING METHODOLOGY IN RESEARCH: STRATEGY AND TACTICS

Having established parameters for defining architectural research, and research in general, the challenge of clarifying "methods" becomes central. In his classic book, *The Conduct of Inquiry*, Abraham Kaplan defines methods as the study of the process, rather than the product, of inquiry.[8] More specifically, he argues for using the term *methodology* for "mid-range" aspects of the research process that are common to a broad range of disciplines. Thus, he is seeking to articulate the processes of inquiry that are simultaneously more *general* than specific techniques of interviewing, archival searches, or data collection and analysis, while also being more *specific* than broad epistemological perspectives that entail assumptions about the general nature of knowledge or being.

Following Kaplan's lead, we use the term *methods* or *methodology* to focus on research processes which are common across the entire range of architectural research, including content areas from the technical to the humanities, and from the most applied to the most theoretical. Figure 1.3 represents a nested set of four frames that describe the conceptual framework in which the level of methodology, or research design, is situated. The outermost framework represents the system of inquiry (sometimes labeled a paradigm or worldview), which entails broad assumptions about the nature of reality, knowledge, and being. For example, the belief system called postpositivism assumes that there is an objective reality that can be experienced and measured. Postpositivism and other systems of inquiry are discussed in considerable detail in Chapter 3.

The next frame represents what we call a "school of thought," a broad theoretical perspective that has significantly influenced multiple disciplines. For example, critical theory and phenomenology operate at this level; and each has significantly influenced the conduct of research in architecture, as well as many other disciplines. These and other schools of thought will be considered and analyzed in Chapter 3

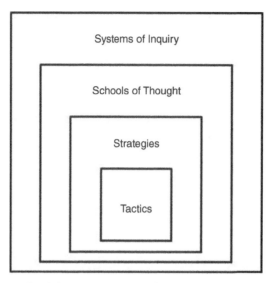

Figure 1.3   The methodological practices of strategies and tactics are framed by broader systems of inquiry and schools of thought.

as well. The adoption of a particular school of thought is likely to influence how research questions are framed, and often imply the use of specific modes of analysis.

Although it is entirely possible to design a research study without aligning it with a particular school of thought, every piece of research is inevitably framed by a system of inquiry, whether explicitly stated or not. Everyone who conducts research is making assumptions about the nature of the world and how knowledge is generated.

Moving on to the relationship between the "mid-range" of methodology and the more specific level of techniques, we have adopted the semantic distinction between *strategy* and *tactics*. This is a common—though not universal distinction—adopted by other authors writing about research methods.[9] Loosely derived from its military origins, the term *strategy* is defined as "the skillful management and planning of anything."[10] This contrasts with the more detailed level of tactics, defined as "any skillful move." In the military sense of these words, *strategy* refers to a nation's overall war plans, whereas *tactics* refers to the disposition of armed forces in combat.[11] In the context of our discussion of research, a strategy refers to the overall research plan or structure of the research study. In contrast, the tactics refer to a more detailed deployment of specific techniques, such as data collection devices, response formats, archival treatment, analytical procedures, and so on.

Thus, we have defined a conceptual model of concentric frames. At the broadest level, the system of inquiry (often linked to a school of thought) frames—but does not predetermine—our choice among a range of methodologies, or strategies. Within any system of inquiry, there are multiple choices of research strategies. Similarly, the choice of research methodology then frames—but does not predetermine—the choice of tactics. Again, multiple tactics are possible within any research strategy. However, there should be coherence and continuity among the four frames of system of inquiry, school of thought (if employed), strategy, and tactics.

We emphasize the conceptual model of the nested framework throughout this book because we firmly believe that it provides a starting point for researchers at all levels of experience, but especially for novice researchers, in refining the conceptual clarity of their inquiry. Indeed, it is not at all uncommon to hear a discussion of research design in which the speaker might remark about his or her choice between using an experimental design and a survey; we would argue that this is mixing up strategy (experiment) with tactics (survey, which is a technique for data collection). Similarly, if someone claims to be doing a phenomenological study, that may accurately reflect the school of thought that frames the research question, but it says nothing about the strategy, the actual plan or organization of the study.

Another term we will frequently use as synonymous with strategy is *research design.* In colloquial terminology, a research design is "an action plan for getting from here to there,"[12] where *here* describes the investigator's research question(s), and *there* describes the results or knowledge derived from the research. In between the here and the there is a set of steps and procedures that may range from being highly prescribed to being emergent as the research proceeds.

More to the point, the term *research design* is one that is particularly appropriate for a readership trained in architecture and/or other design disciplines. In architecture, we often speak of a "parti" in describing the formal organizing concept of a design scheme. Similarly, we often refer to a variety of formal "types"—such as a courtyard form or 9-square plan—that specifies generic spatial relationships (see Figure 1.4). The important point is this: Just as a courtyard plan can be used for such varied purposes as college dorms, houses, museums, or office buildings, a given research design can be employed for a variety of topic areas of architectural research, from thermal comfort studies to analyses of aesthetic theories.

This focus on the formal structure of research designs across a variety of topic areas is also consistent with our goal of providing an integrative framework for architectural research. A common tendency in architecture has been to divide "knowledge" into domains associated with particular subdisciplines. As a consequence, insights derived from research in energy-efficient technologies cannot

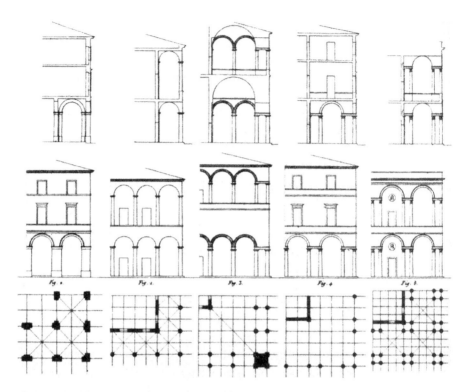

Figure 1.4 The notion of research design as a "type" is analogous to Jean-Nicolas-Louis Durand's development of formal types in architecture.

easily be integrated with insights drawn from aesthetic analyses of exemplar buildings.[13] Yet, we believe that much innovative and needed research in architecture will require integration across such apparently discrete topic areas. By organizing this book in terms of common research designs or strategies, it will be more clearly possible to focus on the commonalities of architectural research across a variety of topic areas and subdisciplinary foci.

In the subsequent chapters of the book, we will address, in turn, each of seven major research strategies, or designs. We have purposefully chosen substantively neutral terms for these research strategies. The intention is to be descriptive of the *structure* of the strategy, and to eschew any assumptions about the subject matter of the research. Readers who scan the table of contents will not see chapter titles containing the familiar terms *theory/criticism research, human behavior research,* or *sustainability research.* Indeed, we hope that this will encourage all of us to think *out of the box.*

Finally, any one book can never be all things to all people. We have intentionally emphasized the level of methodology, or research design, because we believe it is at that level that readers will be most able to appreciate the vast diversity of possibilities in conducting architectural research. Throughout the book we provide examples of how various tactics have been deployed in a broad range of subject areas. Nevertheless, for readers who want to know the ins and outs of survey design, or the best simulation programs for particular technical analyses, we advise readers to begin by reviewing some of the references already cited in our book, supplemented by a search for the abundant literature on all manner of specific tactics.

1.4   WHAT'S NEW IN THE NEW EDITION?

At the beginning of the chapter, we alluded to some of the major shifts over the past decade in the contours of architectural education, practice, and research. In the context of architectural research, in particular, the ebb and flow, substantive emphases, and innovative methodological trends have led us to introduce this second edition of *Architectural Research Methods*. Over the time since the first edition was published we have taken note of comments and suggestions from students and colleagues, in person and often by word of mouth.

While the overall organization of the book remains quite similar, we have made a significant number of changes in the following respects:

- In Part I, we have resequenced, reorganized, rewritten, and added new content to the entire set of five chapters.
- In recognition of the heightened level of discussion on the relationship of design and research, we have expanded on our analysis of this issue, devoting the entirety of Chapter 2 to this topic.
- The many steps in the development of an effective research design are now much more explicitly discussed in two chapters: one on identifying one's research purpose, and another that links the literature review with the pivotal role of the research question.
- Depending on the particular chapter, we have updated varying proportions of the research exemplars we have cited. For example, the chapter on simulation is chock-full of updated exemplars to illustrate several threads of advancement, including increased modeling capabilities, the blurring of modalities in the design process, and the increasing use of 3D and 4D in design concept development.
- In the research strategy chapters that reflect fewer dramatic shifts in either substantive topics or methodology, we have updated a number of citations, but we

have also decided to retain examples of *classic* research studies that are significant in the research tradition of the field. Other studies we have retained in the new edition because they enable us to make a very particular point about the methodological or theoretical issue we aim to illustrate.

- In the visual presentation of the material, we have not only included photos and drawings to reflect newly introduced research exemplars, but we have also redrawn and added new diagrams to clarify theoretical concepts and research processes.

We hope these changes and additions in this second edition serve to enhance the clarity of the material and illuminate the important developments in various domains of architectural research of the most interest to readers.

1.5   THE BOOK AHEAD

1.5.1   *Part I: The Domain of Architectural Research*

Chapter 2 addresses the recurring debate, and the subject of many recent articles and conference sessions, on the relationship of design to research. We analyze the ways in which the two domains of activity are distinct from each other, but likewise share many similar and comparable attributes. From this foundation, we consider the respective roles of research and design in the academic context, with particular attention to recent proposals for how to assess the equivalency of their intellectual and/or creative contribution.

Chapter 3 begins an exploration of commonalities across research strategies by addressing two foundational issues, which apply to research, in general. First, we discuss the range of paradigms—or systems of inquiry—that serve as the epistemological basis for any research study. Within this discussion we consider several frameworks for clarifying the relations between these systems of inquiry. Second, we then examine the similarities and differences in criteria for assessing research quality associated with different schools of thought. Discussion of the specific criteria is framed through a variety of exemplar research studies.

In Chapter 4, we consider the range of purposes for a research study as a starting point in research design. These include contextual purposes, as well as the substantive research purposes—whether geared toward theoretical development or practical application.

In Chapter 5, we discuss the essential, iterative process by which a literature review informs the process of realizing the research question(s), and vice versa. We also underscore the role of the research question(s) as a pivot point in the development of the eventual research design.

1.5.2   *Part II: Strategies for Architectural Research*

Before describing the particular foci of each of the next seven chapters (6 through 12), we describe here their common organizational structure. After a short introduction, we begin with several exemplars of the strategy being examined. In the main body of the chapter, we will discuss the basic characteristics of the strategy, citing further examples of architectural research. With the contours of the strategy clearly in mind, we will discuss some of the common tactics for information gathering and analysis employed within such a strategy. Along the way, we will describe some examples of recent and current research being conducted by students, faculty, and practitioners. A general discussion of the strengths and weaknesses of the strategy concludes each chapter.

Figure 1.5 represents a conceptual model for clarifying the relationship among the several research strategies; as such it also serves as the basis for sequencing the remaining chapters in the book. The basic diagrammatic form is a cylinder.

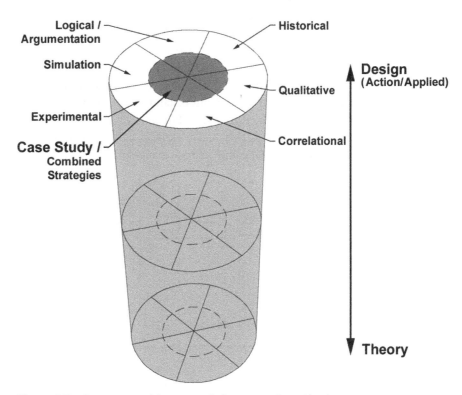

Figure 1.5   A conceptual framework for research methods.

The circular element is defined by pie-shaped wedges, one for each of the six main research strategies. At the center of the circle, there is a "core" that represents case studies and/or combined strategies. The periphery of the circle represents the more distinct and focused exemplars of each particular strategy.

Next, the vertical dimension of the cylinder represents the purpose or outcome of research, defined by the dimension from theory to design (or application). As we have already mentioned, architectural research may be undertaken for different purposes and in different contexts. Sometimes a study of a theoretical concept serves as the initiation of or the outcome of research. Other times, research, particularly in the context of practice, is likely to be initiated with a particular application as the intended outcome.

Finally, a critical feature of the diagram is the sequence of the research strategies within the circle. In the order represented here, each strategy is neighbored by others with common traits. Starting in a clockwise direction with the historical strategy, the diagrammed sequence reflects the chapter order of this book.

Chapter 6 explores the nature of the historical research strategy, which typically draws upon evidence derived from archival or artifactual sources, largely because the research question focuses on a setting or circumstance from the past (see Figure 1.6). In addition, because historical research frequently entails analyses of artifacts or circumstances over time, a narrative form is often employed.

Chapter 7 introduces qualitative research design. Like the historical strategy, qualitative research seeks to understand settings and phenomena in a holistic and full-bodied way (see Figure 1.7). But, whereas historical research seeks discovery through archival and artifactual material from the past, qualitative research typically focuses on social and cultural circumstances that are contemporaneous.

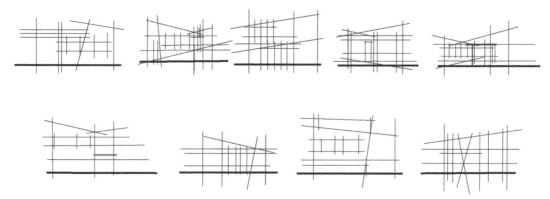

Figure 1.6   A compositional analysis of Popular Modernist housing in Brazil. Drawing courtesy of Fernando Lara.

Figure 1.7 The bedroom window as a place of reverie and withdrawal. From Clare Cooper Marcus, excerpted from *House as a Mirror of Self*, copyright © 1995 by Clare Cooper Marcus, by permission of Conari Press.

Next, in Chapter 8, we move on to the correlational strategy. The signature characteristic of this research design is that specified variables of interest are observed or measured in a particular setting or circumstance. Correlational research, similar to the qualitative strategy, focuses on naturally occurring circumstances, but it makes use of more quantitative data.

In Chapter 9, we explore the nature of the experimental strategy, the research design that is the most completely codified in the research methods literature. Experimental research shares with the correlational design the use of measurable variables, but with a requirement for a treatment controlled by the researcher. For many researchers it stands as the preeminent standard for empirical research because of its precise manipulation of variables (often in a lab setting), with the goal of attributing causality.

Chapter 10 introduces the simulation strategy, which likewise involves control and manipulation of the simulated elements, but it can eliminate the need for empirical testing characteristic of experimental research. The essential characteristic of this research design is that some aspect of the physical environment is recreated in one of a variety of modes, from highly abstract computer simulations to a full-scale, real-life mock-up.

Chapter 11 addresses logical argumentation; it is a strategy that shares with simulation an emphasis on abstraction, but it also entails a self-contained system of logical order. In that regard, it is most similar to the philosophical or mathematical framing of closed systems. Although one uses words or sentences and the other numbers, both represent relatively pure forms of logical argumentation.

And so we come full circle; historical research depends on a constructed logic of interpretation, but that interpretation is based on documents and artifactual evidence, and typically entails a narrative structure.

Finally, in Chapter 12, we find both mixed research and case studies at the core of the cylinder. Although both are ubiquitous as research strategies in architecture, they are of necessity last in our sequence; to employ these overlapping strategies to good purpose requires a working knowledge of the many strategies that are considered in the previous chapters. Increasingly, it appears that researchers across many disciplines are seeking ways to marshal the benefits of two or more research designs. In a similar vein, many other scholars are gravitating toward case study research, a strategy in which a particular setting or circumstance is investigated holistically using a variety of data collection and analysis tactics.

The value of this diagram is as an aid for the researcher in clarifying the nature and structure of his/her proposed study. Just as a schematic diagram or parti in design can serve as a touchstone for the architect throughout the design process, a heuristic device such as this can help the researcher to *define* and *sustain* the essential quality of his/her research design. In principle, we can "locate" on the diagram any research project that you might envision; we invite you to do just that as you begin to explore the possibilities of research design for whatever inquiry you wish to undertake.

NOTES

1. According to the Association of Collegiate Schools of Architecture "Online Guide to Architecture Schools," http://acsa-arch.org/schools/guide-to-architectural-education. Accessed June 28, 2012.
2. "Documents," National Architectural Accreditation Board, www.naab.org/documents/home_origin.aspx?path=Public+Documents\Accreditation. Accessed June 12, 2012.
3. Clifford Pearson, "How to Succeed with Expanded Services," *Architectural Record* (January 1998): 50–55; H. McCann, "Even in a Drought It's Possible to Thrive," *Architect* (February 2010): 18–19; E. Keegan, "First Things First," *Architect* (June 2010): 25–26.
4. Hamilton D. Kirk, "The Four Levels of Evidence-Based Practice," Healthcare Design 3(4), (2003): 18-26.

5. William Clark and Robert Mark, "The First Flying Buttresses: A New Reconstruction of the Nave of Notre Dame de Paris," *Art Bulletin* 66(1) (1984): 47–65.
6. Roger Schluntz, "Design + Energy: Results of a National Student Design Competition," in James Snyder (ed.), *Architectural Research* (New York: Van Nostrand Reinhold, 1984), 39.
7. James Snyder, *Architectural Research* (New York: Van Nostrand, 1984).
8. Abraham Kaplan, *The Conduct of Inquiry* (San Francisco: Chandler, 1964).
9. Groat was first introduced to this vocabulary early in her research career by David Canter, then of the University of Surrey. Although the strategy/tactics distinction is not universally used by research methodologists, a number of authors do make use of it as well (e.g., Denzin and Lincoln, *Handbook of Qualitative Research* (Thousand Oaks, CA: Sage Publications, 1998); Mertens, *Research Methods in Education and Psychology: Integrating Diversity with Quantitative, Qualitative, and Mixed Methods* (Thousand Oaks, CA: Sage Publications, 2010).
10. C. L. Barnhart, *The World Book Dictionary* (Chicago: World Book, 1995).
11. Ibid., 2069.
12. Robert K. Yin, *Case Study Research* (Thousand Oaks, CA: Sage, 1984), 19.
13. Julia Robinson, "Architectural Research: Incorporating Myth and Science," *Journal of Architectural Education* 44(1) (1990): 20–32. See also Michael Joroff and Stanley Morse, "A Proposed Framework for the Emerging Field of Architectural Research," in James Snyder (ed.), *Architectural Research* (New York: Van Nostrand Reinhold, 1984), 15–28.

Chapter 2

Does Design Equal Research?

2.1 INTRODUCTION

In the first edition of this book, we addressed several facets of the relationship between design and research. It is enough here to stake our position on the matter—namely, that there are indeed key differences between the two, which we will elaborate shortly, but then only so we can demonstrate the many similarities and connections between them. In other words, we argue that design and research constitute neither polar opposites nor equivalent domains of activity. Rather, the relationship between the two is far more nuanced, complementary, and robust.

Over the past decade, there has been a particularly lively debate in architecture and allied fields about the extent to which "design" is or should be a template, or more broadly perhaps, a new "paradigm" for research in creative or professional domains. Just within the confines of the peer-reviewed journal, *JAE* (*Journal of Architectural Education*), architectural academicians have taken a notably diverse set of positions on the matter. For instance, in discussing the essential role of research in architecture, Stephen Kieran explicitly describes the relationship between design and research as essentially divergent, but complementary: "Research brings science to our art. . . . To move the art of architecture forward, however, we need to supplement intuition with science."[1] Kieran's discussion of the design research laboratory at the University of Pennsylvania in some ways harkens back to some of the earliest efforts to promote architectural research as voiced in the initial issue of *JAE* in 1947[2] and as represented, for example, by the heyday of the Architectural Research Laboratory at University of Michigan, from its establishment in 1949 through the mid-1970s.[3]

In a second example, author Matt Powers shares with Kieran the assumption that design and research represent essentially distinct domains of activity, but comes to quite a different conclusion about how, or if, the two can be integrated. Indeed, Powers asserts that since research embodies the scientific model of knowledge as "truth" and "fact" based on quantitative data, any overt integration of design and research "diminishes the most important aspects of each activity."[4] Better, he argues that design disciplines work toward the development of a "discipline-dependent scholarship" that moves "away from the shadow of science and toward its appropriate place within academia."[5]

Similarly, author B. D. Wortham argues against research that is "narrowly defined under a scientific rubric," but veers in a slightly different direction by arguing that studio teaching can be research in the sense that "it makes multiple contributions—to the academy, to education, and to the serving and reshaping of society."[6] This view of research as an active contribution to communities, Wortham claims, draws credence from the historical development of land grant universities, and represents a more appropriate model of "discipline-based research."

In a critique of Howard Gardner's theory of multiple intelligences, David Wang and Amber Joplin have proposed yet another way to relate design with research. In explaining why design, curiously, is not one of Gardner's "intelligences," Wang and Joplin proposed that *all* of Gardner's intelligences share implicit traits that are explicit vis-à-vis design. This is because at its most fundamental level, design is related to the innate human ability to plan and pattern any disparate set of inputs toward a comprehensible, or desired, end. In other words, design is a phenomenological "substrate" that permeates "all of Gardner's intelligence categories and thus contributes to their 'end state' manifestations."[7] This is why design cannot be neatly subsumed exclusively under one intelligence category. It should be clear that research, as itself an activity that plans and patterns inputs toward desired ends, is intimately relatable to the human capacity to *design*.

Finally, in a more recent *JAE* article, David Salomon traces the development of the "research studio" as a replacement for the independent design thesis prevalent in many architectural schools.[8] In doing so, Salomon stresses a concept of architectural research that is more pluralistic than most of the previously cited authors, and bears some similarity to Wang and Joplin's position. He sees the research enterprise as encompassing both qualitative and quantitative methods, yielding both "objective truths" and "personal fictions." In other words, both design and research are, he claims, "well-fabricated hybrids."

Although these several examples are by no means fully representative of the diverse points of view in the field, they nevertheless convey some themes common within the architectural academy. One of the most pervasive is a tendency to equate research with a rather narrow view of science as exclusively based on fact and quantitative data, and therefore alien to the intuitive qualities of design. We take a different view of the matter, in at least two respects. First, the range of disciplines commonly implied by the term *science* are in fact more varied in underlying assumptions, methods, and practices than typically appreciated by those outside those disciplines.[9]

Second, we prefer to use the term *research* throughout this book in preference to more focused terms such as *science* or *scholarship*. By research we mean to include works of inquiry occurring across the range of disciplines (sciences, social sciences, the humanities) and professional fields. In this regard, we appreciate the more inclusive perspective expressed in Salomon's article, although we take issue with Salomon's inclination to frame his argument at the level of what we have termed *tactics* (see Figure 1.3), that is, quantitative and/or qualitative analyses. As we indicated in Chapter 1, we believe it is more fruitful to emphasize the broader conceptual level of strategies—or types of research designs—that can be employed across the many topic areas of design research.

2.2   DEFINING DESIGN AND RESEARCH

As is evident from the preceding chapter section, the debate about the equivalence—or lack thereof—between research and design is often contentious and complicated. Moreover, whether explicitly stated or not, many authors (e.g., Wortham, Powers) conflate two issues that are best considered separately: (1) the similarities and/or differences between research and design, and (2) their relative or potential credibility as standards for tenure and promotion in the university context. Both are important issues to address in this context, and for that very reason we aim to disentangle them by discussing them in sequence, moving to the second issue in the later sections of this chapter.

To reprise our introduction to this chapter, we take the stand that design and research are most appropriately and usefully understood as relatively distinct kinds of activity, but they indeed embody many important similarities, including many complementary and overlapping qualities. We will begin by identifying what we believe are the most important distinctions between the two and then describe the many robust similarities they share.

In a somewhat ironic twist, we find ourselves agreeing with some authors whose eventual conclusions we would also dispute. For instance, we very much appreciate Powers's argument that "well meaning [sic] designers and faculty members diminish the value of design by arguing, counterproductively, that design is something it is not, indeed should not aspire to become: research."[10] Yet Powers goes on to argue that there is an underlying epistemological difference between design and research. In contrast, we would argue that both design and research can, and do, occur across a range of epistemological assumptions. Design can be conducted within a postpositivist understanding of knowledge (i.e., usually assumed to reflect the "scientific" method), and research can and does occur within non-"scientific" epistemologies, including what is often referred to as constructivist or subjectivist perspectives.

Throughout this book, we will describe and review many exemplar studies that demonstrate the robust range of architectural and design research across multiple epistemological positions, theoretical schools of thought, and strategies. A detailed discussion of these issues will follow in Chapter 3.

The design (or practice) versus research debate is hardly unique to architecture, and indeed some of the very same discursive positions are found in many other creative or professional fields, including the visual arts, product design, business and consultancy, planning, landscape architecture, and urban design, among others.[11] On one side of this debate, Milburn et al. take a position regarding research in landscape architecture that mirrors Powers's position in architecture: that equating design and research is a disservice to the unique qualities of each, although Milburn et al. do acknowledge that design and research processes have much in common. However, in urban design, Ann Forsyth takes a more integrative approach in looking at how both research and design practice have contributed to innovation in the field. She envisions the potential for urban designers to become "exemplars of interdisciplinary research, serving as the human face of the research turn while expanding and deepening their own body of knowledge."[12]

2.2.1   Design Defined

Over many recent decades, scholars of design theory, researchers, and practitioners have proposed a broad array of definitions to describe the essence of design activity. Two of the most well recognized scholars on the subject are Herbert Simon and Donald Schon. One of Simon's most frequently quoted observations on the nature of design is that designers devise "courses of action aimed at changing existing situations into preferred ones."[13]

Schon, however, maintains that Simon's characterization is too focused on instrumental problem solving with an emphasis on "optimization." Instead, Schon's argument, broadly speaking, is that design thinking is fundamental to the exercise of "reflective practice" in all professions. Following the philosopher Dewey, Schon argues that a designer is one who "converts indeterminate situations to determinate ones."[14] In the more specific instance of the physical design professions (architects, landscape architects, interior designers, etc.), however, Schon conceptualizes their role as making "physical objects that occupy space and have plastic or visual form. In a more general sense, a designer makes an image—a representation—of something to be brought to reality, whether conceived primarily in visual, spatial terms or not."[15]

Several established scholars on design thinking and practice echo Schon's characterization of what physical designers do. Nigel Cross, for instance, argues that "[T]he most essential thing that any designer does is to provide, for those who will make the new artefact, a description of what that artefact should be like. . . . When a client asks a designer for 'a design,' that is what they want—the description. The focus of all design activity is that end-point."[16] Similarly, Bryan Lawson and Kees Dorst, in their book *Design Expertise*, conclude that the "most obvious set of skills employed by all designers are those to do with *making design propositions* [emphasis ours]."[17]

In a similar vein, a characterization that is frequently used to describe design is embodied in one word—*generative.* So, for instance, Cross notes that more experienced designers tend to employ "generative reasoning"; rather than simply finding solutions, designers tend instead to *create* a "generative concept."[18] Likewise, Graeme Sullivan (a scholar of research in art) observes that the artist/scholar John Baldacchino contrasts research and art in the following epigrammatic way: research entails the "search for stuff," while the arts "generate it."[19]

Finally, although both design and research are activities that are typically initiated for a contextually situated purpose, the specific impetus for each is slightly different. In the case of design, the impetus is commonly referred to as a "problem" (e.g., an unmet need for a new building or product) that prompts the development of a designed artifact as a solution that can be achieved in the future. In research, the impetus is typically framed in terms of a "question" to be answered at least in part by examining current or past evidence.

The several themes woven through the commentaries quoted above are highlighted in Figure 2.1 as the primary distinguishing features of design, with the contrasting, but complementary, features of research indicated as well. By "complementary" we mean to emphasize the necessarily reciprocal nature of the design-research relationship. Research can inform design in many ways and at many times in the design process; and the design process and the eventual designed artifact can yield an abundance of questions that lend themselves to many forms of inquiry.

2.2.2   *Defining Research*

In Chapter 1, we briefly discussed some of the primary features of research. Quoting architectural educator James Snyder, who edited one of the first compendiums on

Facets of Difference	Design	Research
Contribution	Proposal for Artifact (from small-scale to large-scale interventions)	Knowledge and/or Application that Is Generalizable (in diverse epistemological terms)
Dominant Processes	Generative	Analytical & Systematic
Temporal Focus	Future	Past and/or Present
Impetus	Problem	Question

Figure 2.1   Matrix of the primary differences between design and research.

architectural research, we defined research as a "systematic inquiry directed toward the creation of knowledge."[20] Remarkably enough, this brief definition remains entirely consistent with characterizations of research in contemporary architectural discourse and academic parlance more generally.

In architecture, for example, Kazys Varnelis posits that "a shared idea of what scholarship is in the university . . . would be in terms of systematic research that produces a 'contribution to knowledge.'"[21] He then uses this definition as a foundation for proposing research studios that would generate "radical results" and help us "reimagine the world anew."[22] Although Varnelis's primary purpose is to apply this definition to the ongoing discourse on research studios, the essence of his definition nevertheless echoes that of Snyder almost 30 years ago.

In the broader academic realm, the definition that the University of Michigan currently provides on its online educational web site for "Responsible Research and Scholarship" also reflects the same two components of both Snyder's and Varnelis's definitions: "systematic investigation" that "contributes to generalizable knowledge." Of significance for our discussion in this book, the university explicitly notes that the term *generalizable knowledge* should *not* be understood as meaning only research that is "hypothesis driven, quantitative, and/or replicable." In other words, the terms *systematic* and *generalizable knowledge* are more broadly construed to apply to research conducted in multiple epistemological frameworks, or systems of inquiry.[23] This wider range of frameworks can be seen later in this chapter, as well as in other chapters of this book.

Similarly, in the architectural context, Salomon's previously cited analysis of research makes the case that research can be understood "as any 'systematic inquiry,' *or* as 'the close study' of something."[24] Just as design "can alternatively be understood as both a rational problem-solving technique or [sic] intuitive aesthetic act," research can be embodied in "multiple modes of inquiry."

Again, as readers will find throughout this book, our definition of research is likewise inclusive of multiple systems of inquiry and theoretical schools of thought. Indeed, we strongly believe that architecture—as well as most design and professional fields—entails such broad multidisciplinary qualities that any one epistemological framework would be inadequate to the task of addressing all the potential research questions within the fields.

2.3 THE COMPARABLE AND SHARED QUALITIES OF DESIGN AND RESEARCH

Having made the case that there are important, necessary, and valuable distinctions to be made between design and research, we now aim to demonstrate the many ways in which they embody comparable and/or shared qualities. By using the term *comparable,* we emphasize features of the two activities that serve similar roles but are not precisely equivalent. And in using the term *shared,* we highlight facets of design and research that maybe are more essentially equivalent but often different in prominence or emphasis. Figure 2.2 summarizes this comparison, and we will highlight them in sequence through this chapter section.

2.3.1 *The Reconstructed Logics of Design and Research*

Over recent decades, both design and research have been the subject of comparable attempts to characterize an idealized model of the sequence and qualities of the

Facets of Similarity	Design	Research
Models of Reconstructed Logic	Systematic Design Process	"Scientific" Method
Multiple Logics	Abductive Inductive Deductive	Abductive (Research Design/Hypothesis Formation) Inductive Deductive
Logics in Use	Generator/Conjecture Model Problem/Solution	Multiple Sequences of Logics, Dependent on Research Questions and Purposes
Scope	Macro/Micro and Mid-level in applied/clinical setting	Big/Medium/Small Theory
Social Context	Situated Practice	Situated Research

Figure 2.2 Comparable and shared qualities of design and research.

processes involved. To clarify the nature of these models, we adopt the term *reconstructed logic* initially proposed by Abraham Kaplan in his classic book, *The Conduct of Inquiry.*[25] Kaplan's purpose was to argue that the idealized notion of the scientific method was an often inaccurate reconstruction of what actually happens in research. Given that Kaplan was writing in the early 1960s, at a time when the positivist epistemological framework was predominant in the sciences and social sciences, his insights are all the more remarkable.

For our purposes in this book, Kaplan's general point is also relevant to comparably idealized notions of the design process that were proposed in the 1960s and 1970s. At that time there was a broad-based advocacy in academia for a more comprehensive design process that would incorporate computing technology, with at least some design theorists anticipating the possibility of essentially automating the entire design process. A related goal behind the proposed systematic model was to ensure that a more fine-grained analytical process would inform design and thereby respond to the increasingly complex nature of architectural projects in a postindustrial society.

In his concise chronicle of this remarkable period in design, Nigel Cross traces how tentatively offered proposals for conceptualizing design became an accepted model for design process that held sway for at least two decades or more. What became widely known as the "systematic design process" is still influential in practice, though much less so now in academia. Never mind that the authors of this model explicitly cautioned that it was *not* intended to replace intuition with logic, but rather incorporate a synthesis of the two.[26]

Nevertheless, in the emergent design methods movement that followed, the systematic design process was broadly accepted as an appropriate "reconstructed logic" consisting of a three-step, potentially iterative, sequence consisting of analysis-synthesis-evaluation (see Figure 2.3). The overall goal was to externalize the logical activities into charts, diagrams, and the like (especially in step 1) so that the designer would be left free to generate ideas and intuitive hunches during the synthesis step, 2. Finally, in step 3, several alternative design solutions would be evaluated according to an array of performance criteria, and the optimum solution selected.

This model of design also gave rise to the concept of "programming" (associated with the analysis step) as a professional niche in architectural practice, and to the "post-occupancy evaluation" (POE) of recently built projects, typically conducted in-house by the architectural firm that designed the project, or by external consultants/researchers. Both of these professional specialties remain important to contemporary architectural practice, but are not as universally employed as some proponents initially imagined.

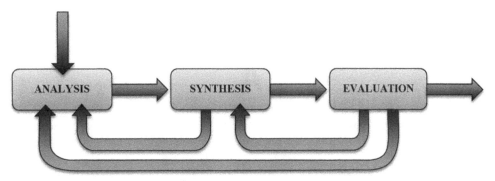

Figure 2.3   The Systematic Design Model. Courtesy of Taylor & Francis.

BOX 2.1

Programming and Evaluation within the Systematic Design Model

J. Christopher Jones, one of the earliest and influential proponents of systematic design, employs the term *black box* to emphasize how the design process itself is often challenging for even a designer to analyze.[a] One way to reduce the mystery of the "black box" is to know as much as we can going into the project, and then evaluate the outcomes of the project after completion so that we can be more informed about the next design effort. The utility of programming is that it aims to maximize the amount of information about a project so that the figural concepts generated can optimally respond to those criteria. These can include an almost boundless list of factors, but much of the early work in programming concentrated on "user needs" as well as energy conservation.[b]

The idea of programming as an effort to maximize knowledge about the figural concepts of design may be seen in Donna Duerk's *Architectural Programming*, a text with the subtitle *Information Management for Design*. In Figure 2.4, Duerk incorporates the three phases of the systematic model of design process with two additional components: the

---

[a] J. C. Jones, *Design Methods*, 2nd ed. (New York: Van Nostrand Reinhold, 1992), 46–51.
[b] Gerald Weisman, "Environmental Programming and Action Research," *Environment and Behavior* 15(3) (May 1983): 383.

(Continued)

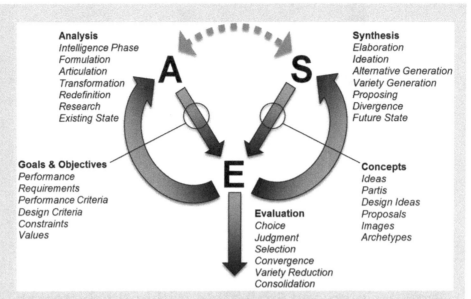

Figure 2.4 The Design Process: Analysis, Synthesis, and Evaluation. Reprinted with permission of Wiley.

performance objectives of the eventual design, and concepts "(design ideas) that develop from the synthesis activities." The same figure (Figure 2.4) also introduces another adaptation of the systematic model, in that "the line between analysis and synthesis is not solid. This is to emphasize that good design ideas do not automatically follow analysis."[c]

Although in-depth programming is most commonly advocated for complex projects with many key determinants unknown or ill defined, almost all design projects beyond ones that make use of existing prototypes (such as big-box stores) involve some programming. Across these variations in the scale and intensity of programming activities, there are multiple viewpoints concerning the extent to which programming is integrated with design development. On the one hand, many advocates for an expansive scope for programming insist that it occur as a separate phase before design activities are initiated.[d] On the other hand, Duerk suggests that for smaller projects and those for which the architect is conducting

[c] Donna P. Duerk, *Architectural Programming: Information Management for Design* (New York: John Wiley, 1993): 18–19.
[d] J. Harvey and J. Vischer, "Environmental Design Research in Canada: Innovative Governmental Intervention." In D. Duerk and D. Campbell (eds.), *EDRA 15, The Challenge of Diversity* (Washington, DC: EDRA, 1984); W. Pena, S. Parshall, and K. Kelly, *Problem Seeking: An Architectural Programming Primer*, 3rd ed. (Washington, DC: AIA Press, 1987).

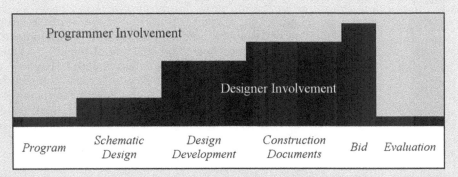

Programmer Involvement

Designer Involvement

| Program | Schematic Design | Design Development | Construction Documents | Bid | Evaluation |

Figure 2.5 Programmer/Designer Involvement in the Design Process. Reprinted with permission of Wiley.

programming activities, there may considerable overlap in the programming and design processes (see Figure 2.5).[e]

At the other end of the design process is post-occupancy evaluation, or POE. After-the-fact data collection is another way of reducing the unknowns of the black box of the design process, at least for future projects. Three kinds of clients tend to commission POEs: those accustomed to developing a series of buildings, those venturing into a new situation with uncertainty, and organizations characterized by an openness to new information.[f] POE can lead to greater understanding of the existing design, with cost-savings ramifications. For example, a POE found that columns in a Phase I office building prevented optimal allocation of secretarial work stations, a problem alleviated in the Phase II design stage. POEs can even be coupled with simulation research. For example, a major engineering firm directed the architect to design their new facility with open office planning. However, the architect was able to persuade the client to first study this idea in a 30-person mock-up of such a space; the resulting noise levels changed the owner's mind back to enclosed office planning.

In a classic book on the methods and procedures of POE studies, Preiser et al. divide POEs into three levels of complexity.[g] An *indicative* POE is one that analyzes as-built drawings, indexing them to safety and security records, and employs interviews of building occupants to understand building performance. An *investigative* POE goes one step further by comparing the existing situation with other comparable facilities and with the

---

[e] Durek, *op. cit.,* p. 19.

[f] Craig Zimring and Polly Welch, "POE: Building 20-20 Hindsight," *Progressive Architecture* (1988): 60.

[g] W. F. E. Preiser, H. Rabinowitz, and E. T. White, *Post-Occupancy Evaluation* (New York: Van Nostrand Reinhold, 1988): 53–65.

(Continued)

prescriptions of the current literature. A *diagnostic* POE involves multi-method tactics (surveys, observations, physical measurements, etc.), all conducted with comparison to other "state-of-the-art" facilities. Readers are referred to their work for more details of each POE type.

The problem with pre and post data collection is obviously that the "episodes" of research are limited to the introduction and the epilogue. The "middle zone," that is, the design process itself, is left unaddressed; a concern that has led other design scholars to propose alternative models.

These efforts to promote a more systematic, comprehensive, and clearly sequenced process were also seen as providing the design professions with a conceptual foundation more comparable to that which supported scientific research. Writing in 1972, Hillier et al. characterized the systematic design model as one that incorporated "as many factors as possible within the domain of the quantifiable" with the goal of replacing "intuition and rules of thumb with knowledge and methods of measurement."[27] They go on to suggest that the impetus for the problem-solving focus of the systematic model of design is based on the two outdated assumptions about the nature of science: "the notion that science can produce factual knowledge, which is superior to and independent of theory; and the notion of a logic of induction, by which theories may be derived logically from an analysis of facts."[28]

In many ways, Hillier et al.'s criticism of the design methods movement of the 1960s and early 1970s links this discussion back to Abraham Kaplan's 1964 book, *The Conduct of Inquiry*, mentioned earlier. Kaplan's critique of the dominant "reconstructed logic" of the social sciences of that era very much mirrors Hillier et al.'s critique of "systematic" design. As Kaplan puts it, "The hypothetico-deductive model reconstruction fails to do justice to some of the logic-in-use, and conversely, some of the reconstructed logic has no counterpart to what is actually in use."[29] In particular, he argues that in the hypothetico-deductive reconstruction "the most important incidents in the drama of science [the formation of hypotheses] are enacted somewhere behind the scenes."[30]

Kaplan then goes on to observe that while "everyone" recognizes that "imagination, inspiration, and the like are of enormous importance in science," the formation of hypotheses is treated as "an extralogical matter."[31] Rather, he argues, the intuition entailed in generating a hypothesis "has its own logic-in-use, and so must find its place in any adequate reconstructed logic." Furthermore, he argues: "To ask for a systematic procedure that guarantees the making of discoveries . . . is surely asking too much."[32] Indeed, the "logic of discovery" embodied in invention can be "cultivated."[33] In sum, Kaplan's stance—not unlike Hillier et al.'s viewpoint on the systematic design model—is challenging the rather limited model of reconstructed logic in science by arguing for an appreciation of the role of intuition in the logic-in-use of scientific discovery.

2.3.2   *The Logics-in-Use in Design and Research*

Significantly, as we have noted in the previous chapter segment, the perspectives of both the design and research literature reveal an implicit convergence with respect to logics-in-use. Indeed, threads of arguments in both literatures draw on (sometimes explicitly, often implicitly) the insights of Charles Sanders Peirce, known as the "father" of the American tradition of philosophical Pragmatism in the late 19th century. Peirce was somewhat of a Renaissance man in that he was also a practitioner of multiple scientific disciplines.[34] Subsequent philosophers and scholars of philosophical Pragmatism include John Dewey and, more recently, Richard Rorty.

BOX 2.2
The Role of Deduction and Induction[a]

To build up a conceptual framework . . . to anchor the variety of approaches that designers take . . . it may be strategic to temporarily suspend the generation of "rich" descriptions of design and instead take a "sparse" account as our starting point. . . . A "sparse" description derived from logic will help us to explore whether design is actually very different from other fields—and should provide us with some insight on the potential value of introducing elements of design practice into other fields. . . . We will describe the basic reasoning patterns that humans use in problem solving by comparing different "settings" of the knowns and unknowns in the equation:

$$\textbf{WHAT} + \quad \textbf{HOW} \quad \text{leads to } \textbf{RESULT}$$
$$\text{(thing)} \quad \text{(working principle)} \quad \text{(observed)}$$

In *Deduction*, we know the "what" (the "players" in a situation we need to attend to), and we know "how" they will operate together. This allows

[a] Reprinted from Design Studies, 32/6, K. Dorst, "The Core of 'Design Thinking' and Its Application," pp. 521-532, (2011), with permission from Elsevier.

(Continued)

us to safely predict results. For instance, if we know that there are stars in the sky, and if we are aware of the natural laws that govern their movement, we can predict where a star will be at a certain point in time.

Deduction: **WHAT + HOW** leads to **???**

Alternatively, in Induction, we know the "what" in the situation (stars), and we can observe results (position changes across the sky). But we do not know the "how," the laws that govern these movements. The proposing of "working principles" that could explain the observed behavior (aka hypotheses) is a creative act.

Induction: **WHAT + ???** leads to **RESULT**

This form of reasoning is absolutely core to the "context of discovery" in the sciences: this is the way hypotheses are formed. Within the sciences, these hypotheses are then subjected to critical experiments in an effort to falsify them. These rigorous tests are driven by deduction. Thus, in the sciences, inductive reasoning informs "discovery," while deductive reasoning informs "justification." These two forms of analytical reasoning help us to predict and explain phenomena in the world. Indeed, though induction contributes to hypothesis generation, philosopher of science C. S. Peirce argues that induction is often an insufficient form of reasoning for hypothesis generation and that abduction is required.

For his part, Kaplan explicitly invokes the heritage of Peirce and Dewey, both of whom sought to explicate the *process* of science [emphasis ours]. Similarly, in a notable 1976 paper on the logic of design, Lionel March discusses the relevance of Peirce's analyses of different categories of inference: deductive, inductive, and especially abductive logic. More specifically, March elucidates Peirce's notion of abductive logic as a type of "synthetic" inference essential to hypothesis generation in science, or as Peirce phrased it: how hypotheses are "caught."[35] In elaborating this concept, March quotes Peirce as follows: "[A]bduction is the only logical operation which introduces new ideas; for induction does nothing but determine a value; and deduction merely evolves the consequences of a pure hypothesis."[36]

In light of Peirce's characterization of abductive logic, March suggests that another term for this type of inference is *productive reasoning,* and as such is an essential characteristic of design thinking. To be sure, March acknowledges the role of deduction and induction in design, summarizing the roles of the categories of inference in this way: "production [abduction] creates; deduction predicts; induction evaluates."[37]

In more recent years, a number of scholars of design studies have also written extensively about the significance of abductive thinking in design process. For one, Nigel Cross in his book, *Design Thinking*, observes that "intuition is a convenient, shorthand word for what really happens in design thinking. The more useful concept ... used by design researchers is abductive: a type of reasoning ... which is the necessary logic of design. It ... provides the means to shift and transfer thought between the required purpose and function and appropriate forms for an object to satisfy that purpose."[38]

BOX 2.3
The Role of Abduction in Design[a]

But what if we want to create value for others, as in design and other productive professions? Then the equation changes subtly, in that the end now is not a statement of fact, but the attainment of a certain "value."

WHAT +   HOW   leads to VALUE
(thing)   (working principle)   (aspired)

The basic reasoning pattern in productive thinking is Abduction. Abduction comes in two forms—what they have in common is that the outcome of the process is conceived in terms of value.

The first form, Abduction-1, is often associated with conventional problem solving. Here we know both the value we wish to create, and the "how," a "working principle" that will help achieve the value we aim for. What is missing is a "what" (an object, a service, a system), that will give definition to both the problem and the potential solution space within which an answer can be sought.

Abduction-1: **???** + **HOW** leads to **VALUE**

This is often what designers and engineers do—create a design that operates with a known working principle, and within a set scenario of value creation. This is a form of "closed" problem solving that organizations in many fields do on a daily basis.

The other form of productive reasoning, Abduction-2, is more complex because at the start of the problem solving process we ONLY know the end

---

[a] Reprinted from Design Studies, 32/6, K. Dorst, "The Core of 'Design Thinking' and Its Application," pp. 521-532, (2011), with permission from Elsevier.

(Continued)

value we want to achieve. This "open" form of reasoning is more closely associated with (conceptual) design.

Abduction-2:   **???**   +   **???**   leads to **VALUE**
                     (thing)   (working principle)   (aspired)

So the challenge in Abduction-2 is to figure out "what" to create, while there is no known or chosen "working principle" that we can trust to lead to the aspired value. That means we have to create a "working principle" and a "thing" (object, service, system) in parallel. The need to establish the identity of two "unknowns" in the equation leads to design practices that are quite different from conventional problem solving (Abduction-1).

One well-known study of logics-in-use in architectural design was conducted by Jane Darke,[39] and has over the years achieved the status of classic study of design process and is now "well-embedded in the literature."[40] Working on her doctorate with established design researcher Bryan Lawson, Darke studied the process by which individual architects went about designing award-winning public housing projects in Britain. What she discovered is that these architects typically came up with a major design idea early on in the process, effectively narrowing down the range of potential solutions.

Based on the observed logics-in-use employed by these architects, Darke's proposed model of design process that has come to be known as the "primary generator" model (see Figure 2.6). The initial primary generator of design is the selection of a "guiding principle" that "enabled the designers to limit the problem to something manageable, to provide a narrower focus in which they could work."[41] This generative concept then serves as the basis of an initial conjecture of the actual design; and that conjecture in turn becomes the basis for evaluating how well the conjecture meets the myriad of detailed requirements of the project. This way of

Figure 2.6 Darke's Primary Generator Model. Courtesy of Taylor & Francis.

designing is essentially consistent with Peirce's notion of abductive thinking as the creative force in reasoning.

Other design scholars also explicitly recognize the essential equivalence of Peirce's general categories of inference in both design and research, especially with reference to the significance of abductive logic. For example, Roozenburg concludes: "Innovative abduction is the key mode of reasoning in design and therefore highly characteristic for this activity. But it is not unique to design. In both science and technology, and in daily life, abductive steps are taken in the search for new ideas."[42] Roozenburg also notes, quoting Peirce, that abductions typically come to us "in a flash," a point that echoes both Kaplan's and Cross's recognition of the role of "intuition" in research and design respectively. Design scholar Panagiotis Louridas takes this line of argument a step farther by concluding that "good science is an art. . . ."[43]

Over the past decade, researchers in various professional fields and/or interdisciplinary areas of inquiry have written as well on the role of abductive reasoning in research. This seems especially true of researchers who identify themselves with either the Pragmatic school of thought (see Chapter 3) and the use of mixed methods in research[44] (see Chapter 12). Typically, researchers who seek to illuminate complex phenomena in real-life settings may not be able to rely on well-established research designs (strategies) and tactics to address the research questions of interest. In this relatively uncertain context, designing the most effective research protocol is not unlike the challenge architects and other designers face in approaching a novel project, and therefore the need to generate innovative hunches and conjectures will be greater.

Nevertheless, as Figure 2.2 suggests, the relative predominance of abductive thinking in physical design is likely to be greater than in the development of a research design or hypothesis generation. Although designers must incorporate deductive and inductive thinking throughout the design process, at least through schematic or design development, abductive thinking is likely to predominate; whereas in research there is likely to be a relatively higher proportion of deductive and inductive thinking throughout the several phases of a study.

One way to understand the relative predominance of these reasoning types in design versus research is to consider the "episodic" nature of each activity. In his 1987 book, *Design Thinking*, Peter Rowe uses the term *episode* to analyze the segments of time and thought employed by the designers he observed as they generated their design schemes for architectural projects. Similarly, researchers typically move through different phases of thinking as they work through various phases of inquiry to discover the answer(s) to the research question(s) posed.

In general, then, designers may well incorporate "episodes" of research activity as they move forward in the more dominantly generative mode of design; and inversely, researchers may well incorporate episodes of "design" (abductive reasoning) in more predominantly analytical reasoning.

To the extent that the "primary generator model" and/or similar analyses of logics-in-use employed by designers are accurate representations of the design process, research episodes may well occur in the midst of evaluating various conjectures—whether a conjecture for the entire project or for segments of it. And what of the systematic design process, which we initially labeled as an idealized reconstructed logic?

To the extent that the model of analysis-synthesis-design is loosely associated in practice with the concepts of programming and post-occupancy evaluations, the model continues to maintain influence in architectural practice. Nigel Cross, among others, has argued that expert designers tend to prefer a breadth-first (as opposed to depth-first) design process, which is more consistent with the primary generator model. However, in "situations where their knowledge is stretched," designers are more inclined to go with a depth-first approach.[45] And this may mean that for novel, complex, and challenging design projects, architects may well find it important to incorporate an in-depth analysis phase at the outset, including multiple episodes of research.

Moreover, in practice, many design projects may be developed through a process that entails either a variation or a hybrid of the two models. A recent project by the architecture firm Perkins & Will demonstrates a more fluid and multifaceted design process than was originally proposed by proponents of the systematic design process. Faced with the need to update their Atlanta office, the firm decided to conceive of the challenge as a "living lab" project that included an extensive pre-/post-occupancy evaluation process. This process incorporated many facets of analysis—from technical performance criteria to operational and aspirational issues. Substantive details of the research conducted in this project are discussed in Chapters 7 and 8.[46]

BOX 2.4

Elaborations of the Primary Generator Model, Framing, and Schemata

Since the publication of Jane Darke's "primary generator" model[a] of 1979 challenged the previously proposed systematic design model, a

[a] Jane Darke, "The Primary Generator and the Design Process," *Design Studies* 1(1) (July 1979): 36–44.

number of other scholars have proposed other formulations that are essentially consistent with the premise of Darke's model. These more recent contributions nevertheless highlight somewhat different qualities or dynamics that may be entailed in the generator-conjecture formulation. They likewise serve as a counterpoint to Simon's "rational problem-solving" model.

Donald Schon's concept of "reflective practice" is described in detail elsewhere in this chapter. In brief, Schon aimed to elucidate how tacit knowledge is intuitively drawn upon by practitioners who must take action in a given situation. This leads Schon to propose a model of how "a reflective conversation with the situation" proceeds from "posing a problem frame and exploring its implications in 'moves' that investigate the arising solution possibilities"[b] (see Figure 2.7). The potential consequences of these moves are then evaluated and new frames or moves may be considered. This formulation of reflective practice is very much consistent with Darke's model, but is more generally applicable to professional practices beyond design.

In a similar vein, Peter Rowe's in-depth investigation of the design processes of three expert architects illuminated yet another implication of the generator model. Like Darke's interviewees, the three architects Rowe studied each in different ways adopted a primary generator as an organizing principle early on, but in some instances these designers also demonstrated a tendency to stick with their initial concept for too long. "Even when severe problems are encountered, a considerable effort is made to make the initial idea work, rather than stand back and adopt a fresh departure."[c] Rowe goes on to observe that in their "attempts to adhere to the 'big idea,'" designers sometimes seemed "to cram the building into the architectural object they were shaping." In other words, while the

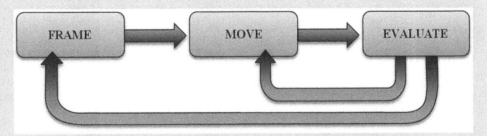

Figure 2.7 Schon's Model of Reflective Practice. Courtesy of Taylor & Francis.

---

[b] Nigel Cross, *Design Thinking* (Oxford, UK: Berg, 2011): 23.
[c] Peter Rowe, *Design Thinking* (Cambridge, MA: MIT Press, 1987): 36.

(*Continued*)

primary generator often seems to serve as an essential kick-start to the design process, it can occasionally delay effective or timely resolution of the design process.

Established scholars of design process Bryan Lawson and Kees Dorst point out the significance of how design students learn, and design experts are able, to "recognise [design] situations" and "draw parallels with situations from other contexts."[d] Drawing on terminology from cognitive psychology, the authors describe how design expertise must rely on the accumulation and cultivation of "schemata." They argue that "[b]ecause design is highly situated, generic solutions usually provide poor outcomes. . . . Designers thus depend on the ability to recognize parallels with well-known situations but also detect subtle variations."[e] The notion of schemata applies not only to individual designers but also to firms. Indeed, the community of professionals within a design firm may share "a common understanding of the relative importance (as the members of the practice see it) of various known schemata." The advantage of such collectively shared schemata is that a coherently conceived design is likely to result from these circumstances, but the downside reprises Rowe's conclusion that designers can stick with a guiding principle for too long or in the wrong circumstances.

Finally, Paton and Dorst's research study of expert designers' experience of briefing processes with their clients (their resulting typology of designer roles is discussed elsewhere in the chapter) returns us to Schon's concept of framing.[f] The authors' general conclusion is that when the designers' roles in the briefing phase are relatively more collaborative, this typically entails a mutual reframing process with the clients and overall the collaborative reframing process tends to yield more innovative design outcomes. Figure 2.8 highlights both the barriers and enablers of this reframing. The barriers include: *fixation* by the clients on their initial idea; a *problem-solving mental model* of design; and a *resistance to the journey* entailed in the design process. Although these barriers were primarily framed in terms of the client, designers may fall prey to these barriers as well. To counter these tendencies, the expert designers generally work to reframe the design "problem" by use of *metaphor or analogy, contextual engagement* (which entails exploring more about the situation with the client), and exploring possible abstract verbal or sketched *conjectures*.

---

[d] Bryan Lawson and Kees Dorst, *Design Expertise* (Oxford, UK: Elsevier, 2009): 148.

[e] Ibid., 164.

[f] Bec Paton and Kees Dorst, "Briefing and Reframing: A Situated Practice," *Design Studies* 32(6) (November 2011): 573–587.

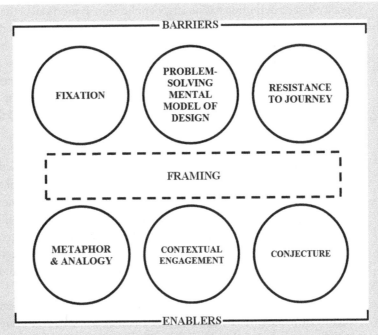

Figure 2.8 Barriers and Enablers to Reframing During Briefing. Redrawn from Bec Paton and Kees Dorst, "Briefing and Reframing: A Situated Practice," *Design Studies* 32(6) (November 2011): 585, with permission from Elsevier.

2.3.3 *The Scope of Design and Research*

Multiple scholars of research and design have conceptualized the variations in the scope and application of each activity by employing terminologies of scale. In the research domain, Gary Moore has employed the terms *big, middle range,* and *small.* So, for example, at the "big" end of the scale are very ambitious theories that explain a large scope of reality. The theory of gravity, which explains both the drop of a coin and the movement of planets, is such a theory. Relativity theory is also such a theory. Truly a large scope of coverage is envisioned by Stephen Hawking's references to GUT ("grand unified theory"). Hawking aims to unify the various fundamental forces in the cosmos (the strong nuclear force, the weak nuclear force, and the electromagnetic force) into a single explanatory framework.[47]

At the other extreme are small, localized explanations for things. "I get depressed when the sky is overcast" may be a kind of small theory. It explains a very localized reality that by definition has no larger application. It meets all of the requirements of a theory, but the explanatory utility in terms of scope is very limited. At this scale, as Moore points out, there may be little functional difference between theory and fact gathering. In other words, if I get depressed when the sky is overcast, the localized domain of applicability (in other words, me) does not require systematic theorizing or, for that matter, research. If the phenomenon is consistent, the relationship between overcast sky and how I feel is sufficient as a set of related facts, and can be simply relied on as a working hypothesis.[48]

Following R. K. Merton, Moore then suggests theories of the "middle range," that is, ones with a scope not grand but also not small. These will not have wide applicability across disciplines; but they do have sufficient applicability to make their claims useful in a scope that is applicable within a discipline. Because of this larger scope, they cannot simply remain as working hypotheses or conjectures; the demand is greater that they be tested and either affirmed or rejected. Some examples of middle-range theory that have been established in architectural research include "defensible space" (see Chapter 8) or the primary generator model of design process discussed in this chapter.

In principle, all research may generate theory across these scales, but in architecture and allied fields, the likelihood is that research will more likely generate middle-range theory than big theory. This is the case for at least two reasons. First, since architecture is a professional field, much of the thrust of inquiry is directed to applied or situated contexts. Second, compared to the research traditions of "purer" academic disciplines, research in architecture and related design and professional fields is relatively newer, and therefore less developed. So, in that sense, there has been less opportunity to refine broader levels of theory that would apply across the multiple threads of architectural research.

More recently, Ken Friedman, a scholar of design process, has similarly described the comparability of research and practice in terms of the scale of application using the terms *macro, midlevel,* and *micro*.[49] In this framework, Friedman argues that "basic" research by definition involves "a search for general principles," which are then "abstracted and generalized to cover a variety of situations and cases."[50] And although basic research may address all three levels of scope, from micro to macro, he argues that applied research tends to be midlevel or micro. Nevertheless, he argues, "applied research may develop or generate questions that become the subject of basic research." Design practice, he asserts, is usually restricted to clinical (or micro-level) research and "generally involves specific forms of professional engagement. . . . In the flow of daily activity . . . , [t]here isn't time for anything else."[51]

In contrast to Friedman's analysis, much of what is often recognized in academia as architectural design theory is envisioned as "big" theory (e.g.,

Le Corbusier's "A house is a machine for living"; or the Modernist "form follows function"); yet we argue that such examples are more properly understood as polemic theory. Since their purpose is to spur the use of a particular generative principle in design, such theories are essentially speculative. To be sure, speculative theory is well recognized in basic research disciplines as a generative instigation for hypothesis testing in subsequent research[52]; yet further research on the viability of speculative design theories in architecture is rare (see Chapter 4).

However, what is commonly referred to as theory in the realm of architectural history is often the application of what we have termed broad cross-disciplinary *schools of thought,* such as critical theory or poststructuralism (see Chapter 3).

In summary, to reference Friedman's position again, any of the three scales of research may generate questions at one or more of the other scales, so in essence each "may test the theories and findings of other kinds of research."[53]

2.3.4   *Situated Design and Research in Action and Collaboration*

Over recent decades, many scholars have written about how the practices of both design and research must be fundamentally understood as activities situated within the social context. In the academic setting, for instance, even students working on individual design projects are engaged within the larger culture of studio practices. And as Dana Cuff's classic book, *Architecture: The Story of Practice,* reaffirmed, the practice of architecture is of necessity a social one, requiring effective engagement with design team members, consultants, and an array of clients and other stakeholders.[54]

Perhaps the most well-known and highly regarded example of this perspective in design practice is Donald Schon's concept of *reflection-in-action.* The term denotes the *actual* need in the professions to solve problems arising out of practical life-contexts.[55] Schon proposes that design activity is a particular instance of reflection-in-action.[56] Schon looks for patterns within context-specific design venues (e.g., a project in a design office, the history of interactions between instructor and student in the studio and its effect on the design). The emphasis is upon the specific design venue as a kind of microculture, complete with ways of doing, implicit understandings, technical terms, and so on, that all arise in the midst of creating a design. What results is a product that is the sum of the reflective actions taken in response to the factors unique to the concrete context.

In research, there has been a long-standing recognition of the importance of research that engages the specificity of real-life situations. *Action research* is a term given to studies that examine a concrete situation, particularly the logic of how factors within that situation relate to each other as the process moves toward a specific empirical goal. The emphasis is on knowledge emerging from localized settings, as opposed to abstract knowledge applicable for many settings. Action research arises out of the social sciences; it has roots in the work of sociologist Kurt Lewin's notion of *field theory*, which basically holds that theoretical knowledge and practical knowledge must inform each other in a concrete context for the establishment of a true domain (field) of endeavor.[57] The applicability of this notion to the generative design process is quite evident.

A more focused version of action research is *design-decision research,* proposed by Jay Farbstein and Min Kantrowitz.[58] In action research, the researcher is still outside of the concrete situation as he or she examines the iterative cycles of actions taken. Design-decision research embeds the researcher more into the actual concrete process; indeed, the authors underline the point that the "researcher" in their model can be the various players of a process themselves. In this sense, "researchers" and "designers" are "one community" and not two: facility programmers, architects, market analysts, communications consultants—in short, any player—can be a kind of "new practitioner" that not only makes decisions but also assesses those decisions from the perspective of research.[59] Farbstein and Kantrowitz give the example of a bank that wished to build a wing outfitted appropriately for its "high-value" customers. But in-depth interviews and focus group discussions revealed that the better approach would be to provide spaces for individualized personal contact, thus avoiding alienating other customers while providing the personal attention the management wanted for the elite clients. It is easy to see how these interventions can aid in the overall design process in an episodic fashion. It is also easy to see how, when design incorporates these approaches, research strategies addressed elsewhere in this book (for instance, in Chapter 7 on qualitative research) can be harnessed for design decisions. Farbstein and Kantrowitz themselves list many "phases" of a building's life cycle to which this approach can be applied: "planning, programming, feasibility studies, design, construction, operation, fine tuning, renovation, maintenance, repair and so forth."[60]

Earlier in this chapter, many of the examples we highlighted regarding the co-existence of design with episodic instances of research implicitly emphasize the single designer. Much has been written recently on the alternative to this paradigm, namely, collaborative design. It is in recognition, at least in part, of the fact that much of architecture emerges as a result of team effort, as opposed to the efforts of a single "star" architect.

Yet more than ever, especially in projects that are increasingly complex, the design process necessarily calls upon the expertise of a wide variety of disciplines. How does this work? And in what ways? How do we understand the role of the architect? Or design team consultants? Or the client? Or the users? Even though much has been written regarding this topic, it is an area that is wide open for more in-depth research. Here, we summarize an exemplar of design process, a theoretical model, and recent research.

In a classic example of collaborative design and research, Charles Moore provides an illuminating account of the work in his St. Matthew's Church project in a suburb of Los Angeles (see Figure 2.9); this is recounted in Andy Pressman's *The Fountainache: The Politics of Architect-Client Relations.*[61] The original church was destroyed by fire, and Moore's firm was hired by the parish with the requirement that any design proposal must be approved by two-thirds of the congregation—one that may have trouble agreeing "what day it was." Moore's solution was to allow the design to emerge by means of collaborating with the congregation in four "open design charrettes" over a period of four months. During this participatory process, many different tactics were used to arrive at a design consensus. These included "awareness walks" of the site, jotting down feelings and observations. Following this, the congregation used found objects (Froot Loops, cellophane, scissors, paper, even parsley) and made various configurations. In the

Figure 2.9 The pergola at St. Matthew's Church, Los Angeles. Designed by Charles Moore. Photograph courtesy of Linda Groat.

second charrette, Moore's team show slides of other church buildings; even though a dark wood building was a pre-charrette favorite, images of a white church by Aalto received many positive votes. During the third charrette, the congregation was given building shapes to work with to express their wishes. The team then took all of these inputs and developed some drawings and a model, all of which they left with the people for a month. In the end, 87% of the congregation approved the design.

Moore's approach reflects many of the characteristics of qualitative research, such as having no preset theory of design strategy going into a research venue, and "living" with the people to develop "thick" accounts of how they perceive things. Moore recalls: "Being a part of making that church was an opportunity to work toward an architecture filled with the energies not only of architects but of inhabitants as well, and helping people to find something to which they can belong. . . ."[62]

Groat has pointed out that traditional images of the architect have often been one of either the architect-as-technician, or the architect-as-artist. Both of these models not only set apart the architect in an individual role (hence perhaps encouraging a "star" quality), they also bring about disjunctures between what architects design and what everyday clients may want. Groat's alternative proposal is that of the architect as a cultivator. Cultivator of what? Says Groat:

> Once we . . . foster environmental values that focus on the common good and reinforce the connectedness of people within an organization, a community, or society as a whole, we are then confronting the essence of cultural life. It is (at this point) that the model of the "designer-as-cultivator" comes into its own.[63]

Groat means to shift the attention from the architect as sole technician or sole artist to a role that is sensitive to a larger communal mission of well-being. She structures her argument by borrowing seven categories of values from organizational theory.[64] The author, Richard Barrett, suggests that, in good organizations, individuals are cultivated to rise above self-interest to take on communal and ultimately global interests of well-being. Groat adapts this model for her proposed paradigm of the architect-as-cultivator (see Figure 2.10). In short, the architect as cultivator encourages three things. He or she emphasizes process, by which Groat means a collaborative and participatory spirit on the part of the architect. Second, the architect as cultivator is one who encourages interdisciplinary design, where different disciplines contribute in concert to a solution; community is inherent in this process. Third, borrowing from the title of Barrett's book, Groat's architect-as-cultivator is one that has "a sensitivity for the cultural as the soul of design."[65] By this is meant a vision for the mission of the common good, with the architect motivating

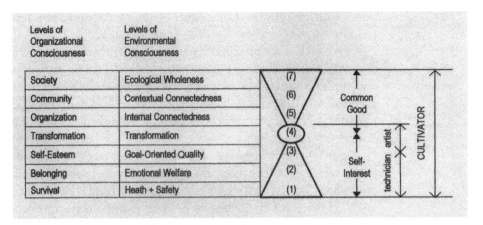

Figure 2.10 Groat's adaptation of Barrett's levels of "consciousness" (from self-interest to global concern) for the architect-as-cultivator's design agenda. Use of original Barrett diagram courtesy of John Wiley & Sons.

his/her team to recognize that quality environments "can only be realized by fully engaging the social and cultural milieu in which it is embedded."

In some organizational situations, however, the collaborative process may occur *only* between the client organization's leader and the designer or design team, thereby not permeating the larger organizational context. There is, for example, a well-documented case of an advertising agency executive collaborating with a well-regarded designer to create a transformative virtual office environment. Although the design goal was to encourage more innovative work and to engender a more communal environment, the employee response was overwhelmingly negative; many struggled to get work done in an environment that felt like a "a cocktail party," fought over too few desks, and desperately tried to define a personal space by displaying family photos.[66] In other words, despite what appeared to be effective collaboration at the top, the design process did not engage the situated organizational context. A similar dynamic seems to have occurred with the design of the Seattle Public Library project, where there appeared to be an effective collaboration between the library leaders and Rem Koolhaas, but much less so with the community at large (see Box 12.2 in Chapter 12).

Just as there needs to be an alignment of organizational values, environmental values, and the architect/designer's role (see again Figure 2.10), there is additionally an essential alignment to the briefing and ongoing design process. Indeed, the entire design engagement process is also influenced by an organization's underlying values, which in turn affects the nature of user participation, how information is to be gathered, and even how design decisions are made.[67]

A research study of expert designers by Paten and Dorst demonstrates a remarkable convergence with Groat's cultivator model.[68] The authors' purpose was to investigate the variety of ways in which designers worked through the project briefing phase with their clients. In their interviews with 15 designers, they asked about the nature of the briefing processes for what the designers deemed to be "typical" and "innovative" projects.

Paten and Dorst's in-depth analysis of these interviews revealed a typology of four designer roles. The designer's least-favored role is that of *technician*, whereby the designer is presented with a well-defined brief and is simply expected to carry this out. In the role of facilitator, the designer accepts the client's established criteria for the project, but is able to devise an appropriate solution for the problem as given. In the third role as expert/artist, the "client is accepted as knowing what they need and the designer is responsible for framing the project with them to achieve a workable outcome." Finally, for all but 4 of the 15 respondents (for whom the expert/artist role was preferred), the designers found the role of the collaborator to be the most satisfying. In this role, "both the client and the designer mutually work on framing the project, in terms of both problem and solution spaces."[69]

This typology is represented in Figure 2.11 and shows that the technician role is characterized by either limited or virtually no collaborative engagement in problem definition, solution formulation, or iterative refinement of the design. By contrast, at the other end of the scale, the collaborator role entails the full engagement of the designer in all three categories of involvement. Interestingly, though some architects or designers may see advantages in the expert/artist role, it actually entails only partial or medium levels of involvement in two of the three categories.

Mode	Point of Entry to Project	Involvement in Problem Space Formulation	Involvement in Solution Space Formulation	Amount of Iteration
Technician	End of planning	No	No	Low
Facilitator	Near end of planning	No	Partial	Low
Expert/Artist	Mid-planning	Partial	Yes	Med
Collaborator	Beginning of planning	Yes	Yes	High

Figure 2.11 Matrix of designer roles. Redrawn from Bec Paton and Kees Dorst, "Briefing and Reframing: A Situated Practice," *Design Studies* 32(6) (November 2011): 583, with permission from Elsevier.

Equally important from the designer's perspective, the examples of projects that entailed the collaborative mode were seen as more diverse and innovative. And the interactions between designer and client were experienced as "highly iterative, transparent and playful." The authors then go on to analyze the type of conversation that occurs between client and designer working in the collaborative mode. In these cases, *"[e]ngineering a dialogical approach,* using a *context-specific language framework* and asking *leading questions* [authors' emphasis] were . . . identified as means to de-structure a situation through language co-creation."[70] The authors also argue that, in addition, employing a "co-created language" serves to establish a level of trust between client and designer.

This dialogic engagement may well lead the client and designer to mutually reframe the nature of the design project, often involving "research on behalf of, and with, the client to reframe the situation (e.g., user-centered design techniques revealing the situation, rather than conforming to a list of functional requirements)."[71] The authors observe that their interviewees expressed curiosity "to find out about the client's world and incorporate that into the situation being framed."[72] Finally, they conclude that such "[s]ituated framing and reframing practices" should be cultivated among expert designers and students alike. "The design professions would do well to collectively reflect on these practices in order to . . . cultivate innovative projects."[73]

2.4   RESEARCH, DESIGN, SCHOLARSHIP, AND SCHOLARSHIP-IN-PRACTICE

There are many external forces driving the interest in relating the domains of research and design. One is the academic environment. Some 20 years ago, Boyer and Mitgang's important work, *Building Community: A New Future for Architecture Education and Practice,* called for a more diverse approach to defining research. They noted that because the academy places more emphasis on traditional research, some architectural faculty felt that design activity is considered less scholarly.[74] In an earlier work, *Scholarship Reconsidered,* they suggested that the traditional model of research as discovery be supplemented by added categories of scholarship in integration, application, and teaching.[75] We agree with Boyer and Mitgang's intent that different categories of intellectual contribution are equivalent, not in kind but in import and value. We noted this in passing in the first edition of this book, but developments since 2002 make this matter more important for this present edition, as will be evident in the following.

Another impetus for relating design to research comes from the profession. The American Institute of Architects now offers considerably more resources for research to its members in comparison to 10 years ago.[76] For example, in 2001, the Latrobe Fellowship, awarded biennially, was instituted by the AIA College of Fellows as a substantial research grant. The 2011 program (for instance) focused on public interest practices, and asked these succinct research questions: What are the needs that can be addressed by public interest practices? How are current public interest practices operating? What is necessary for public interest work to become a significant segment of architectural practice?[77] In 2004, the Research for Practice (RFP) program was instituted, which led to the 2007 Research Summit in Seattle, Washington.[78] It was at this summit that the profession started to develop—in logical argumentation terms—an overall research agenda for the AIA, complete with a set of technical categories for research, e.g., pure basic research, use-inspired basic research, pure applied research and development.[79] It is not clear what these categories exactly mean; the noteworthy point is the effort itself to frame a research agenda.

Also noteworthy is to "increase university research capacity and funding opportunities" as one of the organization's long-range goals.[80] In 2006, the AIA added the Upjohn Research Initiative, encouraging members to submit grant proposals dovetailing research with practice. In 2012, Wang contributed the section on research methods for the *AIA Handbook,* 15th edition. One of the exemplars featured in this article underlines how the Upjohn Initiative brings together practitioners with academic faculty for joint research projects.[81] All of this emphasizes how overlaps between research and design have increased even since the publication of the first edition of this book in 2002.

To return to the academy: the interest in coupling design with research is also driven by institutional pressures. At the university level, there is an increasing trend for architecture faculty to hold the PhD research degree, as distinguished from the practice degrees, the MArch or BArch. (This relates to the second issue that we suggested, at the outset of Section 2.2, to be considered along with technical distinctions between design and research.) A search of the documents of the National Architectural Accreditation Board (NAAB)[82] indicates that the percentage of architectural faculty holding PhD degrees was not even a measure until the 2010 report (at which point it was roughly 17%; the 2011 report has it at 28.5%, although the difference in the reported total number of full-time faculty between the two years is considerable, so the percentage increase is probably not as significant as the numbers suggest).

More anecdotal but probably more indicative evidence of pressure that some design faculty experience can be found on the online NAAB forums. The following example raises a good point: that sometimes the interdisciplinary programs within which architectural faculty reside often do not recognize anything but the PhD.

Thus, the NAAB, according to this individual, should simply convert bachelor's and master's degrees into doctoral degrees retroactively:

> There are several programs throughout the country (and world) where architecture, landscape architecture, planning or design related courses and/or programs are offered under the umbrella of another college. . . . These other departments are not familiar with the architecture structure of "terminal master degrees" . . . . Many M.Arch/B.Arch graduates have lost jobs due to this. Solution: retroactively change the titles to D.Arch.[83]

We certainly do not endorse this suggestion; our task here is to highlight the increasing pressure to recognize research rigor in design inquiry, as evidenced by the increased demand for doctoral degrees, and also to highlight the good work being done to recognize broader definitions of research in relation to design.

To this end, Ellison and Eatman's 2008 report, *Scholarship in Public: Knowledge Creation and Tenure Policy in the Engaged University,*[84] offers good criteria for measuring research rigor of the work of faculty housed within departments that conduct nontraditional research. Based on structured interviews with a wide sampling of U.S. faculty in the arts, humanities, and design, Ellison and Eatman propose several "continuum structures" for accommodating research activity: from scholarship to public engagement, from scholarly to creative acts, a range of choices for being a "civic professional," and a "continuum of actions for institutional change.[85] The authors say this (the italics are theirs):

> The term continuum has become pervasive because . . . it is *inclusive* of many sorts and conditions of knowledge. It resists embedded hierarchies by assigning *equal value* to inquiry of different kinds. Inclusiveness implies *choice*: once a continuum is established a faculty member may, without penalty, locate herself or himself at any point.[86]

Most notable about *Scholarship in Public* is the title itself: it casts public and civic engagement as a mode of research and, among other things, faculty work in theater, art and civic dialogues, historical preservation, urban design, and community development are all offered as examples. The authors define publicly engaged academic work as

> . . . scholarly or creative activity integral to a faculty member's academic area. It encompasses different forms of making knowledge about, for, and with diverse publics and communities. Through a coherent, purposeful sequence of activities, it contributes to the public good and yields artifacts of public and intellectual value.[87]

Key terms and phrases here indicate departure from traditional modalities of scientific inquiry. Most obvious is the word *artifacts*. Ellison and Eatman are explicit in holding that outcomes of research need not be concepts communicated by writing or nomenclature; they can be artifacts such as performances, exhibitions, certainly buildings. "Making knowledge about, for or with" suggests situated and contextual outcomes that do not promise universal applicability, but rather find relevance in particular social-cultural venues. However, even as these modes of research are new, the terms "coherent," "purposeful sequence of activities," and "contributes to the public good" all echo well-known measures of research quality: for example, validity, verifiability, even that elusive word that nevertheless crops up in all discussions about research quality: *robust*. Thus, Ellison and Eatman make clear that these new modes of research should exhibit "relationships of resemblance and unlikeness." By this they seem to mean that, even in their "unlikeness," these new forms of research must be "judged by common principles, standards to which all academic scholarly and creative work is held."[88] They specifically state what these standards ought to be: (1) clear goals; (2) adequate preparation; (3) appropriate methods; (4) significant results; (5) effective presentation; and (6) reflective critique.[89]

BOX 2.5
Public Scholarship in Ritzville, Washington

Since 2005, Professor Janetta McCoy and her students have engaged in interdisciplinary work with the community of Ritzville, Washington (see Figure 2.12). Once a thriving place, this town in rural central Washington has seen a decline in its fortunes since Interstate 90 was gradually completed over the course of the latter half of the last century, reducing Ritzville to no more than an exit off the highway. With state and local funding, McCoy began her work by asking her design students to work with the community in conceptualizing alternatives for an abandoned high school in town. The solutions: a conference center to attract visitors, a microbrewery, a farming museum, and a trade school as a "laboratory for learning about historic preservation." The collaboration stirred considerable interest from the Ritzville community. Says McCoy: "It gets students involved with folks in a rural community who don't look like them, and the process also educates the community about design." Over the years, McCoy's efforts have gone beyond the limitations of semester schedules.

Various funding sources, such as the Ritzville Public Development Authority, have enabled McCoy to run summer studios, hire outside consultants, and pay student workers, all for promoting economic growth through enhancement of the built environment of Ritzville. McCoy's students have conducted feasibility studies, documented the built inventory of the town, and continued to do design projects. One of these involved designs for converting an empty hotel into housing for the elderly; this project generated huge support from the citizens. McCoy and several other faculty now have in place the Rural Communities Design Initiative, which seeks funding sources to support academic design collaboration with rural communities.

McCoy's work, as an example of public scholarship as defined by Ellison and Eatman, can be assessed by the criteria the authors provide: (1) clear goals; (2) adequate preparation; (3) appropriate methods; (4) significant results; (5) effective presentation; and (6) reflective critique.

Figure 2.12 Professor Janetta McCoy (standing in the background, facing left) in her work with the community of Ritzville, Washington. This particular project was for the design of an interactive structure representing the history of Ritzville. Photograph courtesy of Isil Oygur.

Turning to the European scene, in their article "Building a Culture of Doctoral Scholarship in Architecture and Design: A Belgian-Scandinavian Case," Halina Dunin-Woyseth (from the Oslo School of Architecture) and Fredrik Nilsson (from the Chalmers School of Architecture in Sweden) report:

> In September 2003, the Bologna-Berlin policies recognized doctoral studies as the third cycle in European higher education. For the Sint-Lucas School of Architecture (Belgium), this meant developing a new culture, a culture of research and doctoral scholarship. The intentions of the school were to develop experimental, practice-based concepts for this research, rather than to attempt to emulate the discipline-based research that is characteristic of the academic fields.[90]

To this end, Dunin-Woyseth and Nilsson were engaged by Sint-Lucas to develop an eight-module (over two years) curriculum in which practitioners pursue doctoral-level studies in "research by design." This program was implemented in 2006. The eight modules bore these titles: (1) Research Methodologies and Communication; (2) Knowledge; (3) Reflection; (4) Design Cognition; (5) Why/How Design Research?; (6) Artifact, Action and Observation; (7) PhD by Practice; (8) By Design for Design. Based on the "Roskilde Model" for doctoral education developed in Denmark in the 1990s, the approach "consisted of short periods of concentrated . . . teaching by international lecturers, preceded by intense literature studies, and followed by practical exercises such as the writing of essays."[91]

In June 2012, Wang served as the opponent for the public defense of the first doctoral candidate to go through the St-Lucas doctoral system (in collaboration with Chalmers University in Gothenburg, Sweden). The successful candidate, Nel Janssens, is both a practitioner and instructor at St-Lucas. Her dissertation, entitled *Utopia-Driven Projective Research*,[92] takes four conceptual projects—one taking eight years to complete—and derives principles that philosophically advance Cross's theory of "designerly thinking" as well as Lang's work on the deontological nature of much of architectural practice, to wit, that design decisions are made in accordance with the designer's "value-laden" commitments[93] (deontology is discussed in Chapter 4). Although it does not neatly fit into the research strategies addressed in this book, Janssens's approach clearly involves qualitative ethnography and logical argumentation, employing critical theory as a school of thought. The point, however, is that the ethnography is of her own experiences in the practice venues that produced the conceptual projects. Through the lens of standard discipline-based doctorates, Janssens can be (and was) questioned about the circularity of using her own practices as her "samples." But Janssens' work fits all the criteria of Ellison and Eatman's study: its goals were clear; the literature and practice preparation were extensive; appropriate methods were used; the results were significant both in its intended consequence (as a theory of deontological practice that engages and includes the public) and in its unintended consequence (as a pedagogical method for teaching design studios); the presentation was effective; and her work amounted to an engaging critique of design process (as well as itself undergoing reflective critique in the public defense).

Figure 2.13 is a PowerPoint slide used in a seminar for doctoral students Wang conducted at Chalmers University in June 2012.[94] The slide situates the first edition of this Groat-Wang research methods text as one heading of a heuristic matrix

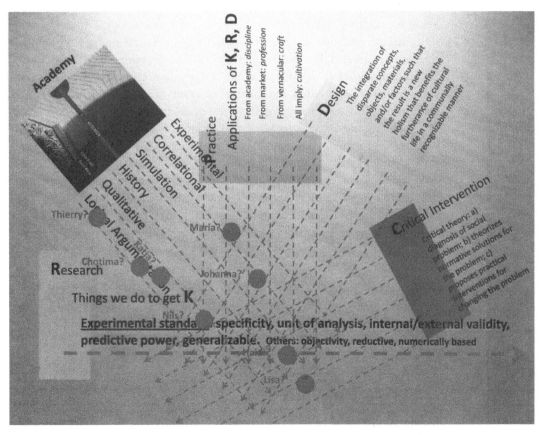

Figure 2.13 A heuristic matrix of different domains of research—including design—with "relationships of resemblance" to standard measures for research quality. The dots represent proposed locations on the matrix where various student dissertation proposals can be situated. Diagram by David Wang.

that includes Practice, Design, and Critical Intervention as the other heads. On the slide, the Groat-Wang book is labeled "Academy," in that the first edition has been primarily used in academic venues for architectural research (among them Chalmers). Readers will recognize the chapter headings covered in the book. The point of the slide is that activity in the Practice, Design, and Critical Intervention domains can also echo—in the vein of Ellison and Eatman's "relationships of resemblance and unlikeness"—the measures for robustness for the research measures outlined in the Groat-Wang strategy chapters. All of this activity, in turn, still harkens back to standards initially established by the positivist tradition, as indicated by the baseline of the heuristic matrix. Finally, the slide then maps the various students' research proposals (the dots) at various points on the matrix. The dot at the far left side represents a project in which the student wishes to frame a broad explanatory theory of how built environments are experienced through time; this can probably be done with logical argumentation strategy as outlined in the Groat-Wang text. But the dot on the far right side represents a topic in which the student wishes to actively alter citizen participation processes in municipal planning venues in Sweden. In other words, at this stage in her development, the application of critical theory—in the sense of the Frankfurt School's formulation of (a) identifying a social problem; (b) proposing normative solutions for the problem; and (c) intervening to change the problem—to a design venue figures prominently in this student's research design. The challenge for her, then, is to achieve robustness in demonstrating "relationships of resemblance" to the measures of research quality found in neighboring domains. We note this European example to underline the rich developments in integrating design inquiry with "research" going on today.

We might also add this: To come full circle back to discussions among U.S. design faculty vis-à-vis academic qualifications, the developments in Europe for bridging design with research bear watching. Ellison and Eatman's new criteria for evaluating rigor in nontraditional public research resonate well with standards being established in Europe. Built or designed work (Ellison and Eatman: portfolios)[95] fits, for example, what Janssens submitted for her doctoral defense. In addition, although Janssens's doctoral committee was comprised of three academic faculty, those faculty came from different schools (in addition to the external "opponent," Wang, from the United States). But the number of players directly involved in her work included practicing architects, two of whom come from architecture firms with in-house research departments. All of this is consonant with Ellison and Eatman's suggestion to "expand who counts . . . in broadening the community of review."[96]

2.5   CONCLUSION

Architectural research, then—and we can be more general to say this about all design research—is experiencing an exciting time of development. Since the first edition of this book, much has emerged in attempts to bridge the gap between design and research as these terms have been conventionally understood. This bears out our view, which, again, is that design and research are neither polar opposites nor equivalent domains of activity; instead, subtle nuances and complementarities exist between the two. At their respective poles, yes, research tends to be more conceptually systematic, whereas design activity makes episodic uses of research (more examples of this are covered in Chapter 4). But as the developments in Europe are beginning to suggest, the "episodic" moniker for research in design is itself increasing in sophistication, as the domains of design and research achieve more nuanced complementarities.

NOTES

1. Stephen Kieran, "Research in Design: Planning Doing Monitoring Learning," *Journal of Architectural Education* 61(1) (September 2007): 31.
2. Turpin Bannister, "The Research Heritage of the Architectural Profession," *Journal of Architectural Education* 1(1) (Spring 1947): 5–12.
3. Avigail Sachs, "The Postwar Legacy of Architectural Research," *Journal of Architectural Education* 62(3) (February 2009): 53–64.
4. Matt Powers, "Toward a Discipline-Dependent Scholarship," *Journal of Architectural Education* 61(1) (September 2007): 17.
5. Ibid., 18.
6. B. D. Wortham, "The Way We Think about the Way We Think: Architecture Is a Paradigm for Reconsidering Research," *Journal of Architectural Education* 61(1) (September 2007): 44–53.
7. David Wang and Ambler Joplin, "The Design Substrate: The Phenomenological Unity Enabling Howard Gardner's Theory of Multiple Intelligences," *Environmental & Architectural Phenomenology Newsletter* (Winter 2009). Also available online at www.arch.ksu.edu/seamon/Wang_Joplin.htm. "Design involves innate processes by which inarticulate needs achieve articulate expressions in social-cultural life. As a noun, 'design' denotes the designed object itself or the act of design. But as a verb, "design" reveals itself to be much more than discrete acts but, rather, includes the inarticulate processes enabling such acts leading to designed objects. It is the phenomenological unity of these inarticulate processes that we call the design substrate."

8. David Salomon, "Experimental Cultures: On the 'End' of the Design Thesis and the Rise of the Research Studio," *Journal of Architectural Education* 65(1) (October 2011): 33–44.

9. Henry H. Bauer, "Scientific Literacy and the Myth of Scientific Methods," in *The So-Called Scientific Method* (Urbana: University of Illinois Press, 1992), 19–41.

10. Matt Powers, "Toward a Discipline-Dependent Scholarship," *Journal of Architectural Education* 61(1) (September 2007): 17.

11. See Graeme Sullivan, *Art Practice as Research: Inquiry in Visual Arts* (Thousand Oaks, CA: Sage, 2010); Lee-Anne S. Milburn, Robert D. Brown, Susan J. Mulley, and Stewart G. Hills, "Assessing Access Contributions in Landscape Architecture," *Landscape and Urban Planning* 64 (2003): 119–129; Howell S. Baum, "Research and Planning Both Have Methods, But Research Is Not Planning," *Journal of Architectural and Planning Research* 22(2) (Summer 2005): 121–128; Ken Friedman, "Theory Construction in Design Research: Criteria, Approaches and Methods," *Design Studies* 24(6) (November 2003): 507–522; Ann Forsyth, "Innovation in Urban Design: Does Research Help?" *Journal of Urban Design* 12(3) (October 2007): 461–473; Tim Brown (with Barry Katz), *Change by Design: How Design Thinking Transforms Organizations and Inspires Innovation* (New York: HarperCollins, 2009).

12. Forsyth, 461.

13. Herbert Simon, *The Sciences of the Artificial,* 3rd ed. (Cambridge, MA: MIT Press, 1996).

14. Donald A. Schon, *Educating the Reflective Practitioner* (San Francisco, CA: Jossey-Bass, 1987), 41–42.

15. Ibid., 41.

16. Nigel Cross, *Designerly Ways of Knowing* (London, UK: Springer, 2006), 15–16.

17. Bryan Lawson and Kees Dorst, *Design Expertise* (Oxford, UK: Elsevier, 2009), 48.

18. Nigel Cross, *Design Thinking* (Oxford, UK: Berg, 2011), 74, 146.

19. Graeme Sullivan, *Art Practice as Research: Inquiry in Visual Arts* (Thousand Oaks, CA: Sage, 2010), 57.

20. James Snyder (ed.), *Architectural Research* (New York: Van Nostrand Reinhold, 1984), 2.

21. Kazys Varnelis, "Is There Research in the Studio?" *Journal of Architectural Education* 61(1) (September 2007): 13.

22. Ibid.

23. Welcome to PEERRS, the University of Michigan's Program for Education and Evaluation in Responsible Research and Scholarship, http://my.research.umich.edu/peerrs/. Accessed June 12, 2012.

24. Salomon, 34.

25. Abraham Kaplan, *The Conduct of Inquiry: Methodology for Behavioral Science* (San Francisco: Chandler, 1964).

26. Nigel Cross, *The Automated Architect* (London, UK: Pion Limited, 1977), 12.

27. Bill Hillier, John Musgrove, and Pat O'Sullivan, "Knowledge and Design," in Nigel Cross (ed.), *Developments in Design Methodology* (New York: John Wiley & Sons, 1984), 245–264.

28. Ibid., 250.
29. Kaplan, 10.
30. Ibid.
31. Kaplan, 10–14.
32. Ibid., 15.
33. Ibid., 16.
34. Spencer J. Maxcy, "Pragmatic Threads in Mixed Methods Research in the Social Sciences: The Search for Multiple Modes of Inquiry and the End of the Philosophy of Formalism," in Abbas Tashakkori and Charles Teddlie (eds.), *Handbook of Mixed Methods in Social & Behavioral Research* (Thousand Oaks, CA: Sage, 2003), 63.
35. Lionel March, "The Logic of Design," in Nigel Cross (ed.), *Developments in Design Methodology* (New York: John Wiley & Sons, 1984), 265–276; N. F. M. Roozenburg, "On the Pattern of Reasoning in Innovative Design," *Design Studies* 14(1) (January 1993), 7.
36. March, 269.
37. Ibid.
38. Cross, *Design Thinking*, 16.
39. Jane Darke, "The Primary Generator and the Design Process," *Design Studies* 1(1) (July 1979): 36–44.
40. Lawson and Dorst, 36.
41. Cross, *Design Thinking*, 16.
42. Roozenburg, 17.
43. Panagiotis Louridas, "Design as Bricolage: Anthropology Meets Design Thinking," *Design Studies* 20(6) (November 1999): 517–535.
44. See Charles Teddlie and Abbas Tashakkori, *Foundations of Mixed Methods Research* (Thousands Oaks, CA: Sage, 2009), 131; Janice M. Morse, "Principles of Mixed Methods and MultiMethod Research Design," in Abbas Tashakkori and Charles Teddlie (eds.), *Handbook of Mixed Methods in Social & Behavioral Research* (Thousand Oaks, CA: Sage, 2003), 193.
45. Cross, *Design Thinking*, 145.
46. J. Barnes and R. Born, *Perkins+Will 1315 Peachtree Street Pre/Post Occupancy* (Atlanta: Perkins+Will Self-Published, 2012).
47. Stephen Hawking, *A Brief History of Time* (New York: Bantam Books, 1988), 74.
48. Gary T. Moore, "Toward Environment-Behavior Theories of the Middle Range," in Gary T. Moore and Robert W. Marans (eds.), *Advances in Environment, Behavior, and Design,* vol. 4 (New York: Plenum Press, 1997), 1–40.
49. Ken Friedman, "Theory Construction in Design Research: Criteria, Approaches and Methods," *Design Studies* 24(6) (November 2003): 507–522.
50. Ibid., 510.
51. Ibid.
52. James Gorman, "'What Is' Meets 'What If': The Role of Speculation in Science," *New York Times,* May 29, 2012, Science section.

53. Friedman, 510.
54. Dana Cuff, *Architecture: The Story of Practice* (Cambridge, MA: MIT Press, 1991).
55. Donald Schon, *The Reflective Practitioner* (New York: Basic Books, 1983), 30–69.
56. Ibid., 76–104.
57. Dorwin Cartwright (ed.), *Field Theory in Social Science: Selected Theoretical Papers by Kurt Lewin* (Chicago: University of Chicago Press, 1976).]
58. Jay Farbstein and Min Kantrowitz, "Design Research in the Swamp," in E. Zube and G. Moore (eds.), *Advances in Environment Behavior and Design,* vol. 3 (New York: Plenum Press, 1991), 297–318.
59. Ibid., 306–307.
60. Ibid., 304.
61. Andy Pressman, *The Fountainache: The Politics of Architect-Client Relations* (New York: John Wiley & Sons, 1995), 59–65.
62. Ibid., 65.
63. L. Groat, "A Conceptual Framework for Understanding the Designer's Role: Technician, Artist, or Cultivator?" in Paul Knox and Peter Ozlins (eds.), *Design Professionals and the Built Environment: An Introduction* (New York: John Wiley & Sons, 2000).
64. Richard Barrett, *Liberating the Corporate Soul: Building a Visionary Organization* (Boston: Butterworth-Heinemann, 1998).
65. Groat, op. cit., 48–49.
66. Ibid.
67. Linda Groat and Lawrence Stern, "Cultivating Organizational Values: A New Model for Workplace Planning," *Journal for Quality and Participation* 23(5) (Winter 2000): 17–21.
68. Bec Paton and Kees Dorst, "Briefing and Reframing: A Situated Practice," *Design Studies* 32(6) (November 2011): 573–587.
69. Ibid., 579.
70. Ibid., 582.
71. Ibid., 580.
72. Ibid., 581.
73. Ibid., 586.
74. Ernest L. Boyer and Lee D. Mitgang, *Building Community: A New Future for Architecture Education and Practice* (Princeton, NJ: Carnegie Foundation for the Advancement of Teaching, 1996), 53–57.
75. Ernest L. Boyer and Lee D. Mitgang, *Scholarship Reconsidered: Priorities of the Professoriate* (Princeton, NJ: Carnegie Foundation for the Advancement of Teaching, 1990).
76. "A History of Research at the AIA," www.aia.org/practicing/akr/AIAB081882. Accessed June 12, 2012.
77. "AIA College of Fellows Awards 2011 Latrobe Prize for Public Interest Practices in Architecture," www.aia.org/press/releases/AIAB087557. Accessed June 12, 2012.

78. "AIA 2007 BoKnoCo Research Summit," http://info.aia.org/researchsummit/about/01.html. Accessed June 12, 2012.
79. Ibid.
80. Ibid.
81. The project is "Main Street Connectivity; Patterns and Processes Linking Urban Commercial Patches." Principal investigators: Edward A. Shriver, Jr., AIA, Principal, Strada Architects LLC, Rami el Samahy, Carnegie Mellon University, Kelly Hutzell, Carnegie Mellon University. See "2011 Upjohn Research Initiative Program—Grant Recipients," http://www.aia.org/practicing/research/AIAB091287. Accessed June 12, 2012.
82. "Documents," National Architectural Accreditation Board, www.naab.org/documents/home_origin.aspx?path=Public+Documents\Accreditation. Accessed June 12, 2012.
83. NAAB Accreditation Review Conference Forum: "Trends in Education," www.naab.org/forum/view_message.aspx?message_id=16&board_id=9&show_archived=&replies=2. Accessed June 12, 2012.
84. Jule Ellison and Timothy K. Eatman, *Scholarship in Public: Knowledge Creation and Tenure Policy in the Engaged University* (Syracuse, NY: Imagining America, 2008).
85. Ibid., ix.
86. Ibid., ix.
87. Ibid., 6.
88. Ibid., ix–x.
89. Ibid., 9.
90. Halina Dunin-Woyseth and Fredrik Nilsson, "Building a Culture of Doctoral Scholarship in Architecture and Design: A Belgian-Scandinavian Case," *Nordic Journal of Architectural Research* 23(1) (2011): 42.
91. Ibid., 47.
92. Nel Janssens, *Utopia-Driven Projective Research*. Doctoral dissertation, Chalmers School of Architecture, June 2012.
93. Jon Lang, *Creating Architectural Theory* (New York: Van Nostrand Reinhold, 1987), 219.
94. David Wang, doctoral research seminar, Chalmers University, Gothenburg, Sweden, June 7, 2012.
95. Ellison and Eatman, 13–14.
96. Ibid., 14–15.

Chapter 3

Systems of Inquiry and Standards of Research Quality

3.1   INTRODUCTION

In Chapter 1, we argued that any researcher's choice of a particular research design is necessarily framed by the researcher's own assumptions about both the nature of reality and how one can come to apprehend it. We have used the term *system of inquiry* to describe these sets of assumptions;[1] another term that is frequently used to describe such assumptions is *paradigm*.[2] Both terms convey the notion of a worldview, the ultimate truthfulness of which cannot be established.

For example, in a study by Stazi et al., the authors present an analysis of solar walls for residential buildings in a Mediterranean climate.[3] The authors' purpose is to investigate how energy savings might be achieved for both winter heating and summer cooling, given that undesired heat gains are especially problematic in climates characterized by hot summers. More specifically, they aim to evaluate the performance of specific solar wall designs through a combination of experimental testing, and subsequent simulation modeling to extend the results by changing the building envelope insulation level (see Figure 3.1). They introduce the details of their research study this way:

> Solar wall is a passive solar system . . . generally made up of south-facing concrete wall painted black on the external surface, an air layer and glazing on the exterior side. Shading devices such as overhangs or movable shutters provide solar radiation control. . . . Trombe wall is a solar wall equipped with vents at the top and the bottom for air-thermo circulation; external dampers provide

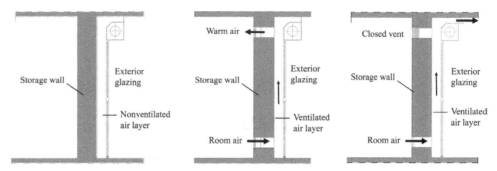

Figure 3.1 Three different solar wall configurations for Stazi et al.'s investigation. Reprinted from *Energy and Buildings* 47, Francesca Stazi, Alessio Mastrucci, and Constanzo di Perna, "The Behaviour of Solar Walls in Residential Buildings with Different Insulation Levels: An Experimental and Numerical Study," 217-229, 2012, with permission from Elsevier. Image courtesy of Francesca Stazi.

external ventilation to the air layer. Typical operation schemes for solar wall and Trombe wall are in [the adjacent figure]. [4]

In this short excerpt, it is clear that the authors have conducted their research within a system of inquiry that assumes the physical reality of objects, whose properties can be accurately specified, their performance measured by calibrated instruments, and the outcomes compared in quantifiable terms. In other words, there is a reality "out there" that we can know and define systematically.

Next is the example of Benyamin Schwarz's study of the design process in the development of nursing homes, examined through three case study projects[5] (see Figure 3.2). The ontological assumptions that frame his research are stated this way:

> [T]his inquiry ... [allowed] access to inherent complexity of social reality. ... A design process cannot be regarded as a world made up of totally objectified elements and observable, measurable facts. Therefore, an effort was made to avoid simplification of the social phenomena of the design process.[6]

Schwarz's commentary reflects his assumption that reality is nuanced by the complexity of social relations, this in contrast to the objectively measured reality as posited by Stazi et al.

Third, and last, is the example of an essay by Jennifer Bloomer titled, "The Matter of Matter: A Longing for Gravity." Bloomer's aim is to "reconsider the notion of longing and more particularly, the place of nostalgia, homesickness, the longing

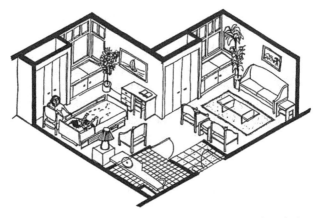

Figure 3.2 Axonometric drawing of the nursing home, the design process for which was analyzed by Benyamin Schwarz. Drawing courtesy of Benyamin Schwarz.

for home, in contemporary Western architecture."[7] She does so by exposing contrasting impulses implicit in our experience of architecture's matter and form. For instance, she argues that on the one hand, nostalgia in contemporary architectural discourse is "a universal genius of new town planning and architectural style."[8] Yet, "on the other hand, nostalgia is covered in refusal. . . . [T]he repression of nostalgia is at the core of the project of modernity."[9] She then goes on to employ a series of poetic evocations of domestic space that reflect these contradictory impulses.

In contrast to the *objective assessment* of physical components represented by Stazi et al.'s study of solar walls and Schwarz's emphasis on the *social dynamics* of design process, Bloomer's exploration of nostalgia is based largely on the *author's poetic evocation* of her own experiences of longing and domestic space.

These three examples clearly demonstrate the great variety of paradigms—or systems of inquiry—within which architectural research is typically conducted. Although Schwarz chose to be quite explicit about the systems of inquiry underlying his particular study, it is far more often the case that researchers are relatively less explicit about their study's ontological assumptions (e.g., Stazi et al. and Bloomer, at least within the works cited). While the experienced researcher is likely to be able to infer the paradigmatic frame of a given study, less experienced readers may be left wondering or confused about why the study was conceived and conducted in a particular way.

Thus, the goals of this chapter are twofold: (1) to provide a conceptual framework for understanding the range of paradigms commonly employed in architectural research; and (2) to clarify the way in which standards for evaluating research quality are substantially dependent on the system of inquiry employed by the researcher.

Why is this important? There are multiple and complementary reasons, dependent to a large extent on the context in which the researcher is situated. For instance, although students in research-focused programs (whether doctoral or MSc) and faculty scholars are likely to be working within a disciplinary subgroup in which broad conceptual frameworks common to that subgroup are well recognized, the researcher may also be tackling a research question of interest to a broader audience. So, clarifying underlying assumptions and quality standards that apply to their work may be essential for the work to reach its broadest audience. Second, whether the researcher is following existing practices of inquiry in his/her subfield or challenging those very practices through the use of atypical research designs and practices, the overall quality of the research is likely to be improved if the researcher is clear-headed about the choices taken.

However, students in professional programs in architecture and design disciplines, or professionals in practice, are likely to engage in research of a more exploratory or episodic quality. In this case, maintaining an overarching conceptual framework across the entire project may be less applicable. Nevertheless, for students, there is an essential opportunity to become familiar with how the underlying premises of the research traditions they may be encouraged to employ are situated within the overall context of research practices. Meanwhile, for practitioners, it is likely that their need to engage in research will vary considerably by project, with the depth and effort involved varying across different phases of a given project. For relatively routine projects, there may be little or no research; for complex and unique projects, there may be a number of research episodes throughout the project. Because the nature of the research may be so varied, it is all the more important for practitioners to have a sense of the many ways given strategies and tactics—perhaps interviews, or the simulation of environments—can be conceptualized and rendered suitable for different purposes.

3.2   FRAMEWORKS FOR UNDERSTANDING MULTIPLE SYSTEMS OF INQUIRY

Because the practice of architecture requires knowledge of a vast array of phenomena—from the physical properties of materials to principles of visual perception—it is hardly surprising that the research subdisciplines within architecture bring with them a full range of paradigms. Indeed, this is also the case within entire disciplinary families—for example, within the sciences, the social sciences, or the humanities. From the perspective of someone in the humanities, "science" may seem to represent a rather monolithic system of inquiry within which a highly standardized set of procedures is adopted; from a scientist's point of view, though, there are vast differences between scientific disciplines with respect to the typical methods employed and their standards for the credibility of evidence.[10] As a consequence, many scholars of research methodology from a variety of disciplines have developed models or frameworks for clarifying the similarities and differences among systems of inquiry.

In the following subsections, we will briefly review several of these frameworks, and then introduce a framework for distinguishing among systems of inquiry that we will utilize throughout the remainder of this book.

In the second portion of this chapter, we will then review standards of research quality articulated through the complementary relationship between systems of inquiry and schools of thought.

3.2.1 Early Frameworks in Architectural Research

In 1984, during the early years of the emergent development of architectural research in the academy, Joroff and Morse sought to review the range and scope of architectural research and provide an integrative framework for clarifying the types or forms of that research. This framework identifies what the authors deem to represent the full range of architectural research areas at the time, organized in a scalar order based on the degree of "systematization" that characterizes the different types of research. This effort is diagrammed as a 9-point continuum, from informal observation on the one hand to laboratory research on the other (see Figure 3.3).[11] In clarifying this concept, the authors suggest that systemization entails two basic ideas: (1) the idea that there is a reality "out there"; and (2) the assumption that to know this reality requires "objective" methods.

Within this conceptual framework, the left side of the model represents a more "subjective" system of inquiry, and the right side the more "objective" system of

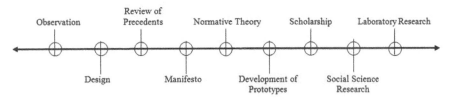

Figure 3.3 Michael Joroff and Stanley Morse's conceptual framework for architectural research. By permission of Michael L. Joroff.

inquiry. Although they introduce the framework as "an overall integrating context for divergent research efforts,"[12] they also propose that such a framework is needed "to distinguish research from other activities in which architects may engage."[13] Indeed, in discussing the examples from the left side of the scale, Joroff and Morse invoke a variety of qualifiers and cautions, none of which are applied to the more objective and systematic examples on the right. For example, they write that when architects review precedents during the design process, "it is an assessment of knowledge gained by others rather than research in the strict definition of the term."[14] Moreover, by equating research with the term *systematic,* and systematic with the belief that there is a reality "out there," they are essentially arguing that "real" research exists only at the objective end of the scale.

A second problematic feature of Joroff and Morse's proposed continuum is that the research types identified on the continuum are hardly comparable, and are in effect a mix of "apples and oranges." For instance, the term *laboratory-type research* invokes an experimental model and shares a place on the continuum with a kind of theory (normative, but what of other theory types?), and observations (a possible data collection tactic). Nevertheless, Joroff and Morse's continuum represents a historically significant effort to identify and validate the potential value and contributions of a multifaceted body of architectural research.

Several years later, in a 1990 *Journal of Architectural Education* article, Julia Robinson characterized the then current state of architecture research as one in which a dichotomous set of paradigms predominated. (Even now, the circumstances she describes are not so very different.) While the stated goal of her article was to offer a means of resolving this dichotomy into a more integrated framework for architectural research, she nevertheless characterized the then current state of architectural research as represented by two rather distinct communities of architectural researchers whose ideas "of acceptable explanation do not necessarily coincide."[15]

The terms by which she chooses to describe these two systems of inquiry are *science* and *myth.* Although both science and myth "are used to explain," the way they do so is quite different. A scientific explanation is typically portrayed as a mathematical description made up of linked fragments; it is thereby atomistic, reductionist, and convergent. Architectural research on topics of technology, engineering, or behavioral issues are seen as representing the scientific paradigm. However, mythic or poetic description is seen as continuous, holistic, divergent, and generative; this paradigm is usually associated with architectural research drawn from an arts and humanities base. This would include much of the scholarly work in the architectural history and design theory areas.

Robinson's intent is to articulate a way forward in architectural research such that the two distinct traditions can be effectively integrated. To this end, she presents the example of a studio project that explores how sensitive design might imbue the qualities of home in institutional settings. This project draws insights from both empirically based survey research and sketch exercises that draw on more intuitive insights about the essential qualities of home (see Figure 3.4 and 3.5).

Although Robinson's use of the *science* versus *myth* terminology is relatively idiosyncratic, the notion of a dichotomous set of research paradigms is commonplace in both architecture and other research disciplines. This dichotomous framework entails implicit associations with ontological and epistemological assumptions, as well as implications for methodological choices, that mirror those described by Robinson.

One of the most common devices for framing such a dichotomous model employs the terms *quantitative* versus *qualitative*. At its most basic level, this terminology assumes that quantitative research depends on the manipulation of phenomena that can be measured by numbers; whereas qualitative research depends on non-numerical evidence, whether verbal (oral or written), experiential (film or notes about people in action) or artifactual (objects, buildings, or urban

Figure 3.4 In her studio teaching, Julia Robinson had her students evaluate institutional living environments, the results of which were subjected to statistical, "scientific" analysis. © ACSA Press, Washington, D.C., 1993.

Figure 3.5 Robinson also had her students sketch a sociable home environment based on the "mythic" qualities that were evoked. Drawing by Michela Mahady. © ACSA Press, Washington, D.C., 1993.

areas). Figure 3.6 represents an abbreviated version of John Creswell's matrix for differentiating quantitative and qualitative research paradigms in the social sciences.[16] Thus, within this model, quantitative research assumes an *objective* reality and a view of the researcher as *independent of the subject* of inquiry. Qualitative research, however, assumes a *subjective* reality and a view of the researcher as *interactive with the subject* of inquiry. On a methodological level, the quantitative paradigm is seen as involving a *deductive* process of inquiry that seeks *cause-and-effect explanations,* whereas the qualitative paradigm necessitates an *inductive* process of inquiry that seeks clarification of *multiple critical factors* affecting the phenomenon.

This dichotomization implicitly persists in more recent characterizations of architectural research. For example, in a 2007 issue of *Journal of Architectural Education,* the journal editors proposed the term *scholarship of design* to serve as more inclusive definition of scholarship and inquiry that was contrasted with "the long-standing rigors of the scientific method"[17] promoted in earlier years of the journal. Similarly, in an article on research studios for a 2011 issue of *JAE,* author David Salomon observed that while research is often equated with "controlled and objective experiments," his aim is to propose a more inclusive definition of research that would entail "multiple modes of inquiry—both quantitative and qualitative."[18]

Unfortunately—though beguilingly simple—the quantitative/qualitative terminology places the emphasis on distinctions at the level of tactics, that is, the techniques for gathering or interpreting evidence or data. And at this level, distinctions between examples of research are often not nearly so clear-cut. Many research

Question	Quantitative	Qualitative
Ontology: What is the nature of reality?	Reality is objective and singular, apart from the researcher.	Reality is subjective and multiple as seen by participants in a study.
Epistemology: What is the relationship of the researcher to that being researched?	Researcher is independent from that being researched.	Researcher interacts with that being researched.
Methodology: What is the process of research?	Deductive process: cause and effect.	Inductive process: Mutual simultaneous shaping of factors.

Figure 3.6 Quantitative and Qualitative Paradigm Assumptions. By permission of Sage Publications. Adapted from John Creswell, *Research Design: Quantitative and Qualitative Approaches* (Thousand Oaks, CA: Sage, 1994), 5.

studies employ a combination of quantitative and qualitative tactics. Even research areas normally associated with a qualitative paradigm, such as architectural history, may necessarily require significant quantitative techniques.[19] For example, in Fernando Lara's study of the acceptance of modern architecture by the Brazilian middle class, a quantitative analysis was conducted based on documentation of the facade elements of 460 houses in Belo Horizonte.[20] In this case, the quantitative analysis complemented interviews and archival material that focused on how and why the houses were built as they were. (For more details on this study, see Chapter 12.)

Even within the family of physical sciences, this dichotomous framework for differentiating systems of inquiry is frequently employed. When the terms *quantitative* and *qualitative* are employed in the sciences, they are often associated with the corresponding terms: *hard* versus *soft* sciences.[21] The implication is that the sciences that depend on numerical measurement (e.g., physics) are hard, while those that rely on description and classification (e.g., biology or geology) are soft.

In our view, however, this dichotomous framework is often misleading. First, as indicated earlier, the reliance on the quantitative/qualitative terminology places undue emphasis on the level of tactics, instead of the characterization of ontological and epistemological assumptions. As numerous examples of architectural research throughout this book will demonstrate, both numerical and non-numerical evidence can be deployed in the service of more than one system of inquiry.

Second, at least as characterized by frameworks similar to that of Creswell's, there is an assumption that each of the two paradigms necessitates a particular research methodology. For example, the quantitative system of inquiry is assumed to be manifested in deductive methodology that seeks to discover cause-and-effect explanations. While not denying that there may frequently be such an association of quantitative data and deductive methods, this is not an invariant and necessary relationship. A system of inquiry will indeed frame the articulation of a research question, but there is not a one-to-one relationship between that system of inquiry and a particular research design. Indeed, in the chapters that follow, we will intentionally include examples of architectural research that employ research designs atypical of that particular topic area and system of inquiry.

Like Robinson, a number of authors in other disciplines seek to resolve the apparent dichotomy of quantitative science and qualitative humanities by incorporating the two epistemologies (and associated data types) into a single research study. For instance, two recent methods books (Creswell and Plano Clark, 2011; Teddlie and Tashakkori, 2009) are entirely dedicated to an examination of how quantitative and qualitative perspectives can be mixed for optimal effectiveness.[22]

3.2.2   *Some Alternative Frameworks*

In contrast, a number of scholars in a variety of disciplines have sought to provide a more fine-grained conceptual framework than the dichotomous model framed by the quantitative versus qualitative dichotomy. One particularly instructive framework is presented in a classic article by Morgan and Smircich writing for a diverse audience of social scientists who, like architectural researchers, are likely to represent the full range of ontological stances.[23] Morgan and Smircich explicitly argue that "the dichotomization between quantitative and qualitative methods is a rough and oversimplified one."[24] They also raise a concern that particular "quantitative" or "qualitative" tactics for gathering or interpreting evidence might be employed for their own sake, without reference to the paradigmatic frame of reference within which they are used. They go on to emphasize the "need to approach discussions of methodology in a way that highlights the vital link between theory and method."[25]

The framework, which Morgan and Smircich propose, is a continuum framed by subjective and objective end points. In contrast to the Joroff and Morse continuum, which simply identifies categories of research, Morgan and Smircich aim to represent the range of paradigmatic assumptions *underlying* research enterprises (see Figure 3.7). Within this framework, they identify and label six paradigmatic positions, indicating for each their core ontological perspectives (concerning the nature of reality), and corresponding assumptions about human nature. Most notably,

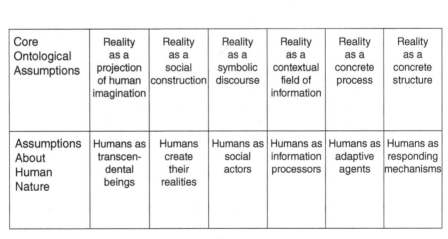

Subjective Approaches ⟷ Objective Approaches

Core Ontological Assumptions	Reality as a projection of human imagination	Reality as a social construction	Reality as a symbolic discourse	Reality as a contextual field of information	Reality as a concrete process	Reality as a concrete structure
Assumptions About Human Nature	Humans as transcendental beings	Humans create their realities	Humans as social actors	Humans as information processors	Humans as adaptive agents	Humans as responding mechanisms

Figure 3.7   Gareth Morgan and Linda Smirich's continuum of research paradigms, 1980. Reproduced by permission of Copyrights Clearance Center.

however, they refrain from specifying particular research designs or tactics that might be associated with these positions. Indeed, they argue that such a one-to-one correspondence between a given system of inquiry and a particular strategy or tactic would be counterproductive.

> [A]ny given technique [or tactic] often lends itself to a variety of uses according to the orientation of the researcher. For example, participant observation in the hands of a positivist may be used to document the number and length of interactions within a setting, but in the hands of an action theorist the technique may be used to explore the realms of subjective meaning of those interactions.[26]

Our own position regarding the relation of systems of inquiry to strategies and tactics is consistent with that articulated by Morgan and Smircich. On the one hand, there should be a coherence and consistency among these characteristics within any given research study. But on the other hand, when a researcher adopts a particular system of inquiry, that decision does not automatically determine either strategy or the tactics for the study. Rather, a variety of both strategies and tactics can be orchestrated in ways consistent with the chosen paradigm.

To illustrate this point, we invoke a rather humorous analogy to a child's toy where a variety of heads, torsos, and legs can be interchanged to create a host of assembled characters (see Figure 3.8). To be sure, some result in improbable combinations of mixed genders and incongruous body forms, just as not all combinations of strategies and tactics make sense within a particular system of inquiry. However, given the selection of a particular "head" (system of inquiry), many options of body parts (schools of thought, strategies, and tactics) can be linked to form a credible and coherent character (research study).

Over recent years, scholars in a variety of other disciplines have similarly sought to identify a more nuanced framework than the quantitative-qualitative dichotomy of epistemological assumptions. For example, social historian John R. Hall, in his book *Cultures of Inquiry* seeks to lay out a "Third Path" beyond the "modern and postmodern methodological debates in the social sciences, history, and the humanities." In doing so, he identifies "a surprising web of affinities and shared problematics" that are "deeply connected, and sometimes dependent upon one another. These connections are often denied by practitioners . . . maintaining the boundaries that mark off some epistemological Other."[27]

Similarly, in his book *The Pursuit of History*, John Tosh tackles the epistemological and methodological traditions of history as a discipline. He describes how through the 19th and well into the 20th century, most historical work was framed by the contrasting traditions of the scientific stance of positivism and the more

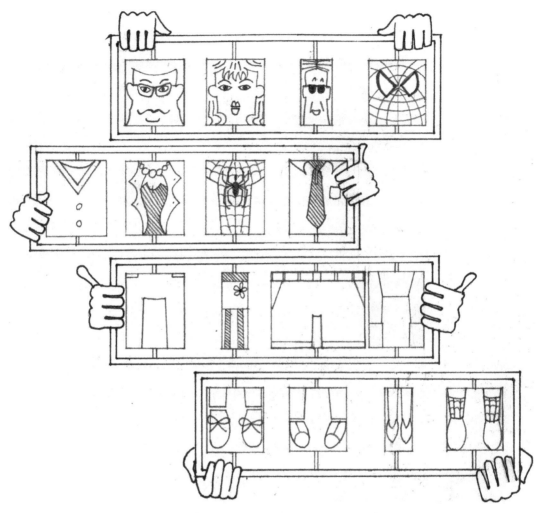

Figure 3.8 Child's toy analogy of integrating different systems of inquiry, schools of thought, strategies, and tactics. Courtesy of Kush Patel.

subjective perspective of Idealism. In more recent decades, history like many other disciplines experienced the "linguistic" or "Postmodern" turn, whereby the potential of achieving any intersubjective agreement in interpreting a given text or source is called into question. While acknowledging the multiple insights and contributions of the radically subjective perspective of the literary turn, Tosh emphasizes two influential trends in recent historical research—social theory and cultural history—both of which represent significant and complementary alternatives to the extremes of Idealism/the literary turn and the scientific tradition.[28]

3.2.3   A Proposed Framework: A Three-Part Continuum

As an alternative to the previously discussed dichotomous epistemological models, we propose a modified continuum that takes into account the perspective of many of the other authors we have already cited. While our proposed continuum (see Figure 3.9) acknowledges the possibility of multiple epistemological and ontological positions along the continuum (e.g., the Morgan and Smircich continuum in Figure 3.7), we identify, for the sake of clarity and ease, three primary epistemological positions. This continuum is bounded by the positivist/postpositivist tradition at one end, and constructivism at the opposite end. The middle ground of the continuum is not so easily labeled because there are multiple labels and schools of thoughts attributed to it by a various academic disciplines. Due to the lack of a widely accepted label, we are using the term *intersubjective* to reflect its interstitial position between the positivist emphasis on objectivity and the constructivist emphasis on subjectivity. This tradition recognizes both the multiplicity of distinct perspectives and the importance of socially shared action and knowledge.

There are several significant challenges in proposing any conceptual framework for the full scope of architectural and design research. First among them is that architecture, as both a discipline and a profession, encompasses an exceedingly multidisciplinary scope that ranges from highly technical research, to analyses of

Objective ◄────────────────────────────────► Subjective

	Positivism/Postpositivism		Intersubjective	Constructivism	
Epistemology	Knower distinct from object of inquiry	Knowing through distance from object	Knowledge framed by understanding sociocultural engagement	Knowledge co-constructed with participants	Knowledge perpetually provisional
Ontology	Assumes objective reality	External reality revealed probabilistically	Diverse realities situated in sociocultural context	Multiple constructed realities	Infinite realities

Figure 3.9   Continuum of research paradigms. Adapted from Mugerauer, 1995; Guba and Lincoln, 1998; Teddlie and Tashakorri, 2009; and Mertens, 2010. Full citations listed in endnotes.

design processes in many cultural contexts, to studies of the history of particular stylistic forms or building types, and a vast array of many other foci of inquiry. Second, over recent years, and certainly since the earlier edition of this book was published, there has been enormous fluidity in the way that different epistemological traditions have been characterized and labeled. Some of this fluidity arises from the differences among the many different academic disciplines that have explicitly addressed these issues. But, in addition, even within particular disciplines or disciplinary groups, there are often great variations in terminology. And finally, even though the range of epistemological traditions is arranged along a continuum, it is nevertheless highly reductive, in effect compressing multiple points of similarities and differences into one primary dimension of difference.

Despite these challenges and disclaimers, it is nevertheless possible to discern some consistent differences among the three primary epistemological traditions, however fluid the labels and underlying premises may be. We would argue that in order to advance the potential contributions of architectural research over the long term, it is both practical and essential to illuminate the paradigmatic perspectives that inform our field.

Positivism/Postpositivism   At the objective end of the continuum lie ontological positions that assume the existence of a reality that can be objectively described or measured. Historically, positivism was characterized by what many would describe as a "naive" belief in a reality "out there" that can be fully known, while the currently more prevalent stance of postpositivism is characterized by a more nuanced belief in an "out there" reality that can only be known within some level of "probability."[29] And whereas positivism has assumed that objectivity can be achieved in the research process; postpositivism presumes that objectivity is a legitimate goal that may be imperfectly realized. Postpositivists also acknowledge that the experimental model typically used in the natural sciences is often inappropriate for research involving people. As a result, modifications and accommodations may have to be made in research practices, particularly the use of quasi-experimental and correlational strategies. (See Chapters 8 and 9 for details.) In addition to these basic positivist notions are the complementary assumptions that values should remain outside the conduct of inquiry (or at least can be controlled), and that it is possible to identify causal factors for observed phenomena.

In the context of architectural research, the positivist tradition is the most influential mode of research in the technical domains of the field, such as energy conservation practices or structures. These are topics of research in which there is an assumed consensus that the physical properties of materials or the processes of mechanical systems can be objectively measured or, at the very least, that such measurements can *practically* be assumed to reflect reality. Nevertheless, though relatively rare, there are examples of research on technical topics that draw from nonpositivist epistemological traditions; some of these examples will be discussed in later chapters of this book.

In other areas of design research, such as those involving people's responses to particular settings, the influence of the positivist tradition is more contested. Even so, research that measures the extent to which multiple, measured variables account for particular actions or social outcomes is likely to assume a probabilistic understanding of reality.

Intersubjective   At the middle segment of our continuum, the essence of this paradigmatic orientation is that the world is known, intersubjectively, through sociocultural engagement. Ontologically, it assumes that although there are multiple diverse viewpoints regarding sociocultural realities, it is nevertheless possible to achieve shared understandings of those realities.

In contrast to the objective segment of the continuum, the intersubjective perspective assumes that it is neither possible nor necessarily desirable for research to establish objectivity within a value-free stance. Rather, researchers recognize the significance of values and meaning in framing the goals of the research and/or interpreting the results.[30] And in contrast to the positivist paradigm, causality is assumed to be just one of many possible relations or interactions within the phenomena under study. More important, any causal relationship should be socially and historically situated.

For architectural and design research, this perspective would foreground the values and intentionality of people's actions and interpretations of meaning at all scales of environments, including how these transactional relations are situated in the larger social or historical context. For instance, this perspective might be employed to elucidate a community's interpretation of civic meaning in a new library or city hall. Another study might explore the contested dynamics among members of a design team for a major architectural project.

Constructivism   At the right, or subjective end, of the continuum lies the set of ontological and epistemological assumptions described as constructivism. Within the past decade, many authors have come to employ the term *constructivism* in preference to several other labels—naturalistic, qualitative, or interpretive—that had been previously used interchangeably to describe this approach to research.[31]

As advocates of constructivism, Denzin and Lincoln summarize this paradigm as entailing a "relativist" ontology, whereby multiple realities are understood as being socially constructed.[32] Whereas the positivist tradition assumes the potential of an objective reality, and the intersubjective paradigm foregrounds the transactional nature of meaning and action in a socially situated context, constructivism adopts a subjectivist epistemology whereby knowledge emerges as the researcher(s) and respondents co-create understandings of the situation or context being studied. In environmental and design research, the constructivist approach would seek to elucidate in-depth insights and interpretations of a given setting from the perspectives of the individuals who experience that environment.

A more radical version of the constructivist paradigm holds that a virtually infinite number of realities can be presumed. Knowledge can be only temporarily or provisionally established, and is soon to be reinterpreted. In the social sciences or the humanities, this version of constructivism often takes the form of in-depth textual analyses of either documents or interview materials; "hegemonic" interpretations are reconsidered in the light of what is or is not stated in a text. In architectural or environmental design research, artifacts, buildings, and settings are often the "texts" that are the subject of interpretation and reinterpretation.[33] In its most radical form, interpretations are always provisional and fluid; no shared or common understanding can be established. As theorist Robert Mugerauer concludes, "[S]ince there is always the delay and deferral of meaning, while signs (inescapably) indefinitely refer to one another," "no meaning"—as opposed to multiple meanings—is revealed.[34]

3.2.4   *The Complementary Nature of Research Framed by Diverse Systems of Inquiry*

Finally, and most importantly, the larger intent of Figure 3.9 is to convey the stance to which we are committed in writing this book, specifically that each system of inquiry can provide an appropriate and useful frame of reference for architectural research. Good research that yields important theory or significant practical applications can be achieved within any one of these paradigmatic clusters. Likewise, adherence to a particular system of inquiry—however esteemed within a particular subdiscipline of architectural research—is no guarantee for achieving high-quality research. In that, the analogy to architectural style is directly pertinent; though we may individually prefer to design in a particular style, we have to acknowledge that there are both good and bad exemplars of that style. Adherence to Classicism or Art Deco, Postmodernism or Neo-Modernism, does not in and of itself assure quality.

3.3   MEASURES OF RESEARCH QUALITY

In an inherently interdisciplinary field, such as architecture, a common tendency is for researchers, who might work primarily or only within one system of inquiry, to evaluate research from a different system of inquiry according to the standards of quality they know best. For example, researchers whose work falls clearly within the positivist paradigm may nevertheless tend to judge research done in either a constructivist or intersubjective paradigm by the standards they themselves employ. Not surprisingly, this can lead to a lot of heated arguments about whose work is really "research" and whose is not. In such instances, the potential benefits of tackling research topics in architecture from a variety of perspectives are virtually negated.

Instead, we believe it is far more productive to evaluate quality in architectural research according to the standards that have been developed by methodologists working within the various paradigmatic traditions. Although the quality standards for the positivist/postpositivist paradigm have been codified for many years, the effort to articulate standards of quality appropriate for alternative paradigms remains a continuing project; in recent decades, it has yielded numerous articles and chapters across many disciplines. Perhaps the most influential early exemplar of this effort is embodied in a 1981 journal article by social scientist Egon Guba. Figure 3.10 presents the typically recognized quality standards of the positivist/ postpositivism paradigm alongside Guba's proposed standards for what he termed at the time a *naturalistic* paradigm.

A second important feature of the matrix in Figure 3.10 is that the relevant quality criteria (in the left column of the matrix) are "generic" terms that are not associated with any particular system of inquiry.[35] The obvious purpose in doing so is to avoid privileging the terms and concepts associated with any one paradigm. Nevertheless, there is legitimate criticism that this matrix still privileges the postpositivist paradigm standards by forcing the identification within the naturalistic paradigm of terminology essentially comparable to those postpositivist standards.[36]

Indeed, from a historical perspective, Guba's proposed quality standards represent an explicitly binary alternative to the then dominant positivist/postpositivist system of inquiry. Since the publication of Guba's article, many researchers and scholars have acknowledged the significance of Guba's contribution in the articulation of quality standards outside the postpositivist tradition. However, a number of scholars (including Guba himself) have over recent years have offered either refinements or alternatives to the "naturalistic" standards for particular domains of research; these will be discussed later in this chapter. Nevertheless, we believe that Guba's proposal remains a useful introduction to the principles of quality standards in research.

3.3.1   *Quality Standards within a Postpositivist System of Inquiry*

For better or worse, many readers are likely to be at least somewhat familiar with the standards of quality identified with the objective paradigm. This is because they

Standard	Positivism / Postpositivism	Naturalistic
Truth value	*Internal validity* Equivalence of data of inquiry and phenomena they represent	*Credibility* Check data with interviewees; triangulation—multiple data sources of data collection
Applicability	*External validity* Generalizability	*Transferability* Thick description of context to assess similarity
Consistency	*Reliability* Instruments must produce stable results	*Dependability* Trackability of expected instability of data
Neutrality	*Objectivity* Methods explicated; replicable; investigator one-step removed from object of study	*Confirmability* Triangulation of data; practice of reflexivity by investigator

Figure 3.10 Comparative analysis of quality standards, 1981. By permission of Egon Guba.

have been codified, discussed, and presented in methodology texts for many years. And as alluded to earlier, because the standards that apply to other systems of inquiry have been less explicitly codified, or codified more recently, there is often the tendency among researchers to apply the "objective" standards to research executed within the other systems of inquiry. Although we believe this tendency is a mistake, we have nevertheless chosen to begin with the objective paradigm, simply because it already is a starting point for many researchers.

Internal Validity   Although there are many subcategories of internal validity, the fundamental issue is whether the key concepts and operations of the study are truthful representations of the object of study. For example, we might ask whether a housing satisfaction questionnaire really measures residents' satisfaction with their housing. This requires a clearly stated definition of what would constitute housing satisfaction and a rationale for the correspondence between the question items and that definition. Or, perhaps, we have reason to develop a new housing questionnaire. We might want to make sure that the results using that questionnaire correspond to a previously developed questionnaire on housing.

In the case of Stazi et al.'s study of solar walls referred to at the beginning of this chapter, the authors carry out their testing of a Trombe wall system used as a nonventilated solar wall in winter, and a Trombe wall with cross-ventilation and shaded by roller shutters and overhangs in summer. This experimentation was conducted over several years at a case study residential site in Italy. Data from the experimental model was then used as a basis for the development of a simulation model; such that "the first simulation was run to reproduce the 'as built' condition. ... Once the model had been validated, it was then possible to calculate results for the whole year, including measurements of indoor air temperatures, solar walls surface temperatures, and heating energy consumption."[37] In other words, the authors employed both experimental data and numerical simulations in concert to assess the validity of the Trombe solar wall measurements.

External Validity   The question behind this criterion is whether the results of the study are applicable to the larger world. Or, at least, what are the defining contextual constraints within which the results are valid? In the case of the solar wall study, the authors are quite specific and clear in stating that the window designs were tested at a case study residential site in Italy. Based on these climatic conditions and the subsequently calculated simulation model, the authors conclude that solar walls are shown to (1) be superior compared to conventional walls in both energy savings and comfort in winter; and (2) achieve adequate performance, with cross-ventilation adaptations, in summer.

What if we want to use this experimental Trombe wall design in New York or California? We have two choices. At a more informal level, we might compare the climate data for New York or California with that of Mediterranean Italy; we would then make a calculated judgment about the degrees of similarity in climate. We might well conclude that the climates of California and Italy are similar enough to expect the same results; similarly, we might conclude that the New York climate is too dissimilar to assume comparable results. In that case, we might seek to expand the original study and employ additional experiments to run the numerical simulation using the New York climate data.

Reliability   The concept of reliability is concerned with the consistency of the measurements or findings. Within the objective paradigm, the assumption is that the research methods would yield the same results, if the study were conducted under the same conditions. What might we say, then, about the reliability of the solar wall study? In this case, since the research concerns relatively stable physical objects and properties, the window performance data would be expected to be quite reliable, so long as the physical conditions of the experiments and simulation remain the same. Nevertheless, the authors conclude their article by acknowledging that additional experiments are being carried out so as to provide more complete data on how the performance and management of ventilated Trombe walls can be improved during the summer months.

However, other architectural studies using an "objective" system of inquiry frequently have, as the focus of study, conditions or social phenomena that will necessarily require a greater examination of reliability. If, for instance, we consider again the example of housing satisfaction research, we might expect similar results in a study in which a sample of residents are surveyed initially, and then again a week or two later. In this instance, the similar results would suggest reliability; inconsistent results would suggest unreliability of the questionnaire. However, if the survey were administered to the same group a year or two later, after major changes in the housing management occurred, then we would expect that changes in the survey results might well occur. We would then attribute the lack of consistent or stable results to a fundamental change in the conditions of the study rather than to a lack of reliability of the survey instrument.

Objectivity   Consistent with the "objective" system of inquiry, the goal for the research procedures is to keep the potential bias or interference of the researcher out of the process. This is achieved by strict specification and administration of the relevant procedures. Typically, the researcher utilizes standardized measurement instruments—whether questionnaires or calibrated equipment; the sequence and process of experimental manipulation are highly regulated. In the case of the Stazi et al. study, the researchers carefully specify the experimental and simulation procedures, provide detailed diagrams and photographs of the Trombe solar wall configuration, and extensive charts reflecting the results of the Trombe wall performance assessment. Within the text, other information is provided, such as the dimensions, materials, the devices for regulating air temperature, and so on. Armed with these specifications, another researcher could choose to replicate the study, thus providing yet another test of these results.

3.3.2.   *Quality Standards within a Naturalistic System of Inquiry*

The second column in Figure 3.10 reflects Egon Guba's proposed set of quality standards for what he termed *naturalistic inquiry*.[38] In introducing what he calls "criteria for assessing trustworthiness," Guba has identified a number of key charac-teristics of naturalistic inquiry, among them the recognition of multiple realities, as opposed to a single reality; the assumption that generalizations are not necessarily possible in all instances; the understanding that a research design may emerge as the research proceeds; and the belief that the researcher and the respondent influ-ence and are influenced by each other.

Guba subsequently proposed yet another alternative set of quality standards for naturalistic research.[39] However, because of the heuristic value of the originally developed criteria and their influence on the literature on research methodology, we will present them here for discussion and comparison to the postpositivist standards.

The standards of quality that Guba has proposed represent substantially differ-ent criteria—though presented in parallel structure—from those associated with the postpositivist system of inquiry. Moreover, Guba provides examples of several concepts or procedures for meeting each of these criteria, but given the summary nature of this discussion, we will simply highlight the most essential points.

Credibility   The idea behind credibility is to establish truth value by taking into account the natural complexities inherent in the situation or circumstance being studied. In other words, credibility entails a more holistic approach to the research problem. Two particularly important ways of demonstrating truth value are trian-gulation and member checks. The former involves the utilization of a variety of data sources, multiple investigators, and/or a combination of data collection techniques in order to cross-check data and interpretations. The latter involves checking the data and interpretations with the respondents and groups from whom the data were solicited, a process that Guba claims "goes to the heart of the credibility criterion."[40]

If we return now to Schwarz's study of nursing home design, we find that he reports triangulation but not the use of member checks. To be specific, Schwarz achieves triangulation in two distinct ways. First, although he provides details of three separate case studies, he reports that these are three of a total of eight case study facilities. In other words, his conclusion that the architectural model used for nursing homes is misguided and unduly compromised by code regulations and reimbursement systems is strengthened by his being able to demonstrate this dy-namic in multiple instances. Second, within each case study, Schwarz indicates that his data derive from:

> [M]ultiple means such as open-ended interviews, document collection, par-ticipatory observation, and visits to built facilities. . . . Key informants included care-providers, owners, architects, gerontological consultants, staff members,

committee and board members, state regulators, residents of nursing homes and their families.[41]

Transferability   Like generalizability—its corresponding term in the postpositivist paradigm—transferability has to do with the extent to which the conclusions of one study can be applied to another setting or circumstance. To achieve transferability, Guba argues, one must provide a sufficiently "thick" description such that relative similarity of the two contexts can be adequately. assessed. In the nursing home study, Schwarz is careful to emphasize the particularities of the settings he studied, while at the same time he suggests the likelihood that similar themes would likely emerge through research in other nursing home settings:

> In [this] tradition . . . , researchers are cautious not to generalize because of the personal nature of their observations and specificity of the measurements made in the fieldwork. In most cases, fieldwork can produce results that would not necessarily be replicated by other researchers. Because of the nature of in-depth studies, the themes, results, and conclusions are real and accurate, primarily within their original context. Although no comprehensive generalization was intended in this study, it is safe to assume that the themes described in the three cases are not unique in other design processes of nursing homes.[42]

Dependability   The notion of dependability suggests that there is a fundamental consistency within the data, but it also takes into account "apparent instabilities arising either because different realities are being tapped or because of instrumental shifts stemming from developing insights on the part of the investigator-as-instrument [of research]."[43] The primary device for ensuring dependability is, according to Guba, the establishment of an "audit trail." The audit trail documents all the processes by which data were collected, analyzed, and interpreted; this might include interview and observation notes, drawings and diagrams that track people's activity patterns in a building, the investigator's daily journal notes, and so on.

In the publication format of Schwarz's study, it is not possible to verify the extent to which Schwarz may have established a comprehensive audit trail. However, one can infer from his discussion of the data analysis that a substantially complete audit trail may well have been established:

> The analysis process followed the grounded theory approach [see Chapter 7 for details] in the steps described by Chesler.[44] The data were transcribed, coded, and categorized in a search for themes. Due to the limited scope of this article, the themes from the three cases presented here depict only issues related to

regulations and the reimbursement system of long-term care settings. These themes are major anchoring points of the world's [sic] views of the actors in the design process. Quotes are given in their natural form to capture the character of the fieldwork.[45]

Confirmability   Contrary to the notion of ensuring the investigator's objectivity, Guba argues instead for the confirmability of data and interpretations. This, he maintains, can be achieved through a combination of triangulation and reflexivity on the part of the researcher. We have already discussed the use of multiple methods, sources, and investigators to establish triangulation. Reflexivity requires the investigator to reveal his/her epistemological assumptions, their influence on the framing of the research question, and any changes in perspective that might emerge during the course of the study.

In the example of Schwarz's study, his efforts to establish triangulation have already been noted. And although he does not provide the full measure of reflexivity suggested by Guba, he nevertheless makes his stance clear by articulating the system of inquiry within which his research is situated.

3.3.3   *Quality Standards among Selected Schools of Thought and Disciplines*

In recent years, a number of authors across a variety of fields have articulated specific quality standards for research that falls within the continuum of intersubjective or constructivist paradigms. Figure 3.11 represents a sampling of the quality standards usually associated with particular disciplines and/or exemplary "schools of thoughts" outside the positivist/postpositivist tradition.

Sources listed in the bottom row of Figure 3.11 are cited elsewhere in this chapter and therefore listed in the endnotes, except for the following: Linda Finlay, "A Dance Between the Reduction and Reflexivity," *Journal of Phenomenological Psychology,* 39 (2008): 1–32; Linda Finlay, "Debating Phenomenological Research Methods," *Phenomenology & Practice* 3(1) (2009): 6–25; Amadeo Giorgi, "A Phenomenological Perspective on Certain Qualitative Research Methods," *Journal of Phenomenological Psychology* 25(2) (1994): 190–220; Martha S. Feldman, *Strategies for Interpreting Qualitative Data* (Thousand Oaks, CA: Sage, 1995).

Recall that in Chapter 1, we defined schools of thought as broad theoretical perspectives that have significantly influenced multiple disciplines. In Figure 1.4 we diagrammed a relationship of nested squares whereby systems of inquiry represent the broadest assumptions that frame the research enterprise. Within that broader framework, the adoption of a particular school of thought is likely to influence how research questions are framed. Although it is entirely possible to

Perspectives / Standards	History	Pragmatism	Transformative	Phenomenology	Constructivist	Radical Constructivist / Poststructuralist
Truth Value	Sources never complete but use of multiple sources	Tools of inquiry refined in light of communal meaning	Maintain diversity with target groups, check data with interviewees	Precise description of phenomena	Ontological "authenticity" enlarges personal constructions and credibility	Truth is undecideable, remains within play of signification
Applicability	Tension in history between focus on unique events and generalization	Established through process of validation; truth happens to an idea	Cultural sensitivity can ensure applicability; erode ignorance	Search for essences	Transferability, educative authenticity leads to improved understanding of others	Dissemination is perpetually unfulfilled, meaning and absence of all signified
Consistency	Insight and interpretation dependent on individual scholar	Seek agreement via action	Data collection designed for identifying potential benefits for excluded group(s)	Researcher's free imaginative variation	Dependability, tracking expected instability of data	Only instability is possible, each interpretation sows seeds of its undoing
Neutrality	Scrutinize assumptions (reflexivity)	Investigator interprets meaning framed by larger purposes (reflexivity)	Reflexivity with emphasis on power differentials	Reflexivity and bracketing (reductive focus)	Reflexivity	Author produces fiction, inventing styles and meanings as needed
Situatedness	Attention to entire historical context	Inquiry situated in transactional engagement and larger purposes	Situating inequalities and issues of social justice in historical context	"Intentionality" as essential character of consciousness	Emphasis on natural settings	Interpreting is entirely situated within "textual" analysis
Sources	Tosh, 2011	Maxcy, 2003; Teddlie and Tashakkori, 2009	Guba and Lincoln, 1998; Mertens, 2010; Teddlie and Tashakkori, 2009	Finlay, 2008, 2009; Giorgi, 1994	Denzin and Lincoln, 2008; Guba and Lincoln, 1998; Teddlie and Tashakkori, 2009	Feldman, 1995; Mugerauer, 1995

Figure 3.11 Quality standards among exemplar schools of thought and disciplines. Adapted from sources listed in figure.

design a research study without aligning it with a particular school of thought, virtually every research study is framed by a system of inquiry, whether explicitly stated or not, that implies basic assumptions about the nature of reality and knowledge. Nevertheless, when researchers *do* identify their work as associated with a school of thought, the associated conceptual framework often influences not only how the research question is framed, but also the use of particular research tactics, including the choice of relevant sources or data, as well as the use of particular analytical tools.

If we very briefly consider each of the terms identifying the disciplinary domains and schools of thought represented in Figure 3.11, we can get some sense of the overall conceptual complexity of the several exemplars. For consistency with the previous matrix of quality standards (Figure 3.10), we are using the same generic terms for aspects of quality coined by Guba. However, few of the authors make any specific references to these particular labels; we have simply categorized the various authors' comments according to these terms for ease of comparison. Indeed, the standards identified by the individual columns often overlap and/or are virtually identical to some of the standards in other columns. As a consequence, there may be instances where a particular study might be appropriately interpreted as fitting under more than one perspective.

Most important, although this matrix may appear to be organized as a continuum similar to Figure 3.9 (systems of inquiry), this is not the intended reading of the matrix. Rather, we would argue that the arrangement of the several columns within the matrix represents a rather fluid positioning of the quality standards represented. In other words, the relative positioning of, for example, the emancipatory perspective is not meant to imply that all studies identified with that perspective are necessarily less intersubjective or more subjective than research from a pragmatist perspective. Although it may well be possible to define a "central" epistemological tendency for each school of thought along an intersubjective–constructivist continuum, it is also true that any given research study within that school could justifiably be located at the different ends of such a continuum. In other words, while there is often an identifiable paradigmatic tendency within a given school of thought or disciplinary domain, that tendency is not determinative.

To begin, then, the matrix column at the right side of the matrix identifies the quality standards articulated by the historian John Tosh. He is the author of a classic book on the practice of historical inquiry titled *The Pursuit of History*, now in its fifth edition. Because his intention is to identify the more discipline-specific and overarching principles of historical research, his proposed standards are less clearly affiliated with a particular school of thought. Overall, Tosh, like many historians, argues that excellent historical research depends on the insight and interpretive skill of the historian. Nevertheless, he argues that the overall quality of that research can be reinforced by, among other things: the willingness of the historian to scrutinize his/her assumptions (reflexivity); the use of as many sources as possible in the face of typically limited sources; and the use of a "hypothesis" (in a generic sense of the word) while being open to contrary evidence.[46]

Moving to the second column, the term *pragmatic* is used in two complementary senses. In the more generic sense of the term, some researchers argue that this epistemological perspective is primarily a theoretical rationale for the use of a mixed methods (quantitative/qualitative) research strategy. (See Chapter 12 for extended discussion of mixed methods.) Other researchers more explicitly draw on the philosophical roots of Pragmatism, initially articulated in the late 19th and early 20th centuries by such theorists as Charles Sanders Peirce and John Dewey. In general, pragmatism assumes that "humans live in a common world that is nevertheless nonobjective."[47] It is social "transactions" that enable us to understand both "the existence of multiple subjective realities while at the same time seeking agreement via action." This emphasis on a "transactional" relationship between meanings and actions leads to a "prospective" stance embodied in the question: "What difference would it make to us if the statement were true?" In other words, the pragmatist researcher is concerned with the value and efficacy of the outcomes of the research enterprise for the larger community.[48]

BOX 3.1

A Pragmatic Analysis of New Urbanism and Suburban Decentralization

In a 2009 study, Brian Christens explicitly draws on a philosophically pragmatist approach to analyzing the competing models of suburban decentralization and new urbanism (see Figures 3.12 and 3.13).[a] He argues that much of the ongoing discourse on this topic has mistakenly focused on evaluating which side of the argument has marshaled "the more objectively appealing theories and facts." Rather than employing a research approach based on "theoretical/empirical objectivity" (usually associated with the postpositivist paradigm), Christens argues that it is more

[a] Brian Christens, "Suburban Decentralization and the New Urbanism: A Pragmatic Inquiry into Value-Based Claims," *Journal of Architectural and Planning Research* 26(1) (Spring 2009): 30–43.

(Continued)

Figure 3.12   Typical street in Orchard Village with a lack of housing diversity and sidewalk, garages facing street. Courtesy of Joongsub Kim.

appropriate to adopt a research approach that explicitly addresses the underlying *values* inherent in the two neighborhood models. To this end, Christens argues that research in the tradition of pragmatism leads to conclusions that are

> situational and tentative—they are "true" only for a particular place and time and in relation to a certain set of goals. . . . [P]ragmatism envisions a philosophy engaged in the task of theorizing attainable values as both means and ends toward which everyday individual and structural efforts might be dedicated.

Thus, Christens's aim is *not* to draw conclusions about the extent to which of the two neighborhood models is better or more effective, in general. Rather, he identifies the following research questions to be posed against each of these neighborhood design concepts:

1. What are the beliefs that inform this approach?
2. If we are to adopt these beliefs in specific instances, what are the values for which we are working?
3. And why should we—in this context—believe these values to be worthy of our actions (and beliefs)?

Figure 3.13 Typical street in Kentlands with a mix of diverse housing types, sidewalk, and no garages facing street. Courtesy of Joongsub Kim.

In addressing the first two questions, Christens's detailed analysis leads him to conclude that the values most commonly associated with suburban decentralization include "the pursuit of paradise, economic liberalism, private property rights/transportation, functional aggregation, and *bonding* with communities of individuals with perceived similarities." In comparison, the values most often articulated as a basis for new urbanism include "social equity, the common good, *bridging* of social groups, sustainability, community, and a vibrant public." Christens suggests that although these value sets do not always or necessarily represent oppositional poles of values, they nevertheless represent a distinct difference in emphasis.

To address the third research question, Christens first reminds us that the "pragmatist approach to a project is to ask which beliefs work in practice in certain contexts." For instance, he highlights author David Brain's suggestion that proponents of new urbanism might better eschew the notion of "community" and aim instead to achieve "civility," a concept that "involves a level of trust and capacity for social relation that makes collective decision-making possible." Moreover, new urbanism's relative emphasis on physical design qualities is not likely to be sufficient to achieve some of the generally desired transformations in economic or social domains. However, the inability of suburban decentralization to serve as a catalyst for the values of bridging relations across social groups,

(Continued)

environmental conservation, and a more vibrant public sphere "necessi-tates the search for alternatives."

In conclusion, he argues that in moving forward with specific neighbor-hood development proposals, all involved would do well to maintain "an experimental habit of mind." Rather than looking for an ultimate solution, it would be far more effective to seek "modest practical steps" that would assimilate differences between the competing neighborhood models.

In the third column, a common alternative label for transformative is emanci-patory. As such, this perspective emerged in recent decades in response to concerns among scholars in a number of disciplines who began to point out the unconscious dominance of racial, ethnic, gender, and Western-focused biases in the vast major-ity of research. Typically, this approach promotes social justice by focusing on the dynamics of power and marginalization as they affect less dominant groups; as well, it seeks to highlight the historically and socially situated context in which the study respondents find themselves.[49] In architectural research, this would, for example, include studies that investigate the extent to which individuals and groups experi-ence equitable access to various settings.

Depending on disciplinary traditions, many scholars whose work can be cate-gorized as within the transformative perspective strongly identify their work as "critical theory." This school of thought is derived from the work of several genera-tions of German philosophers and social scientists associated with the Frankfurt School (including such influential theorists as Jurgen Habermas and Herbert Marcuse) who drew substantially from the Marxist tradition. In a broader context, many scholars who employ feminist, critical race, or postcolonial perspectives frame their work under the umbrella of Critical Theory.[50]

Much influenced by the heritage of German philosophy and the Marxist tradi-tion, the initial aim of the Frankfurt School scholars was to go beyond the estab-lished domains of philosophy and social sciences to achieve a more integrative theoretical stance that is simultaneously "explanatory, practical, and normative."[51] In doing so, they sought to "transform contemporary capitalism into a consensual form of social life."[52] In more recent developments, the work of Jurgen Habermas has been particularly influential; many of the major tenets of his work are seen as consistent with the perspectives of American Pragmatists including Dewey and Rorty. For example, embedded in Habermas's emphasis on the role of "communica-tive action" is the assumption that "rationality" is not about acquiring knowledge but rather about how practical knowledge enables the cultivation of social relation-ships, a stance that foregrounds the practical goal of solving problems.[53]

BOX 3.2

A Transformative Perspective on the Practice of Julia Morgan

Diane Favro's study of the well-known, early-20th-century California architect Julia Morgan (1872–1957) embodies the premises and standards of the transformative school of thought.[a] By way of introduction to her study, Favro first cites a quotation from a 1931 interview with Julia Morgan in which she is asked about women's contribution to the field of architecture. Morgan demurs and comments that women professionals had so far contributed little or nothing, though they might in the future. Favro then compares these comments with the response of Linda Nochlin, who in 1972 was asked why there had been no great women artists, to which Nochlin replied that "as a disenfranchised group, women artists had limited opportunities for greatness." Favro then goes on:

> Thus, Nochlin correctly deduced the question itself is inappropriate. Women architects similarly have been evaluated according to masculinist criteria. To be accurate, every evaluation of female practitioners must consider how gender affected their careers, designs, and recognition.

With this introduction, Favro is clearly signaling that her study of Morgan will challenge existing orthodoxies regarding how the careers of architectural practitioners in general, and women in particular, are assessed. (See Figure 3.14, an example of one of Morgan's significant projects.) Throughout the article, she very explicitly weaves the historical situatedness of gender issues as they were lived by women during Morgan's lifetime. For example, she describes the anomaly of Morgan's being one of the few American students among her almost entirely male colleagues to actually receive a diploma from the Beaux Arts. Morgan, Favro argues, was tenacious in doing so "to overcome the disadvantages incumbent with her gender." Favro then goes on to suggest that other characteristics of her professional life—such as her downplaying of her gender in her professional role, maintaining a low profile, developing a repeat business with influential women clients—were strategies adopted because of the social construction of gender at that time.

Favro makes the point that previous research had often criticized Morgan for many of the attitudes and practices described above, including her lack of "a signature style or theory." But, Favro argues, "her accommodation was a logical response to the professional situation faced as a

---

[a] Diane Favro, "Sincere and Good: The Architectural Practice of Julia Morgan," *Journal of Architectural Education* 9(2) (1992): 112–128.

(*Continued*)

Figure 3.14 One of Julia Morgan's well-known buildings at Asilomar, California. Photograph courtesy of A. Melissa Harris.

trailblazer." In this regard, Favro reframes the conventional interpretation of Morgan's role and stature in the profession, thereby providing an important educative function.

Consistent with the transformative perspective's imperative to promote positive change in social and cultural practices, Favro's analysis makes it clear that she is challenging the historically situated value system evident during Morgan's lifetime. But, more important, she also argues that the values Morgan embraced and promoted deserve to be at the heart of contemporary architecture. Favro concludes her article this way:

> Morgan deserves recognition for all her skill at crafting a profitable, large-scale, and enduring career despite the obstacles presented by her

> gender. . . . Reacting to preconceptions about women's roles . . . [she] emphasized livability, cost effectiveness, durability, client-satisfaction, and user needs. Difficult to document, non-visual in content, transient, and associated with women, these concerns historically have earned little praise. . . . If these aspects of architecture are thought unimportant, then perhaps the priorities of the architecture profession, not the gender of the architect, should be evaluated.
>
> There is no doubt that Favro seeks to provoke changes in the values, attitudes, and practices of architecture as it is currently conceived and practiced.

Next, the phenomenological tradition has long been influential in architectural research; it is, however, a mode of inquiry that is challenging to situate among other schools of thought, due in part to its relatively unique conceptualization of "subjectivity." Phenomenology is a philosophical tradition that has its roots in the works of German philosophers, particularly Heidegger and Husserl; in architecture, this perspective is most notably represented by the European scholar Christian Norberg-Schulz in his books on topics of dwelling and place, and more informally by many authors and architects who less explicitly adopt its conceptual framework.

A number of scholars, both in architecture and in other disciplines, take the position that phenomenology is fundamentally intersubjective in that it "involves a belief that shared understanding is possible."[54] At the same time, phenomenology emphasizes the holistic depth of the participant's or author's experiences; from them, generalizations are made about the essence of such experiences. In architecture and environmental design research, this of course highlights a person's experience of built form and place. To the extent that generalizations about an environmental experience are derived from the insights of a single person, this tradition is often open to being labeled as "subjectivist" by some theorists. However, to the extent that personal preconceptions are held in abeyance, the emphasis may be more "intersubjective."

As described earlier in this chapter, the term *constructivist* has in recent years been used in preference to other previously used terms such as *naturalistic* or *interpretive.* With that heritage in mind, Guba and Lincoln describe the quality standards for constructivism with reference to Guba's original criteria for trustworthiness, noting as well constructivism's emphasis on methodological procedures for studying phenomena in their natural settings.[55] In addition, Guba and Lincoln propose additional criteria that intentionally reject any implied comparison with postpositivist standards. The authors propose to emphasize the notion of authenticity, manifested in several ways: ontological authenticity, which enlarges personal constructions; educative authenticity, which leads to the improved understanding of others; catalytic authenticity, which stimulates action; and tactical authenticity, which empowers action. These criteria for authenticity are incorporated in several cells of the constructivist column of the matrix.

Finally, the quality standards for a more radical version of constructivism are represented in the last column of the matrix. This perspective is often referred to as a poststructuralist or postmodern school of thought (not to be confused with the architectural style). Consistent with the hypo-subjective epistemological and ontological premises of poststructuralism described earlier in the chapter, the quality standards highlight the scholar's interpretive creativity in illuminating the impossibility of any fixed meaning of the "text" being analyzed, while simultaneously giving license to produce "fiction." In the social sciences or humanities, the text may be an existing document, archival material, interview transcript, or the like. In architectural and environmental research, the "text" is typically a building, designed artifact, or larger setting.[56]

The essay by Jennifer Bloomer described at the beginning of this chapter represents an example of this poststructuralist perspective. For instance, she maintains that the "repression of nostalgia is at the core of the project of modernity."[57] Although this statement is essentially consistent with the standard interpretation of Modernism, she quickly upends that interpretation by arguing that the intensity of Modernism's repression of nostalgia in effect amounts to "a fetishization of an imagined absence." In other words, underlying Modernism's insistence on "form" expressed by "glossy smooth skin" only hides a repressed longing for the solidity of "matter."[58]

Bloomer's essay also employs a repetition of word play, another common device in poststructuralist analysis. Specifically, she weaves together the experience of nostalgia in domestic space with an interplay of the words *mater* (mother in Latin) and *matter* expressed in a masonry, climate-sensitive home.[59] Underlying this layering of interpretation is the metaphoric connection of the feminine to the repressed fecundity of architectural matter in general, and in domestic space in particular. In this way, Bloomer proposes an unexpected interpretation of Modernism that depends on her unique exploration into the imagined space between intended and unexpressed or repressed meaning.

In sum, the sampling of quality standards across multiple disciplines and the work of a diverse set of scholars demonstrate that the codification of research standards across the intersubjective/constructivist paradigms continues to be a work in progress. Advocates for these paradigms might well argue that the range and diversity of standards represent not only a robust development of these research traditions but also an appropriate sensitivity to the contextual differences among disciplines and topics of inquiry. However, researchers working in the postpositivist tradition would likely argue that the continuing influence of that tradition is at least in part due to the relative consensus achieved in the codification of those standards. Each of these positions may well make an accurate point; in the end, architectural and design research is all the richer for the contributions of these multiple research traditions.

3.4   CONCLUSIONS: LOOKING AHEAD

Over the course of this chapter, we have sought to demonstrate how the researcher's affinity for a particular system of inquiry is likely to frame the choice of a school of thought, the way in which the research question is posed, the selection of a research design, the tactics of information gathering and analysis, and even the practices of the researcher as he or she conducts the inquiry. Although we will not always specify the particular research paradigm framing the various exemplar studies cited in the seven chapters on research strategies that follow (Chapters 6 through 12), we suggest that readers will nevertheless find it useful to keep in mind these paradigmatic perspectives and associated quality standards when considering the underlying assumptions and diverse contributions of the research reviewed.

NOTES

1. Donald Polkinghorne, *Methodology for Human Sciences* (Albany: SUNY Press, 1983).
2. Norman Denzin and Yvonna Lincoln, *Handbook of Qualitative Research* (Thousand Oaks, CA: Sage, 1998).
3. Francesca Stazi, Alessio Mastrucci, and Constanzo di Perna, "The Behaviour of Solar Walls in Residential Buildings with Different Insulation Levels: An Experimental and Numerical Study," *Energy and Buildings* 47 (2012): 217–229.
4. Ibid., 217–218.
5. Benyamin Schwartz, "Nursing Home Design: A Misguided Architectural Model," *Journal of Architectural and Planning Research* 14(4) (1997): 343–359.
6. Ibid., 347.
7. Jennifer Bloomer, "The Matter of Matter: A Longing for Gravity," in D. Agrest, P. Conway, and L. Weisman (eds.), *The Sex of Architecture* (New York: Harry N. Abrams, 1996), 161.
8. Ibid., 162.
9. Ibid.

10. Henry H. Bauer, "Scientific Literacy and the Myth of Scientific Methods," in *The So-Called Scientific Method* (Urbana: University of Illinois Press, 1992).

11. Michael Joroff and Stanley Morse, "A Proposed Framework for the Emerging Field of Architectural Research," in J. Snyder (ed.), *Architectural Research* (New York: Van Nostrand Reinhold, 1984), 15–28.

12. Ibid., 21.

13. Ibid.

14. Ibid.

15. Julia Robinson, "Architectural Research: Incorporating Myth and Science," *Journal of Architectural Education* 44(1) (1990): 20.

16. John Creswell, *Research Design: Qualitative and Quantitative Approaches* (Thousand Oaks, CA: Sage, 1994).

17. "Editorial: Plus Ca Change, Plus Ca Change," *Journal of Architectural Education* 61(1) (2007): 3.

18. David Salomon, "Experimental Cultures: On the 'End' of the Design Thesis and the Rise of the Research Studio," *Journal of Architectural Education* 65(1) (2011): 34.

19. John Tosh, "History by the Numbers," in *The Pursuit of History* (London: Pearson Education Limited, 2002), 244–270.

20. Fernando Lara, *Popular Modernism: An Analysis of the Acceptance of Modern Architecture in 1950s Brazil.* PhD dissertation, University of Michigan, Ann Arbor, 2001.

21. Bauer.

22. John W. Creswell and Clark V. L. Plano, *Designing and Conducting Mixed Methods Research* (Los Angeles: Sage, 2011); Charles Teddlie and Abbas Tashakkori, *Foundations of Mixed Methods Research: Integrating Quantitative and Qualitative Approaches in the Social and Behavioral Sciences* (Los Angeles: Sage, 2009).

23. Gareth Morgan and Linda Smircich, "The Case for Qualitative Research," *Academy of Management Review* 5(4) (1980): 75–91.

24. Ibid., 499.

25. Ibid., 499.

26. Ibid., 498.

27. John R. Hall, *Cultures of Inquiry: From Epistemology to Discourse in Sociohistorical Research* (Cambridge, UK: Cambridge University Press, 1999), 4.

28. John Tosh, "The Limits of Historical Knowledge," in *The Pursuit of History* (London: Pearson Education Limited, 2010): 175–213.

29. Donna Mertens, *Research Methods in Education and Psychology Research and Evaluation in Education and Psychology: Integrating Diversity with Quantitative, Qualitative, and Mixed Methods* (Thousand Oaks, CA: Sage, 2010).

30. Teddlie and Tashakkori, 88.

31. Norman Denzin and Yvonna Lincoln, *Collecting and Interpreting Qualitative Materials* (Los Angeles: Sage, 2008); Teddlie and Tashakkori; Mertens; Creswell and Plano.

32. Denzin and Lincoln, 32.

33. Robert Mugerauer, *Interpreting Environments: Tradition, Deconstruction, Hermeneutics* (Austin: University of Texas Press, 1995); Jacques Derrida, "A Letter to Peter Eisenman," *Assemblage* 12 (1990): 7–13.

34. Mugerauer, xxxv.

35. Egon Guba, "Criteria for Assessing the Truthworthiness of Naturalistic Inquiries," *Education Communication and Technology Journal* 29(2) (1981): 76–91.

36. Egon Guba and Yvonna Lincoln, "Competing Paradigms in Qualitative Research," in Norman Denzin and Yvonna Lincoln (eds.), *The Landscape of Qualitative Research* (Thousand Oaks, CA: Sage, 1998), 213.

37. Stazi et al., 220.

38. Guba.

39. Guba and Lincoln, 213–214.

40. Guba, 85.

41. Schwartz, 347.

42. Ibid., 355, 356.

43. Guba, 86.

44. Mark Chesler, "Professionals' Views of the 'Dangers' of Self-Help Groups," Working Paper 345 (Ann Arbor: University of Michigan, Center for Research on Social Organizations, 1987).

45. Schwartz, 347.

46. Tosh, "The Limits of Historical Knowledge," 206–208.

47. Spencer Maxcy, "Pragmatic Threads in Mixed Methods Research in the Social Sciences: The Search for Multiple Methods of Inquiry and the End of the Philosophy of Formalism," in Abbas Tashakkori and Charles Teddlie (eds.), *The Handbook of Mixed Methods in Social & Behavioral Research* (Thousand Oaks, CA: Sage, 2003), 59.

48. Abraham Kaplan, *The Conduct of Inquiry: Methodology for Behavioral Science* (San Francisco: Chandler, 1964), 43.

49. Mertens, *Research and Evaluation in Education and Psychology*; Donna Mertens, "Mixed Methods and the Politics of Human Research: The Transformative-Emancipatory Perspective," in Abbas Tashakkori and Charles Teddlie (eds.), *The Handbook of Mixed Methods in Social & Behavioral Research* (Thousand Oaks, CA: Sage, 2003).

50. James Bohman, "Critical Theory," in Edward Zalta (ed.), *The Stanford Encyclopedia of Philosophy* (Spring 2012 ed.): 1–2.

51. Ibid., 2.

52. Ibid., 2.

53. Ibid., 8.

54. Mugerauer, 16.

55. Guba and Lincoln, 213.

56. Mugerauer, xli.

57. Bloomer, 162.

58. Ibid.

59. Ibid., 163.

Chapter 4

What's Your Purpose? From Theory Building to Design Application

4.1   INTRODUCTION

Having explored the complementary and interwoven relationship between research and design in Chapter 2, we now consider the challenge of turning a general topic or interest area into an actual research "design." (By design here we mean the conceptual framework of research strategy and tactics that comprise the rationale for pursing the answers to a researcher's targeted research questions.) This is a multistep and highly iterative process, which will be outlined in the course of the next two chapters. In this chapter, we argue that the first step in this process necessarily entails a thoughtful consideration of the multiple layers of *purpose* underlying any research study. These purposes have to do with *both* the contextual backdrop of the study *and* the goals of the research itself. The contextual purposes answer questions such as: What motivates this research? Who is the audience? What are the anticipated impacts, or contributions, of the outcomes of the research? Paired with these contextual questions are questions related to the theoretical purposes for the research. Is it to create new theory? Or does it expand an existing theory either by refining it or applying it to new venues? And if the project is to culminate in a design, how does that relate to the use of theory? It should be clear that both sets of questions can be and are linked in a variety of ways (see Figure 4.1).

In this chapter, we address contextual and research purposes and conclude with a section on application (various ways research purposes are operationalized in research approaches). Chapter 5 will address research questions more explicitly, and how literature review plays an important role in determining these questions.

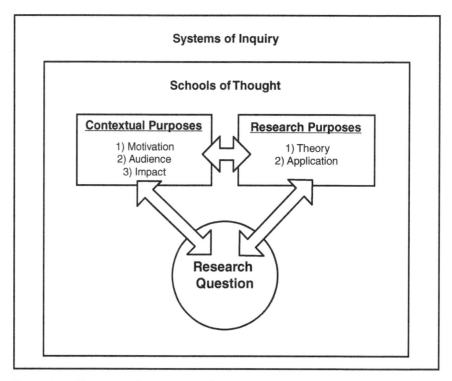

Figure 4.1 The research questions of a study are intimately related to external factors motivating the study (contextual purposes) as well as the theoretical framework and hoped-for applications (research purposes) of the study. Both domains are in turn framed by the researcher's commitment to a school of thought and a system of inquiry. Diagram courtesy of Linda Groat.

4.2   CONTEXTUAL PURPOSES

A considerable body of literature on research procedures would suggest that the first step in designing a study is to conceptualize a general area of interest into a research question, or set of research questions. (Again, the formulation of research questions is the topic of Chapter 5.) But turning a general interest or topic area into the research question (or questions) that will eventually frame the entire research project entails a careful consideration of one's purpose. In other words, in order to transform a general topic into a successful research project, one must attend to first principles and ask: why *am* I doing this research? As Newman et al., the authors of an insightful chapter on research methods, explain:

The research question alone will not produce links to methods unless the question is thought through seriously, as well as iteratively, and becomes reflective of purpose. In other words, . . . the research question is necessary but not sufficient to determine methodology. By considering the question and purpose iteratively, one can get to a design or set of designs that more clearly reflect the *intent* [our emphasis] of the question.[1]

A further advantage of clarifying one's purposes at the outset of the research design process is that the legitimacy and eventual impact of research are likely to be strengthened by the conceptual consistency between (1) the stated research purposes, (2) the research question(s), and (3) methodological design. As Newman et al. put it: "Strong consistency grounds the research findings and helps ensure that audiences have confidence in the findings and implications of the research studies."[2] This is true whether the audience includes fellow students, faculty colleagues, clients, design or policy decision makers, or the general public.

Serious consideration of the various contextual purposes of any research project will inevitably entail a set of interconnected questions. Among the most important questions are: (1) What is the motivation for this research? (2) Who is the audience for the study? and (3) What is the potential or intended impact of this research once it is completed?

In the following chapter subsections, we examine in detail how these foundational questions begin to frame and define the context of a research project. And although we will discuss these questions in sequence, we assume that in practice it will be necessary to cycle back and forth between these questions. So, for example, answering question 2 may result in rethinking the answer to question 1, and possibly lead to a reconsideration of the scope and nature of the original topic area.

4.2.1   What Are the Motivations for This Research?

To begin, the answer to the question "what is the purpose of this research project?" will necessarily be influenced by the context in which the study is being conducted. For instance, a student in either a research studio or research methods course may well be asked to conduct an individual study or group research project. Or, in the context of a professional practice, a designer may be responsible for pursuing a research question entailed in some aspect of a specific design project, and/or at the behest of a client. All of these circumstances define some sort of *practical* mandate that dictates or constrains the topic or scope of the research.

However, some researchers may be situated in contexts where it is possible, perhaps encouraged, to pursue a topic of strong *personal interest*. For many students in either research master's or doctoral programs, this may well be the case. And many, perhaps most, academic faculty are deeply motivated to pursue areas of inquiry that are of significant personal interest, often supported by either university or external funding. Similarly, depending on the particular nature of some design firms, an increasing number of professionals maintain research units within or in association with their design firms. Often, these endeavors enable the practitioners to pursue research that will enhance the knowledge base for specific building types, lead to product patents, or identify innovative uses of emerging technologies.

In other words, the reason(s) for taking on any given research project may be either highly personal or very practical. In many cases, however, the purposes of a particular study may incorporate both personal and practical concerns, either in equal measure or perhaps with more emphasis on one versus the other.[3]

4.2.2   *Who Is the Audience?*

Although the identity of the study's eventual audience may be implicitly suggested by the personal and/or practical reasons for undertaking the research project, it is nevertheless important to clarify explicitly who might be expected to be interested in or influenced by the proposed study (see Figure 4.2).

At one extreme, at least initially, some researchers envision an audience of one—themselves. For instance, a student may decide to take on an independent study project on a topic of great personal interest, such as tracing the morphological development of a small town in the Pyrenees that she visited during a semester abroad. However, if the student sees the benefit of working with a faculty advisor and/or receiving academic credit, then there is at least an audience of two. And if the research project is done in the context of a larger class, then the class as a whole is also an audience with respect to class discussions or project presentations.

Taking this situation a bit more broadly, an additional number of faculty and students may be invited as an audience for the class presentations. So, although the student may have initiated the project as a personal quest, the concept for the project might well be expanded. In this case, the student may need to consider how the morphological analyses might be influenced by and contribute to an understanding of the larger set of class projects. If the student's project is the only morphological analysis within the class, the student may want to clarify the benefits of such analyses in general, beyond the specifics of the particular town studied. If, however, everyone in the class is researching the morphologies of different sites and towns,

Figure 4.2 Any research, whether it culminates in a written work or a design presentation, must take into consideration the intended audience. The project shown here, "Children's health and built environment: Regreening the grounds of an elementary school," is described in the next chapter (Box 5.4). Photograph courtesy of David Wang.

then the student may want to focus on the similarities and differences of her analysis in relation to the entire set of sites.

Many examples of research in architectural practice may also have relatively small audiences. Often, the architect is expected by the client to conduct one or several episodes of research to resolve practical problems for a specific project. In the early years of Groat's career, the design of a 2,000-worker campus for a major corporation entailed several discrete segments of research, including simulation of the curtain wall system in earthquake conditions due to the presence on the site of a fault line; materials research for the application of long-lasting color to the aluminum cladding; and user research involving full-scale office mock-ups for development of a new purpose-built furniture system. Although the actual design of the building was widely disseminated in the architectural press, the research components of the project were proprietary and disclosed only to the client representatives.[4]

Ed Shriver, principal at Strada Architects in Pittsburgh, reports a good example of research in a practice context that began with a focused audience (the client) and resulted in a larger audience.[5] Initially commissioned by a major tenant to design commercial space in the city, Shriver developed lot maps of the commercial establishments in the blocks surrounding the site of the project. These patterns stirred his interest to index them to various sorts of rental, traffic, and demographic data to see if relationships could be discerned that might be of use to commercial tenants in more general terms. Shriver's interest resulted in a subsequent (2011) AIA Upjohn Applied Research Grant, as he teamed with architectural researchers from Carnegie-Mellon University to further study how a variety of data could inform commercial patterns in several urban locations in the Pittsburgh area.[6]

At the other end of the spectrum, many notable research studies are undertaken with the intention of addressing the interests of multiple and/or large audiences. This was certainly the case when Oscar Newman conducted his classic study of the relationship between crime and the formal configuration of low-income public housing projects prevalent at the time.[7] As a result of his research, Newman and his team were able to demonstrate that less crime occurred in mid-rise housing projects than in high-rise housing. Details of the methodological aspects of this research are presented in Chapter 8, but for now the important point concerns the broad and multiple audiences addressed by Newman's work. Because there were already major concerns among policy makers, law enforcement agencies, and the public about the suitability of the high-rise typology for low-income populations, Newman's research was funded by a grant from the U.S. Department of Justice. After three years of study, the resulting book was widely disseminated to planners and urban policy makers. In addition, the study was also of much interest to architects, especially so since a number of notable architects of the time had designed public housing projects. As a consequence, excerpts of Newman's study were also published in one of the premier architectural journals at the time; for this publication, the coverage included discussion of specific design features that would reinforce residents' capacity to notice and mitigate criminal activity.[8]

Most research studies, however, are likely to address audiences of a more intermediate scope and complexity. In an academic setting, students in research master's or doctoral programs, as well as faculty, are likely to pursue research that addresses a relatively focused scope. In other words, the typical audiences for such academy-based research include some combination of specialty area audiences through peer-reviewed journals or conferences, discipline-wide audiences, and sometimes interdisciplinary audiences.

Research is occasionally published in professional architectural or other design magazines, but more commonly is segregated into a research awards issue. One example of a research study that addressed both academic and professional audiences was Groat's study of contextual design principles. The purpose of the research was to elucidate laypeople's conceptualization of contextual compatibility through their responses to architectural exemplars representing several distinct contextual design strategies theorized at the time. A discussion of the compositional design qualities preferred by laypeople was initially published in a special issue on context and change in one of the professional magazines,[9] and, subsequently, articles that focused on methodological and theoretical issues of environmental cognition were published in scholarly venues.[10]

4.2.3   *What Is the Potential or Likely Impact of This Research?*

Finally, the third dimension of contextual purposes in research is its imagined impact. One way to put the issue of impact in direct terms for each researcher is to pose the question: What do I hope to accomplish by doing this research? And more particularly: Will my audience(s) come to think differently about the topic of my research? Or will people be more inclined to take action regarding a particular situation? Perhaps with respect to a design process, or designed environment? As the next chapter addresses, the likely outcomes of a proposed research design should be envisioned from the very beginning. It is one factor affecting the research framework itself. We now turn our attention to this framework.

BOX 4.1

Contextual Purposes: Motivation, Audience, Impact

Topic: My dissertation examines questions of space and social meaning in two significant post-1968 European modes of architectural practice: the work of Belgian architect-writer Lucien Kroll and Swiss-French architect-theorist Bernard Tschumi.[a] The research draws connections between the spatial writings of French sociologist Henri Lefebvre and the design work of Kroll and Tschumi as they relate to politics of space, agency, and everyday life. The study investigates two seminal works: Lucien Kroll's La Maison Medicalé (La Mémé; Figure 4.3) in Woluwé-Saint-Lambert,

[a] Kush Patel, *Practicing Lefebvre: How Ideas of Social Space Are Realized in the Works of Lucien Kroll and Bernard Tschumi*, PhD dissertation, University of Michigan, Ann Arbor, 2013.

(Continued)

Figure 4.3   La Maison Medicalé (La Mémé) in Woluwé-Saint-Lambert, Brussels: Lucien Kroll designed the exterior as a framework such that students could create and change their own façade by choosing among its various finishes, sizes, and removable panels. Image (and text) courtesy of Kush Patel, PhD student, University of Michigan Taubman College of Architecture and Urban Planning.

Brussels, and Bernard Tschumi's Parc de la Villette in Paris, and evaluates their respective approaches to engaging wider social meanings against Lefebvre's spatial framework. Through literary analysis, the dissertation brings to light the social issues at stake in each of the two projects under study. Through fieldwork and qualitative study, the research offers an empirical basis to a broad philosophical discourse on social space.

Motivation: Despite the ebb and flow of different ideologies, for many academics and practitioners of architecture, the concept of space and its relationship with society has remained fundamental to the development of architectural knowledge. This is because space and its social meaning is an enduring construct around which the knowledge of architecture is formed and advanced. Hence I have been motivated to examine the limits and potentials of architectural frameworks that engage social and political dimensions of space. I am interested in investigating architectural approaches to producing spatial conditions that speak to diverse social meanings.

Audience: The primary audience of my research is my interdisciplinary dissertation committee, comprising members from specialty areas within the discipline, namely, architectural design, environment-behavior studies, and architecture history and theory; as well as members specializing in urban planning theory and continental philosophy. My larger aim is to reach a wider audience of socially conscious and civic-minded design theorists and practitioners. By discussing the social story integral to each case study, I hope to provide an alternative reading of leading works of architecture in ways that help outline the material limits and potentials of social and political mindedness. This, I expect, will speak to the intellectual interests of both academics and designers.

Impact: For the discipline and practice of architecture, my research will offer a way to reconsider the social dimensions of space by addressing questions of voice and agency, and going beyond the commonly held view of space as a formally designed object. Additionally, by reintroducing social and political meanings of space into the processes and products of architectural work, my research will provide a rethinking of the boundaries of socially motivated design thinking and practice. Throughout, one of the goals of this dissertation is to develop Lefebvre's critical theory of space in directions that are useful for architecture.

4.3   CATEGORIES OF THEORY

As shown in Figure 4.1, the second category of purposes concerns those that are inherent or intended in the nature of the research itself. In these terms, we can identify a spectrum of goals—from those that are concerned with a contribution to theory building to those that emphasize application in specific contexts. Although these purposes may loosely correspond to the potential impact of the study for various audiences as discussed earlier, the intent here is to highlight how the goals of application and/or theory serve as threads that are woven through the research design of the entire research project. In this section, we address aspects of theory that affect developing a research design. In the next section, we address matters of application. Taken together, theory and application can serve as the starting points as well as the ending points of research. For example, a researcher may frame the goal of his/her study as a way to test how a particular theory may serve to explain a particular environmental phenomenon under investigation. The theory in question might have to do with environmental cognition, principles of urban centers as heat islands, or the role of a particular social theory in the design strategies of particular architects. Alternatively, a researcher may choose to focus primarily on the identification and significance of particular environmental qualities and features as they might be applied to specific designed contexts.

The word *theory* comes from the Greek *theoria*, which means to behold, to contemplate, from a removed distance. This term is then contrasted with the Greek *praxis*, which has more to do with action or activity. There is, then, a contrast between the contemplative quality of *theoria*, in which we stand apart from the object we are contemplating, and *praxis*, in which we are engaged actively with the object. Implicit in this contrast is the fact that *theoria*/contemplation is something that precedes *praxis*/action, in the sense that the former informs the latter. Because we have *theoria*, we know how to *praxis*. But this leads to the further observation that *theoria* and *praxis* are not simply sequential to each other; instead, they relate cyclically. Out of our *praxis* informed by *theoria*, we gain new insights for subsequent *theoria*; so the process is ongoing.

It should be clear that *theoria/praxis* relate intimately to the contextual purposes just addressed. For instance, if the intended audience is largely academics, *theoria* can possibly be both the beginning and ending points of a research design (we provide examples in the next section). In this instance, *theoria* is likely to be systematic, approaching the level of philosophical discourse, while the *praxis* aspect might be in the form of recommendations at the conclusion. But if the intended outcome is a physical building, use of *theoria* is likely to be episodic, with care taken to select the correct theoretical venue in which to situate justifications for design action (*praxis*). Or research can be undertaken for specific applications in concrete venues; the firm Carpman Grant Associates, for example, applies wayfinding theory to physical design in case-specific venues, as we note later in this chapter.

We begin our consideration of theory by simply referring to the common definition of the word found in the Merriam-Webster Dictionary:

1. The analysis of a set of facts in their relation to one another.
2. Abstract thought: speculation.
3. The general or abstract principles of a body of facts, a science, or an art (for example: music theory).
4. *a)* A belief, policy, or procedure proposed or followed as the basis of action; an ideal or hypothetical set of facts, principles, or circumstances.
5. Plausible or scientifically acceptable general principle or body of principles offered to explain phenomena.

6. *a)* A hypothesis assumed for the sake of argument or investigation; *b)* an un-proved assumption: conjecture; *c)* body of theorems presenting a concise systematic view of a subject.

This definition is helpful because its various shades of meaning can be grouped under three general headings for our purposes, as shown in Figure 4.4.

These columns are not hermetically sealed one from the other (i.e., there are overlaps in what they mean), but they offer a useful heuristic for comprehending theory. By explanatory theory we generally mean not only theories that emphasize prediction or causality, but also theories that illuminate the role of social processes and interpretation (see Chapter 3). Normative theory, as its name implies, are theories that explain and describe conventional actions based upon a "norm"; examples are given later in this chapter. Polemical theory is an enormously relevant body of theory in motivating subjective affirmations of architectural design; hence, we term it here design-polemical theory. As the Merriam-Webster definition says, these theories are inherently abstract and speculative. But if they do their job, they produce what rhetoricians Chaim Perelman and L. Olbrechts-Tyteca call "the adherence of minds"[11]; again, examples are provided later. Finally, the definitions under the columns in Figure 4.4 are broad descriptions of theory that apply to all three shades of meaning. We now summarize these types of theory.

Explanatory Theory	Normative Theory	Design-Polemical Theory
(5) Plausible or scientifically acceptable general principle or body of principles offered to explain phenomena [we expand this definition in this chapter]	(4) A belief, policy, or procedure proposed or followed as the basis of action; an ideal or hypothetical set of facts, principles, or circumstances	(2) Abstract thought: speculation
(1) The analysis of a set of facts in their relation to one another		
(3) The general or abstract principles of a body of facts, a science, or an art (for example: music theory)		
(6) a) A hypothesis assumed for the sake of argument or investigation; b) an unproved assumption, conjecture; c) body of theorems presenting a concise systematic view of a subject		

Figure 4.4 Merriam-Webster (numbered) definitions of "theory" arranged under three headings. The definitions below the columns apply to theory in all three of the columns.

4.3.1   *Explanatory Theory*

Of our three categories, this term probably is the most expansive. After all, all theories explain and describe their object. Here we use the term *explanatory* to broaden the term beyond positivism and/or postpositivism. (For clarity on this matter, refer to our thoughts about the spectrum of possible systems of inquiry in Chapter 3.)

As for positivist outlooks, here is a simple example. Consider a piece of framing lumber, say, a 2″ × 8″ Douglas fir joist, very typically used to build floors in residential construction in the United States. We know so much about the behavior of this material that we are confident that a 2″ × 8″ in Boston and its 2″ × 8″ counterpart in Los Angeles will behave in the same way, other factors being equal. If loaded in the same fashion, the resulting behaviors in both cases will be statistically indistinguishable. Many materials used to construct houses depend on this kind of theoretical knowledge, for instance, the U-value of wall insulation, the dependability of coatings on electrical wiring, the bearing strength of concrete foundations. We do not want any significant variations in how these materials will perform. Now, theories explaining and describing the behavior of these materials relate more comfortably to certain kinds of research strategies, experimental research being the most obvious (see Chapter 9).

There was a time when "research" was mostly limited to discovery of theories that explain a phenomenon so thoroughly that its behavior can be predicted without significant variance (hence the definition in the first column in Figure 4.4: "plausible or scientifically acceptable general principle or body of principles offered to explain phenomena"). The outlook assuming that all phenomena can be described and explained this way is called positivism. But as noted in previous chapters, research scholarship has become much more inclusive across the spectrum of systems of inquiry.

For instance, in our treatment of history research (Chapter 6), we cite Professor Matthew Cohen's tactic of combining archival data with minute measurements of the San Lorenzo Basilica in Florence to yield a novel explanation of the structure's medieval proportional system; this is an important departure from the received view that San Lorenzo is an exemplar of *Renaissance* proportions. Cohen's is very much an explanatory theory of the formal characteristics of an artifact, namely Brunelleschi's San Lorenzo.[12] (Actually, Cohen's method leads him to propose an alternative attribution for the architect of San Lorenzo, as we explain in Chapter 6; see Box 6.4.)

Finally, consider Herbert Gans's *The Levittowners,* which is an iconic example of *in situ* descriptions and explanations of the life of a particular culture, or cultural

BOX 4.2

"Reconfiguring the User": Framing a New Explanatory Theory

How do designers process information about users? To answer the question, Isil Oygur[a] embedded herself in two architectural firms, two industrial design firms, and two interaction design firms (i.e., web site designers). In each, she conducted ethnographic research in how designers interacted with their target users. Oygur drew from three existing theoretical frameworks:

1. Karin Knorr-Cetina's book *Epistemic Cultures*,[b] which posits that knowledge construction in cultural contexts depends on machineries of knowledge production.
2. The literature in constructivist learning theory posits that everything we learn is an interpretation of our own experience and prior knowledge in some way. This understanding helped further explain the dynamics of knowledge production.
3. Oygur also referenced Susan Leigh Star and James R. Griesemer's theory of *boundary objects*.[c] Boundary objects are conceptual frameworks that fall in between disciplinary domains; they are "malleable" enough to accommodate the epistemic frame of each domain while staying integral to their own essential theoretical makeup. An architectural plan, for example, can be a boundary object: it is understandable to both designer and user, but in different ways.

Here is what Oygur found (see Figure 4.5). User input provided to designers ranges from "given" (e.g., the program document) to "constructed information" (e.g., information from the user that requires interpretation, such as a range of color preferences); from "concrete" (e.g., strictly specified, such as four-year-old kids' attention spans) to "abstract" based on the nature of user information (e.g., personas classified according to Internet usage patterns). As the diagram shows, Oygur mapped these types of input

---

[a] Isil Oygur, *Reconfiguring the User: How Designers Process User Information*, PhD dissertation, Washington State University, May, 2012.
[b] Karin Knorr-Cetina, *Epistemic Cultures: How the Sciences Make Knowledge* (Harvard University Press, 1999).
[c] Susan Leigh Star and James R. Griesemer, "Institutional Ecology, 'Translations' and Boundary Objects: Amateurs and Professionals in Berkeley's Museum of Vertebrate Zoology, 1907–39," *Social Studies of Science* 19(3) (August 1989): 387–420.

(Continued)

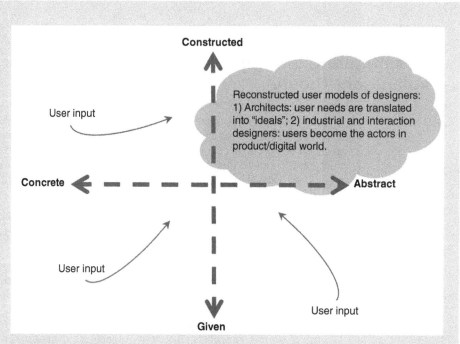

Figure 4.5 Diagram of Isil Oygur's theory of how designers (architects, industrial designers, interaction designers) "reconfigure" the user. Diagram by David Wang as directed by Isil Oygur, based on data collected for her dissertation.

on two axes. She found that no matter what kind of user input comes in, designers tend to "reconstruct user models," and *all reconstructed user models fall within the Abstract/Constructed quadrant.* Architects reconstruct user models that are characterized by "ideals," which are abstractions of "user flow" and "preferred imagery" (e.g., what forms and materials the design should be expressed by). In contrast, industrial designers and interaction designers reconstruct users as a medium central to the proper functioning of the design solution and experience. In all cases, the reconfiguration of the user into an Abstract/Constructed phenomenon defines the user knowledge production in design.

context.[13] Gans embedded himself in Levittown for two years, partaking of the life of the town as one of the residents, albeit journaling his observations and thoughts constantly. The resulting account in his book *The Levittowners* is a description of the multilayered social-cultural interactions of that particular context. Now, we might say that this kind of *theoria* is predictive in that it stirs confidence that if we were to return to this kind of Levittown (what might be called a "suburban" setting, although today's suburbs are a great deal more varied than Gans's Levittown), we would find the kinds of interactions that Gans found, everything else being equal. But this is not really as germane an "outcome" as the satisfaction of the pure explanation (and description) of what Gans found in that significant artifact of post-World War II America.

4.3.2   Normative Theory

We return to our 2″ × 8″ Douglas fir example, but now focus our attention on floor joist framing (or wall framing for that matter). In the United States, we space our floor joists and wall studs at one per every 16 inches. This practice is so standard that floor boards and wall boards are fabricated in 4 feet by 8 feet sheets, so that a board's edges exactly match the joist and stud spacings for ease of nailing. Now, if we were to build a house with floor joists spaced 17 inches apart, would the floor collapse? No, it would not. How about spacing them at 18 inches apart? The floor will be "bouncier" but probably still not collapse. How about at spacing joists at 24 inches apart? Well, this is not recommended. But we don't recommend spacing them at 17 inches either, because much more material will be wasted in having to cut the standard-sized floor and wall boards designed to fit 16-inch spacings. And the building inspector will not approve our work if the joists are not spaced at 16 inches. All of this is based on a *culturally accepted* practice of spacing floor joists.

The point here is that we are dealing with a very different kind of theory, one that falls more under the definition of theory in the second column of Figure 4.4: "a belief, policy, or procedure proposed or followed as the basis of action; an ideal or hypothetical set of facts, principles, or circumstances." The theory that describes and explains the praxis of laying joist and stud spacings at 16 inches is a *normative* theory in this sense. The word *norm* or *normal* is embedded in this term, because normative theory describes and explains practices that are so normally accepted that they have become conventional. In fact, one trait of conventionalized practices is that we are not aware they have a theoretical dimension at all; they are simply the ways things are done. And yet embedded in conventional actions are many theoretically assumed factors. Normative theories do not claim strict prediction; for example, if floor joists are spaced 17 inches apart, normative theory says nothing about the floor collapsing. But it does say that extra effort and expense will result, because everybody else involved in building houses—manufacturers, suppliers, builders, regulators—are all working within the conventional practice of 16-inch spacings for floor joists.

Normative theories inform much of what is done in architectural offices. For example, reference to established architectural typologies often sets the pace for design projects (see Figure 4.6).[14] The American Institute of Architects recently established an online resource of "Best Practices" that represent "the collective wisdom of AIA members and related professionals."[15] The web site links to a wide variety of specific cases that amount to "a compendium of relevant knowledge gained from experience." Practitioners can look to them as exemplars to guide practice. For instance, under the heading of "Sustainability," one best practice is *Energy Design Guidelines for High Performance Schools.*[16] The expectation is that these guidelines set a normative standard for the design of these schools.

The extent to which normative theory complements and intersects with explanatory theory is significant for the development of architectural research. As design theorist Ken Friedman puts it: "Because design knowledge grows in part from practice, design knowledge and design research overlap; the practice of design is one foundation of design knowledge."[17] In other words, many normative theories that are now embedded in architectural practice may be derived from earlier advances in explanatory theory; and conversely, the evolution of normative theories in different contexts or circumstances may prompt reexamination of explanatory theories.

4.3.3   *Design-Polemical Theory*

In his book *Creating Architectural Theory*, Jon Lang says, "The normative statements of designers are by, definition, value-full."[18] This is normative in a slightly different sense than understood as descriptions of conventionalized practices. By normative Lang means to underline the point that designers make "deontological statements which, when applied to practice, can be seen in the designs that result."[19] The *Stanford Encyclopedia of Philosophy* says: "In contemporary moral philosophy, deontology is one of those kinds of normative theories regarding which choices are morally required, forbidden, or permitted. In other words, deontology falls within the domain of moral theories that guide and assess our choices of what we ought to do (deontic theories)."[20] Lang's usage of the term aligns with this definition; designers are guided in their actions by "value-full" convictions of how a design problem should be (or ought to be) addressed or solved. These value-full convictions stem from a range of cultural variables, including the designers' attitudes toward society, people, the natural environment, technology, and also the design professions themselves.[21] Together, these variables inform an "ought to" attitude on the part of the designer (i.e., design

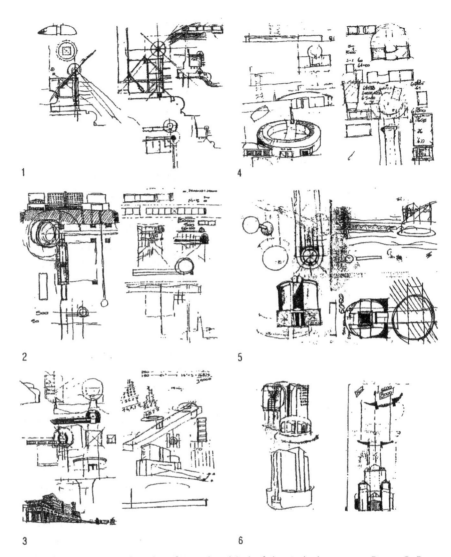

Figure 4.6 Progress sketches from the third of three design teams Peter G. Rowe studied in situ as the teams generated their design solutions. Here, the drawing sought to resolve the tension between a desire to conform to Burnham's Chicago master plan and a programmatic wish to extend the project into the lake. Rowe found that much of what architects do is informed by normative guidelines and practices: references to precedent, references to established typologies, and working out conflicting themes by iterative sketching. From Peter Rowe, *Design Thinking* (Cambridge, MA: MIT Press, 1987), 23.

ought to be this or that). Lang gives two examples from Frank Lloyd Wright's tenets for good house design:

> First: To reduce the number of necessary parts of the house and the separate rooms to a minimum, and make all come together as enclosed space—so divided that light, air and vista permeate the whole with a sense of unity.... Ninth: Eliminate the decorator . . .[22]

It is not difficult to detect a moralizing tone in Wright's statements. This "ought to" posture is a very common tendency in design thinking; indeed, Lang cites Ulrich Conrad's *Programs and Manifestoes on 20th-Century Architecture* as a compendium of examples of deontological positions vis-à-vis design.

All told, the deontological tendency fits the definition in the third column of Figure 4.4: "abstract thought: speculation." This is not to denigrate this kind of theorizing; it only underlines the difference between this kind of theory compared to explanatory theories and normative theories. The persuasive force of theories in the first two columns comes from their general applicability and, in the case of column two, their widely accepted utility. The persuasive force of deontological theories, in contrast, resides in polemics, that is, in a designer's ability first to express a conviction for his/her own designs, but ultimately in the adherence to the designer's point of view by a large audience. We address the tactics of polemics for design in Chapter 11.

An interesting dynamic exists between normative theories, as defined in the second column of Figure 4.4, with normative-deontological theories as defined by Lang. Example: When Wang was in architecture school at the University of Pennsylvania, the architect Norman Foster came to teach a guest studio. At the end of the project assignment, all of the student designs more or less looked like Norman Foster projects. The point is that some leading designers—their ideas—*create* norms for a wide population of designers, norms that at the outset were not conventional ways of doing things (*à la* column 2). Indeed, the distinction is precisely in the fact that the ideas are new. In Wright's case, at a time when *conventional* design practice was of residential rooms walled off from one another, Wright promoted an "ought to" of open and fluid spaces, exemplified in the Prairie Houses of the first decade of the 20th century. Wright's views did not immediately influence residential design in the United States for a variety of reasons (some of which were personal to Wright's life at the time), but Wright's "ought to" ideas, particularly of fluid spaces, had important bearing on the development of the International Style in Europe.

At one level, the potential significance of design-polemical theory resides in its ability to persuade its audience, ultimately to influence design conduct on an extended scale. As previously noted, Wright was enormously influential. Foster continues to be as of this writing, although arguably, he is probably not of the stature of Wright in terms of overall influence. "Ought to" design-polemical theories that have influenced large communities of practitioners and large bodies of work are quite important in what constitutes architectural history. Indeed, in his book on architectural theory, Paul-Alan Johnson observes that "what is called [architectural] theory has more to do with certain arguments and ideas aimed at persuading others to particular beliefs and values."[23]

In the broader context of architectural research, design-polemical theory can work in tandem with both normative and explanatory theory, and all three types of theory can inform and be informed by each other. First, researchers working with explanatory theory can seek to understand the large cultural ideas that in turn shape design-polemical theory. Similarly, in the research domain, Abraham Kaplan notes that "[t]he works of the mind are all of one piece," in that the development of the research enterprise is affected by "the thought of the period on matters of religion, politics, art and whatever."[24] Put another way, even those working in explanatory theories participate in the same cultural percolations that drive design-polemical theories.

Second, recall again that our dictionary definition of theory includes "abstract thought/speculation" as part of its domain; again, this characterizes design-polemical theorizing. But our view is that the "ought to" element of design-polemical speculation should be informed by as much explanatory (perhaps even normative) theoretical backing as possible. Moreover, the importance of speculation in research is also foundational to the discussion of abductive reasoning in inquiry by Peirce, March, and subsequent authors (see Chapter 2).

Third, designers themselves can become more practiced in researching the factors shaping the contemporary zeitgeist. There is much in the literature indicating that creative design does not arise *de novo*, but rather as a result of sustained exposure to design education.[25] This includes awareness of cultural trends, and how to harness them for expression in design as something to be cultivated.

Finally, using design-polemical theory as an opportunity for developing new explanatory theory remains a potentially significant research trajectory that is too often overlooked. As already discussed, many notable design-polemical positions have become so influential in practice that they are eventually accepted as normative theory. Although many scholars may debate the logic or theoretical import of design-polemical theories current at the moment, there are fewer in-depth inquiries into the strengths and weaknesses of such theories as they are manifested in built form and/or in lived experience. But such inquiries have the potential for producing new explanatory theory that could inform future developments in normative and design-polemical theory. This is not only a missed opportunity for aspiring researchers, but too often a weak link in the development of a more holistic and robust research tradition for the design fields.

One recent example of research that examines the impact of design-polemical theory as it is manifested in notable architectural projects is Kush Patel's study described in Box 4.1. Patel examines—both theoretically and empirically—how Bernard Tschumi's and Lucien Kroll's individual interpretations of Lefebvre's concept of social space result in very different qualities of lived spatial experience. In a slightly different vein, the predictive accuracy of a widely discussed design-polemical theory was tested out in a study by Groat and Canter. In this case, the authors took on Charles Jencks's contention that Postmodern buildings (intended to express meanings more accessible to the public) would be distinctly more appreciated by nonarchitects than Modernist buildings. The authors found that although a few Postmodern buildings were genuinely appreciated by nonarchitects, there was no clear-cut preference or appreciation for the Postmodern style.[26]

All of this is to say that the design-polemicism that often characterizes architectural design decisions could be harnessed to achieve more clarity of social meaning if architects were more knowledgeable about how the general public, as well as culturally distinct constituencies, experience the many dimensions of lived space. Indeed, a reason for this book is to suggest various ways for obtaining this knowledge.

BOX 4.3

OMA's "Bigness": A Design-Polemical Theory

OMA's theory of "Bigness"[a] exemplifies design-polemical theory. Rem Koolhaas posits that we live in such a diverse, multicultural, and *cybernetically* powerful global reality that architecture simply limited to localized physical sites is no longer adequate as an expression for the times. Instead, design must somehow respond to the Bigness of a global culture enabled by the instant and limitless connectivity of the Internet.

---

[a] Rem Koolhaas /OMA, "Bigness, or the Problem of Large" [1994]. In Harry Francis Mallgrave and Christina Contandriopoulos (eds.), *Architectural Theory, Volume II: An Anthology from 1871–2005* (Malden, MA: Blackwell, 2008), 566–568.

This is why Koolhaas's buildings tend not to relate very obviously to their immediate physical surroundings. Consider the Seattle Public Library, or the CCTV Tower in Beijing (Figure 4.7). These edifices are "world buildings" in the sense that they can "fit" or not "fit" into any localized site. They are responding to larger—BIGGER—cultural realities than the limitations of a city block. (Refer to Box 12.2 for challenges that arose in community involvement vis-à-vis this project.) It is instructive to place this OMA theory, which accommodates the technology of the computer (cybertechnology), with theories at the dawn of the 20th century, which sought to accommodate the machine. Coming to mind is Wright's "Art and Craft of

(a)

Figure 4.7   Rem Koolhaas OMA: Seattle Public Library (a); CCTV Tower, Beijing (b). OMA's theory of "Bigness" conceives of a global cyber-contextual siting of buildings rather than simply responding to localized physical sites. This results in buildings that are essentially interchangeable with regard to locale: the form in (a) can be in Beijing, and vice versa. Photographs courtesy of David Wang.

(Continued)

(b)

Figure 4.7   *(Continued)*

the Machine."[b] In this well-known talk given at Hull House in Chicago in 1901, Wright sought to incorporate the aesthetics of the machine into his organic ideas of architectural design. In this speech, Wright sought to justify his theory by appealing to larger democratic ideals: to wit, that the machine enables architectural design to benefit all people rather than just an elite. A century later, architects like Rem Koolhaas, MVRDV, and Greg Lynn, to name a few, seek to incorporate cybertechnologies into their designs by means of polemics.

---

[b] Frank Lloyd Wright, "Art and Craft of the Machine," in Edgar Kaufman and Ben Raeburn (eds.), *Writings and Buildings* (Cleveland, OH: World, 1960), 55–73.

4.4   MULTIPLE PURPOSES: THEORY BUILDING AND/OR DESIGN
APPLICATIONS?

In Chapter 1, we introduced a diagram (Figure 1.7) of the several research strategies (profiled in coming chapters) in relation to an axis of purposes, from theory building to design application. While it is certainly true that a single study can be initiated or result in both theoretical and applicative purposes, it is more often the case that there is a relatively stronger emphasis on one or the other. Whatever the case, a good research design reflects clear articulation of the researcher's purpose, whether theory and/or application.

In this section, we consider examples of how theory was used (or the extent to which it was used) to align with the purposes of each project. We first consider examples of generating new theory from existing theory; many times this is the case when the audience is comprised of researchers and/or academics. Second, we turn our attention to perhaps the other extreme: applying theory to inform a specific building design in architectural practice. In this case, the practicalities of client demands and budgetary restrictions usually call for more episodic applications of theory. Third, we consider how theory is used in a design consultancy, focusing on targeted theoretical themes applied very specifically to enhance built environments. Here again, the use of theory tends to be selective rather than broad. Finally, we consider another example of theory in service to architectural design at project scale, this time in a student MArch thesis. In student cases with fewer real-world constraints, theory can be more broadly applied to design decisions, although in a more interpretive manner.

4.4.1   *From Theory to New Theory*

Isil Oygur's doctoral research featured in Box 4.2 is an example of building from existing theory to generate new theory. Oygur's ethnographic research took three theories (epistemic culture, boundary objects, and constructed knowledge; see box) to develop a new theory of how designers "reconfigure" their users into various abstract constructs. None of the existing theories explicitly address design per se. Oygur's contribution is weaving these threads into her own theory of how users are "reconfigured" in the design process. Research like this draws systematically on theory, and the new theory proposed is itself systematic. Oygur's immediate audience is her doctoral committee, which is a harbinger of the peer reviewers who will decide on her future submissions to academic journals. All of this is to say that the specific purpose of Oygur's research is to make a contribution to the research/academic literature; the "application" in this sense is the new theory itself. Put another way, rather than the new *theoria* having immediate *praxis* implications,

Figure 4.8 Alhusban measured student designers in all five years of the BArch curriculum as they took part in a controlled design exercise (of a beach house). Measurements consisted of photographs, recordings of spoken information, and the drawings, over elapsed time. This information was then charted in LCM maps. The upper image shows the room with the equipment. At lower left is one of the students doing the exercise. Alhusban also measured faculty (at lower right) to compare the difference in quantity of creative leaps. Photographs courtesy of Dr. Ahmad Alhusban, Hashemite University, Jordan.

academic research of this nature often generates issues for future research, implicitly or explicitly, as the new theory is applied to practice. For example, one of Oygur's 18 concluding observations is this: "The existence of an in-house research department (in a design firm) is not a guarantee that the designers will focus more on the users; nor does it guarantee that all designers (in the firm) will construct an identical user."[27] This finding not only invites further research to explore its validity; it may also influence practitioners' assessments of how best to gather research data.

Another example of developing new theory from extant theory is Ahmad Alhusban's doctoral dissertation on "the creative leap" in architectural studio education. Alhusban drew from an existing theory (limited commitment mode, LCM),[28] but the current literature largely applies LCM to the design of smaller-scale objects, generally in the realm of industrial design. Alhusban adapted it to the design of entire buildings in the schematic design phase by studying architectural students in all five years of a BArch professional program (Figure 4.8). One of Alhusban's findings was that divergent thinking ability—the ability to attend to many different design threads simultaneously—is one measure of the frequency of "creative leaps." Additionally, Alhusban found that increased experience also increases the number of these leaps, hence showing that "creative leaps" are not totally spontaneous out-of-the-blue events.[29] (See Chapter 2 on design logics.) Again, in research of this type, the emphasis in the outcome is the new theory that emerges; *praxis* is often stated as a series of recommendations for application. For instance, Alhusban's findings led him to suggest, as a matter of *praxis*, that more experienced teachers teach first-year design studios, so that beginning students can be immediately exposed to the rich variety of creative leaps in seasoned designers.

BOX 4.4

Architecture and Cultural Capital

Jennifer Chamberlin's dissertation, *The Cultural Reproduction of Architecture: Examining the Roles of Cultural Capital and Organizational Habitus in the Socialization of Architectural Education*, is an example of a study that draws from extant theory to frame new theory.[a] It is particularly notable because it features three steps in a theoretical line of development.

[a] Jennifer Chamberlin, *The Cultural Reproduction of Architecture: Examining the Roles of Cultural Capital and Organizational Habitus in the Socialization of Architectural Education*, PhD dissertation, University of Michigan, Ann Arbor, 2010.

(Continued)

The first step takes as primary theory the concept of cultural capital as elaborated by the French sociologist Pierre Bourdieu.[b] According to Bourdieu, cultural capital constitutes a significant form of power in any society. It is manifested in a variety of traits: behaviors, experiences, credentials, social networks, and attitudes. Most important, Bourdieu sees cultural capital as being *embodied* in individuals, typically acquired through multiple cultural milieus, and most typically from birth. Whereas economic wealth can be acquired and possessed, those with cultural capital only have to be what they are.

The second step is a development of Bourdieu's theory, as represented by the work of Garry Stevens, a professor of architecture at University of Sydney. As articulated initially in a journal article and subsequently in a book titled *The Favored Circle*, Stevens adapts Bourdieu's argument to the context of architectural education.[c] Using archives of existing demographic data from his own university context and a British university, Stevens elucidates how cultural capital may significantly influence the initial acceptance rates of architectural students as well as their eventual success, or lack thereof, in school and the profession. The primary thesis of his research is that architecture, compared to many other professional fields, is relatively *less* permeable to prospective students with lower levels of cultural capital.

Because of the limited scope of the evidence Stevens cites in his research, Chamberlin sought to investigate in greater depth its applicability in the U.S. context. This is the third theoretical step: Chamberlin's development of the extant theory in the literature. To this end, she compared the experience of architectural students at two U.S. universities: one where the overall level of cultural capital of the student population was relatively high, and the other where the level of cultural capital was measured to be lower.

Although the scope of Chamberlin's entire study is too multifaceted to fully summarize in this context, one set of findings, in particular, yielded a potentially significant refinement in the theoretical implications of cultural capital. Through the statistical tactic of K-Means Cluster Analysis, three groups of students were identified based on differences in their levels of cultural capital. One group, cluster #3, clearly emerged as the "high cultural capital" group, but the other two groups of students were not as easily defined (see Figure 4.9). Of these two groups of students, cluster #1 had far higher levels of parental education (compared to cluster #2), approaching the levels for cluster #3. Measures of childhood cultural pursuits, however, suggest that the differences between clusters #1 and #2 were less pronounced. Nevertheless, the overall profile of cluster #2 suggests that these students'

[b] Pierre Bourdieu, *Distinction: A Social Critique of Taste* (Cambridge, MA: Harvard University Press, 1984).

[c] Garry Stevens, *The Favored Circle: The Social Foundations of Architectural Distinction* (Cambridge, MA: MIT Press, 1998).

exposure to creative arts led to activities entailing more active engagement. The emergence of the cluster #1 group especially was a substantial finding because these students did not fit neatly into the dichotomy of high versus low cultural capital that both Bourdieu and Stevens present.

In sum, Chamberlin's research enabled her to contribute to theory building in interdisciplinary research on the effects of cultural capital in educational settings. The effect of both quantitative and qualitative differences in cultural capital in the experience of architectural education can now be tested in additional architectural settings or in other professional fields. A secondary outcome of Chamberlin's research is the potential of case-specific analyses to suggest institutional improvements in each school's architectural program.

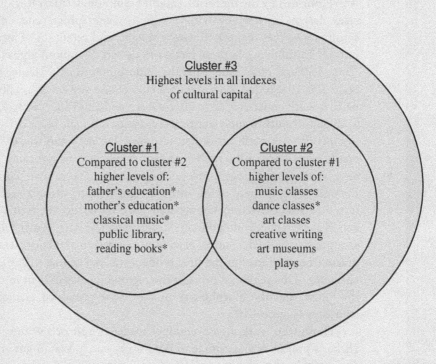

Figure 4.9 Among the three clusters of students, cluster #3 reflects the highest level of cultural capital in all measures. While there is some overlap of measurement levels between clusters #1 and #2, items indicated by asterisks represent significant levels of differences between the two groups at a 95% level of confidence. Diagram courtesy of Jennifer Chamberlin and Linda Groat.

4.4.2   *From Theory to a New Building in an Architectural Practice*

In contrast to developing new theory from existing theory in an academic venue, the goal of architectural practice is to build buildings. The purpose is quite specific because the audience is quite specific: the client. While iconic architects whose works appear in magazines and history books might claim to substantially realize their architectural theories in their bodies of work, it is more generally the case that architects use design theory in targeted ways to respond to the practical constraints unique to each project and client. This usually means more episodic instances in adapting theory (we elaborated on this point in Chapter 2).

Austin Dickey's Canyon House serves as a good illustration. This project grew in part out of the architect's commitment to the theory of Critical Regionalism. Promoted by the theorist Kenneth Frampton, Critical Regionalism emphasizes designs in keeping with a region's geographical and cultural history, sensitivity to that region's climate and light, and retention of local tactile attributes.[30] Faithfulness to these factors in design, Frampton argues, increases the "boundedness" of a locale, what the philosopher Martin Heidegger calls dwelling.[31] The 10 wooded acres of the Canyon House site are unusually fissured with narrow basalt crevices of up to 20 feet deep, and 5 to 15 feet wide. Dickey saw this as an opportunity to apply a critical regionalist rationale to his design by embodying this site feature in his design response. Dickey's aim was to "translate" the tactile experience of the site's abundant small canyons right into spatial experiences of the morphology of the house. To this end, a "canyon" corridor serves as the organizing element of the entire design, creating distinct sectors not unlike how the basalt crevices define separate portions of the site itself. Originally conceived as a basalt corridor, the corridor-canyon was later changed to concrete masonry units; this is an example of an ideal expression of theory meeting up against practice constraints. But the final product was in keeping with the geographical character of the region; it brought the region's quality of light into the spaces of the house, and the morphology of the house remained tactilely true to the landscape (Figure 4.10).

Those who work in conventional academic research venues might exclude Dickey's project as an example of rigorous research. We do not argue this point essentially, but two points in response are in order. First, the very project of writing a book on *architectural* research methods implies that conventional paradigms of academic research have to be stretched to accommodate what scholars like Nigel Cross have called "designerly" ways of thinking and knowing (again, see Chapter 2).[32] Here, our goal is to survey how theory is used to inform a variety of

Figure 4.10   The Canyon House. Critical Regionalist theory embodied in architectural design. Photographs courtesy of Austin Dickey, Copeland Architecture & Construction, AIA.

Figure 4.10   *(Continued)*

different purposes and applications, and we mean to include in this chapter examples of how practitioners get from theory to built form. Second, globally, if not in the United States, serious efforts are being made to comprehend design practice as a form of research. In Chapter 2, we saw this in the Belgian-Scandinavian case, where design- and practice-based doctoral education has been enacted into curricula.[33] Fueling this need is recognition that architectural knowledge is inherently "projective," which is to say its mode of inquiry involves insight into future

conditions, not just present or past conditions, and bringing those future conditions into fruition.[34] This fits with what was mentioned earlier: the deontological
nature of practice-based design-polemical theorizing.

BOX 4.5

Theory Influences in the Fernan Ranger Station: A Testimonial (Sam Rodell, Architect, AIA)

What my clients experience as "theory" is pretty basic stuff. People tend to find authors like Christopher Alexander and Sarah Susanka to be revelatory. From there, we might bridge to Michael Benedikt or Louis Kahn; I just see where our discussions lead us. Getting a client engaged at a theoretical level early in a project—not in a condescending or manipulative way, but in a truly earnest search for clarity relevant to them—pays huge dividends over the whole life of the project. I find myself going into the construction phase with huge equity in trust and credibility if I have succeeded in getting my clients enrolled in the world of ideas at the front end.

In this ranger station for the USDA Forest Service (Figure 4.11), the work of Christopher Alexander, Robert Venturi, and Charles Moore served to clarify architectural aspirations that had emerged out of our interviews with the Forest Service staff and their desire to express the character of their culture in a positive way to the public. For example, conversations about making the building welcoming to the public, the public entry easy to locate and use, and making meeting rooms available for community use, including after hours, were directly informed by these patterns from Alexander's *Pattern Language*: Positive Outdoor Space (#106), Main Entrance (#110), Reception Welcomes You (#149); Small Meeting Rooms (#151), and Rooms to Rent (#153). Other patterns referenced for welcoming the public included Wings of Light (#107), Paths and Goals (#120), Short Passages (#131), and Small Services without Red Tape (#81). I also referred to the work of Venturi and Moore to show our clients prominent public projects that actively used symbolic and traditional elements in design. Moore: St. Matthew's Episcopal Church, Pacific Palisades, California. Venturi: Lewis Thomas Laboratory and Gordon Wu Hall, Princeton University. And, of course, the work of these architects influenced me and served to open up the possibilities of overtly "decorative" elements in architecture . . . the cult of Modernism was still very powerful when this project was done, in 1988.

(Continued)

Figure 4.11   Fernan Ranger Station, Coeur d'Alene, Idaho (1988). Photograph courtesy of Sam Rodell, Architect, AIA.

4.4.3   From Theory to Built Environments: Use of Theory in a Design Consultancy

By a design consultancy we mean organizations that offer design services for a wide variety of built environment needs. These needs are specific, rendering the kind of theory each consultancy draws upon to be targeted. One example is Carpman Grant Associates, Wayfinding Consultants (CGA).[35] Founded in 1986 by Janet R. Carpman and Myron A. Grant,[36] CGA is a good example of theory being used in service of focused environmental needs (see Box 4.6 and Figure 4.12). In CGA's case, the firm has completed hundreds of wayfinding projects (such as sign design, map design, and wayfinding staff training) for over 70 client organizations throughout the United States and Canada, including health care facilities, historic and cultural facilities, educational facilities, office facilities, and government facilities. Carpman and Grant have also innovated key definitions and unique methodologies in developing pragmatic approaches to reducing disorientation in confusing places. These have been summarized in numerous articles, along with two books authored by Carpman and Grant: *Design that Cares: Planning Health Facilities for Patients and Visitors*[37] and *Directional Sense: How to Find Your Way Around.*[38]

Several pioneers laid the foundation for Carpman and Grant's work, specifically for their view that the physical environment significantly influences a range of behaviors and emotions. They therefore use social science theory and methods to discover large and small truths about how human beings interact with physical spaces, improving the quality of built environments for users. Kevin Lynch coined the term *wayfinding* in his seminal *Image of the City*[39] and described characteristics, such as nodes and landmarks, that make a place imageable. Romedi Passini, along and with Paul Arthur, defined wayfinding behavior, including decision making and decision execution, and explored the connection of wayfinding to architecture.[40] Jerry Weisman both pointed out architectural aspects of wayfinding (such as views to the exterior; decision points; and features such as artwork, lighting, and color that reinforce signage) and noted the importance of the management of a wayfinding system.[41] Marvin Levine theorized about the orientation of You-Are-Here maps and provided research evidence of its importance in assisting people in finding their way.[42] Stephen Kaplan and Rachel Kaplan developed useful theory, one aspect of which is how navigating takes up a great deal of "space" in one's head (and requires more effort) when an environment is unfamiliar, but as one learns it, navigation feels easier and is less taxing to the brain.[43] John Zeisel conducted applied research, wrote, and taught about the importance of involving users in design, and adapted classic sociological methods, such as observation and interviewing.[44] Mike Brill created ways to apply people-place theories and methods to solving problems, such as effective workplace design.[45] He founded and led BOSTI, a problem-solving consulting firm. Richard Saul Wurman wrote about issues of design in relation to information itself: that information design (including signs and maps) can help or hinder the ability of users to understand and make use of it.[46]

BOX 4.6

A New Wayfinding System for the Massachusetts State House

The original Massachusetts State House was completed in 1798 by self-taught architect Charles Bulfinch. Many additions followed, including a rear annex in 1831, and east and west wings in 1914–1917. Perched on 6.7 acres, the State House overlooks the Boston Common in the center of

(Continued)

Boston; it remains the working seat of state government as well as the most visited tourist destination in Massachusetts.

Two features made wayfinding particularly difficult: the annex and the main building do not connect on some floors; and tightened security as a result of the terrorist attacks of September 11, 2001, resulted in only 3 of the original 21 entrances remaining open, with the main public entrance—leading to key tourist destinations—closed. In addition, a host of contributing factors made wayfinding a challenge, such as little attention to citizens with disabilities and a series of outdated circulation systems.

CGA conducted detailed wayfinding design and operational analyses (including visitor interviews, management interviews, and staff focus groups), prepared a wayfinding plan, and designed new exterior and interior wayfinding signs[a] and You-Are-Here maps (see Figure 4.12). Informed by the participation of representatives of the disability community, the project team made recommendations about how wayfinding could be made easier for people with mobility, vision, hearing, and cognitive disabilities. These included designing new signs; removing outdated signs and maps; providing information about accessible entrances, restrooms, and assistive technology; enhancing accessible entrances and drop-off areas; providing tactile maps; and conducting staff training.

Here are some insights to come out of this project:

1. A systematic approach to wayfinding is needed, rather than focusing on signs alone.
2. Attention is needed to both design and operational aspects of a wayfinding system.
3. Ongoing audit/evaluation of a wayfinding system is needed as situations, locations, and priorities change.
4. Involvement of users and managers can and should be part of wayfinding system assessment and planning.
5. Implementation of wayfinding system elements can be phased.
6. The design of a good wayfinding system does not have to compromise either function or aesthetics.
7. Wayfinding ease can be improved even in the most challenging architectural and operational environments.

---

[a] Signs were designed by CGA's environmental graphics design partner, Nicolson Associates, Bloomfield Hills, MI.

Figure 4.12   Shown here are user interviews and staff focus groups, along with examples of exterior and interior signs and You-Are-Here maps that comprised part of the new wayfinding system. © 2012 Chapman Grant Associates, used with permission of the Massachusetts State House.

Box 4.6 showcases an example of CGA's work at the Massachusetts State House, Boston. Patrick Reed, then Deputy Superintendent for Administration, Bureau of State Office Buildings for the Commonwealth of Massachusetts, had this to say about the outcome: "beyond aesthetics, finally, after many years of confusion, people understand where they're going and can figure out how to get there—no small feat in a building that was notoriously disorienting for the thousands of tourists, legislators, lobbyists, and others who passed through it every day." Carpman Grant's work illustrates the targeted way theory can be used to enhance users' experiences with environmental design.

4.4.4   *From Theory to Design in Architectural Studio Education*

We now consider theory in relation to architectural design in the case of an MArch student thesis. Here, theory can once again be applied broadly (if not systematically) to the outcome, which is usually the design of an entire building, or at least a project at this scale if not larger. But ultimately, the transition from theoretical constructs to formal gestures in these cases is necessarily interpretive, rooted in the designer's value-full deontic decisions. We noted earlier that design-polemical theories gain their validity through adherence to the designer's deontological point of view by a large audience. In a student case, that audience is largely his committee, and secondarily his peers.

Eric Williams's MArch thesis sought to situate the design of a winery at the intersection of several key theoretical issues (Figure 4.13). He first drew from Heidegger's *Question Concerning Technology*[47] to establish the fact (and the consequences) of today's common cultural practice of thoroughly depending on technology to alter nature for human convenience. Heidegger (and Williams) argue that this impoverishes cultural life. Given the fact that we cannot return to a pretechnological culture to overcome this problem, Williams looked to a solution offered by the philosopher Albert Borgmann,[48] one that accommodates the use of technology in culture so long as it is subservient to "focal practices." Focal practices are activities that emphasize craft over machine production, and the sanctity of cultural practices over commodified technological convenience. Williams then introduces his technical term *terroir*, meaning "taste of the earth." With this term, Williams pivots to winemaking as an opportunity to embody focal practices that necessarily blend "a narrative of climate, soil type, and topography." This becomes the theoretical rationale behind his winery design as an expression of resistance to the blind use of technology for mass production.

Williams chose to use *terroir's* blending of indigenous natural elements as the theoretical key towards elevating a series of functions associated with winemaking into focal practices. This ranges from visitor observation of harvesting ("visitors can see traditional crushing contrasted with mechanical crushing and engage in the focal practice of the harvest"); to participation in winemaking ("visitors will be able to harvest, press, rack, and riddle grapes from the vineyard"); to connoisseurship ("visitors will be able to create their own blends of wine from various varietals. As they meander through the art gallery, they can explore blended examples of craft and commodity technology"); to picnics ("visitors can climb the stairs to the roof garden, pick their produce, and hand it to the chef so that it may be prepared in their meal"); to concerts, which are traditional at this winery throughout the summer months ("This focal practice is architecturalized by the new amphitheater which is carved out of the landscape mimicking the original contour lines").[49]

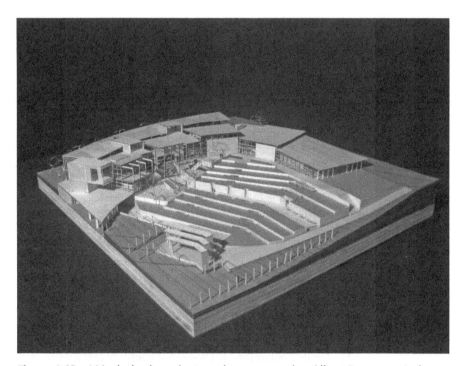

Figure 4.13   MArch thesis project: a winery expressing Albert Borgmann's theory of "focal practices." Image courtesy of Eric Williams.

4.5 CONCLUSION

This chapter has addressed the intricate connections between research purpose, theory building, and design application. We pointed out the distinction between contextual purposes, which tend to be external (considerations of motivation, audience, and anticipated impact), and theoretical purposes, which are internal to the nature of the project (is it to expand a theory? is it to create new theory? or does it use theory to inform a specific design?). It should be clear that the ultimate intended purpose determines the selection of a research design and, further, how theory relates to both. In the next chapter, we add to this mix by considering the framing of research questions, and the role of literature review.

NOTES

1. Isadore Newman, Carolyn S. Ridenour, Carole Newman, and George M. P. DeMarco, Jr., "A Typology of Research Purposes and Its Relationship to Mixed Methods," in Abbas Tashakkori and Charles Teddlie (eds.), *Handbook of Mixed Methods in Social & Behavioral Research* (Thousand Oaks, CA: Sage, 2003), 167–188.
2. Ibid., 167.
3. See Joseph A. Maxwell, *Qualitative Research Design: An Interactive Approach*, 2nd ed. (Thousand Oaks, CA: Sage, 2005).
4. "IBM's Santa Teresa Laboratory," *Architectural Record* (August 1977): 99–104.
5. David Wang telephone interview with Ed Shriver, Strada Architects, April 19, 2012.
6. American Institute of Architects 2011 Upjohn Research Initiative Program—Grant Recipients, "Main Street Connectivity; Patterns and Processes Linking Urban Commercial Patches." Researchers: Edward Shriver, Kelly Hutzell, and Rami el Samahy. www.aia.org/practicing/research/AIAB091287. Accessed May 2, 2012.
7. Oscar Newman, *Defensible Space: Crime Prevention through Urban Design* (New York: Macmillan, 1972).
8. Oscar Newman, "Alternatives to Fear," *Progressive Architecture* (1972): 92–100.
9. Linda Groat, "Public Opinions on Contextual Fit," *Architecture: The AIA Journal* (November 1984): 72–75.
10. Linda Groat, "Contextual Compatibility in Architecture: An Issue of Personal Taste?" in J. Nasar (ed.), *The Visual Quality of the Environment: Theory, Research, and Application* (Cambridge, UK: Cambridge University Press, 1998), 228–253.
11. Chaim Perelman and L. Olbrechts-Tyteca, *The New Rhetoric, A Treatise on Argumentation* (Notre Dame and London: University of Notre Dame Press, 1969), 13–17.
12. Matthew Cohen, "How Much Brunelleschi?: A Late Medieval Proportional System in the Basilica of San Lorenzo," *Journal of the Society of Architectural Historians* 67 (2008): 18–57.

13. Herbert Gans, *The Levittowners: Ways of Life and Politics in a New Suburban Community* [1967] (New York: Columbia University Press, 1982).
14. See Peter G. Rowe, *Design Thinking* (Cambridge, MA: MIT Press, 1987), 1–37.
15. AIA Best Practices, www.aia.org/practicing/bestpractices/index.htm. Accessed May 29, 2012.
16. AIA Best Practices, "Energy Design Guidelines for High Performance Schools," American Institute of Architects, www.aia.org/aiaucmp/groups/ek_members/documents/pdf/aiap017470.pdf. Accessed May 29, 2012.
17. Ken Friedman, "Theory Construction in Design Research: Criteria, Approaches, and Methods," *Design Studies* 24(6) (November 2003): 512.
18. Jon Lang, *Creating Architectural Theory* (New York: Van Nostrand Reinhold, 1987), 219.
19. Ibid.
20. "Deontological Ethics," in *The Stanford Encyclopedia of Philosophy*, http://plato.stanford.edu/entries/ethics-deontological/. Accessed May 3, 2012.
21. Lang, 222–230.
22. Frank Lloyd Wright, cited in Lang, 219.
23. Paul-Alan Johnson, *The Theory of Architecture: Concepts, Themes & Practices* (New York: Van Nostrand Reinhold, 1994), 13.
24. Abraham Kaplan, *The Conduct of Inquiry: Methodology for Behavioral Science* (San Francisco: Chandler, 1964): 21.
25. See, for instance, V. V. Kryssanov, H. Tamaki, and S. Kitamura, "Understanding Design Fundamentals: How Synthesis and Analysis Drive Creativity, Resulting in Emergence," *Artificial Intelligence in Engineering* 15 (2001): 329–342; C. Wang, "On the Inspiration of Creative Thinking for Engineering Students," *Information Technologies and Application in Education: First IEEE International Symposium* 1 (2007): 443–448; L. Zeng, R. W. Proctor, and G. Savendy, "Can Traditional Divergent Thinking Tests Be Trusted in Measuring and Predicting Real-World Creativity?" *Creativity Research Journal*, 23(1) (2011): 14–37.
26. L. Groat and D. Canter, "Does Post-Modernism Communicate?" *Progressive Architecture* (December 1979): 84–87.
27. Isil Oygur, *Reconfiguring the User: How Designers Process User Information*, PhD dissertation, Washington State University, May 2012, 197.
28. See M. Kim, Y. Kim, S. Lee, and A. Park, "An Underlying Cognitive Aspect of Design Creativity: Limited Commitment Mode Control Strategy," *Design Studies* 28(6) (2007): 585–604.
29. Ahmad Alhusban, *What Does the Architectural Creative Leap Look Like through a Conceptual Design Phase in Undergraduate Architectural Design Studio?* Doctor of Design dissertation, Washington State University, May 2012, 150–154.
30. K. Frampton, "Towards a Critical Regionalism: Six Points for an Architecture of Resistance," in H. Foster (ed.), *Postmodern Culture* (London: Pluto Press, 1983) : 16–30.
31. Martin Heidegger, "Building Dwelling Thinking," in David Farrell Krell (ed.), *Basic Writings* (New York: HarperCollins, 1993), 347–363.

32. Nigel Cross, *Designerly Ways of Knowing* (London: Springer-Verlag, 2006); Nigel Cross, "Designerly Ways of Knowing," *Design Studies* 3(4) (October 1982): 221–227.

33. Halina Dunin-Woyseth and Fredrik Nilsson, "Building a Culture of Doctoral Scholarship in Architecture and Design: A Belgian-Scandinavian Case," *Nordic Journal of Architectural Research* 23(1) (2011), 41–55.

34. Halina Dunin-Woyseth and Fredrik Nilsson, "Building (Trans)disciplinary Architectural Research—Introducing Mode 1 and Mode 2 to Design Practitioners," in Isabelle Doucet and Nel Janssens (eds.), *Transdisciplinary Knowledge Production in Architecture and Urbanism* (Dordrecht: Springer, 2011), 79–96.

35. A significant portion of the text of this section, along with the text of Box 4.6, was supplied by Janet R. Carpman, PhD, of Carpman Grant Associates, Wayfinding Consultants, Ann Arbor, MI.

36. See www.wayfinding.com

37. Janet R. Carpman and Myron A. Grant, *Design that Cares: Planning Health Facilities for Patients & Visitors,* 2nd ed. (San Francisco: Jossey-Bass, 2003).

38. Janet R. Carpman and Myron A. Grant, *Directional Sense: How to Find Your Way Around* (Boston: Institute for Human Centered Design, 2012).

39. Kevin Lynch, *Image of the City* (Cambridge, MA: MIT Press, 1960).

40. Romedi Passini, *Wayfinding in Architecture* (New York: Van Nostrand Reinhold, 1984); see also Paul Arthur and Romedi Passini, *Wayfinding: People, Signs, & Architecture* (New York: McGraw-Hill, 1992).

41. Gerald D. Weisman, *Way-finding in the Built Environment: A Study in Architectural Legibility.* PhD dissertation, University of Michigan, Ann Arbor, 1979.

42. Marvin Levine, "You-Are-Here Maps: Psychological Considerations," *Environment & Behavior* 14(2) (1982): 221–237.

43. Stephen Kaplan and Rachel Kaplan (eds.), *Humanscape: Environments for People* (Belmont, CA: Duxbury Press, 1978).

44. John Zeisel, *Inquiry by Design: Tools for Environment-Behavior Research* (Monterey, CA: Brooks Cole, 1981).

45. Mike Brill, with Stephen Margulis, Ellen Konar, and BOSTI, *Using Office Design to Increase Productivity,* vol. 2 (Buffalo, NY: Workplace Design and Productivity, 1985).

46. Richard Saul Wurman, *Information Anxiety* (New York: Bantam Books, 1989).

47. Martin Heidegger, "The Question Concerning Technology," in D. F. Krell (ed.), *Basic Writings* (San Francisco: Harper, 1992), 307–341.

48. Albert Borgmann, "Focal Things and Practices," in *Technology and the Character of Contemporary Life* (Chicago: University of Chicago Press, 1987), 196 cf.

49. Eric Williams, *Architectural Terroir: Blending Techné and Technology in Winery Design.* MArch Monograph, Washington State University, 2009.

Chapter 5

What's Your Question?
Literature Review and Research Design

Chapter 3 addressed broad conceptual frameworks of research: systems of inquiry and schools of thought. Chapter 4 addressed the contextual and internal (theory and application) purposes of research; these were captured by the diagram in Figure 4.1. This present chapter addresses the specific research question or questions that every research design must have, and how literature review helps to frame these questions. To this end, we expand Figure 4.1 as shown in Figure 5.1.

Figure 5.1 adds two new factors: the literature review box at the upper right of the figure, and the strategies and tactics boxes at the bottom of the figure. This chapter addresses how literature review informs the framing of research questions, which act as pivot points in the development of an eventual research design. All of Part II of this book, beginning with Chapter 6, addresses strategies and tactics of research design.

A note to readers who are *not* intending to embark on a long or extensive research project; on the face of it, this chapter's focus on literature review and the framing of research questions may initially seem to be of limited relevance to your circumstances. Indeed, as we have already acknowledged, for those whose primary purpose is a physical design outcome, research is likely to be of a more episodic nature, specific to questions arising across different phases of the design process. Nevertheless, we would argue that the issues addressed in this chapter concerning how to cultivate one's clarity of thought, purposes, processes, and outcomes are equally relevant—no matter whether you are contemplating a mini-study in the midst of a design project or envisioning a multiphase research enterprise.

141

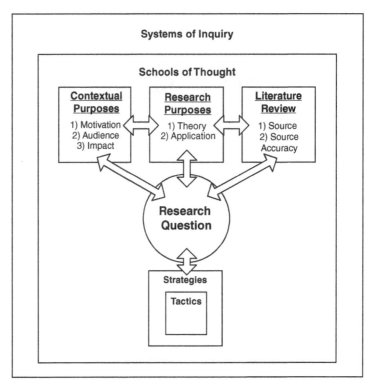

Figure 5.1 The research question as a pivot point in the development of the research design. This figure adds to Figure 4.1 by highlighting the role of litera-ture review in framing the research question or questions.

5.2   LITERATURE REVIEW COMPARED TO ANNOTATED BIBLIOGRAPHY

Literature reviews and annotated bibliographies are the stepping-stones toward framing concise research questions. Annotated bibliographies demonstrate knowl-edge of the general literature relevant for the researcher's area of interest. In con-trast, literature reviews synthesize themes within that literature. These syntheses entail assessment and critique of existing perspectives, but also offer new ideas. From these ideas emerge original research questions. Figure 5.2 itemizes some other differences.

There is a difference, then, between a researcher's literature *awareness*, repre-sented by the annotated bibliography, versus what he or she ultimately writes as a

Annotated Bibliography	Literature Review
1. A bulleted list of relevant titles usually in alphabetical order by author.	1. Often written in prose/narrative form, either as a stand-alone document or as a section of a larger research document.
2. Seeks to be comprehensive.	2. Is selective, grouping related references into common themes or points of view that pertain to the research question(s) addressed in the larger document. Or: stand-alone literature reviews can be references directing readers to relevant sources.
3. Each entry is summarized in a few sentences or short paragraph, usually with comments by the researcher on how the reference influences or relates to his/her area of interest.	3. The selected references are explained in support of, or in other ways servant to, the researcher's research design: theoretically, methodologically, as examples of related work, etc.
4. Usually does not make comparisons between references; nor does it seek to synthesize themes.	4. It is the job of literature reviews to group themes, synthesize ideas, explain different schools of thought, or trace historical development of an idea or theory.

Figure 5.2 Comparison between annotated bibliography and literature review.

literature review, which reflects further development toward the new knowledge the researcher intends to contribute in his/her research.

For student researchers, both annotated bibliographies and literature reviews drive home the point that no idea is so new that it is not already relatable to a substantial literature. The goal is to identify that literature and become familiar with it (to gain literature awareness), and then to internalize that literature so as to propose original research questions. In the United States, this is one way to explain the rationale behind the coursework portion of graduate research curricula, in contrast to the research portion after the coursework has been completed and whatever candidacy exams have been passed. Coursework develops literature awareness on the part of the student. It cultivates an ingrained sense that, while all good research requires original thinking, no research can be conducted *de novo*; all research grows out of, and should contribute to, relevant literature. The ensuing research period of a student's training is usually when general literature awareness is refined into specific research questions; literature review(s) aid in this process.

BOX 5.1

Annotated Bibliography: From General Literature Awareness to a Focused Research Topic

It is important in the research process to develop a way to keep track of annotated references. This might be in either written or electronic format or both (see also Box 5.2). An annotated bibliography is a formal compilation of these references, and helps the researcher move from general literature awareness to a focused research question. The following is an entry in an annotated bibliography of Dr. Ahmad Alhusban. Early in his studies, Alhusban was already interested in what the design thinking literature calls "the creative leap." As his familiarity with this literature increased, one gap he noted was the limited amount of material on the creative leap in conjunction with architectural design (as opposed to industrial design). The following entry comes from an annotated bibliography he submitted as an assignment in a doctoral readings class in his second year. It was about this time that he began to learn about Limited Commitment Mode, a tool that he ultimately used in measuring the different magnitudes of the creative leap in first- to fifth-year architectural students.

Kim, M., Kim, Y., Lee, S., & Park, A. (2007), "An underlying cognitive aspect of design creativity: Limited Commitment Mode control strategy," in Design Studies, 28(6), 585–604. This study used the Limited Commitment Mode (LCM) to test for differences in process between expert and student designers. LCM theory posits that in solving a series of design sub-problems, a designer can put any one sub-problem on "hold" to attend to another sub-problem, returning to the first at a later point. The researchers addressed two questions. One was whether adeptness in LCM control improves the creativity of the design product. Another was whether there are differences between experts and students in the use of LCM. Methods included experimental and statistical analysis, "think aloud" protocol analysis, video cameras, voice recorders, and a video capturing program. The sample included 4 industrial designers with over 5 years of experience (expert group) and 4 graduate students without practical design experience (student group). The results: First, expert designers used LCM control strategy more actively than student designers. Second, expert designers arrived upon design concepts later than student designers. Third, the later the design concept was decided, the more creative the final project. Finally, expert designers drew from different cognitive sources than student designers; these differences being reflected in the degree of creativity of the final solution.

Applicability to research interest: 1) This article provides an opera-tionalizable definition of creativity; 2) A good example of research into constraints versus design solutions; 3) The authors chart how design ideas emerge; 4) A good example of protocol analysis; 5) Describes how to construct a coding theme; how to draw an LCM flow graph; how to make statistical correlations using the Spearman test due to small sample size.[a]

The standard elements of an annotated bibliography entry are here. First is the citation of the work in full. This is followed by a general descrip-tion of the article's intentions. The article's guiding questions are identi-fied, along with methods used and a summary of the findings. Alhusban then itemizes how the article informed his thinking.

_____

[a] Ahmad Alhusban, Annotated Bibliography submitted for DDes 563 Reading, Spring 2011.

Defining the research question or questions, then, is the researcher's goal vis-à-vis the literature. In his book *Qualitative Research Design,* Joseph Maxwell notes that it is the research questions that "directly link to all other components" of the re-search project. If the questions are too broad, there is "no clear guide in deciding what data to collect." If the questions are too narrow, they may "leave out many things that are important to the goals of the study."[1] Literature review, then, plays a key role in reducing a large body of literature to a collection of references having direct bearing on a research topic; it is in this refining process that research ques-tions emerge. When the questions are defined, when their relevance is explained, when the methods for answering them are operationalized and the outcomes are reported and interpreted, when all of this is achieved, a contribution of new knowl-edge is made to a general body of literature. So, while literature awareness can be relatively passive, critical thinking is the active element in writing a literature review. Annotated bibliographies and literature reviews are essential to the process by which the researcher initially identifies and iteratively refines the research question(s) central to his/her project. In this process, other questions ought to be asked, like these:

1. What are the main lines of knowledge already established in my interest area?
2. What leading theories inform these lines of knowledge?
3. Are there obvious differences in points of view (different schools of thought)?
4. What is the ideological lineage(s) of ideas I am interested in?

5. Who are the leading thinkers and/or what are the iconic works in this field?
6. Can any of the established findings be applied in new ways, in new settings?
7. Are there gaps in this interest area that the literature, so far as I can see, does not cover?
8. Do current events suggest that leading works can be updated in light of new developments?
9. What do all of the above have to do with my research interest? How does each entry shed light on the direction I should go? What does entry X teach me? What insights does it offer? What weaknesses can I improve upon?

Again, these are not themselves the research questions. They are assessment questions that aid in selecting from a general literature (as perhaps represented by bibliographies) more specific threads to pursue. Note that the latter questions in the preceding list are more activist in nature; that is, answering them may well lead to specific research questions.

BOX 5.2

A Note about Note Taking

The proliferation of electronic resources has made access to sources easier. But digesting what the sources say requires the same hard work—or hand work—as in the days of the card catalog. We are referring to note taking, and having a system of organization and retrieval (see Figure 5.3). Annotated bibliographies and literature reviews are made much easier when the researcher has a systematic way of noting points made in references. Jacques Barzun and Henry Graff make the point that a researcher's notes are (or ought to be) his/her thoughts about the literature being read. In this way, Barzun and Graff elevate note taking from simply copying down references from texts; whether too much or too little makes little difference. "Am I simply doing clerk's work or am I assimilating new knowledge and putting down my own thoughts? To put down your own thoughts, you must use your own words, not the author's."[a] From these thoughts come the purpose of the study, or, in Maxwell's terms, from these thoughts emerge research questions.[b] Additionally, thoughts often occur when the books are not around; they need to be jotted down quickly, or many of them are forgotten. There are many different ways to take notes and file them.

[a] Jacques Barzun and Henry F. Graff, "The ABC of Technique," in *The Modern Researcher,* 6th ed. (Stamford, CT: Thomson Wadsworth, 2004), 15–36.
[b] Joseph A. Maxwell, *Qualitative Research Design* (Thousand Oaks, CA: Sage, 2005).

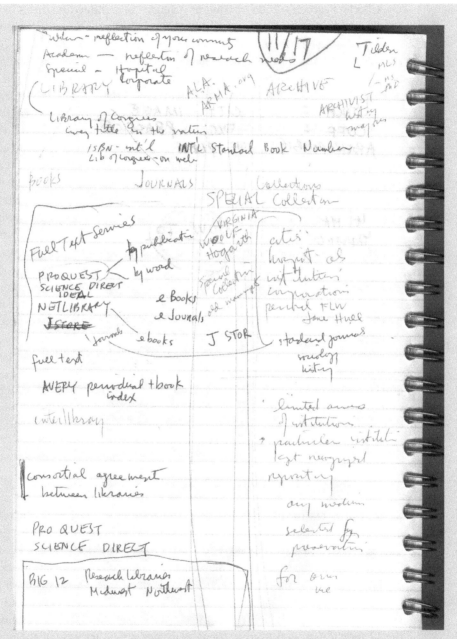

Figure 5.3 Shown here is a page of notes from Wang's dissertation research in 1997. For that work, daily notes jotted down were placed into an accordion folder with many divisions, each marked with the projected chapters of the dissertation. The notes were placed in the appropriate sections.

Cherie Peacock's 2005 master of science in architecture thesis is titled *Dwelling Well: An Application of Christopher Alexander's Theory of Wholeness to Investigate Occupant Affective Responses to Homes Incorporating Renewable Natural Resources.*[2] The first thing to note is the specificity of the title. Thesis and dissertation titles are usually long because they are the result of an iterative process in which research questions were sharpened to answer just this issue, and not other ones. (John Creswell suggests a 12-word limit for research titles.[3] But 12 words are a rule of thumb; the key is precision.) The iterations in refining the research title go hand-in-hand with refining the research question; all of this comes from engagement with the literature. Beginning researchers often mistake a general area of interest for a specific research topic. When Wang first met with Peacock, the answer to the question "what do you want to research?" was, "I want to research sustainability." This broad topical area resulted, several years later, in the above titled work.

Peacock's background was in environmental engineering, and she came into the program with an interest in green efficiencies in residential design, and an entry-level awareness of relevant literature. During her coursework period, she was exposed to Alexander's writings; specifically, she found that a theme in Alexander's interest in developing his Pattern Language was a desire to achieve "wholeness."[4] Another literature source was Clare Cooper Marcus's tactic of having occupants sketch their feelings about their homes rather than report them in words.[5] (See Box 7.1.) Both were important in Peacock's assessment questions about the sustainability literature. Can Alexander's theory of wholeness be applied to occupants of off-grid homes? Can Cooper Marcus's tactic of drawing feelings be used to graphically capture feelings of "wholeness"? (Many of Cooper Marcus's own examples seem to capture negative affective conditions.) These assessments drove iterations of the research questions in the course of Peacock's work.

5.2.1   Types of Research Questions

To even further refine the title, it is helpful to consider Maxwell's types of research questions in application to the Peacock example.[6] Maxwell posits three pairs of questions. The first pair is generic versus particularistic research questions. Generic research questions imply answers to a general set of factors. Peacock's title implies a generic question: What are occupant affective responses to homes incorporating renewable natural resources? But, in fact, Peacock considered 12 cases, ranging from straw bale homes to homes with passive heat storage systems, and the 12 individuals who lived in them. A particularistic framing of the question might be: What are the occupant responses in 12 cases of naturally built homes? Maxwell notes that this is the difference between samples and cases. A sampling approach implies statistical ability to generalize to a broad population from the samples, while a case study approach limits the findings more to just the cases. A particularist would criticize Peacock for implying a generic result when her approach was in fact particularistic.

Here is Maxwell's second pair: instrumental versus realist research questions. Peacock's formulation of her title presumes a realist approach, to wit: realists "treat unobserved phenomena [in Peacock's case the affective feelings of the occupants] as real, and their data as evidence about these, to be used critically to develop and test ideas about the existence and nature of the phenomena." And so a realist question might be this: "What are the affective responses of occupants living in off-grid, naturally built homes?" An instrumentalist approach, in contrast, would be concerned about keeping the data to only that which is observed, and not making implied inferences about them. Hence, an instrumentalist research question would be: "What are the reported affective responses of 12 occupants living in their off-grid, naturally built homes?"

Maxwell's third pair is variance versus process research questions. A variance question for Peacock's study can be: "Do occupants of off-grid, naturally built homes experience wholeness factors at the same level as experienced by occupants living in conventionally built homes?" Peacock may have discovered certain factors motivating her informers to move to their off-grid homes, but clearly her aim was not to answer this sort of variance question. Her study was a better fit for answering questions of a process nature: "What factors spurred her informers to live in off-grid homes?" And, "What traits do folks who live in off-grid, naturally built homes share in common, if any?"

In any of these hypothetical questions, the reader should appreciate how specific they are, and that they come only after quite a bit of spade work has been done in becoming familiar with the general literature in this domain.

5.2.2   *What to Do? versus What Is the Case?*

A matter related to asking assessment questions—on the way toward developing research questions—is seeing the difference between What is the case? versus What to do? This is particularly true for those in the design disciplines. The former suggests a more theoretical goal and the latter a more applied goal. As such, these two types of questions reprise the issues of purpose addressed in Chapter 4, and diagrammed in Figure 1.7. Here is a what-to-do posture: *"Designing more off-grid homes will enhance affective responses to residential settings."* Many designers think of research in these action terms. But note that this what-to-do statement is not a question; indeed, a what-to-do posture is not prone to asking questions; it is instead a call to action. In Peacock's case, being personally committed to off-grid residential living (at the time she lived in a straw bale house herself), she began her program of study with more of a what-to-do approach. Put another way, she wanted to be an advocate for living off-grid. Even though advocacy is now accepted within certain schools of thought (for instance, in critical theory, introduced in Chapter 3), generally speaking, the nature of research leans more toward a what-is-the-case posture. Peacock's thesis, and the questions suggested earlier that apply to her topic, all fit within a what-is-the-case approach. This is because by the time she was researching her thesis, she saw that answering what-is-the-case questions could help her (and others) comprehend why promoting off-grid living is desirable, as a thing to do. This is because a what-is-the-case approach usually yields knowledge of a more generalizable nature, so that it can be applied intelligently in future what-to-do settings.

5.3   AN INTERACTIVE PROCESS

One challenge in writing about literature review and research questions is the necessarily linear nature of any written document. Put another way, reading *about* literature review can easily create the illusion that we are dealing with a step-one, step-two, step-three process. But this is not the reality. Gaining awareness of a general literature, writing literature reviews, and developing research questions—these almost always go on simultaneously. It is a symphonic process. Or to put it less elegantly, the process is usually messier than we would like. Maxwell calls it an *interactive* process, meaning that research questions only tend to clarify in midst of an active process of research: "researchers often don't develop their eventual research questions until they have done a significant amount of data collection and analysis."[7] In addition, all sorts of things are going on in the life of the researcher; among those should be instances of becoming aware of the literature, and instances of gaining critical insight into that literature. Those instances happen piece by piece, and usually not in any controllable order. In his published output thus far, this author (Wang) can recount in almost every case fortuitous encounters—hallway chats with colleagues, giving a lecture and an unrelated thought crops up, searching in the library but a volume *from some other field* strikes him as relevant—that ultimately led to significant insights for a research project. Conversely, not a few times an article is half drafted, but literature surfaces showing that someone else has already pursued the topic. It forces substantial change in direction.

To underline the interactive and nonsequential nature of developing research questions from the literature, consider this chart:

To Do

	1. Thinking	2. Finding	3. Sorting	4. Writing
A. Topic	•General interest area •Interest threads •What is the research question? •What is the justification? •Range of sources •Titling	•References from articles •Trails •Talking to key people •Database searches •Identifying exemplars •Dissertation data bases •Sources from coursework •Grey sources	•Primary/secondary •Schools of thought •Gaps •Comparing/Relating •Deepening •Supporting arguments •Opposing arguments	• Annotations •Recording /Retrieval •Foldering / Titling •Draft topical sentences •Draft abstracts •Table of contents •Chapter structure •Potential research questions
B. Theory (systems of inquiry & schools of thought)	•What epistemological assumptions? •What philosophical foundations? •Related fields (level of interdisciplinarity)	• Interdisciplinary links •Exemplary thinkers •Exemplary theories •Exemplary works •Contacting people	•How has this line of theory evolved? •Where does it come from? / lineage •Find examples •What related theories?	• Write out how this line of theory affects your topic • Potential research questions • Titling
C. Method	•What strategy? •What tactics? •Appropriate sources for this methodology	•Literature resources (on method) •Exemplars from the literature •Contacting people	•What strengths/ weakness in the key sources? •What is doable?	•Diagramming •Potential research questions •Titling
D. Outcomes	• Theory, such as new or refined explanation or model. • Application, such as design guidelines or tools. • Or both.	•Exemplars	•Is this still what I want to do? •Check my titling	•Literature awareness •Other new works •Future research •Supplemental articles

*(Row label at left, rotated: **To Clarify**)*

Figure 5.4   Awareness of literature-related issues in "real time," leading to literature review and framing research questions. Chart by David Wang.

Figure 5.4 is a matrix with things to do arranged in columns (Thinking, Finding, Sorting, Writing) and things to clarify arranged in rows (Topic, Theory, Method, Outcomes). At the intersections are some action items related to those junctures. The key to using this matrix is to realize that all of the intersections are more or less simultaneous concerns for the researcher. This is why we say that this matrix describes an awareness of literature-related issues in "real time." For example, an experienced researcher, upon being presented with a general interest area (A/1, Thinking/Topic, at upper left) may well be able to guide someone by envisioning a research question (4/A,B,C). Or an interdisciplinary linkage in the potential question (B/1) can immediately generate a possible title for the research, or chapter headings in a dissertation (A/4, Thinking/Writing, at upper right). And that particular arrangement of chapters arises because of an awareness of what can be left for future research (D/4, Outcomes/Writing, at lower right). A benefit of knowing a body of literature is having a sense of the gaps, of what looks like a potential contribution, and what ideas can open up new lines of inquiry.

For a less experienced researcher, part of the learning process is developing the knack for seeing this "lay of the land" (Figure 5.4) in "real time." Students often feel overwhelmed by having a general interest in something—let us say, again, "sustainability." But then, how do we get from general interest to specific questions? The matrix is one way to answer this question. It doesn't reduce the work required, but it begins to clarify what work must be done. For any one particular project, the work is doing the action items from juncture to juncture on the matrix. A research-oriented mind is trained by repeated exercises in linking these connections all at once. In what follows, we will address handling the literature through the categories of Topic, Theory, Method, and Outcome (the rows in the matrix). But the caveat must be that, at any one juncture, the concerns of the other junctures are also in play. Reference to the junctures will be made by letter/number, as in A/1 for Topic/Thinking.

5.3.1   *Research Questions in Relation to the Literature*

Again, at the early stages, a proposed topic is usually too broad. But as we saw in Peacock's case, even at the initial stage, some threads are already motivating the research interest (still A/1). Immersion in the relevant literature, coupled with asking assessment questions, gradually moves the researcher's thinking toward developing the research questions. So, what literature is the researcher already aware of? In these readings are no doubt references to track down (A/2); these references can be the first links in developing a trail (A/2). A trail is a series of sources commonly linked by references the researcher comes across (see Box 5.3). Together, they deepen understanding of a theme while increasing awareness of how that theme is being addressed in the literature. Trails can begin fortuitously; one reference leads to another. Or they can be intentional: look in the index of a book for an entry of interest; go to that section; it will most likely have references to other related texts or sources.

Other ways to immerse oneself in the literature include word or topic searches in databases (A/2). Even in the 10 years since the first edition of this book (2002), electronic databases have become much more accessible. Of course, the Internet itself is an extremely useful, albeit unregulated and non-peer-reviewed, search resource. Aside from its general search engine, Google has many scholarly books available on line (including the first edition of this book). This resource can at least be searched to determine whether or not ordering hardcopy versions is necessary. There is also Google Scholar, linking to many peer-reviewed articles. The standard caution to young researchers is to not use such online references as Wikipedia, because its open access nature is not rigorous enough to vet the information on its pages. But Wikipedia can be a useful starting point for searches, because its entries are a good way to find key words, which can then be used to search journal data-bases such as Avery Index, or PsychInfo, ProQuest, or JStor.com. From these data-bases, many trails can be started. Wikipedia should not be cited as an ending reference (that is, do not cite it in publications as an endnote, footnote, or bibliog-raphy entry). But there is no harm to using it as a starting point for searches, and this approach can apply to any unvetted Internet source.

Thesis or dissertation databases, such as available on WorldCat.com, are also informative. Key word searches often lead to relevant titles. Additionally, if for no other reason, time spent on getting acquainted with dissertation titles is a good way to cultivate the imagination toward capturing one's own research interest by titling—see below. (Still A/2, but also awareness of A/1 and A/4 with regard to titling.) There is a rigor in dissertation titles that makes them satisfying to read. Again, the titles reflect substantial periods of work to get to an arrangement of words that specify a concise focus. Here is the title of this author's dissertation (1997): *A Cognitive-Aesthetic Theory of Dwelling: Anchoring the Discourse on the "Concept of Dwelling" in Kant's* Critique of Judgment. There is a reason for the fre-quent use of the colon in these titles. The first words capture the essence of the overall argument; sometimes it is a technical term unique to the study. The wording after the colon is usually a concise elaboration of what the technical term means.

Note also that dissertation or thesis titles are usually different from book titles. Book audiences tend to be larger and more diverse, so book titles are often more general in tone. Books tend to encompass more; within a book can be a range of topics thematically interconnected in something like what Howard Gardner calls a domain.[8] An example of this, currently on the author's desk, is Edward Said's *Orien-talism*.[9] Look in dissertation databases and you will not find one-word titles like this. Neither will academic journal articles be titled in this generalist manner. "Ori-entalism" may well be the technical term on the left side of a colon in a dissertation title, but it will not be the only word in that title.

Titling is itself a tactic in getting from general literature awareness to a specifi-able topic (A/1, A/4). In the researcher's imagination, there ought to be a symbi-otic relationship between the first drafts of a topic statement with the title. The title guides the statement; drafting the statement may alter the title. Both are readily changeable, as provisional research questions change. But taken together, finding alignment between the two becomes a clarifying force. There is a visionary element here. Imagine your research document complete; there it is in a journal or in some bound format. What is the title? This author often tells his students that on his computer desktop are folders labeled only with future (provisional) article titles. The folders are empty because there is not yet a clear idea what the contents will be. "Kuhn on Architectural Style" began this way.[10] There was an inkling to find parallels between Thomas Kuhn's theory of the behavior of scientific paradigms with shifts in design styles; both seem to behave in similar cultural ways. The folder began empty with a provisional title, and it collected references, and half-page attempts at an opening paragraph, perhaps a draft of the article's anticipated conclusions, until, some three years later, a conceptual framework for an article became clear. Usually, draft titles and draft contents are like conceptual putty that get worked and reworked; both change as the overall form gets clearer. The key is to keep the title and the contents reflective of each other. The point is this: in "real time," titling exercises should take place at the very beginnings of engagement with the literature (A/1). How would you title your research today? Of course, it will change many times. But title the research as it stands today.

A related exercise is to draft a table of contents. This presumes a multichapter work. Or if it is to be a journal article, envision the subsections. The time to do it is today, not later (A/4).

Barzun and Graff make the point that as awareness of the literature increases in relation to a topic, conceptual demarcations will appear.[11] For example, for any topic there are primary and secondary sources. Primary sources are those that in one way or another are the headwaters of the topic under study. They are the original sources that, relative to the topic, are not essentially commentary *about* it, but rather provide the substance of what other sources, relative to the same topic, comment *upon*. Those other sources, then, are the secondary sources. In Peacock's *Dwelling Well* example, the title makes clear that Christopher Alexander is a primary source. Consider Figure 5.5; the diagram illustrates the hierarchy of sources that informed this author's doctoral dissertation.

From the author's dissertation title, it is clear that Kant's works, particularly the *Critique of Judgment*, are primary works.[12] The title also indicates that Norberg-Schulz's works on architectural phenomenology are also primary.[13] The diagram maps the flow of the original philosophical material in Kant's works, how this material was digested by a network of commentators and analysts (the secondary sources) and, finally, how a new theory was framed from material taken from both the primary and secondary sources. Also shown is the necessary engagement with the line of thinking via Norberg-Schulz, to which the new theory was a response. Note the designation of Heidegger as a secondary source. Although a primary source for Norberg-Schulz, Heidegger was a secondary source relative to the research on Kant.[14] This does not mean that original Heidegger material did not play a part in the dissertation; certainly it did, because the critique of the Norberg-Schulz material demanded it. But relative to the actual topic of inquiry centered around Kant's philosophy, Heidegger's works were secondary sources. Arranging the literature into primary and secondary and even tertiary sources is integral to framing the logic of a research project. Diagramming such as this can be taking place fairly early in the "real time" of engaging with the literature.

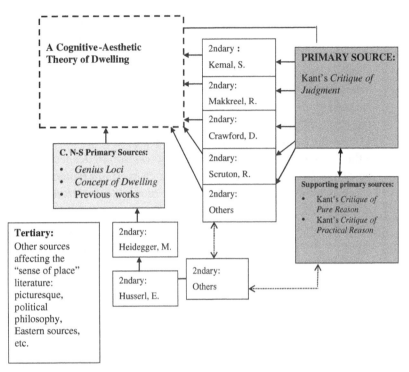

Figure 5.5 Diagram of hierarchy of sources for a research dissertation titled *A Cognitive-Aesthetic Theory of Dwelling: Anchoring the Discourse on the "Concept of Dwelling" in Kant's* Critique of Judgment. (Primary works shaded.)

There are many other ways to sort the general literature (A/3). O'Leary suggests developing a hierarchy, from background literature, to moderate, high, and highest relevance.[15] This again presumes that the researcher is gaining a feel for relevance *in relation to what*. Comparing and contrasting how two or more sources treat the same topic may yield critical discernments for gaps that can be further developed. Identifying opposing points of view is another: how is it possible that the same topic can generate opposing views? Is there a way to integrate the views? This might be a gap. As a body of literature becomes familiar, sorting it in different ways may well open the way toward concise research questions.

5.3.2 Theory in Relation to the Literature (with an Emphasis on Interdisciplinary Linkages)

For purposes here, theory (row B in Figure 5.4) can be understood as broad systems of inquiry and/or schools of thought (already illustrated in Figures 3.9 and 3.11 in Chapter 3). For example, different schools of thought may have opposing points of view on the same topic (B/1). A structuralist may analyze a cultural context within a relatively stable network of social signs (examples: Levi-Strauss, or Baudrillard in the *The System of Objects*).[16] But a poststructuralist will insist on assessments of institutional power in determining cultural meaning, and may express "incredulity towards meta-narratives" (examples: Michel Foucault, or Edward Soja).[17] So, the researcher will need to identify his/her theoretical framework (B/2). Is it structuralist or poststructuralist? Or is an objective reality independent of social construction presumed? Who are the exemplary thinkers? And what are the exemplary works leading the way in this approach (B/2)? How do these sources in turn deepen understanding of the topic (A/3)? How do they shape the research questions (column 4/A, B, C)?

Another way of saying this is that since any idea is relatable to a body of literature, almost all research builds on theoretical foundations already in place. The researcher should situate his/her idea in the ideological lineage it belongs to (B/3). Figure 5.6 shows how Norberg-Schulz is situated in a network of literature. This has to do with mapping the "family tree" of ideas in which Norberg-Schulz's works can be placed. Obviously, this is another way to sort through the literature: mapping out all of the ideological tentacles of key theoretical lines of reasoning.

Ideological family trees are now even more important because they often transcend disciplinary boundaries. The term *interdisciplinary* (B/1) is now so well received, there is always demand for research that bridges traditional disciplines. In Box 5.3, the research is conducted in the Individual Interdisciplinary Doctoral

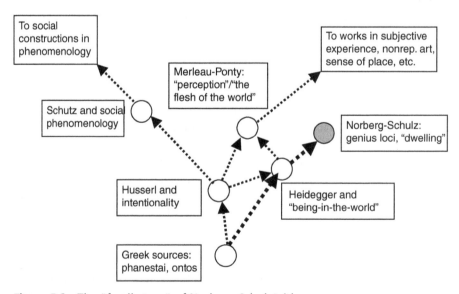

Figure 5.6 The "family tree" of Norberg-Schulz's ideas.

Program (IIDP) at Washington State University. The student has degrees in interior design and has taught art history. Her dissertation uses the history strategy (see Chapter 6) to access "sense of place" in four cultural venues in American history. She was familiar with literature addressing this topic in the design disciplines (for instance, Schneekloth and Shibley's *Placemaking*, or Oldenburg's *The Great Good Place*), but she needed perspectives on "place" that were not specifically tied to building typologies or even physical places.[18] (The subtitle of Oldenburg's book is itself a listing of these typologies: cafes, coffee shops, bookstores, hair salons, and so on).[19] Box 5.3 recounts in the student's own words how one of her trails of research led to the historian David Glassberg's *Sense of History: The Place of the Past in American Life*, the fifth chapter of which provides six characteristics of "place" specifically *not* indexed to physical forms or typologies.[20] (In fact, Glassberg makes a claim that might surprise those coming at "place" only from a design perspective: even fast food establishments can provide sense of place![21] This is quite another point of view than can be found in a work designers know well; James Howard Kunstler's *Geography of Nowhere*, where a Red Barn restaurant is summarily dismissed as "an ignoble piece of shit."[22]) This illustrates how different theoretical lenses can view the same reality differently, and how interdisciplinary research is valuable in developing theories that can accommodate apparently divergent points of view.

BOX 5.3
Trail of References in the Literature

The following is from an e-mail exchange between the author and Dana Vaux, PhD candidate in the Interdisciplinary Independent Doctoral Program, Washington State University. Vaux has undergraduate and graduate degrees in interior design, as well as a background in teaching art history. Her dissertation uses the history strategy (see Chapter 6) to uncover four cases of "sense of place" in American history: preindustrial, industrial/modern, postmodern, and "cyber." Vaux's argument is that "sense of place" is not so much indexed to physical attributes of places as it is to people's subjective affections. In Figure 5.7, Vaux was asked to describe how she pursued one trail in the literature that specifically helped her frame this argument. The column entries at left are Vaux's own words; the entries at right are the references Vaux tracked, along with this author's commentary in italics.

(Continued)

Vaux	Author Comments/References
I spent a couple of hours yesterday morning trying to figure out the genesis of that trail of references. I thought it was in Confino's article, but couldn't find a reference in that article to Glassberg. I looked in some of the other history articles as well, and didn't find it. So . . . I think it went like this:	*Vaux is referring to* Alon Confino, "Collective Memory and Cultural History: Problems of Method," *American Historical Review* 102(5) (1997): 1386–1403.
I searched JSTOR with keywords, "sense of place" and "history" (JSTOR is the best search engine for the *Journal of American History*).	www.jstor.org/www.journalofamerican-history.org/
I found a book review on Glassberg's *Sense of History* (which I can't find now). It piqued my interest in the book, but it did not mention the "place and placelessness" issue so I didn't save the reference. I decided to look through more book reviews on the results list to see what else I could find (they were untitled so I had to open each separately).	*This comment by Vaux, along with the one in the first box above, illustrates the "real-time" challenges of tracking a theme in the literature. What is instructive is how even these "misses" (e.g., "I thought it was in . . . but couldn't find a reference," "it did not mention [my interest] so I didn't save the reference," etc.) can be part of the search. Note how in each case Vaux took action in response to a dead end.*
Then I found a second book review that mentioned Glassberg's book. It specifically mentioned his chapter on place and place-lessness (obviously of interest to my research), and his "award-winning article" that forms the introductory chapter:	Paula Hamilton, "Review of 'Sense of History' by David Glassberg," *Journal of American History* 89(2) (2002): 733–734.
I searched in the WSU article search engine and found Glassberg's 1996 article:	David Glassberg, "Public History and the Study of Memory," *Public Historian,* 18(2) (1996): 7–23.
I read the article, thought it was worthwhile as a reference and found his book in the WSU catalog:	David Glassberg, *Sense of History: The Place of the Past in American Life* (Amherst, MA: University of Massachusetts Press, 2001).
In Glassberg's notes on Chapter 5, I found a reference to an article of Clare Cooper Marcus's of which I was not aware and will apply to my research.	Glassberg, 113–114. Clare Cooper Marcus, "Environmental Memories," in I. Altman and S. Low (eds.), *Place Attachment* (New York: Plenum Press, 1992), 87–112.
Hope this helps. I'm sure I have many more "research trails" ahead, so I'll try to keep note of some of them.	

Figure 5.7 Developing a trail in the literature. Courtesy of Dana Vaux.

From the last chapter (Box 4.2), Isil Oygur's research is another example of developing interdisciplinary linkages from the literature. Oygur ethnographically embedded herself in the offices of designers and architects to report on how design decisions were made *in situ*. During a meeting with her interdisciplinary committee, a professor from Systems Information made reference to how the candidate's dissertation needed to be a "metatheory," meaning a theory devised to analyze theoretical systems.[23] The other members of the committee (from architecture, interior design, and education, and an external member who is from industrial design) were expecting a grounded theory as her final outcome (see Chapter 7 for discussion of this school of thought). The question in committee arose: how does "metatheory," as understood by one discipline, differ from "grounded theory," as understood by other disciplines? Instinctually, the committee might have sensed that the difference is the one conventionally accepted, to wit, that metatheory is an umbrella under which grounded theory can exist. But there was no certainty on whether or not this was the case in this particular conversation. In any event, it highlighted the fact that the student must make clear how she was using these terms. In her own words, here is how Oygur resolved the disparity in light of the literature (this is from an e-mail):

> Within the context of my study, meta-theory is a "grand theory" that is already existing; it is a theory about theory. On the other hand, grounded theory refers to the theory that I have been developing from my data (I am using the grounded theory as it was defined by Glaser and Strauss and as it has been used in the social sciences).[24] To give an example, after coding my data, I realized that designers identify different conceptual user models at different phases of a design project. Based on this finding, my grounded theory is that "the user is a constructed phenomenon in the design process." In order to explain how this theory works in a larger framework, I used Cetina's "epistemic cultures" as a metatheory.[25] Cetina explains that it is necessary to study knowledge production in order to understand the use of knowledge. Within knowledge production, she defines a concept called "reconfiguration." According to reconfiguration, in each disciplinary context, things are redefined based on needs. For example, in design contexts, a user can be reconfigured in the form of a post-it or mock-up. So I am using "epistemic culture" as a meta-theory to develop my own grounded theory underneath it.[26]

Throughout all of this in "real time," we are *writing* (B/4). It is evident even from the quoted e-mail that this particular student—as the author knows from four years of working with her—is adept at writing. Her e-mail was sent back within hours of the author's query asking her to state how her work was handling the difference between the terms, so it represents a point of view that had already been put into words.

A recurring tendency in student research is talking rather than writing. The discussions can indeed be stimulating. But, unwittingly, semesters can go by with students having meetings with faculty advisors discussing the literature, or cutting-edge ideas, or methods (both strategies and tactics)—all of this without writing anything. In the course of a busy semester, it is often easy for the faculty advisor(s) to miss the fact that student X faithfully meets with the needed faculty every week, but hasn't produced any writing. Students should be reminded that the time to start writing is not next week; it was yesterday.

What writing should be done? Titling, aligning titles with topical statements, enlarging them to drafts of abstracts, projecting tables of content, chapter structures, and so on (see A/4). Theoretical thinking probably cannot draw real nourishment from the literature until attempts are made to write down how relevant theories are informing the research.

There is also diagramming; see C/4. As thinking and writing about research progresses in real time, it is helpful to be diagramming the logical structure of a proposed research design. But diagramming is most required in considerations of methodology, to which we now turn.

BOX 5.4

Children's Health and Built Environment: Regreening the Grounds of an Elementary School

Amy Boudinot's MArch thesis project culminated in a building design (see Figure 5.8), but began as the design of an academic syllabus. Concerned about childhood obesity and diabetes, Amy collaborated with medical school faculty in the WWAMI program (WWAMI is the program that facilitates medical school education in Washington, Wyoming, Alaska, Montana, and Idaho) to develop a course for medical students focusing on environmental design and health. Getting from literature awareness to literature review in her project entailed five stages ("stages" because these searches of literature were roughly sequential, but much of it was occurring synchronically):

Stage 1: A review of university course offerings across the country underlined a lack of courses that integrate environmental design with medical education.
Stage 2: Amy then conducted searches for articles addressing the integration of health with design in education. This search uncovered key articles such as Nisha D. Botchwey and Susan E. Hobson, "A Model

Curriculum for a Course on the Built Environment and Public Health: Training for an Interdisciplinary Workforce," *American Journal of Preventive Medicine* 36 (2009): S63–S71.

Stage 3: Then the task was to see how childhood obesity and diabetes are covered in the literature; there is a wealth of information in this area. The literature shows that the problem spiked in the 1980s, correlating it to technological developments that encouraged more sedentary lifestyles brought about by iPods, cell phones, video games, computers, portion size increases, soda consumption, and an increased school day (5 to 7 hours). Exemplary reference: Lisa R. Young and Marion Nestle, "The Contribution of Expanding Portion Sizes to the US Obesity Epidemic," *American Journal of Public Health* 92(2) (2002): 246–249.

Stage 4: Academic publications addressed linkages between diabetes and obesity with sedentary lifestyles. Exemplary reference: Matthew Salois, "Obesity and Diabetes, the Built Environment and the 'Local' Food Economy," *Munich Personal RePEc Archive* (2010): 1–28.

Stage 5: Throughout this process, Amy was searching the literature for built exemplars of schoolyard design. A fortuitous event here was her discovery of Fernanda Fragateiro's design of a playground when Amy traveled to Portugal. Exemplary reference: J. E. Dyment and A. C. Bell, "Grounds for Movement: Green School Grounds as Sites for Promoting Physical Activity," *Health Education Research* 23(6) (2008): 952–962.

Figure 5.8 Design for Moran Prairie School, Spokane, WA. Photograph and information courtesy of Amy Boudinot, MArch student, Washington State University.

5.3.3   *Methodology in Relation to the Literature*

Concomitant to clarifying research questions from a general literature is also the project of identifying a methodology for that emerging topic (the C row in Figure 5.4). This book frames research methodology into strategies (types of research designs) and tactics (the means for collecting and analyzing information). For purposes of literature review, the point is that any broad topical area can be focused down to any number of different strategic approaches, or research designs. Part II of this book describes, in detail, seven research strategies (and the tactics they typically employ) common to research in architecture and allied fields. Without getting into the descriptive details of the various strategies, we simply observe at this point that consideration of potential methodological choices is an important component of the literature review process.

Substantial bodies of literature exist just to address methodologies, quite apart from literature having to do with the potential topic itself. Each of the options suggested earlier in this chapter leads to different literature on methodology. Thinking about the method (C/1) forces a clarification of many other "real time" junctures (A/1, A/2, A/3, A/4, B/1, B/2, B/3, B/4) in moving from general literature awareness towards a specific topic.

It should be easier by now to see the difference between general literature awareness and literature review. By the time the literature review can be written, the researcher ought to be able to say this or that specific reference is important because it stands in some clear logical relationship to the proposed research questions. Relative to theory and topic, exemplars of similar research (B/2) in this vein will be identified in the literature review. In addition, the literature review will also have annotations relative to potential choices of methods (C/1) and exemplars (C/2).

Consideration of method will also lead to assessments of whether or not a topic is feasible (C/3). Some titles (A/4) sound ideal, but they would require unreasonable demands on time, or money. If the research involves human subjects, what ethical barriers must be addressed? What approvals are needed?[27] Are there examples of simplified approaches in the literature, perhaps using less invasive tactics? Some student work simply cannot take on research involving human subjects in longitudinal studies (those taking a long time). Perhaps the literature contains examples of how to abridge time periods in order to get at the same kinds of results.

Recently, the author was involved in a master's thesis that sought to correlate the visual design of neighborhoods with crime prevention on urban college campuses. Early on, this had the look of a focused topic. The potential literature was clear: Oscar Newman's work on defensible space, and Wilson and Kelling's "broken windows" theory.[28] But how can we operationalize this domain into a manageable master's thesis? In the initial thinking, the student wanted to select college campuses internationally for comparison. Even though she was an international student with travel to her home country built into her schedule, the idea was still not feasible. Then how about several urban campuses across the United States? This still meant quite a bit of time and money. For a master's thesis, it was decided to do in-depth correlations between police crime records indexed to specific locations on a single urban college campus local to the student's residence. [29] (See Chapter 8 on correlational research.)

With respect to C/3, the present author has proposed a way of mapping research methodology. This not only aids in thinking through the differences between strategy and tactics, it is also a "where we are" visual guide during the research process.[30] For example, Ellen Berkeley's "Boston City Hall" is a fairly well-known article that uncovered differences between expert opinions in comparison to users' views about Boston City Hall.[31] Berkeley acquired her qualitative data from interviews, archives, popular media, and expert opinions. In the left map in Figure 5.9, the qualitative strategy is the vertical spine, while the several tactics are the horizontal notations.

On the right of Figure 5.9 is a map of a student's proposed research. Her research question: *What are the personality profiles of developers who converted old urban buildings into housing units?* The map lays out a sequence of steps that the student pursued, including the initial literature review, a series of case studies (see Chapter 12), and the logically derived explanatory framework.

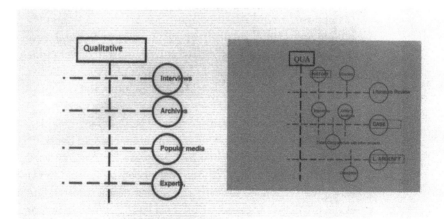

Figure 5.9 Maps of qualitative research strategy. Left: Method map of Ellen Berkeley's research on Boston City Hall. Right: Method map for a student's investigation of alternative housing in reclaimed urban buildings. This material is reproduced with permission of John Wiley & Sons, Inc. These diagrams first appeared in "Diagramming Design Research," *Journal of Interior Design* 33(1) (2007): 33–43.

5.3.4   Outcomes in Relation to the Literature

At the outset, we said that an experienced researcher will be able to discern in the early stages (A/1–4) between a potential topic and implications it has for future work (D/1). Put another way: a topic cannot become clear if everything else associated with it is also in the foreground. One way to put factors into the background (so as to bring a topic clearly into relief) is to ask: What kind of outcome am I aiming for (D/1)? In any case, the question of outcome should be asked as early as A/1. Intended outcomes can range from highly theoretical (a new or refined explanation or model) to applied (perhaps design guidelines) or both (see Chapter 4). The researcher's interest at A/1 determines the methods (C/1), all of which shape the anticipated outcomes (D/1).

In the case of Ahmad Alhusban (Box 5.1; see also Figure 4.8), the early interest (A/1) lay with what the design thinking literature calls "the creative leap." But much has been done in this field by Nigel Cross and others associated with the journal *Design Studies*. So from the very beginning, questions related to refining his interest had to do with whether or not there are gaps in this literature to fill (A/3). (Also in this kind of research are questions of feasibility, C/3. In Alhusban's case, the complexities of "protocol analysis" of architects in action ultimately led to the decision to limit the research to architectural students in all levels of the design studio in an academic setting.) One apparent gap is the limited amount of material on the creative leap in conjunction with *architectural* design (as opposed to industrial design). Box 5.1 features an entry from an annotated bibliography Alhusban did in his second year of doctoral studies. The point is that literature awareness, now located at D/4, must to be very much at play in the early stages of determining a topic. Alhusban's outcomes are both a theory (of how the creative leap works in all levels of the architectural design studio) and a tool for measuring such leaps.

Consider another example of how an initial general idea at A/1 changed because of an increasing awareness of the literature, and hence what was needed as an outcome (D/1, D/4). When he first began his doctoral work, Bryan Orthel, another Interdisciplinary PhD candidate, knew he wanted to work in the area of historic preservation. At the early stages, that meant research into preservation policy at the municipal, regional, or national level. A possible outcome was some sort of critique of preservation standards, or perhaps a new set of guidelines (D/1).

However, growing awareness of the literature highlighted a difference between existing standards, as such, and the reason for having such standards at all. Through the study of literature that became exemplars in his study, Orthel realized that written standards only represent regulatory decisions *about* material forms (historic buildings, monuments, etc.), but not the immaterial cultural forces that determine preferences for one material object over another. In Orthel's own words: "The physical aspect of material culture is readily recognized, but the intangible, social ideas and beliefs attached to the physical things are less clear." Orthel's focus began to clarify (D/3) around not so much a set of guidelines for historic preservation, but rather a theory explaining historic preservation *consciousness*. That is to say, Orthel came to realize that communities preserve not objects but memories of themselves and of their localities. In sum, historic preservation is motivated by a need to preserve communal identity prior to any motivation to preserve a physical object or to craft preservation standards.

BOX 5.5
Preservation of Historical Identity

Bryan Orthel's theory that preservation of communal identities motivates the preservation of physical artifacts is illustrated by this photo montage of markers on the front of the First Presbyterian Church in Lexington, Kentucky (Figure 5.10). In his own words in the caption, Orthel describes these markers. Key references that focused Orthel's thinking from preservation standards in general to preservation consciousness include (the comments in brackets are Orthel's annotations):

Bruner, Edward M. "Abraham Lincoln as Authentic Reproduction: A Critique of Postmodernism," *American Anthropologist* 96(2) (1994): 397–415. [methodologically opaque, but a strong critical analysis of public perception of heritage tourism] Hodge, Christina. "A New Model for Memory Work: Nostalgic Discourse at a Historic Home," *International Journal of Heritage Studies* 17(2) (2011): 116–135. [narrative analysis of public documents and media reporting; good critical analysis of effect of interpretation on public understanding of history] Hoskins, Gareth. "A Place to Remember: Scaling the Walls of Angel Island Immigration Station," *Journal of Historical Geography* 30 (2004): 685–700. [critical analysis of limitations of American preservation approach] Lieb, Jonathan I. "Separate Times, Shared Spaces: Arthur Ashe, Monument Avenue and the Politics of Richmond, Virginia's Symbolic Landscape," *Cultural Geographies* 9 (2002): 286–312. [strong narrative description and geographic analysis of a specific case of active history]

(*Continued*)

Figure 5.10 The First Presbyterian Church in Lexington, Kentucky, displays four markers near the building's main entrance emphasizing history, preservation, and identity. In this small area, the church members publicly claim identity as a religious group (informational sign, left top), provide a contextual chronicle identifying their history in the city's development (historical marker, right), note their building (and by extension their selves) as important to preserve (National Register notice, rectangular, center), and frame social association within the community (local preservation marker, oval, left bottom). At the same time, each marker also positions the church and its members in the present. All images courtesy of Bryan Orthel, PhD, Kansas State University.

Another recommended activity in D/4 is reading articles of a more general nature. This might not be a direct link to literature having to do with the research project at hand. But in any line of work, clarity in writing is essential. In research writing, there are additional elements to learn. When is it best to cite a source in support of the author's claims? When is it not necessary? How can addressing differing sources in the literature energize the writing in this section? When is it proper to include a citation in the text? When should it be placed in the endnote? When is a writer *over*-citing sources, such that the author's own voice—not to mention his/her own point of view—does not come through? All of this is part and parcel of the task of engagement with the literature for purposes of research. William Zinsser's *On Writing Well* should be read and re-read by anyone wishing to write nonfiction works.[32]

5.4   CONCLUSION

Finally, a word about passion. A researcher's passion for his/her topic applies to any of the chapters of this book, but it seems particularly fitting to mention it in this one. Without passion for the topic, it is difficult to engage meaningfully with the literature. Without passion, fact finding in a general literature may be accomplished, perhaps even to a responsible degree. But without passion, it is difficult to critically process large bodies of literature into original research questions to pursue. Without passion, the discipline of learning the literature is not there. Without passion, the fortuitous encounters somehow do not occur. Why? Because thoughts and heart are elsewhere, so when something potentially fortuitous happens, it doesn't occur to the researcher that it has. By passion we mean a compelling interest in a topical area such that the interest itself becomes a spawning ground for new ideas. John Zeisel uses the words *inspiraton, imagination, and intuition;* he calls it the ability to have "preconceptions."[33] Zina O'Leary spends an entire chapter on research as a creative process; it calls for fluency and flexibility in handling new and old ideas, or engaging in remote associations between elements that would not ordinarily be linked. [34] (See also Chapter 2 on creative process in design and research.)

Often, the researcher's passion brings him or her to make environmental decisions as well; to get oneself into a venue that is conducive to spawning new ideas. Aspiring writers move to New York; aspiring actors go to Hollywood. Of course, each must do what life circumstances allow for; our point is that the passionate researcher seeks to maximize opportunities to go "where the fish are swimming." If that is not New York, at least it is willingness to spend long hours in the library (or the electronic equivalent). All of this recalls Mihály Csíkszentmihályi's theory of flow: "concentration is so intense that there is no attention left over to think about anything irrelevant . . . . [S]elf-consciousness disappears and the sense of time becomes distorted. An activity that produces such experiences is so gratifying that people are willing to do it for its own sake."[35] Csíkszentmihályi's theory emphasizes that creativity is not an isolated phenomenon; it happens best in optimal cultural, which is to say, collective, venues. The passionate researcher maximizes exposure to such venues.

In conclusion, through the course of the five chapters that form Part I of this book, we have introduced our readers to a series of conceptual diagrams which aim to clarify both the role of methodology in research and the initial steps in the development of research question(s). With regard to the former, we have represented methodology as situated within a nested relationship, framed by larger worldviews and theoretical schools of thought. With regard to the latter, we have outlined an iterative process in which defining one's purposes and exploring the limits and focus of the topic work together in concert, leading ultimately to the articulation of clear research question(s). Refer again to Figure 5.1. The diagram summarizes the major issues we have addressed in Part I, as well as introduces the strategy chapters in Part II. Note that the research questions serve as a pivot point toward the identification, perhaps discovery, of the most appropriate strategy and tactics for answering those questions.

NOTES

1. Joseph A. Maxwell, *Qualitative Research Design* (Thousand Oaks, CA: Sage, 2005), 65–67.
2. Cherie Lynette Peacock, *Dwelling Well: An Application of Christopher Alexander's Theory of Wholeness to Investigate Occupant Affective Responses to Homes Incorporating Renewable Natural Resources.* Master of science in architecture thesis, Washington State University, 2005.
3. John Creswell, *Research Design: Qualitative, Quantitative, and Mixed Methods Approaches*, 2nd ed. (Thousand Oaks, CA: Sage, 2003), 24.
4. Christopher Alexander, *The Timeless Way of Building* (New York: Oxford University Press, 1979).
5. Clare Cooper Marcus, *House as a Mirror of Self* (Berkeley, CA: Conari Press, 1995).
6. Maxwell, 70–76.
7. Ibid., 65.
8. Howard Gardner, *Intelligence Reframed: Multiple Intelligences for the 21st Century* (New York: Basic Books, 1999), 82.
9. Edward W. Said, *Orientalism* (New York: Vintage Books, 2004).
10. David Wang, "Kuhn on Architectural Style," *Architectural Research Quarterly* 13 (2009): 49–58.
11. Jacques Barzun and Henry F. Graff, *The Modern Researcher*, 6th ed. (Stamford, CT: Thomson Wadsworth, 2004), 26–31.
12. Immanuel Kant and Werner S. Pluhar, *Critique of Judgment* (Indianapolis, IN: Hackett Publishing, 1987).
13. Christian Norberg-Schulz, *Genius Loci: Towards a Phenomenology of Architecture* (New York: Rizzoli, 1980).
14. Martin Heidegger, *Being and Time*, trans. John Macquarrie and Edward Robinson (New York: Harper & Rowe, 1962).
15. Zina O'Leary, *The Essential Guide to Doing Research* (London/Thousand Oaks/New Delhi: Sage, 2004), 71.
16. Claude Lévi-Strauss, *Structural Anthropology* (London: Allen Lane, 1958); Jean Baudrillard, *The System of Objects* (London: Verso, 2005).
17. Jean-Francois Lyotard, *The Postmodern Condition,* trans. Geoff Bennington and Brian Massumi (Minneapolis: University of Minnesota Press, 1984), xxiv. Examples include Michel Foucault, *Discipline and Punish: The Birth of the Prison* (London: Allen Lane, 1976); and Edward Soja, *Postmodern Geographies: The Reassertion of Space in Critical Social Theory* (London: Verso, 1989).

18. Lynda H. Schneekloth and Robert G. Shibley, *Placemaking: The Art and Practice of Building Communities* (New York: Wiley, 1995); Ray Oldenburg, *The Great Good Place: Cafes, Coffee Shops, Bookstores, Bars, Hair Salons and Other Hangouts at the Heart of a Community* (New York: Marlowe & Co., 1999).

19. Oldenburg.

20. David Glassberg, *Sense of History: The Place of the Past in American Life* (Amherst: University of Massachusetts Press, 2010), 111–127.

21. Ibid., 123.

22. James Howard Kunstler, *The Geography of Nowhere* (New York: Touchstone, 1993), 124.

23. *The American Heritage Dictionary of the English Language, 4th ed.,* updated in 2009 (Boston: Houghton Mifflin, 2000).

24. Barney G. Glaser and Anselm L. Strauss, *The Discovery of Grounded Theory: Strategies for Qualitative Research* (New Brunswick [U.S.A.]: AldineTransaction, (1967 [2008]): 1: "the discovery of theory from data—which we call *grounded theory*—is a major task confronting sociology."

25. Karin Knorr Cetina, *Epistemic Cultures: How the Sciences Make Knowledge* (Cambridge, MA: Harvard University Press, 1999): 1: "This book is about epistemic cultures: those amalgams of arrangements and mechanisms—bonded through affinity, necessity, and historical coincidence—which, in a given field, make up *how we know what we know.*"

26. Isil Oygur, PhD, e-mail to David Wang, November 12, 2011. Italics and endnote references were added.

27. Virtually every university (especially those that conduct federally sponsored research) has established mandatory, institutional procedures: (1) to protect the confidentiality and well-being of human subjects; and (2) to review the proposed research design of any study involving the use of human subjects.

28. James Q. Wilson & George L. Kelling, "Broken Windows: The Police and Neighborhood Safety," *Atlantic Monthly* (March 1982): 29–38.

29. Xin Lin, *Exploring the Relationship between Environmental Design and Crime: A Case Study of the Gonzaga University District.* Master's in landscape architecture thesis, Washington State University, August, 2010. www.dissertations.wsu.edu/Thesis/Summer2010/x_lin_072310.pdf. Accessed November 14, 2011.

30. David Wang, "Diagramming Design Research," *Journal of Interior Design* 33(1) (2007): 33–43.

31. Ellen Berkeley, "More than You want to Know about Boston City Hall," *Architecture Plus* (February 1973): 72–77, 98.

32. William Zinsser, *On Writing Well: The Classic Guide to Writing Nonfiction,* 25th ed. (New York: HarperCollins, 2001).

33. John Zeisel, *Inquiry by Design* (New York and London: W. W. Norton, 2006), 36–37.

34. O'Leary, 3.

35. Mihály Csíkszentmihályi, *Flow: The Psychology of Optimal Experience* (New York: HarperPerennial, 1991), 71–90.

Part II

Seven Research Strategies

Chapter 6

Historical Research

6.1   INTRODUCTION

In his study entitled "The Home," Adrian Forty cites a character in an 1888 fictional work entitled *Mark Rutherford's Deliverance.* Here is Mr. Rutherford:

> "at the office . . . nobody knows anything about me, whether I was married or single, where I live, or what I thought upon a single subject of any importance. I cut off my office life in this way from my home life so completely that I was two selves, and my true self was not stained by contact with my other self. (At) . . . the moment the clock struck seven . . . my second self died, and . . . my first self suffered nothing by having anything to do with it. . . . I was a citizen walking London streets; I had my opinions . . . I was on equal terms with my friends; I was Ellen's husband; I was, in short, a man. . . ."[1]

Forty presents a case that, from 1850 to 1950, the concept of the home underwent significant changes, bringing about transformations in how the home as a material object came to be designed. Forty provides four headings, each describing a period within this larger time span. For each, he interprets how social-cultural factors brought about material expressions of "home." The first heading (and the only one we review here due to space) is "A Place for Anything but Work." The Industrial Revolution drew many from the countryside to the city to work in the factories. This had the impact of separating home from workplace as two distinct concepts in the communal mind for the first time. The craftsman who worked at home now became a laborer in the factory, where his freedom was curtailed and he was "subordinated . . . to the rules and directions of the managers." This, in addition to the oppressive working conditions, underlined the sense of separation between

Figure 6.1   London home in 1893 (from Adrian Forty): "a palace of illusions . . . ." By permission of Royal Commission to the Historical Monuments of England.

workplace and home. As a result, the home began to take on connotations of retreat, of an idealized realm in which the worker is anything but a worker. Figure 6.1 is an image from Forty's study, showing a London home interior in 1893. It shows how the home had become "a palace of illusions, which encouraged total dissociation from the world immediately outside."[2]

6.2   TRAITS OF HISTORICAL RESEARCH OLD AND NEW

Forty's example exhibits traits of history research both old and new. In his book, *The Pursuit of History*, John Tosh observes that historians are "as true as they can be to the surviving evidence of the past."[3] But as we shall see in this chapter, old (perhaps received) ways of narrating this evidence have been challenged by new perspectives—generally subsumed under the heading of "the cultural turn"—that have greatly expanded what constitutes "evidence from the past." Let's consider here how Forty's example illustrates both traditional as well as these new perspectives.

1. History research brings into view something from the past. Because the "something from the past" is not empirically accessible, the history researcher must use various tactics for unearthing evidence from a time and a world not his or her own. In Forty's case, a fictional account from the past—an account nevertheless representative of those times—and a photograph of a home interior are two examples of data he looked to for his interpretation. We will discuss more of these tactics in this chapter.

2. Interpretation. Forty's interpretation is just that: an interpretation. This is to say that aside from evidence from the past, the historian's point of view is a key part of history research and narration. There is a technical as well as a theoretical aspect to the project of interpretation. Technically, evidence from the past abounds, and the researcher must know where to look for it and how to look for it; this is the technical aspect.[4] The researcher must also know how to arrange the evidence in an interpretative framework, and interpretation perforce requires theoretical commitments. In recent years, due to the "cultural turn" in history research (addressed throughout this chapter), the role of schools of thought becomes all the more important.

3. Narrative. The output of history research is not verse, or essay, or some other literary form; the output is narrative. This may seem obvious, but "narrative" in historiography requires its own discipline. The recent publication of *The Fiction of Narrative*, a retrospective of the work of Hayden White from 1957 to 2007, underlines how the topic of historical narrative can fund the output of a scholar's entire life's work.[5] Precisely because historiography concerns realities not present, White's insight is that it stands at the nexus between reportage, simplistically conceived, and story. We will return to White in section 6.3.

With a view towards the "new" in the current practice of history, Tosh cites two influential bodies of theory. The first is the "cultural turn," whereby historians seek to interpret cultural meaning, drawing insights from cultural anthropology. A second body of theory derives broadly from various social theories, but particularly from the Marxist tradition.[6] As part of this tradition, architectural and urban historians have been drawn to a spatial turn, which will be described in more detail shortly.

4. The cultural turn.[7] Forty's study of social factors that brought about changes in home interiors is part of a significant widening, in the later decades of the 20th century, in subjects previously regarded as unfit for historical analysis.

Early in the century, in the words of Georg Iggers, "historians shared the optimism of the professionalized sciences generally, that methodologically controlled research made objective knowledge possible."[8] This viewpoint assumed that something like a single history of the world can be framed, given enough evidence.

The cultural turn is a significant reaction against this view as the 20th century played out. The historian Geoff Eley outlines the following characteristics of the cultural turn:

   a. Attention paid to gender issues.
   b. The influence of Michel Foucault's work on power, knowledge, and regimes of truth in relation to social history.
   c. A departure from the French *Annales* approach to history, which was an earlier "turn" away from narrow political history to a broader variety of social and cultural issues, including the cultural outlook of periods.
   d. The emergence of cultural studies as a focus of history research.
   e. An active dialogue between anthropology and history.[9]

Perhaps more descriptively, the cultural turn can be characterized by an outlook that the literary theorist Jean-Francois Lyotard (1924–1998) casts as "incredulity towards meta-narratives."[10] And so in the 2005 epilogue to his book, Iggers describes a "turn from macrohistories to paying greater attention to smaller segments: to the lives and, significantly, to the experiences of little people."[11] Thus the cultural turn encourages focus on local, vernacular realities rather than, for instance, national histories. It shifts attention from privileged outlooks to what can be called everyday, or popular, culture. As well, the cultural turn values what is stored in memories and subjective "geographies" as opposed to, or in addition to, what is only captured in documents. Tosh refers to the cultural turn as a fundamental "reorientation in the priorities of historians."[12]

Tosh indeed opens his chapter on the cultural turn by addressing its impact on art history and material culture. Specifically, "art" is widened to include "a vast range of everyday detail—clothing, implements, buildings—that are incidental to the artist's purpose but included in the interests of verisimilitude or 'background.'"[13] Forty's study, for example, focuses on vernacular home interiors, along with all sorts of everyday artifacts such as sewing machines and popular ads, as worthy of historical inquiry. Another example is Daniel Bluestone's study of the life and times of a 19th-century Chicago structure, the Mecca. Built initially as an innovative apartment building in 1891, Bluestone tells the story of how the Mecca over the years became part of Chicago's blighted "Black Belt," ultimately to be demolished in 1952 after decades of resident resistance. In its place was constructed Crown Hall, the modernist home of the architecture school of the Illinois Institute of Technology. Bluestone's narrative is an example of the cultural turn not only because it focuses on the interests of an underrepresented population residing in a structure not normally considered canonical architecture, but also because Bluestone explicitly documents the blindness of the "dominant" culture to the Mecca as a culturally significant artifact.[14]

Another example of how the cultural turn encourages consideration of artifacts can be seen in Dolores Hayden's *The Power of Place: Urban Landscapes as Public History*. Her chapter "Place Memory and Urban Preservation" catalogues how the history of brass workers in Waterbury, Connecticut, and the lives of laundry workers in New York's Chinatown all become subjects for research as "public history." Hayden considers examples of buildings that are "mundane, battered, and constantly reused" as candidates for historic preservation. In the same chapter, even public art is related to history research: Hayden describes an installation in a building in Charleston, South Carolina, in which the floor is painted to indicate the "spatial experience of African Americans over three centuries."[15] Box 6.1 considers an example of what happens when the perspectives of multiple groups of people come into play in an architectural project with historic overtones.

BOX 6.1

Competing Historical Perspectives at CentrePointe, Lexington, Kentucky

The cultural turn rejects the possibility of totalized, single histories. Instead, it recognizes that history can be narrated from multiple points of view. This pasture was once a city block containing 15 buildings dating from the 1820s to the 1940s. The buildings were demolished in 2004 and 2008 in preparation for a proposed high-rise redevelopment. But conflict arose over different understandings of the block's history; the debates continued even after the building demolitions, and the proposed redevelopment was delayed. Here are some of the differences. The developer denied the historic value of the demolished buildings: "It's not like Lincoln ever shopped there."[a] A city official questioned the very definition of history: "The historic fabric is important to downtown, but right now I don't think anybody can say what the historic fabric is."[b] One

[a] Tom Eblen, "We Need to Balance Past, Future in Historic Preservation Debates," *Lexington Herald-Leader* (Lexington, KY), March 3, 2012.
[b] Ryan Hrvatin, "Letter to the Editor: Historic Block," *Lexington Herald-Leader* (Lexington, KY), April 6, 2008.

(Continued)

Figure 6.2   Competing views of "history" meet at this "pastured" city block in the heart of Lexington, Kentucky. Information and image courtesy of Bryan D. Orthel, PhD, Kansas State University.

individual asked, "How can a building dating back to 1826 not be historical?"[c] Many members of the community had personal histories with this locale. University students campaigned to prevent the demolition of buildings they valued as social gathering places. Civil rights demonstrations in front of a Woolworth store that was on the block received less attention during the debate over demolition, but it was an important part of the block's history for the African-American community. In response to the demolitions, members of the community held a public funeral for the buildings. New organizations have been created to advocate for different aspects of the community's history, and the public discussion of the redevelopment continues.

[c] Mari Adkins, "Comment in Response to 'There's a Lot of History on CentrePointe Block,'" *The Bluegrass and Beyond* [blog], June 23, 2008 (1:02 PM), http://tomeblen.bloginky.com/2008/06/22/theres-a-lot-of-history-on-centrepointe-block/

5. The spatial turn. Related to the cultural turn—and this can be seen in both Bluestone's and Hayden's examples—is the spatial turn.[16] Artifacts cannot be front and center without consideration of space. For Bluestone, the Mecca and other Chicago apartment houses "represent an uneasy combination of public space and private realm."[17] And Hayden holds that that public history cannot be separated from an engagement with the politics of space.[18] Hayden is drawing from Henri Lefevre, who posited that a culture's unreflective perception and use of space is "at once indistinguishably mental and social, which comprehends the entire existence of the group concerned."[19] For instance, Lefevre contrasts the empty Greek agora with the object-filled Roman Forum, drawing from this contrast the Greek preference for unity while the Romans organized spaces toward different functions.

The spatial turn can be seen in the work of Edward Soja. The first edition of this book cited his "Los Angeles, 1965–1992," which is an in-depth portrait of the city's multicultural communities during the time bracketed within those years.[20] Soja's analysis was implicitly spatial (see Figure 6.7). Soja has since written about post-1992 Los Angeles describing, in explicitly spatial terms, how Los Angeles is now transformed into "a hive of community-based organizations and grassroots activism." Soja argues that this evolution came about because of disenchantment, at the grassroots level, about the failure of government leadership as exemplified in the events that led up to the 1992 riots.[21] For our purposes, it is enough to note that, in the cultural and spatial turns, both physical objects along with subjective constructions of the space that they are found in (or that produced them) become key issues in historical analysis.

6.3   THE STRATEGY OF HISTORICAL RESEARCH: HISTORICAL NARRATIVE

How is history narrated, and in what ways can we be confident that history narration is robust and believable? In this chapter section, we will note similarities between historical narrative and literary constructions. But this does not negate the fact that historical accounts should not violate the interconnectedness of things temporally and spatially in what R. G. Collingwood has termed "the one historical world."[22] Edmund Morris's 2000 biography of Ronald Reagan, entitled *Dutch*,[23] illustrates the problem that arises when a historical narrative's coherence is violated. Morris chose to place a fictional character into his account of Reagan's tenure in the White House. While this may have some literary value, it is problematic as historical narrative.[24] Morris's work is an instructive case of how a historical narrative might have overstepped its bounds into fiction. Here we summarize three perspectives on historical narration.

6.3.1   *History as Constructed of Narrative Sentences*

Arthur Danto posits that the nature of historical accounts finds expression in *narrative sentences*. A narrative sentence is one that involves two situations separated by time. For example, the statement "The Thirty Years War began in 1618" is a narrative sentence; it involves an E-1, which is 1618, and an E-2, which is the year 1648.[25] Making this statement before 1648 would make no sense. To illustrate his point further, Danto asks us to imagine an absolutely objective and exhaustive account of the flow of history documented by what he calls an Ideal Chronicle Machine, a gadget that rolls out *the* account of all possible events as time progresses. We could imagine the machine rolling out the Ideal Chronicle (the IC) of *all* the events of 1618. But even though all events are accounted for, the *identity* of the event we call the Thirty Years War cannot emerge via the IC, either at the 1618 mark, or as the IC rolls by the year 1648. Denizens within the 30-year period would have no idea they are in such a 30-year period. Only an observer removed from the objective flow of the IC could point to the flow, cull out the relevant facts as he or she sees them, and construct an account called the Thirty Years War. That construction is necessarily by narrative sentences.

Consider this statement made about Frank Lloyd Wright by William Cronon: "The faith of the Lloyd Joneses was more than just a religion for Wright; it also schooled him in the moral rhetoric that would forever shape his speech and writing."[26] This is a narrative sentence. It involves two temporal conditions: (1) the "faith of the Lloyd Joneses," his mother's family that was no doubt a factor in his early life; and (2) "the moral rhetoric that would forever shape his speech and writing." To be able to make the statement, Cronon must be standing at a point in time after Wright's life. Cronon's position is also a privileged one, for by making such an assessment of the Lloyd Joneses' influence upon Wright's "moral rhetoric," he discounts other possible influences upon that rhetoric. (Figure 6.3 pictures Wright's mother's family.)

F. R. Ankersmit notes several consequences of Danto's theory of narrative sentences. One is that just by making a thread of events "discernible" against the anonymous backdrop of the IC, a historical narrative not only represents a past event; there is a sense in which the representation is more primary than the represented. This is because, again, in the IC, there really is not anything that is "the represented"—until a narrative represents it.[27] Ankersmit thus notes the metaphoric power of the narrative sentence: the historian, by weaving his/her narrative, creates accounts of past times necessarily unknown to the people of those times. He cites Danto's point that the statement "Juliet is in the sun" is certainly not the same as referring to the same sun as "a body of hot gases."[28] The point is that the descriptive

Figure 6.3 Wright's mother's family: "The faith of the Lloyd Joneses . . . would forever shape his speech and writing" (William Cronon on Frank Lloyd Wright). Courtesy of Frank Lloyd Wright Preservation Trust.

power of the historian in framing his/her narrative is enormous. Cronon, in another place, says this:

> In the act of separating story from non-story, we wield the most powerful yet dangerous tool of the narrative form. It is a commonplace of modern literary theory that the very authority with which narrative presents its vision of reality is achieved by obscuring large portions of that reality.[29]

6.3.2   *Historical Narratives in Relation to Literary Constructions*

As to the nature of the narrative itself, W. B. Gallie said this some time ago: "every genuine work of history displays . . . features which strongly support the claim that history is a species of the genus Story."[30] Gallie goes on:

> The systematic sciences do not aim at giving us a followable account of what actually happened in any natural or social process: what they offer us is idealizations or simplified models. . . . But history, like all stories and all imaginative literature, is as much a journey as an arrival, as much an approach as a result . . . every genuine work of history is read in this way because its subject-matter is felt to be worth following—through contingencies, accidents, setbacks, and all the multifarious details of its development. . . .[31]

Gallie is not saying that the historical narrative is identical to fiction; he is highlighting an essence of historical accounts. A story has a beginning, a development, a conclusion; it is an account of a set of events and details that carry the reader along in a coherent drama. Gallie holds that it is the same with historical accounts. That is why we enjoy reading them over and over again, even though the outcome is known.

Perhaps the leading proponent of historical narrative as a form of story is Hayden White. Of course, White draws distinctions between historical narration and fiction, and in the course of a career-long apologetic for his views he outlines a substantial philosophy of historiography. In a 1998 essay simply entitled "Storytelling,"[32] White first outlines objections—levied by Fernand Braudel and Roland Barthes—against treating historical accounts as stories. These critiques, on White's analysis, assume that the elements of story are imposed on a set of events. The profundity of White's response is that the essence of story is not imposed on historical events. Instead, somehow history-as-story is, first, itself a *mode* of knowledge and, as such, second, is something human beings participate in even as we organize our lives (or, if you will: even as we "make history"). To illustrate, we can easily imagine saying: "Today I will do this and that because my goal is to achieve such and such." Or on a grander scale: "We want to pass this bill so all can have access to healthcare." The point is that we organize our lives towards achieving certain ends; these organizing threads are not unlike the stuff of stories. White's argument is that human beings are inherently motivated by a story-narrational way of processing the inputs and outputs of their lives. In this sense, when a historian recounts a set of events, it is possible, on White's view, "to discover the 'real' story or stories that lie embedded within the welter of 'facts' and to tell them as truthfully and completely as the documentary record permits."[33]

In further answer to the critique against historical narration as story, White draws from the Danish linguist Louis Hjelmslev to distinguish different levels of narration, specifically the Form of the Content and the Substance of Expression.[34] The Form of the Content has to do with what can be regarded as the "facts" of a set of events. The Substance of Expression, however, has to do with "the plot-type" of the contents narrated by the historian. White uses an example from politics to illustrate the difference—and in process to affirm the legitimacy of his view of history as story. Many politicians use a rags-to-riches story to legitimize their campaigns, and the public recognizes this device. But if a politician uses the life story of another politician for his own, the public would reject this tactic as unacceptable, as has happened, White points out, in U.S. political campaigns (White cites Senator Joe Biden's 1988 presidential campaign as an example). The rags-to-riches story relates to Substance of Expression. Copying the facts of another politician's life for one's own is merely reporting the Form of the Content of a set of events, and this is not acceptable. In sum, White places great emphasis on the legitimacy of selecting a plot-type, or a Substance of Expression, for historically narrating a set of facts.

The selection of a plot-type is what White calls *emplotment*. Robert Doran, editor of a 2010 reader of White's works, defines emplotment as follows: "To emplot events means to organize and arrange them according to a recognizable story-type, which entails a reduction to the number of possible story-types available in a given culture. . . . White posits a reduction to four story archetypes: Romance, Tragedy, Comedy, Satire."[35] We can question why just these four typologies, and not others. But the key for us is this: White is not saying that the historian is free to impose any storyline on a set of facts of history. He is positing a sympatico relationship between actors and their narrators such that both are motivated by a storyline sense of how to proceed. It is instructive to revisit Danto's Ideal Chronicle in light of White's view. While we can agree with Danto that the IC, taken as an abstract whole, is blind to individual narrative threads within itself, White's insight is that the historian's narrative task is not to invent accounts from a position purely outside of the IC (even though he or she is), but rather to find sympathetic threads between his/her narration and "real" stories that might have been motivating actors within the IC. This calls for imagination.

6.3.3   *The Role of Imagination and Comprehension in Historical Narratives*

R. G. Collingwood's *Idea of History* was published in 1946, so it is somewhat dated; it clearly precedes the cultural turn in history studies, and it reflects early and mid-20th century attitudes about the possibility of a totalized history (of which more later). The British historian Barbara Taylor, for instance, has this to say about Collingwood's ideas:

> Today, Collingwood's account of historical consciousness seems wonderfully prim. Human thought—that is, the stuff of history, as Collingwood defines it—is composed of reasoned reflection only: anything else that we find knocking about in our minds—"irrational elements, impulses and appetites"—belong to our animal nature and are therefore outside history. "They are the blind forces and activities in us which are part of human life . . . but not parts of the historical process: sensation as distinct from thought, feelings as distinct from conceptions, appetites as distinct from will."[36]

These limitations notwithstanding, Collingwood's theory of the historical imagination bears mention here because it is still relevant to the discourse on historical narrative. By historical imagination Collingwood is not primarily saying that historians must have this kind of imagination—although they should. By the term, Collingwood primarily means to say that the very existence of culture demonstrates the human capacity to think reflectively about the progress of time and the contents that emerge from that process. Nature does not think; people do; culture is the result of that thinking. Collingwood's position can be related to Kant's observation that natural processes seem like "purposiveness without a purpose," while the human rational faculties can think "determinate thoughts" and freely choose moral actions based on those determinations. It is this latter capacity that brings Collingwood to distinguish between "outer" and "inner" thinking. Nature's processes are merely outer. But human actions, and hence all of human culture, is the result of the inner capacity to reflect upon the human situation. History conceived properly, then, is a science of culture. The historian's task is to enter into this "scientific" frame of thinking in order to write history. This is Collingwood's theory of the historical imagination in the macro sense. In Collingwood's day, psychology was coming into its own as an academic discipline.[37] This motivated Collingwood, a professor of philosophy at Oxford (but also a historian), to sharpen his definition not only about the imagination's role in framing historical narrative, but also about the importance of the historical imagination itself as the way towards grasping the total pattern of human thinking (of which endeavors in other fields, such as art or religion or science, capture only in part).

At the individual level, then, a historian's imagination must indeed place himself or herself in the thoughts of the actors being described in the historical narrative. Aside from any datedness Collingwood's output may have today, this is obviously still relevant. Again echoing Kant, Collingwood argues that the human imagination has an inherent ability to comprehend past phenomena in coherent wholes, and he makes interesting connections between this ability and the ability to create art. Says Collingwood: "the historian . . . is always selecting, simplifying, schematizing, leaving out what he thinks unimportant and putting in what he regards as essential. It is the artist, and not nature, that is responsible for what goes into the picture. . . ."[38] Collingwood's point is this: The product of this imaginative-narrative activity, as historical narrative, is not "weak knowledge." Rather, precisely because of the legitimacy of the human imagination when it functions in this way, the result is valid and robust knowledge.

A critique of Collingwood's position has been set forth by none other than Hayden White. It is not clear, says White, how one gets from the imagined constructions of individual historians to a "science" of human affairs. "There exists no reference outside the mind of the historian by which propositions may become the common property of the society that Collingwood hoped to serve."[39] But White underlines Collingwood's importance. As culture continues to evolve and becomes, in White's words, "more violent," we may need to reconsider Collingwood's theory of the historical imagination at the macro scale.

6.4 THE STRATEGY OF HISTORICAL RESEARCH: SOME SCHOOLS OF THOUGHT

With the cultural turn as well as the spatial turn, the diversity of possible interpretations in history research only increases. This is even before yet another "turn" is thrown into the mix: the linguistic turn. It is no exaggeration to say that many of the ideological threads of the 20th century concerned the meaning of words, or more precisely, the putative inability of words to represent originals. If words cannot represent originals dependably, aside from other implications, one result is that meaning is necessarily localized rather than totalized. Meaning becomes culture-dependent only; transcendent truth is not possible. Subjective meaning increases in relevance while objective meaning is questioned as to the extent of its objectivity: objectivity for whom? Most readers will recognize threads of poststructuralism, if not deconstruction, in this view. The earlier chapters of this book make clear that research can be conducted within different "schools of thought." In our view, poststructuralism can be regarded as a school of thought. Here we address it, along with some other schools of thought, vis-à-vis history research.

6.4.1 *Positivist Explanations of History: A "Covering Law"*

We saw how Collingwood aimed for a "science" of history by means of the historical imagination. This is to say that, as recently as the earlier part of the 20th century, empirical science largely held sway as the measure of how to achieve true knowledge. This was manifested in history research in the belief that a single history of the world was possible, given enough empirical evidence. Even as the law of gravity has universal applicability, historians also held to a "covering law" for a single totalized history of human events. A chief proponent of this view was Carl Gustav Hempel (1905–1997), who was active in the Berlin Circle in the 1920s.[40] The Berlin Circle, along with the Vienna Circle, promoted empirical verification using the assumptions of scientific method as the exclusive means to gain true knowledge. Said Hempel: "There is no difference . . . between history and the natural sciences: both can give an account of their subject matter only in terms of general concepts."[41] Thus, in Hempel's view, we do not yet have truly rigorous historical accounts. We only have *explanation sketches*, because any account is as yet unable to identify the covering law behind the phenomena it is describing. When a covering law *is* discovered, to explain an event covered by the law is tantamount to predicting future events of that kind.[42]

Also in the positivist vein is Karl Popper (1902–1994). Popper rejects the possibility of large-scale predictions. His *Poverty of Historicism* holds that the growth of human knowledge is not predictable, and so neither are actions based upon future knowledge.[43] Only small-scale predictions are conceivable in the realm of the social sciences. Popper calls this "piecemeal engineering," by which the social scientist, much like the natural scientist, takes small steps based upon *available* knowledge, observing the results, correcting mistakes, and eschewing any grand "utopian" claims to general predictions of the future, which Popper terms *prophecy.*[44]

Any notion of a covering law enabling a totalized history is now out of date. But it remains relevant for several reasons. First is simply that history research is not only about what philosophy of history current researchers espouse; it is also about understanding what actors in past historical venues understood about history. For example, emphasis on "scientific method" predisposed many to think causally about the history of design. This tendency is particularly strong in theories that emerged during or after the Industrial Revolution. Eugene-Emmanuel Viollet-le-Duc (1814–1879) revisited Gothic structures to explain their forms as the rational expression of necessary structural forces (see Box 6.2). As well, Auguste Chiosey (1841–1904) was influenced by Viollet-le-Duc's rationalism. In his *Historie de l'architecture* (1899), architectural form, as *effect*, is the result of the rational processes of construction, as *cause:* "Style does not change according to the caprice of . . . fashion, its variations are nothing but those of processes . . . and the logic of methods implies the chronology of styles."[45]

BOX 6.2
Causal Thinking in Architectural Design: Viollet-le-Duc

Eugene-Emmanuel Viollet-le-Duc (1814–1879) was one of the leading thinkers to assess architecture from a rationalist point of view. The images in Figure 6.4 are from his *Lectures on Architecture.* Consider Viollet-le-Duc's rationalist deductions on the style of the copper vessel. Its appearance: "exactly indicates its purpose . . . it is fashioned in accordance with the material employed . . . the form obtained is suitable . . . (for) the use for which it is intended. . . ." There really is only one way in which the copper vessel could be optimally designed, and human reason could achieve this expression by deductive processes. In the same vein, Viollet saw the architecture of the Gothic period as an expression of the reasoned analysis of structural forces. In short, form is the effect of structural principles, as cause. Analytical drawings such as the one shown here of Notre Dame Cathedral fill the pages of his works (see Figures 6.4a and 6.4b).

Figure 6.4a Illustration of copper vessel from Lecture VI of Viollet-le-Duc's *Lectures on Architecture*: "Thus . . . this vessel has style . . . first, because it exactly indicates its purpose; second, because it is fashioned in accordance with the material employed," etc. In short, here is an argument from *cause*.

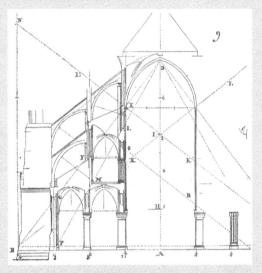

Figure 6.4b Diagram from Viollet-le-Duc's *Dictionnaire Raisonnée* highlighting the rational factors behind Gothic framing.

6.4.2   *History as the Movement of Absolute Spirit*

Another interpretive approach, derived from the philosopher G. W. F. Hegel, holds that history is the ongoing evolution of a communal consciousness or mind (*geist*, translated "mind" or "spirit"). Hegel posited a communal consciousness that is the sum of the consciousnesses of all individuals in a society at any one time—only the whole is more than the sum of the parts. This corporate consciousness, if not a mind of its own, at least has attributes of volition. It is this larger-than-the-sum-of-the-parts quality to the communal consciousness that is represented by the word *spirit*. The single subject is always enmeshed in this much larger *zeitgeist* (spirit of the time) than he or she is able to fully comprehend. The influence of this approach upon architectural history at the turn of the 20th century was enormous. Typical is this kind of wording from Le Corbusier:

> A great epoch has begun. There exists a new spirit. Industry, overwhelming us like a flood which rolls on towards its destined end, has furnished us with new tools adapted to this new epoch, animated by the new spirit.[46]

Modernists, in effect, assumed that their time was the fulfillment of Hegel's idea that the evolution of absolute spirit will culminate in a condition of complete knowledge. Many works of history from this period, such as those by Pevsner and Giedion, are colored by this assumption of the Modernist *zeitgeist*. The title of Giedion's text, *Space, Time and Architecture*, is itself illustrative of the epistemological assumptions of the work.[47] In a new release of Pevsner's *Pioneers of Modern Design*, Richard Weston says this in the introduction:

> Gradually, the zeitgeist assumes a life of its own, cast as an individual but pervasive driving force behind art. The history of art in turn came to be seen as a succession of styles leading inexorably to a culminating vision, followed by a period of decline . . . this conception lurks everywhere in Pevsner's text.[48]

Heinrich Wolfflin's influential study, *Renaissance and Baroque*, which posits explanations as to why the former style evolved to the latter, is an earlier example of this kind of application of the Hegelian system.[49] Readers would do well to study this work, and see in it a forerunner of Giedion's and Pevsner's outlooks.

The Hegelian approach can also render the backdrop behind specific individuals and their work more theoretically meaningful. The cliché description of someone being "a man of his times" has theoretical roots in this view. Even though the movement of communal spirit tends to devalue individual lives as such, Hegel invested heavily in special individuals as agents that bring about change. When dealing explicitly with history, Hegel calls such a person a *world historical individual*. The progress of communal spirit is thus advanced by these individuals.

> The historical men, the world historical individuals, are those who grasp just such a higher universal, make it their own purpose, and realize this purpose in accordance with the higher law of the spirit. . . .[50]

The artist stands in a similar position as one who is able to "grasp the higher universal," so as to "realize this purpose" in material forms. Of Alberti, for instance, Jacob Burckhardt (Wolfflin's teacher at the University of Basel) said this: "of his various gymnastic feats . . . we read with astonishment how, with his feet together, he could spring over a man's head; how in the cathedral he threw a coin in the air till it was heard to ring against the distant roof; how the wildest horses trembled under him. . . ."[51] Quite a fellow, that Alberti! More recently, and certainly more soberly, Robert McCarter's biography of Frank Lloyd Wright casts him as the architect at "the defining moment," by which is meant Wright's pivotal role in creating an American architecture throughout the 20th century.[52]

6.4.3   *Structuralist Approaches to History*

With structuralism we enter into the theoretical undergirding of the linguistic turn. Structuralism traces to Ferdinand de Saussure (1857–1913), who revolutionized linguistic studies. De Saussure's thesis for language is that word-signs, as well as the components of word-signs (e.g., letters, in the case of alphabetized systems), are only meaningful when standing in relationship to other such signs. The entire network of these relationships constitutes a *langue,* the totality of the structural system, while any iteration of an instance of the *langue* is a *parole.* The atomic components of the *langue/parole* system are the *phonemes,* or the sound-images that make up the actual "material" of the language system. Systems of meaning—language systems, such as English or Chinese, for example—have their own organic properties. The structural nature of these systems is that they are self-contained, self-regulating, and self-transformative.[53] For example, the English language defines a clear, albeit widely diffused, conceptual area of containment. It operates by a coherent set of rules that make reference to nothing outside of the system; it is self-regulating, and it evolves purely according to immanent conditions. We can discern several ways this manifests itself: new words emerge (e.g., "byte"); new meanings are assigned to existing words (e.g., "mouse," or "surf"); and words fall out of daily use (e.g., "thee"). Thus, second, language is self-transformative. Third, language signs are themselves arbitrary; it is a sign's relationship to other signs that carry meaning. Peter Caws puts it this way: "[T]he chief characteristic of the phoneme is simply that it is different from all the other phonemes—what it is in itself is a matter of comparative indifference."[54] No reference to anything external to the system is necessary for meaning; meaning arising out of internal relationships is in this sense arbitrary, dependent only upon the agreement of the community that assigns such meaning. This is the briefest explanation of structuralism. (Terence Hawkes provides an accessible overview in his *Structuralism and Semiotics.*[55])

Consider now this observation made by Mihály Csíkszentmihályi about the Renaissance artist and architect Raphael:

> The creativity of Raphael fluctuates as art historical knowledge, art critical theories, and the aesthetic sensitivity of the age change. According to the systems

model, it makes perfect sense to say that Raphael was creative in the sixteenth and in the nineteenth centuries but not in between.[56]

By a systems model, Csíkszentmihályi holds that creativity emerges out of a network of cultural factors, among these a recognizable set of symbolic rules, an individual who manipulates these rules in an original fashion, and a network of gatekeepers who recognize the novel value of the individual's contributions. This is a structuralist posture. Note that creativity is no longer rooted in the person of Raphael and his actions, but only in how he, and his output, stand in relation to a certain set of cultural factors. A similar example—perhaps the one that gives theoretical context to Csíkszentmihályi's position—is George Dickie's institutional theory of art. "By an institutional account I mean the idea that works of art are art because of the position they occupy within an institutional context,"[57] and not by any inherent attributes of the works themselves.

BOX 6.3
What Advertisers Know: A Structuralist Analysis

One day, the French Enlightenment philosopher Denis Diderot (1713–1784) was given an elegant robe by a friend. The robe contrasted with the ratty furnishings of Diderot's study: the desk was old, the curtains were stained, and so on. Not long after receiving his gift, all the furnishings of Diderot's study were updated to match the quality of the robe. Grant McCracken calls this "the Diderot Effect," and uses it to diagnose the power of advertising. Material objects are carriers of social meaning. A consumer wants to "maintain a cultural consistency in his/her complement of consumer goods." In Diderot's case, the robe was a "carrier of privileged meaning," which led Diderot to "make all the rest of his possessions consistent with it."[a] With this in view, advertisers can persuade a consumer to upgrade his/her system of objects of meaning. "Impulse buys" are of this nature, and they may exert the Diderot Effect on other objects in the consumer's system of objects of meaning. For example: a consumer trades in his Chevrolet for a BMW, and two months later he buys a Rolex watch. The BMW is what McCracken calls a "departure purchase": it had the effect of upgrading the constellation of objects

[a] Grant McCracken, *Culture and Consumption: New Approaches to the Symbolic Character of Consumer Goods and Activities* (Bloomington and Indianapolis: Indiana University Press, 1988), 118–129.

defining the consumer's identity. Or: a consumer can be reminded to *maintain* his/her current constellation of objects of meaning, which would entail purchases as "ballast." Say a consumer replaces his current Chevrolet with a new Chevrolet. In McCracken's terms, this is maintaining a Diderot Unity. Either case entails a purchase. The chart shown in Figure 6.5 arranges in rows systems of material objects that define individual identities. Advertisers know that someone who wears a Rolex watch is more likely to drive a high-end automobile, dine at high-end restaurants, and perhaps vacation on the French Riviera. Another way to think of this is to consider what kind of magazine would carry ads for BMWs: they would more likely be found in *National Geographic*, and less likely to be in, say, *Seventeen* magazine.

The above is a structuralist analysis. Note that meaning resides not so much in objects themselves, but in how multiple objects stand in relation to each other. More specifically for history, one can assess how a culture advances and changes as a result of small (but numerous) Diderot Effects introduced into the system.

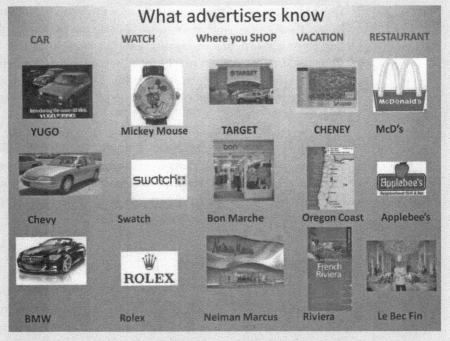

Figure 6.5 Systems of material objects: meaning is generated as they relate to each other. Image by David Wang.

There is also deep structure, from Noam Chomsky's theory of how the mind generates language. Chomsky holds that the mind has innate abilities to organize the world and to frame that organization into language. From these "deep structures," Chomsky generates a set of algorithms from which sentences are constructed. This theory has also been used to explain the generation of architecture. The reasoning is that architectural forms, as universal as human language, must also be generated from innate orientations within the mind. Broadbent et al. cite four such mental orientations of "structures": the building as container of human activities, the building as a modifier of climate, the building as a cultural symbol, the building as a consumer of resources.[58] These "structures" offer a basis by which built forms throughout history could be assessed in a way that is not limited by the bounds of any particular culture.

Another appeal to deep structure is the idea that the mind has embedded orientations that are expressed *geometrically* in the visible realm. Henry Glassie's taxonomy of the objects of Anglo-American folk architecture adapts Chomsky's theory of deep structures in this way:

> Down from the level of the observable there is a continuum of abstraction that becomes less detailed and more powerful as it modulates to lower planes ... at the lowest level of organization—a level comparable to that on which Chomsky's kernel sentences may be found—there are base concepts that are specific structures of geometric entities to which designing rules are applied in order to derive the structures of specific components—the types of which actual artifacts are examples.[59]

Glassie proposes that an impressive range of Anglo-American folk architecture may be formally explained by a set of geometric "rules" that derive from a base concept of an "axially ordered pair of squares." For example, "a quantitative study revealed that 99.2 percent of the 2,193 barns surveyed could be understood in terms of this bilaterally symmetrical, tripartite concept . . . ."[60]

6.4.4   *Poststructuralist Approaches to History*

Poststructuralism rejects transcendentally constant bases for meaning. Instead, it holds that "reality" is a by-product of "discourse," and hence subservient to it. For Michel Foucault, for instance, historical periods come and go, each period understood as a web of discourses, only to be replaced by another period, understood as another web of discourses. This rejects a universal or transcultural understanding of "reality," in which certain ideational benchmarks remain constant (e.g., "progress," "heaven," "nature," "man," and so on). Hence Lyotard's "incredulity toward metanar-ratives" noted earlier.

What is discourse? Poststructuralism understands discourse as something like the cultural manifestations of the trafficking of thought, distributed into various topical foci. These in turn are maintained by tacitly agreed-upon ways of seeing, reified into expressions of institutional power, such as political or economic structures, a moral code, the news media, the ecclesiastical class, and so on. Foucault refers to "practices" such as economics, technology, or politics as "conditions of formation" that make "human nature" possible. In other words, Foucault sees "human nature" itself as a discursive product of a fairly recent Western way of seeing.

Since poststructuralism sees material products of culture as parts of a larger immanent discourse, any historical assessment of architecture in this strategy is necessarily an assessment of social-cultural discourse as well. As in the Hegelian school of thought, the individual artist may not be fully aware of the forces of corporate consciousness acting upon him or her. But in a departure from Hegel, there is no obligation to a general sense of progress, or even necessarily to any sense of holistic communal identity. Any overarching coherent view of reality, in Lyotard's words, is replaced by "clouds of narrative language elements . . . each of us lives at the intersection of many of these."[61]

We have cited Soja's recent work on the spatial turn vis-à-vis Los Angeles. The first edition of this book cited his earlier study of Los Angeles in the period 1965–1992. This earlier work remains a good example of a poststructuralist approach.[62] Two turbulent dates bracket Soja's study: the Watts riots of 1965 and the riots related to the Rodney King incident in 1992. Soja narrates the Los Angeles of 1965–1992 as six intermeshed realities that involve everything from geographically distributed "exopolises," each different, and larger, than the actual incorporated municipalities, to "flexcities" that are geographies related to shifts in patterns of economic production, to "cosmopolises" that, though local, depend on the global economy. These then are intermeshed with social hierarchies that are "no longer easily definable by simple racial, ethnic, occupational, class, or immigrant status."[63] To this is added the police structure that inhabits this complex reality to enforce an unquiet peace. Finally, on all of this is overlaid an endless agglomeration of "simcities" ("Korealand, Blackword, Little Tijuana . . . Funky Venice").[64] The reader is left with a sense of the density and complexity that is Los Angeles (see Figure 6.6). It reinforces the poststructuralist idea that meanings and "knowledges" are products of a cultural time and place. For what it takes away in negating the idea of transhistorical knowledge, poststructuralism gives back in grasping the immanent knowledge operating in any particular cultural-temporal space more deeply.

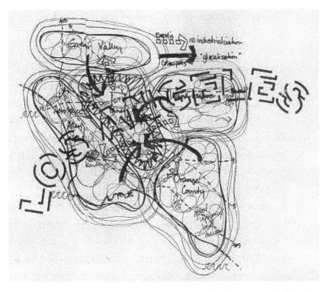

Figure 6.6 A student's graphic interpretation of Soja's analysis of Los Angeles. Courtesy of Angela Feser.

6.5   TACTICS IN HISTORICAL RESEARCH

In the sixth edition of *The Modern Researcher*, Jacques Barzun and Henry Graff make the following observation:

> It is from historical scholarship that the world has taken the apparatus of foot-notes, source references, and bibliography, which validate what is stated. It is from writers of history that others have learned to sift evidence, balance testimony, and supply verification.[65]

Barzun and Graff's book takes us soberly to the tactical side of history research, which entails the hard work of gathering historical data. Not nearly as glamorous as the larger schools of thought just considered, this is the "grunt work" required for writing narrative sentences. Put another way, if the historian is indeed to occupy a privileged position of culling a narrative thread out of Danto's Ideal Chronicle, if he or she is to emplot historical narrative successfully *à la* White, hard tactical work of the kind described by Barzun and Graff is indispensable. Sifting evidence entails tracking down sources. Balancing testimony and verification entails keen evaluation of the evidence. And writing the narrative is an ongoing compositional discipline. Indeed, Barzun and Graff's quoted statement suggests that history writing set the original

Identification	Organization	Evaluation/Analysis
Facts versus ideas	Researcher's mind	Audience
Fact finding	Accuracy	Attribution
Being a detective	Love of order	Clarification
Library	Logic	Check for falsification
Internet	Honesty	Bias
Catalogues	Imagination	Self-criticism
Encyclopedias	"Cross-questioning"	
References	Compilation	
Chronology	By topic	
Maps	By time	
Current opinion	By internal logical order	
Colleagues, "experts"	Verification	
Note taking	Composing	
	Paragraph, chapter, part	
	Use plain words, sentences	
	Tone and rhythm	
	Art of quoting	

Figure 6.7 A representative list of tactical concerns in history research mentioned in Jacques Barzun and Harry F. Graff, *The Modern Researcher,* 6th ed. (2004).

standards of accuracy for any kind of report writing. In sum, if a novice researcher is confused about the differences between writing history versus writing fiction at a theoretical level (perhaps at the level of strategy), it is at the tactical level that the differences clearly stand out. The discipline of collecting and interpreting data in history research, guided by the researcher's "historical imagination," is quite intense. Figure 6.7 outlines some of the themes covered in Barzun and Graff's book; we highly recommend the book itself as a guide for conducting history research at the tactical level.

In distinction to categories of *handling* the evidence (identification, organization, evaluation), here are some categories for *types* of evidence: determinative, contextual, inferential, and recollective evidence.

6.5.1   *Determinative Evidence*

Of primary importance is evidence that situates the object of study in a particular time and a particular place. Dates are one obvious type of determinative evidence.

For example, Barzun and Graff give this example as a fact: "Thomas Jefferson was born on April 2, 1742."[66] But in most cases with architectural research, often we have the artifact or structure itself. Indeed, James Ackerman makes the distinction between social historians who "reconstruct in imagination a human situation [which] cannot be directly experienced," and art historians who do the same thing, but only as a tool toward understanding the empirical work of art, which is still with us" (Ackerman includes architecture as part of art history research).[67] For architecture, often archaeology plays an important role. Figure 6.8, for example, shows the evolving plan over the centuries of the Abbey Church of St. Denis north of Paris.

An excellent example of using the building itself as determinative evidence is Matthew Cohen's study of Brunelleschi's Basilica of San Lorenzo in Florence:

> By using measurements subjected to rigorous analysis as a primary source in the study of the Basilica of San Lorenzo, this investigation arrives at novel conclusions pertaining not only to architectural proportion but, unexpectedly, to the question of attribution as well.[68]

Cohen's approach is straightforward: why not measure the building to see what it tells us, as opposed to scholarship that *only* relies on archival information and

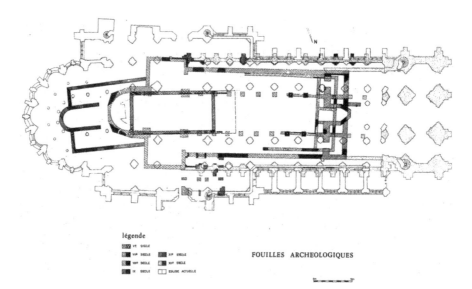

Figure 6.8 The abbey church of St. Denis in its various iterations: the evolving plan through time, based upon archaeological evidence. From Brankovic Branislov, *La Basilique de Saint-Denis: Les etapes de sa construction.* Courtesy of Editions du Castelet, Boulogne, France.

(perhaps idealized) theories? Cohen's measurements suggest that San Lorenzo contains a medieval proportional system that is based on mathematically irrational ratios. San Lorenzo is widely regarded as a Renaissance building, but on determinative evidence, Cohen finds that it does not have a proportional system most scholars consider to be Renaissance. This goes against the widely promulgated view of thinkers such as Rudolf Wittkower, to wit, that Renaissance buildings were designed around a commensurable system of numerical proportions.[69] Since Cohen's method has not yet been applied to any Renaissance building, furthermore, it suggests that we may not know with any degree of certainty what kinds of proportional systems Renaissance architects actually used.

Cohen himself underlines the importance of archaeology in his findings. In the postscript to his article, Cohen conceives of architectural history research as a midway point between architecture itself (in that the building at hand can be evaluated by the conventional architectural factors for any building: dimension, structure, materials, and the like), art history (i.e., the use of documentary evidence), and archaeology.[70] A building in its extant condition and the same building in its archaeological condition, coupled with documentary evidence, form a "disciplinary triad" (Cohen's term) that can effectively uncover new historical knowledge. (See Box 6.4.)

Traditionally, photographs may also serve as determinative evidence, but advancements in digital technology reduce a photograph's dependability. For example, the Associated Press issued this story:

> A negative of the 1906 photograph depicting the first person to scale Mount McKinley proves the climber actually was standing 15,000 below the summit. . . . Dr. Frederick Cook claimed he took the picture of his companion, Edward Barrill, after the pair scaled the Alaskan peak, which at 20,320 feet is the highest peak in North America. But researcher Robert Bryce told the Times that a print made from Cook's original negative shows geographical features in the background that were cropped when the explorer published the photograph. . . . Bryce found the photograph in some of Cook's papers recently donated to the archives at Ohio State University. [71]

This is dated compared to what can now be done with digital technology and imaging software. Today guidelines continue to evolve on the admissibility of photographs in legal proceedings.[72] But history research in general has always relied on photographs as a source of determinative evidence: it not only provides social context, but also often situates the topic in its natural context, which leads to contextual evidence.

6.5.2   Contextual Evidence

In architectural history research, cultural factors synchronic to the artifact under study provide contextual evidence about the artifact. Consider Otto von Simson's study of Abbot Suger, the innovator of the renovations of the Basilica of St. Denis. Von Simson claims that the abbot's decisions about the portal design of the west facade of the church may have been influenced by the Platonic ideas of Bernard of Clairvaux: "the increasingly cordial relations between the two men suggest that the art of St. Denis may reflect Bernard's ideas."[73] From archival evidence Simson first situates the building in time: "Suger's church, it will be recalled, postdates his reform of the monastery, undertaken at the insistence of St. Bernard."[74] Simson then uses other architectural objects as contextual evidence. He compares the St. Denis portal design with the portal of the abbey church at Beaulieu in Languedoc, built shortly before the St. Denis portal, in the 1130s. The Languedoc design is one of "turmoil. . . . Innumerable figures seem to be crowded into a narrow space; the Apostles and angels . . . in wild agitation." This was a style that St. Bernard found to be "most offensive." The St. Denis portal, in contrast, is "serene and calm . . . clarity and simplification is [sic] noticeable throughout," reflective of the Platonic peace of an ideal world. Finally, Simson's argument is built on extant letters between St. Bernard and Suger.[75] "Bernard addresses Suger as his 'dearest and most intimate friend'; and unable to visit him, he requests the dying man's blessing."[76]

In Cohen's case, to show that San Lorenzo's proportions were intentional rather than coincidental, Cohen set the rule that "the proportion must appear in documentary sources relevant to the early fifteenth century, or closely resemble other proportions that do."[77] To this end, Cohen assembles an impressive amount of evidence on the extent of the medieval knowledge of geometry and arithmetical fractions. With these as background, Cohen analyzed the nave arcade dimensions of San Lorenzo. He first specifies the actual dimensions drawn from his measurements, and then demonstrates that they compare to a sequence of numbers widely known at the time of the basilica's construction: "any educated person of the early fifteenth century would have recognized the progression 1, 9, 13, 17 as a small . . . piece of a vast network of similar progressions, all interrelated according to the principles of Boethian number theory."[78] This is contextual evidence. It also relates to the next kind of evidence.

6.5.3   Inferential Evidence

Sometimes, by proximity of date and reasoned interpretation, one fact can be posited as very likely to be linked with another fact, even though "hard" connections of a determinative or even contextual nature may not be available. Consider this: Wright's Robie House is one of the 20th century's best-known architectural works.

Figure 6.9 Frederick Robie, with driver, in the Robie Cycle Car, designed and built several years before the construction of the Robie House. Courtesy of Frank Lloyd Wright Preservation Trust.

But for a study of how the house came to be, the photograph of Frederick Robie in his Robie Cycle Car may be more informative than photographs of the house itself.[79] Robie's car speaks to the kind of man that would be attracted to building the Robie house (see Figure 6.9). Robie was an industrialist conversant with what technology can provide in the way of objects that connote progress—and one not afraid to realize them: integrated ventilation systems, an attached garage, and structural steel cantilevers. The car bespeaks of such a forward-looking man.

BOX 6.4

"How Much Brunelleschi?": Use of Inference in Historical Research

Other threads of new inquiry come from Cohen's measurements at San Lorenzo.[a] For instance, visual observation revealed a wide variance in

[a] Matthew A. Cohen, "How Much Brunelleschi? A Late Medieval Proportional System in the Basilica of San Lorenzo," *Journal of the Society of Architectural Historians* 67 (2008): 18–57.

(Continued)

the quality of the stonework detailing in the basilica, suggesting different phases of the work (see Figure 6.10). From this, Cohen infers haste in the less developed sections of the structure, which he relates to the shifting agendas of the patron, Cosimo de Medici.[b] Perhaps more significantly, Cohen's measurements—again coupled with archival information—suggest that the architect of record after about 1422, Filippo Brunelleschi, owed a lot to the *capomaestro* who preceded him on the project beginning in about 1421, Matteo Dolfini.[c] Dolfini, a cleric as well as an architect, appears to have been more indebted to a medieval metaphysics of number

Figure 6.10   Images on the left are of detailing on the western bays of San Lorenzo, while the images on the right are from the eastern bays. From this striking difference in quality, Cohen infers a significant gap in time during construction. By permission of Matthew A. Cohen.

[b] Ibid., 21–33.
[c] Ibid., 41–43.

than the more practical Brunelleschi. Because much of the foundations of San Lorenzo had already been set in place by Dolfini by the time Brunelleschi took over as *capomaestro*, Cohen argues strongly that this is the reason for some of the proportional imperfections of the final project—imperfections that can be detected only through careful analysis of detailed measurements (e.g., Brunelleschi's Renaissance arches in the nave resulted in a slightly lower profile than the medieval pointed arches Dolfini's foundation dimensions originally called for). Cohen's work reminds us that buildings are not productions of pure theory—especially if the theory comes centuries after the fact—but artifacts that bear the imprint of the complicated percolations of synchronic cultural processes. It is all there in the masonry, as it were, if we only know how to observe, and infer. We suggest a term for this tactic: *acute observation*. Acute observation is systematically detailed measurements of historical buildings, used in concert with documentary material, to produce narrative sentences having analytical power.

6.5.4   Recollective Evidence

To use the Robie example again, much of what we know about the events that led up to Frederick Robie's collaboration with Wright comes from an interview Robie's son conducted with his father some 53 years after the construction of the house. This interview can be found in Leonard Eaton's book *Two Chicago Architects*.[80] With recollection, all of the previous kinds of evidence may be involved. Recollection can lead to determinate information such as dates, and it can yield contextual information. It is also inferential in nature, since the interviewee is drawing inferences about those facts in time past. The validity of recollective evidence, then, depends significantly upon who the interviewee is, what role he or she played relative to the object under study, what credibility he or she currently has, and how much of what he or she says can be corroborated by other evidence.

But the analyst must be on guard. The interview of his father conducted by the younger Robie is illustrative. The older Robie characterized his selection of Wright this way: "I became rather interested in his views . . . and I thought, well, if he was a nut, and I was maybe, we'd get along swell."[81] Robie also said selecting Wright was "the best business deal I ever made."[82] The first comment reinforces the inference that Robie and Wright both had maverick temperaments. As to the second statement, the analyst must assess how much of this position is the result of the influence of Wright's stature upon Robie's "recollections" half a century later. This caution seems warranted by the following Robie recollection of the typical residence at the turn of the century:

> The idea of most of those houses was a kind of conglomeration of architecture, on the outside, and they were absolutely cut up inside. They were drafty . . . . I wanted no part of that. I wanted rooms without interruptions. I wanted the windows without curvature . . . I wanted all the daylight I could get in the house, but shaded enough by overhanging eaves . . . . I certainly didn't want a lot of junk—a lot of fabrics, draperies, and what not . . . I finally got it on paper . . . and displayed them to friends . . . they thought I had gone nuts."[83]

But this sounds like Mr. Wright himself! Wright led the way for "rooms without interruptions," he brought natural light into the interior (although other of his works, *and not necessarily the Robie,* are good examples of this), and Wright hated drapes. In other words, Robie's recollections may be more of a Wrightian manifesto than they are a report of the actual events, in light of what Wright's stature had become 53 years since the Robie project. The interview in history research has the effect of a hall of mirrors, interpretations upon interpretations. Even Robie's recollection of the "facts" may be more of an interpretation, informed intimately by subsequent developments.

6.6   CASE STUDY IN TACTICS: "INCA QUARRYING AND STONECUTTING" BY JEAN-PIERRE PROTZEN

Protzen researched Incan construction technique, from quarrying stones to their installation. We used this case in the first edition of this book; it still remains a good compendium of tactics to access the past. The reader is asked to become familiar with Protzen's article, which appears in the May 1985 issue of the *Journal of the Society of Architectural Historians* (references to this article in this chapter section will only be by page number).

Tactic 1: On-site familiarity. Protzen acquired knowledge of his topic by firsthand visits. From these came sketch maps, measurements and drawings, recordings of "innumerable blocks," field notes, and slides (footnote, p. 161). Figure 6.11 shows some drawings sketched on site. On-site familiarity was essential for framing conjectures that, in the completed narrative, achieved the weight of informed opinion. For instance, from the capital Cuzco, the physical distance of the two quarries Protzen researched led him to surmise that "the choice of rock type must have been of utmost importance to the Incas, or they would not have quarried sites so difficult of access and so far away" (p. 162).

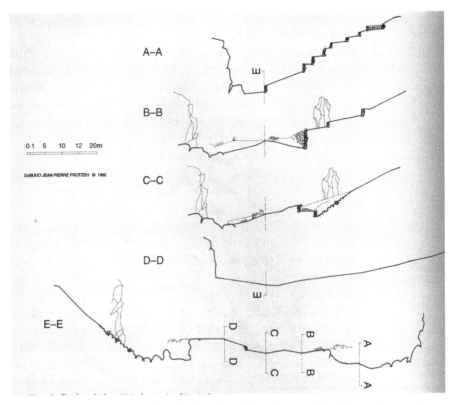

A–A

B–B

0.1 5   10   12   20m

DoBUUO JEAN PIERRE PROTZEH © 1982

C–C

D–D

E–E

Figure 6.11 Protzen's sectional drawings, based upon site observations, of one of the Inca quarries. Courtesy of Jean-Pierre Protzen.

Tactic 2: Use of documents. Protzen refers to other studies either to corroborate his own findings or as a foil to what he observed. For instance, he cites a work by George Squire, who wrote of the Kachiqhata quarry in 1863. The fact that the earlier report "matches my own observations very closely" lends credence to Protzen's assessments because it describes the site conditions more than 100 years closer to the actual period under study. This same tactic is used again later in the article, when Protzen cites Jose de Acosta's 1589 observations of fitted joints in a masonry wall ("without much mortar ... it was necessary to try the fit many times") to defend his theory that the Inca masons did not use many sophisticated tools (p. 179; see also the reference to Outwater on the lack of tools, pp. 165–66).

Tactic 3: Visual comparisons. Visual comparisons uncover site information that cannot be found any other way. For example, the two quarries Protzen studied

(Katachiqhata and Rumiqolqa) yielded different qualities of stone. The coarse-grained rocks from Katachiqhata were used in the buildings of the "religious sector," while the flow-banded andesite from Rumiqolqa, which is easier to be extracted in slabs, was used for sidewalks (p. 165). Also, at Rumiqolqa, Protzen saw traces of how the rocks were quarried by means of a channel cut into the top of a cantilevered portion, and then holes worked into the channel of considerable depth. This also corroborates a report of the same technique surmised by Squires a century before (p. 169).

Tactic 4: Material evidence. Protzen looks to the artifacts themselves for evidence to support his hypothesis that the chief method of Inca stone dressing was by pounding. He noted that whitish coloration of the pitmarks on the stones was consistent with the heat produced in pounding. Furthermore, he noted that the pitmarks were finer as they got closer to a joint edge (see Figure 6.12). He theorized that they were made by "smaller hammers to work the edges." He found evidence to support this in the smaller slivers that lay in the surrounding area ("limiting myself to chips that I could pick up with my fingers, I found 43 slivers" [p. 175]). Also, the artifacts allowed Protzen to hypothesize how the eyeholes so common in Inca masonry were made. "They exhibit a conical shape of either side of the perforated stone. This suggests that the pounding had been started from both sides until there remained only a thin membrane to be punched out." Based on this, Protzen suggests his alternative to a theory of Bingham's, who suggested that the holes were bored with bamboo "rapidly revolved between the palms of the hands" (p. 176).

Tactic 5: Comparison with conditions elsewhere. Protzen looks to similar conditions in cultures elsewhere to speculate on technique, this based on assumptions that there are a limited number of ways pre-industrial cultures can dress large masses of stone by hand. Of the evidence at Kachiqhata: "The cutting marks on these and other blocks are intriguing. They are very similar to those found on the unfinished obelisk at Aswan, and the technique involved must not have been very different from the one used by the Egyptians, who used balls of dolerite to pound away at the workpiece until it had the desired shape" (p. 165).

Tactic 6: Local informants and lore. Protzen depended on local lore to identify the west quarry of Kachiqhata as "the real quarry of Ollantaytambo" (p. 166). However, Protzen often cites local information just to question it or disagree with it. For instance, regarding certain needle-like blocks found at a quarry termed the Llama Pit, the author rejected the local opinion that they were for bridge construction (p. 167). He based his own view upon, again, educated conjectures from visual observation. The point is that local informants and lore constitute a supply of data that the researcher can use in ways that help his/her narrative.

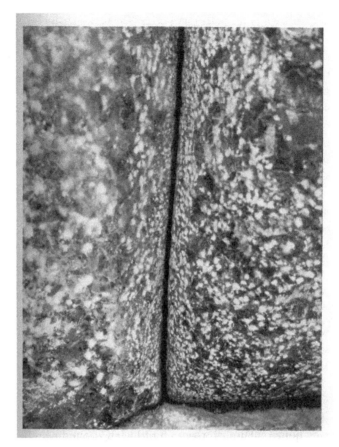

Figure 6.12   This image from Protzen shows the pitmarks he observed diminishing in size as they get nearer the joint. Courtesy of Jean-Pierre Protzen.

Tactic 7: Reenactment/testimonial. Probably the most persuasive of Protzen's tactics are his reenactments of the work the Inca stonemasons performed (see Figure 6.13). Based on his visual observations, Protzen reenacted both the dressing of the stones and the erection of a large masonry wall. In the first instance, he tested his theory that systematic pounding was the method of dressing by using a hammer of metamorphosed sandstone on a raw block of andesite. He learned the efficacy of different angles of pounding, as well as the utility of gravity as an aid in maneuvering a 4-kg hammer. In the second instance, Protzen tested his idea of how large stones were fitted together in a wall of irregular jointure. He found that the

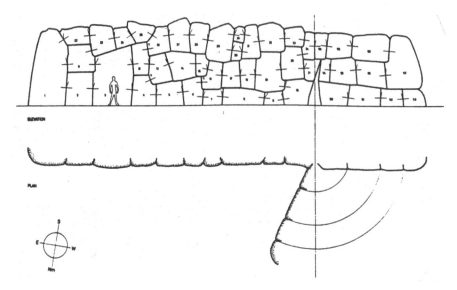

Figure 6.13   A Protzen drawing showing wall construction. Protzen enacted construction procedures to demonstrate his hypothesis that each new course can be cut to fit the profile of the course below it. Courtesy of Jean-Pierre Protzen.

dust produced from the pounding of a bedding joint got compressed when an upper stone was placed on the bed, indicating where further pounding was required. "Through repeated fitting and pounding, one can achieve as close a fit as one wishes" (p. 179).

The outcome of these reenactments is reported with the strength of a testimonial. With respect to the dressing of the andesite block, "the work from rough block to the stage with one face dressed took me only 20 minutes" (p. 173). This persuades the reader that pounding alone by a crew of trained persons can produce, without sophisticated tools, large amounts of dressed stone in a reasonable amount of time.

Tactic 8: Identification of remaining questions. Clearly stating what one does *not* know in the face of present evidence can actually make a narrative more robust; this applies in general to any kind of research report. Here, after summarizing the local lore on an area designated as "quarrymen's quarters," as well as critiquing the view of another analyst (Harth-terre) on this subject, Protzen simply says that "the significance . . . of these structures remains to be established" (p. 164). And against his theory that the Inca did not use many tools in their stonemasonry,

Protzen acknowledges examples "throughout the territory that I explored" where there appear to be clear cases of saw cutting and/or stone polishing. "What tools they used for this I do not yet know" (p. 178). Far from negating the validity of his ideas, Protzen's admission of ignorance on these matters underscores his credibility. Future theories explaining the presence of sawed stone at certain locations may fit in as a corollary to his larger theory of pounding, as opposed to anything that would negate his ideas.

6.7   CONCLUSION

History research accesses evidence from the past, and this chapter provided an overview of what is entailed. At the strategic level, schools of thought affect how past conditions are interpreted. Tactically, history research entails fact finding, fact evaluation, fact organization, and fact analysis. It requires an interpretive imagination that nevertheless does not spill over into fiction, but is rather guided by a mind that Barzun and Graff describe as having a love for order. It entails being aware of different kinds of judgments that can be made once enough evidence has been garnered. It entails the imaginative identification and use of specific tactics to access the object under study, as illustrated by Protzen's efforts. Above all, again at the strategic level, history research requires the framing of a narrative that is at once holistic, in the sense that a story is holistic.

We conclude with one more example (see Box 6.5) to illustrate how advancing computer technology helps history research.

BOX 6.5

Visualizing Auschwitz: "Placing History" with GIS Technology

As part of an interdisciplinary project exploring the geographies of the Holocaust, art historian Paul B. Jaskot and geographers Chester Harvey and Anne Kelly Knowles have been building 2D and 3D digital models of the concentration camp and urban environment at Auschwitz. The initial questions guiding their research related to visibility: What parts of the camp were most thoroughly documented by SS photographers? How

(Continued)

visible were prisoners from guard posts inside Birkenau, the largest and most geometrically laid out part of the camp? Were some parts of the camp relatively hidden from the surveillant gaze of camp guards? Figure 6.14 was developed out of these early questions. The cones of light on the map (right) show the approximate positions and points of view of SS photographers when they took the two photographs (left), which record the arrival of Hungarian Jews by train at Birkenau in May 1944. Connecting the photos to a map helped the team to begin to interpret SS attitudes toward their victims, what they thought was important to record, and how the photos might be used as evidence to reconstruct both the built environment and prisoner experiences in the camp.

The idea of using visibility analysis to study Auschwitz inspired a more ambitious project, still in development. Using a variety of visual sources,

Figure 6.14   At right is GIS plan of the Auschwitz camp. Cones in the plan are viewing angles, projecting what the camp guards can see, as represented by the photographs. Photographs by permission, United States Holocaust Memorial Museum; courtesy of Yad Vashem collection. Plan is courtesy of Professor Anne Kelly Knowles. Text by Anne Kelly Knowles, with Paul B. Jaskot and Chester Harvey.

Harvey and Jaskot conceived of a detailed digital plan of the camp and the town of Auschwitz based on a GIS database of individual buildings. Nazi architectural plans located buildings within the camp and, just as importantly, enabled the team to enter dates of when buildings were planned or actually constructed. Photographs taken from American bombers flying over Auschwitz provided a base map for the general layout of the camp near its completion in 1944, while high-resolution aerial images from the city of Warsaw's GIS office made it possible for Harvey to place many buildings precisely. He used computer-aided design (CAD) as well to construct digital 3D models of the barracks and other key structures, such as the crematoria. The goal of using the digital model to estimate which areas of the camp were easiest to keep under surveillance was superseded when the team realized that they could use the buildings database to study a whole new set of questions: namely, which structures were planned but never built, and which were built out of urgent necessity to carry out the Nazis' genocidal plans? The researchers are now focusing on these questions, as well as using the database to study Auschwitz as a dynamic, sometimes even chaotic construction site—far less settled than the common conception of a concentration camp as a grimly static place. Construction activity may account for why the peak period of construction at Birkenau coincided with a significant spike in the number of escapes from Auschwitz. The digital model, holding the footprints of both idealized plans and the built reality of Auschwitz, is crucial for distinguishing Nazi architectural ideals from the realities on the ground.

Text by Anne Kelly Knowles, Geography Department, Middlebury College, Paul B. Jaskot, Department of Art and Art History, DePaul University, Chester Harvey, Rubenstein School of Environment and Natural Resources, University of Vermont.

Strengths	Weaknesses
Historical research remains a storied and elevated mode of inquiry. As noted by Barzun and Graff, its standards of reportage have traditionally set the standards for documentation, citation, format, and so on, for other modes of qualitative writing.	As noted throughout this chapter, history is an interpretive enterprise, so that any one particular study on a topic is no doubt one point of view on that topic. For those digesting a historical narrative, then,
History is also a unique mode of inquiry in that it is probably the only research strategy whose topic of inquiry does not "exist" in any empirically accessible way. Of course the advantage of art-architectural history research is that the artifact in question is often still with us in some form.	It is necessary to weigh not only the report itself, but also the theoretical frame of the analyst.
History at the tactical level is commonly used in other research strategies, so the how-to's of data procurement are important to know even for researchers using other strategies.	Multiple histories of any one topic are probably needed for a full-orbed account of that topic.

Figure 6.15   Strengths and weaknesses of historical research.

NOTES

1. Adrian Forty, "The Home," in *Objects of Desire* (London: Thames and Hudson, 1986), 100.
2. Ibid., 101.
3. John Tosh, *The Pursuit of History*, 5th ed. (Edinburgh Gate, UK: Pearson Education Limited, 2010), 206–207.
4. How history researchers procure their evidence has itself become a topic of extensive study. For example, see Margaret Stieg Dalton and Laurie Charnigo, "Historians and Their Information Sources," *Colleges & Research Libraries* 65(5) (2004): 400–425; Wendy Duff, Barbara Craig, and Joan Cherry, "Historians' Use of Archival Sources: Promises and Pitfalls of the Digital Age," *The Public Historian* 26(2) (2004): 7–22.
5. Hayden White, *The Fiction of Narrative: Essays on History, Literature and Theory 1957–2007*, Robert Doran (ed.) (Baltimore, MD: Johns Hopkins University Press, 2010).
6. Tosh, 215.
7. A good summary of the cultural turn is provided by Geoff Eley, "Taking the Turn," in *A Crooked Line: From Cultural History to the History of Society* (Ann Arbor: University of

Michigan Press, 2008), 121–133. Eley outlines the following characteristics of the cultural turn: (1) attention paid to gender issues; (2) the influence of Michel Foucault's work on "power, knowledge and regimes of truth" in relation to social history; (3) a departure from the French *Annales* approach to history; (4) the emergence of cultural studies as a focus of history research; and (5) an active dialogue between anthropology and history.

8. Georg G. Iggers, *Historiography: From Scientific Objectivity to the Postmodern Challenge* (Middletown, CT: Wesleyan University Press, 1999), 2.

9. Eley, 121–133.

10. Jean-Francois Lyotard, *The Postmodern Condition*, trans. Geoff Bennington and Brian Massumi (Minneapolis: University of Minnesota Press, 1984), xxiv.

11. Georg G. Iggers, "Epilogue," op. cit., 2005, 150.

12. Tosh, 248.

13. Ibid., 250. To Tosh's list, Eley adds the "cultures and economies of consumption and entertainment," citing as examples film, photography, video, television, extending into commercial media (such as advertising, comic books, magazines). "Feminist scholars explored the relationship of women to popular reading genres (including romances, family sagas, and gothic novels). . . ." Eley, 130–131.

14. Daniel Bluestone, "Chicago's Mecca Flat Blues," *Journal of the Society of Architectural Historians* 57(4) (1998): 382–403.

15. Delores Hayden, "Place Memory and Urban Preservation," in *The Power of Place: Urban Landscapes as Public History* (Cambridge, MA: MIT Press, 1995), 44–78.

16. See Ralph Kingston, "Mind over Matter: History and the Spatial Turn," *Cultural and Social History* 7(1) (2010): 111–121.

17. Bluestone, 382.

18. See Hayden, 41–42.

19. Henri Lefevre, *The Production of Space*, trans. Donald Nicholson-Smith (Oxford, UK: Blackwell Publishers, 1994), 240.

20. Edward Soja, "Los Angeles, 1965–1992," in Allen J. Scott and Edward Soja (eds.), *The City: Los Angeles and Urban Theory at the End of the Twentieth Century* (Berkeley: University of California Press, 1996), 426–462.

21. Edward Soja, "Seeking Spatial Justice in Los Angeles," in *Seeking Spatial Justice* (Minneapolis: University of Minnesota Press, 2010), 111–155; citation is from page 112.

22. R. G. Collingwood, *The Idea of History* (London and New York: Oxford University Press, [1940], 1956), 246.

23. Edmund Morris, *Dutch: A Memoir of Ronald Reagan* (New York: Random House, 2000).

24. For instance, see this June 5, 2004, critique by John O'Sullivan, "Not the Authorized Biography," in *National Review Online*; http://old.nationalreview.com/flashback/jos200406052119.asp. Accessed July 21, 2011.

25. Arthur Danto, *Narration and Knowledge* (New York: Columbia University Press, 1985), 152.

26. William Cronon, "Inconstant Unity: The Passion of Frank Lloyd Wright," in Terence Riley and Peter Reed (eds.), *Frank Lloyd Wright, Architect* (New York: Museum of Modern Art, 1994).

27. F. R. Ankersmit, "Danto, History, and the Tragedy of Human Existence," *History and Theory* 42 (October 2003): 291–304.

28. Ibid., 301. Ankersmit is citing Arthur Danto, *Transfiguration of the Commonplace* (Harvard University Press, 1981), 179.

29. William Cronon, "A Place for Stories: Nature, History, and Narrative," *The Journal of American History* 78(4) (1992): 1349.

30. W. B. Gallie, *Philosophy and the Historical Understanding* (New York: Schocken Books, 1964), 66.

31. Ibid., 67.

32. Hayden White, "Storytelling" (1998), in *Fiction of Narrative*, 273–292.

33. Ibid., 282.

34. Ibid., 287–290.

35. Robert Doran, "Introduction: Humanism, Formalism and the Discourse of History" (2010), in *Fiction of Narrative*, xxiv.

36. Barbara Taylor, "How Far, How Near: Distance and Proximity in the Historical Imagination," *History Workshop Journal* 57 (Spring 2004): 117–122.

37. James Connelly and Alan Costall, "R. G. Collingwood and the Idea of a Historical Psychology," *Theory & Psychology* 10(2) (2000): 147–170.

38. Collingwood, *The Idea of History*, 236. Collingwood's derivation for the historical imagination largely comes from Kantian sources. In his *Critique of Pure Reason*, Kant holds that the imagination is one of the mind's *a priori* faculties and that the imagination has reproductive and productive modes (see Kant, *Critique of Pure Reason*, A100–A102, A118). In the *Critique of Judgment*, Kant adds to the imagination's powers by positing it as *the* faculty involved in the creation of objects of art. (See Kant *Critique of Judgment*, Sec. 1, 203.) Collingwood's "historical imagination" is derived from these sources; it has the ability to picture things that are not empirically seen at the moment, and the end result of its work may be likened to art.

39. Hayden White, "Collingwood and Toynbee," in *Fiction of Narrative*, 15.

40. See Mauro Murzi, "Carl Gustav Hempel (1905–1997)," in *Internet Encyclopedia of Philosophy*, www.iep.utm.edu/hempel/. Accessed April 16, 2012.

41. C. G. Hempel, "The Function of General Laws in History," *Journal of Philosophy* 39 (1942): 35–48.

42. Ibid., 39. "The preceding considerations [on prediction in scientific theories] apply to *explanation in history* as well as in any other branch of empirical science . . . . [T]he expectation referred to is not prophecy or divination, but rational scientific anticipation which rests on the assumption of general laws" (Hempel's italics).

43. Karl Popper, *The Poverty of Historicism* (London: Routledge & Kegan Paul, ARK Edition, 1986).
44. Ibid., 42–49.
45. See Reyner Banham, *Theory and Design in the First Machine Age*, 2nd ed. (New York: Praeger, 1967), 24.
46. Le Corbusier, *Towards a New Architecture*, 1931 trans. F. E. Etchells (New York: Dover Publications, [1931] 1986), 227.
47. Nicholas Pevsner, *An Outline of European Architecture* (Baltimore, MD: Penguin Books, [1943], 1974). Also Sigfried Giedion, *Space, Time and Architecture* (Cambridge, MA: Harvard University Press, [1949], 1967).
48. Richard Weston, "Introduction," in Nicholas Pevsner, *Pioneers of Modern Design, 1936* (New Haven and London: Yale University Press, 2005), 8.
49. Heinrich Wolfflin, "The Causes of Change in Style," in *Renaissance and Baroque,* trans. K. Simon (Ithaca, NY: Cornell University Press, 1966), 73–88.
50. Hegel, *Reason in History*, trans. R. S. Hartman (New York: Liberal Arts Press, 1953), 38–39.
51. Jacob Burckhardt, *The Civilization of the Renaissance in Italy*, trans. S. G. C. Middlemore (New York and London: Harper and Brothers, 1860).
52. Robert McCarter, *Frank Lloyd Wright* (London: Reaktion Books, 2006), 7–8.
53. Ibid., 15–17. Hawkes cites Jean Piaget.
54. Peter Caws, *Structuralism: The Art of the Intelligible* (Atlantic Highlands, NJ, and London: Humanities Press International, 1988), 72.
55. Terence Hawkes, *Structuralism and Semiotics* (Berkeley: University of California Press, 1977).
56. Mihály Csíkszentmihályi, *Creativity: Flow and the Psychology of Discovery and Invention* (New York: HarperCollins, 1996), 30.
57. George Dickie, "The Institutional Theory of Art," in Noel Carroll (ed.), *Theories of Art Today* (Madison: University of Wisconsin Press, 2006), 93.
58. Geoffrey Broadbent, R. Bunt, and C. Jencks, *Signs, Symbols and Architecture* (New York: John Wiley & Sons, 1980), 137.
59. Henry Glassie, "Structure and Function: Folklore and Artifact," *Semiotica* 7 (1973): 328.
60. Ibid., 329.
61. Lyotard, *The Postmodern Condition*, xxiv.
62. Edward Soja, "Los Angeles, 1965–1992," in Allen J. Scott and Edward Soja (ed.), *The City: Los Angeles and Urban Theory at the End of the Twentieth Century* (Berkeley: University of California Press, 1996), 426–462.
63. Ibid., 446.
64. Ibid., 454.
65. Jacques Barzun and Henry F. Graff, *The Modern Researcher* (Belmont, CA: Wadsworth Cengage Learning, 2004), 5.

66. Ibid., 102.

67. James Ackerman, "The Nature of Art History," in *Art and Archaeology* (Englewood Cliffs, NJ: Prentice Hall, 1963), 127–130.

68. Matthew A. Cohen, "How Much Brunelleschi? A Late Medieval Proportional System in the Basilica of San Lorenzo," *Journal of the Society of Architectural Historians* 67 (2008): 18–57.

69. Ibid., 17, 44.

70. Ibid., 44.

71. "Ascent of McKinley in 1906 Doubted," *Spokane Spokesman-Review* (November 27, 1998). Associated Press wire service.

72. For an overview on how digital imaging technology complicates once-assumed representations of "reality," see Jol A. Silversmith, "Photographic Evidence, Naked Children, and Dead Celebrities: Digital Forgery and the Law," ThirdAmendment.com, www.thirdamendment.com/digital.html. Accessed August 1, 2011.

73. Otto von Simson, *The Gothic Cathedral* (Princeton, NJ: Princeton University Press, 1988), 56–58, 111.

74. Ibid., 111.

75. Ibid., 110.

76. Ibid., 112.

77. Cohen, 19.

78. Ibid., 28.

79. For example, Daniel Hoffman's study of the house benefits greatly by inclusion of a photograph of the car. Donald Hoffman, *Frank Lloyd Wright's Robie House* (New York: Dover, 1984), 3. (Italics added.)

80. Leonard K. Eaton, *Two Chicago Architects and Their Clients: Frank Lloyd Wright and Howard Van Doren Shaw* (Cambridge, MA: MIT Press, 1969), 126–133.

81. Ibid., 9.

82. Ibid., 131.

83. Ibid., 127.

Chapter 7

Qualitative Research

7.1 INTRODUCTION

In her influential and classic book, *Architecture: The Story of Practice,* Dana Cuff provides in-depth descriptions and analyses of architectural practice.[1] Throughout the book, she recounts in great detail the many interactions and processes that architects experience on a daily basis. With these observations as a foundation, she brings to light many of the underlying contradictions of the profession. These include, for example, the profession's tendency to celebrate the creative talent of the individual architect, even while most architects work in collaborative settings to bring to life complex building projects.

In introducing her study, Cuff describes in considerable detail how she went about her research. First and foremost, she persuaded three Bay Area firms to let her observe and participate in the life of the firm over a six-month period. In these settings, she observed meetings, interviewed firm members, participated in casual conversations, and took part in many informal social activities (see Figure 7.1). Throughout these interactions, Cuff maintained two important principles: (1) that she sought to understand the dynamics of the profession from the point of view of the participants; and (2) that, at the same time, such insiders' perspectives had to be balanced by her "outsider's observations."[2] But while Cuff insists on grounding her work in the empirical reality of her observations, she also highlights the role of interpretation and meaning. As she puts it:

> Philosophically, what I value . . . is [a] rejection of positivist notions of the social world, embracing interpretation, meaning in context, interaction, and the quality of the commonplace.[3]

Figure 7.1   Architects, clients, and consultants meeting an essential aspect of the design process. Courtesy of Kevin M. Daly.

In her dissertation study, Donna Wheatley has investigated the extent to which the alignment between the spatial qualities of workplaces and intentional corporate branding has been achieved from the perspectives of different stakeholder groups.[4] This is a topic of significant interest for architects and designers who regularly grapple with how to embody the goals and values of corporate clients in built form, through spatial qualities suitable for both the culture of the organization and the work practices and sensibilities of the employees. As Wheatley pointedly states:

> [A]ligning spatial qualities of workplaces with corporate branding is an explicitly practiced strategy. [T]here is often the expectation for architects to integrate corporate values into their designs with the expectation that users will respond in a favorable way to the clients. However, there is little in the way of studies that examine the success [of such a design strategy].[5]

Given the global prevalence of corporate branding, Wheatley selected six major projects designed by architects in Australia, China, and Great Britain (see Figure 7.2). Since her research question fundamentally centers on the interpretive sensibilities and experience of the various stakeholders (architects, client, and users), Wheatley sought a research design that would elicit each individual's interpretations of the environment in their own terms. For this reason, she developed an in-depth interview protocol employing sets of visual images that would elicit the participants' metaphoric associations their workplace—categories of images that included art, interiors, sculpture, food, color, and so on. Participants at each site were asked to select one or two images from each set of image categories that reflected their feelings about the design and experience of the workplace. In addition to being asked to sort these selected images into groupings meaningful to them, participants were also asked to select specific images in response to more focused questions.[6] The resulting interview texts were then

Figure 7.2   Case 1 located in Shanghai, China: exterior view and open meeting space (7.2a and b); and Case 2 located in Sydney, Australia: exterior view and significant interior space (7.2c and d). Courtesy of Donna Wheatley.

coded for *every* expressed association between environmental qualities and participant interpretations.[7]

7.2   THE STRATEGY OF QUALITATIVE RESEARCH: GENERAL CHARACTERISTICS

What both the Cuff and the Wheatley studies have in common is that they can be categorized as qualitative research. Although this research design can actually be manifested in a variety of formats, several common attributes can be identified. Norman Denzin and Yvonna Lincoln, authors of a highly regarded, three-volume handbook on qualitative research, offer the following "generic" definition of qualitative research:

> Qualitative research is multi-method in focus, involving an interpretive, naturalistic approach to its subject matter. This means that qualitative researchers study things in their natural settings, attempting to make sense of, or interpret phenomena in terms of the meanings people bring to them. Qualitative research involves the studied use and collection of a variety of empirical materials.[8]

Another feature of qualitative research that is also frequently cited in the research methods literature is an underlying emphasis on an inductive process. Creswell describes this tendency in the following way:

> [W]e ask open-ended research questions . . . , shaping the questions after we "explore. . . . Our questions change during the process of research to reflect an increased understanding of the problem.[9]

Five key components of qualitative research, articulated in the previous quotations, can be identified. We will consider each of them in turn, using examples from architectural research to illustrate these points.

7.2.1   *An Emphasis on Natural Settings*

By "natural settings" is meant that the objects of inquiry are not removed from the venues in which they typically exist as part of everyday life. Cuff's primary material came from her in-depth observations and interactions at three architectural firms over a six-month period of time. In the Wheatley study, the value of the research lies in its ability to uncover the similarities and differences in the interpretations of the various stakeholder groups in each of the six workplaces studied. In both of these cases, the researchers used research tactics that engaged people within the context being studied, while the context itself was studied in its natural state.

7.2.2   A Focus on Interpretation and Meaning

In both the Cuff and the Wheatley studies, the authors not only ground their work in the empirical realities of their observations and interviews, but they also make clear that they, as researchers, play an important role in interpreting and making sense of that data. To reiterate one of Cuff's points (quoted earlier), she intentionally employs methodological practices that embrace interpretation and meaning in context. Similarly, Wheatley notes that the in-depth engagement with participants fostered communication and understanding, while the detailed coding process of the interview texts fundamentally depended on her interpretive skills.[10]

7.2.3   A Focus on How the Respondents Make Sense of Their Own Circumstances

In the descriptions of the Cuff and Wheatley studies, it is clear that the researchers aim to present a holistic portrayal of the setting or phenomenon under study as the respondents themselves understand it. Cuff, for example, offers extensive and detailed descriptions of interactions among the multiple players in client meetings. Similarly, an essential aspect of Wheatley's study is to explore each participant's interpretation of the workplace in his/her own terms; this includes elucidating the extent to which the various stakeholders' understandings converge, or not.

In another exemplar of qualitative research, Linda Groat and Sherry Ahrentzen conducted a series of in-depth interviews with faculty women in architecture, the results of which were published in the *Journal of Architectural Education*.[11] For their part, Groat and Ahrentzen specifically sought to understand faculty women's perceptions in terms of three aspects of their experiences in architecture: their attractions to architecture as a career; their experience of either discrimination or encouragement both in practice and as faculty members; and their visions for the future of architectural education.

7.2.4   The Use of Multiple Tactics

Denzin and Lincoln refer to this characteristic of qualitative research as bricolage, and the research as bricoleur. A *bricolage* is "a pieced-together, close-knit set of practices that provide solutions to a problem in a concrete situation."[12] The idea of bricolage implicitly suggests that qualitative researchers will employ a range of tactics that are both particular to the context being studied, and of course appropriate to the research question(s) being asked.

A good example of a multitactic qualitative study may be seen in Karen Keddy's study of the experience of a hospital surgical unit from the perspective of the nursing staff. Keddy sought to conduct research that would serve as an antidote to the prevalent tendency in health care research to focus primarily on operational efficiency. Rather than focusing on how nursing staff's productivity might be increased through design interventions, Keddy sought to provide a more holistic understanding of "the physical nature of nursing work and the physical environment from the nurses' perspective."[13]

To explore these issues, Keddy employed a wide variety of tactics, including structured, in-depth interviews, location mapping, photo-documentation, architectural inventories, place-centered behavioral mapping, and focused observations, and an image-based visual exercise called an "experiential collage."[14] The intention of the collage exercise (see Figure 7.3), conducted after the initial interview, was to elicit "insights into how a nurse actually feels about what she thinks and what she does as well as what it means to her . . . , a means of making different perspectives about the socio-spatial nature of nursing work visible."[15]

Taken together, this set of data collection tactics focuses not so much on quantities of easily measured and known activities, but on the experiential qualities and conceptualizations of the nurses' work. As a result, this study was able to reveal the "hidden activities many nurses perform which are not measured or even included in such inventories as work sampling."[16]

To be sure, not all qualitative research studies rely on such a diverse array of tactics to investigate the research question. However, even in research studies where one primary mode of inquiry is used, secondary tactics are typically employed. For example, although Cuff depended primarily on fieldwork observations of three different firms especially in work meetings (documented in 600 pages of notes), she also interviewed firm members, chatted casually with people, did drafting and other work activities, and participated in many informal activities with firm members.[17] Similarly, although Groat and Ahrentzen's research on faculty women depended extensively on an in-depth interview protocol of key questions and optional follow-up questions, the authors also incorporated insights from an earlier quantitative survey questionnaire and archival statistics from the national architectural faculty organization.[18]

7.2.5   *Significance of Inductive Logic*

As Creswell argues in a quotation cited earlier in the chapter, the research questions investigated through a qualitative study frequently evolve in an iterative process.

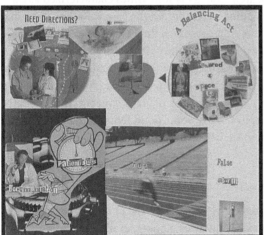

Figure 7.3   Examples of experiential collages. Courtesy of Karen Keddy.

The initial formulation of a question is typically refined in the light of ongoing interviews or observations; this enables the researcher to test out emerging insights: for example, by adding new or follow-up questions to the interview, and conducting observations at different locations or times of day. [19] (See also Chapters 2 and 11 for more details on inductive logic.)

Such is the case with Groat and Ahrentzen's study of faculty women. The analysis of the one- to two-hour interviews required a long, interactive process of identifying key themes, the development of an elaborate coding scheme, and eventual synthesis into the textual narrative for their article. The published article not only reports on the key themes culled from the "visions" section of the interview, but also grounds these themes through illustrative quotations from individual faculty women. Only after the major themes were identified did the authors turn to consider the remarkable parallel to the recommendations of the 1996 Carnegie Foundation study of architectural education.[20] To be specific, five of the seven themes Groat and Ahrentzen identified correspond to those from the Carnegie study: ideals of a liberal education, interdisciplinary connections, different modes of thought, communicative design studios, and caring for students. Groat and Ahrentzen conclude that "these recommendations constitute a consistent and powerful argument for the visions for architectural education that any number of individual faculty women have been valiantly advocating for many years."[21]

Although the qualitative research strategy is sometimes characterized as *exclusively* inductive, many researchers point out that is not the case.[22] Rather, it is a matter of degree of emphasis. Whereas other research designs are more likely to rely more heavily on deductive logic (e.g., experimental or logical argumentation), qualitative research tends to emphasize a holistic exploration of complex situations and environments where testing and deduction of sequenced or causal relations are unlikely. However, the often-iterative sequence of data collection, interpretive processes, and theory building implies that at some point tentative conclusions and theories and may be tested out in more deductive sequences.

7.2.6   *Other Aspects of Qualitative Research Strategy*

To review, then, the strategy of qualitative research is one of first-hand encounters with a specific and defined context. It involves gaining an understanding of how people in real-world situations "make sense" of their environment and themselves; and it depends on, rather than rejects, the researcher's interpretation of the collected data. Finally, it achieves this understanding by means of a variety of tactics, employed through a primarily inductive process. Other typical characteristics of the qualitative strategy are listed in Figure 7.4.

Although the origins of qualitative research are primarily in social and human science-based fields, readers of this chapter may already see that this research design bears many similarities to historical research in architecture (see Chapter 6). Indeed, both strategies seek to describe and/or explain socio-physical phenomena within complex contexts, and both seek to consider the relevant phenomena in a

Holistic. Qualitative research typically aims "to develop a complex picture" that "involves reporting multiple perspectives, identifying the many factors involved in a situation, and generally sketching the larger picture that emerges." (Creswell, p. 39)

Prolonged Contact. With its emphasis on fieldwork, qualitative research typically entails "investment of time sufficient to learn the culture, understand context, and/or build trust and rapport." (O'Leary, p. 115)

Open-Ended. Qualitative research tends to be more open-ended in both theoretical conception and research design, such that "the initial plan for research cannot be tightly prescribed, and that all phases of the process may change or shift" during the fieldwork or data collection. (Creswell, p. 39)

Researcher as Measurement Device. Since there is relatively little use of standardized measures such as survey questionnaires, the researcher is "essentially the main 'measurement device' in the study." (Miles & Huberman, p. 7)

Analysis through Words or Visual Material. Since an emphasis on descriptive numerical measures and inferential statistics is typically eschewed, the principal mode of analysis is through words, whether represented in visual displays or through narrative devices. (Miles & Huberman, p. 7)

Personal or Informal Writing Stance. In contrast to the typical journal format of experimental or correlational studies, the writing style of qualitative work is typically offered in a "literary, flexible style that conveys stories . . . without the formal academic structures of writing." (Creswell, p. 40)

Figure 7.4 Additional attributes of qualitative research. Sources: John W. Creswell, *Qualitative Inquiry & Research Design: Choosing among Five Approaches* (Thousand Oaks, CA: SAGE, 2007); Matthew B. Miles and A. Michael Huberman, *Qualitative Data Analysis* (Thousand Oaks, CA: SAGE, 1994); Zina O'Leary, *The Essential Guide to Doing Your Research Project* (Thousand Oaks, CA: SAGE, 2010).

holistic manner. Even more telling, perhaps, is that Denzin and Lincoln's major edited book on qualitative research strategies includes a chapter titled "Historical Social Science" by Gaye Tuchman.[23] A major facet of Tuchman's argument is that earlier formulations regarding the distinction between history and sociology have been largely abandoned. She then concludes: "What remains in both fields is recognition that research is an interpretive enterprise."[24]

There are, however, at least two major differences between the qualitative research design and the historical strategy, as defined within this text. Perhaps the most obvious is the temporal focus; whereas qualitative studies tend to focus on contemporaneous phenomena, historical research by definition focuses on environments or contexts that were created in the past. Second, the data sources and collection techniques are also likely to be different. Whereas qualitative researchers more often incorporate data sources that involve people through interviews and observation, historians more routinely rely on written documents and physical sources.

Despite these differences in focus, the relationship between qualitative and historical research designs demonstrates once again how permeable the boundaries are between the various research strategies. In this case especially, the two are easily compatible in architectural research. Moreover, aspects of one can successfully augment the characteristics of the other. For example, some historical research may advantageously incorporate a greater focus on the social impact of particular buildings, styles, or city forms. Likewise, studies of contemporaneous environments may profit from more extensive analyses of historical archives and/or of the physical artifacts themselves. This potential for combined strategies will be taken up in greater detail later in this book. (See Chapter 12 on combined strategies.)

7.3   STRATEGY: FOUR QUALITATIVE APPROACHES

In this section, we address three relatively distinct schools of thought common to qualitative research in architectural and environmental research: ethnography, phenomenological inquiry, and grounded theory (sometimes known as the constant comparative method). In addition, we will describe more recent trends in which scholars have sought to integrate aspects of the several schools of thought.

In each of the following subsections, we first summarize the basic characteristics of each qualitative approach, including a discussion of the strengths and weaknesses of each. We then point out examples from architecture and architectural inquiry that offer ready connections to each approach.

7.3.1   *Ethnography*

Ethnographic research emphasizes in-depth engagement with site-specific settings, most especially through active and thorough observation. Although ethnographic fieldwork was initially and primarily associated with the discipline of anthropology, it has also been adopted by a number of other disciplines, including sociology, human geography, organization studies, educational research, and cultural studies.[25]

True to its anthropological roots, ethnographic methodology emerged in the early 20th century through the work of several anthropologists who aimed to establish a "natural science of society" that could "furnish an objective description of a culture."[26] In contrast to the "desk" anthropologists of the time who based their speculations purely on secondary sources, the proponents of ethnography sought to ascertain the "natives'" point of view, within the context of their own culture.

Although early ethnographic research reflected Western interest in non-Western societies through the prism of the positivist intellectual paradigm of the time, more recent ethnographic work in a variety of disciplines has sought to investigate various subcultures within both Western and global societies through a naturalistic paradigm, often employing a transformative school of thought.

The overall characteristics of ethnographic work are fully consistent with the broader definition of the qualitative strategy presented earlier in this chapter, including holistic exploration of a setting, including context-rich detail; the reliance on unstructured (i.e., not precoded) data; a focus on a single case or small number of cases; and data analysis that emphasizes the interpretation of "the meanings and functions of human action."[27]

Perhaps the most distinctive aspect of ethnographic fieldwork is its tendency to rely on "observation" as its primary mode of data collection. Although observation is a common tactic within both qualitative and other research strategies, ethnographer Giampietro Gobo argues that what distinguishes observation in ethnography is "the more active role assigned to observation."[28] If the researcher is relatively uninterested in understanding the symbolic meaning embedded in cultural life, she may choose to employ *nonparticipant* observation so as not to interfere with the ongoing actions and behavior of the people be studied.

More commonly, the researcher is likely to employ *participant* observation. This term is frequently used to refer to a situation in which the researcher plays a naturally occurring, established role in the situation under study. For instance, the researcher's identity might be known by few or many, or revealed in more or less detail. Moreover, the researcher may participate to a greater or lesser degree in his apparent role; or he may take the stance of either an insider or outsider. Thus, participant observation can encompass enormous variation in how the researcher chooses to observe and participate in the phenomena being studied.

Cuff's study of architectural practice serves as a good example of the ethnographic approach to qualitative research. She is quite explicit in describing her research as following ethnographic principles. As she puts it:

> [M]ost current ethnographic studies look at patterns of interpretation that members of a cultural group invoke as they go about their daily lives. Into the general knot of making sense of the world, an ethnography ties ideas about the group's knowledge, its beliefs, its social organization, how it reproduces itself, and the material world in which it exists.[29]

Moreover, as mentioned earlier in this chapter, Cuff's in-depth study of three architectural firms entailed a robust and active engagement participant observation, which included observing and note taking at design team, client, and consultant meetings; a variety of office work such as drafting and model making; and numerous informal social occasions.

A doctoral dissertation in architecture offers another example of ethnographic research. In response to the ongoing modernization of her native Thailand, Piyarat Nanta sought to discover the extent to which people's place experience of their traditional vernacular homes in a rural region of central Thailand had been transformed through the changing sociocultural context of the past 50 years.[30]

With this goal in mind, Nanta interviewed 2 members of each family in 15 vernacular houses in a rural village area of Baan Krang, where rice farming occupies over 95% of the arable land.[31] Because she sought to understand the temporal transformation of each home, most respondents were elderly, but were typically assisted by a younger family member who was interviewed as well. In addition, she also interviewed five master house builders and two master carpenters. Her initial semistructured interview with the families (which were video recorded and later transcribed) yielded insights on the history of the house, daily activities, occupants' perceptions of their homes, and historical and contemporary social changes.[32]

These interviews served as a springboard for subsequent observation and artifactual documentation. In addition to observing the life style of the family and the home in use, Nanta took careful note of physical modifications made to the home to accommodate their changing life patterns. The artifactual documentation entailed photography, videotapes, and annotated plan layouts of the interior, exterior, and immediate landscape. Once the contemporary house layout was documented, family members were asked to recall the house form historically, and the separate historically based annotated layout was produced (see Figure 7.5). To augment the historical perspective on farming life, Nanta conducted a survey of nearby Buddhist temple murals, which depict the dynamics of the domestic and social lives of the farmers, as well as physical features of their dwellings.

Overall, Nanta's research is a classic example of the ethnographic approach to qualitative research which foregrounds the active role of observation, while also employing "ancillary sources" such as interviews, artifactual documentation, and historical archives.[33] In a broader perspective, Nanta's research is consistent with the general characteristics of qualitative research, particularly its inductive emphasis. This is evidenced in the way she has layered her in-depth analyses of the families' daily life and routines; the meaning and interpretations of home; and the house form as it evolved over generations. Taken together, in a holistic way, she is able to conclude that the experience of place in these vernacular homes has evolved from a hierarchical to an integrated space; from being a container for ancestral memory to

Figure 7.5 Transformation of two Thai vernacular dwellings. Historical dwellings are shown at the top with contemporary versions below. Courtesy of Piyarat Nanta.

a physical structure that symbolizes status; and from constant family interaction to transspatial family relations—or, in sum, from the house as the center of the social group and rice production to the house as sanctuary.

7.3.2 *Phenomenology*

Phenomenological inquiry is arguably the most well-known and established strand of the qualitative research utilized in architectural research. It derives from both the phenomenological tradition of German philosophers (e.g., Husserl and Heidegger, among others) and more recent versions of phenomenology influential in the social sciences. Among these, the sociologist Alfred Schutz attempted to develop a "phenomenological sociology" that would serve as a bridge between traditional sociology and Edmund Husserl's philosophical phenomenology.[34]

A defining quality of this work, as described by John Creswell, is that researchers aim to clarify the essential or underlying meaning of experience, "where experiences contain both the outward appearance and inward consciousness based on memory, image, and meaning."[35] Similarly, Schwandt identifies the goal of phenomenological inquiry as seeking an understanding of "the complex world of lived experience from the point of view of those who live it."[36] Following Husserl, the Cartesian duality of subject and object is collapsed by presuming that "reality" is embodied in the meaning of an object in subjective consciousness. A basic principle underlying such an inquiry is the concept of "bracketing," whereby the researcher sets aside any prejudgments and relies on his/her intuition and imagination to uncover the universal or essential qualities of the phenomena.

From the perspective of the architectural field, a significant advantage or attraction to phenomenological inquiry results from the premise that consciousness is understood to be directed toward an "object," the reality of which is inextricably linked to one's consciousness.[37] And this, of course, may include the physical environment. As such, phenomenology can be seen as having more kinship with architectural research than other qualitative approaches that have originated with a more exclusive focus on people's interactions unmoored from the physical context.

Within the environmental design fields, David Seamon, editor of the long-standing newsletter *Environmental & Architectural Phenomenology*, has identified three ongoing strands of research over the past five decades: (1) hermeneutical; (2) first-person; and (3) existential.[38] The research described by the first category, hermeneutic inquiry, includes a number of the classic phenomenological texts that have been influential in architecture and allied disciplines, such as Norberg-Schulz's *Genius Loci* and subsequent books, Thiis-Evensen's *Architectypes in Architecture*, and Edward Relph's *Place and Placelessness*. Within the hermeneutic category, Gaston Bachelard's book *The Poetics of Space*, from 1958, represents a truly classic work.[39] Bachelard uses textual analysis of poignant vignettes from literature and poetry to weave an interpretive analysis of dwelling. Because such works depend primarily on a combination of argumentation and/or textual analyses, studies of this kind are discussed in Chapter 11.

The second and third strands of phenomenological inquiry, however, represent research within the qualitative research strategy. As Seamon explains, in first-person phenomenological inquiry "the researcher uses her own firsthand experience of the phenomenon as a basis for examining its specific characteristics and qualities."[40] A classic example of this type of inquiry is Francis Violich's comparative analysis of place experience in five Dalmatian towns. Through a variety of tactics, including mapping, sketching, and journal entries, he identified first the key spatial features that contributed each town's character, and concluded his analysis with a composite set of qualities that contribute to a sense of place.[41]

In a similar vein, Ingrid Stefanovic sought "to provide a phenomenological reading" of two very different towns: the Croatian town of Cavtat, and the Toronto suburb of Missasauga. Although the towns represent a significant contrast in spatial and temporal qualities, Stefanovic concludes that "some convergence of images in our descriptions . . . may shed light on the appeal of genuine sense of place."[42] Indeed, she finds that both communities share a strong expression of center; the significance of nature within the built environment; an expression of self-identity; the experience of enclosure; and reference to the larger scale of environments within which they are situated.[43]

The immediacy and experiential depth of first-hand studies such as these can often be informative, insightful, and sometimes inspirational for design professionals. Nevertheless, first-hand studies are not without their challenges. Methodologically, the researcher aims to "bracket" his/her prejudgments to arrive at an understanding of the "essence" of the experience that transcends individual subjectivity. Or, as Schwandt puts it, phenomenological research must struggle with "[t]he paradox of how to develop an objective interpretive science of subjective human experience."[44]

The challenge is even more complicated when architects and designers, as the researchers, apply their subjectivity to illuminate the "essence" of a given place experience. A considerable body of design research has demonstrated critical differences between expert and lay experiences in a variety of settings and contexts.[45] Similarly, people who experience a building or landscape with different purposes in mind (an errand versus recreation; or a business meeting versus building maintenance) are likely to experience the setting in fundamentally different ways.[46] So, for purposes of design practice, first-hand phenomenological studies may well spark an imaginative design concept, but they may not yield sufficient insight for designers faced with the dynamics of a complex, multifaceted design project.

BOX 7.1

Qualitative Research: A Phenomenological Approach to Research Design

Clare Cooper Marcus's study of people's attachments to their homes, *House as a Mirror of Self*, is a good example of what one might call "applied phenomenology."[a] This book builds on work that she began many years ago with the publication of a now-classic article entitled, "The

[a] Clare Cooper Marcus, *House as a Mirror of Self* (Berkeley, CA: Conari Press, 1995).

(Continued)

House as a Symbol of the Self."[b] Her approach to this material is particularly attractive in that she finds ways to access the phenomenological unity between a subject and her home—and finds ways to write about it—without using much of the typical jargon found in more explicit phenomenological writings. Because of her lack of use of the usual jargon, the following citation from the introduction to her book is actually somewhat atypical, but it is useful in unveiling the phenomenological moorings of her methodology:

> So far as I was able, I attempted to approach this material via what philosopher Martin Heidegger called "pre-logical thought." This is not "illogical" or "irrational," but rather a mode of approaching being-in-the-world that permeated early Greek thinkers at a time before the categorization of our world into mind and matter, cause and effect, in-here and out-there had gripped . . . the Western mind. I firmly believe that a deeper level of person/environment interaction can be approached only by means of a thought process that attempts to eliminate observer and object.[c]

Marcus was dissatisfied early in her research because her work had dealt primarily with house, but not home. It was not until a friend of hers "talked to the desert" that she discovered a way by which precognitive realities of the "house-self dynamic" could be unearthed. She then embarked on tactics that involved asking a subject to talk to her house, and then to have the house "talk" back to her, supplemented by her respondents' attempts to capture the feelings in graphic form (see Figures 7.6, 7.7, and 7.8).

When Cooper Marcus turned to graphic exercises, as well as "talking to" rather than "talking about" environments of attachment, a phenomenological world opened up. For example, one individual, Bill, chafed at her suggestion that his love for remodeling was a "hobby." Bill's response: "The word hobby is an annoying word to me . . . this is not a hobby . . . this is a fundamental part of our existence."[d] His insistence that the work of his hands is a "fundamental part of our existence" is profound in its conveyance of a sense of ontological unity between himself and his environment. In studies of a phenomenological nature, such use of words may also be data.

---

[b] Clare Cooper Marcus, "The House as Symbol of the Self," in J. Lang et al. (eds.), *Designing for Human Behavior: Architecture and the Behavioral Sciences* (Stroudsburg, PA: Dowden, Hutchinson & Ross, 1974).
[c] Clare Cooper Marcus, *House as a Mirror of Self*.
[d] Ibid., 61.

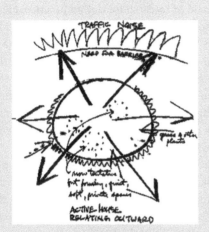

Figure 7.6 Drawings by the interviewees. Illustrations originally appeared in *House as a Mirror of Self* by Clare Cooper Marcus, used with permission of author.

Figure 7.7 Drawings by the interviewees. Illustrations originally appeared in *House as a Mirror of Self* by Clare Cooper Marcus, used with permission of author.

Figure 7.8 Drawings by the interviewees. Illustrations originally appeared in *House as a Mirror of Self* by Clare Cooper Marcus, used with permission of author.

In this light, Seamon's third category of existential-phenomenological research is likely to be the most pertinent strand of research for design practice. He defines this category as focusing on "the specific experiences of specific individuals or groups in actual situations or places."[47] The assumption behind this type of phenomenological inquiry is that when individual descriptive accounts are thoughtfully analyzed and considered collectively, meaningful themes will be revealed so long as the researcher remains "open to their guidance and speaking, their disclosure, when we attend to them."[48] This quotation is a particularly evocative way to highlight the sensibility among many researchers who value the commitment to use of an inductive process in qualitative research.

Maire O'Neill's study of Montana ranch families' place experiences over two generations is a good example of Seamon's existential phenomenology category. Within a conceptual framework informed by well-known precedents in the phenomenology literature (e.g., psychologist Erwin Straus and geographer Yi-Fu Tuan), she focuses on the haptic sensibilities of the body (perceptions gained by movement, touch, etc.) experienced by three families who were third- to fifth-generation residents of their ranches. Through in-depth open-ended interviews, she posed questions "intended to initiate a monologue that allowed participants to consider the buildings and landscape in their own terms."[49]

By carefully scrutinizing the interview transcripts, O'Neill was able to uncover the "modes of perception and understanding people were thinking about, recalling and describing their space."[50] From these interview monologues, she derived a taxonomy of the types of knowledge the ranchers unself-consciously employed to recall their place experience: visual, haptic, familial, and cultural. In addition, the ranchers' recall of the spatial qualities of the ranches over generational time revealed a remarkable stability of circulation patterns and spatial placement of buildings (see Figure 7.9). As O'Neill observes, this continuity of place form and memory through generations embodies Seamon's concept of "place-ballet as part of an integrated pattern of life that in itself defines the place."[51]

Although O'Neill's conclusions for this specific setting type are not likely to be immediately useful to designers or architects in practice, the underlying principles are indeed relevant to practice. Designing with sensitivity to the haptic experience of place from multiple subjective perspectives can contribute to the quality of many design projects. O'Neill also argues that the insights from this study have important implications for architectural and design education:

> [U]nwittingly, the teaching and learning process of the design studio may completely override a variety of culturally or individually based perceptual characteristics that might otherwise enrich . . . the work. By cultivating awareness of a

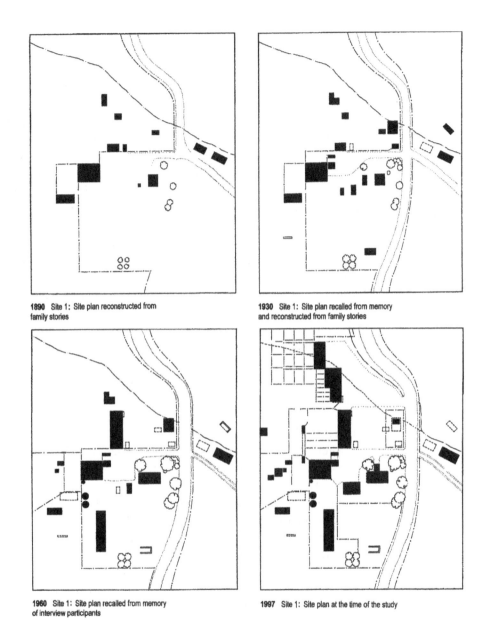

1890 Site 1: Site plan reconstructed from family stories

1930 Site 1: Site plan recalled from memory and reconstructed from family stories

1960 Site 1: Site plan recalled from memory of interview participants

1997 Site 1: Site plan at the time of the study

Figure 7.9 Transformation and continuity of family ranch site plan. Illustration courtesy of Maire O'Neill. Permission courtesy of Wiley.

range of haptic sensibilities, designers can more appropriately consider how insiders really experience place.[52]

Finally, a range of phenomenological research derived from cultural studies and human sciences provides a complementary foundation for research in architecture and design. Earlier in the chapter, a brief mention was made of the contributions of Alfred Schutz, a sociologist and author of the book, *The Phenomenology of the Social World*. His intention was to elucidate the process of intersubjective understanding, and the process by which it is co-constructed. This project, subsequently taken up by Garfunkel, has been termed *ethnomethodology*.[53] In a study by Auburn and Barnes, the authors seek to demonstrate how such an approach can illuminate the intersubjective processes by which place meaning is contested and/or affirmed.[54] Taking the example of in-depth analyses of complaints of transgression by travelers through a rural residential neighborhood in Britain, the authors argue that some phenomenological concepts such as place identity or place attachment focus too exclusively on mentalist interpretations, and potentially minimize the role of a more holistic *action* orientation that accounts for people's *purposes* within the context of others' actions.

Ethnomethodology also highlights an important potential for research that focuses on the processes of design and planning practices. As qualitative researcher Lynn Butler-Kisber observes, a number of professional disciplines are attracted to such an approach because of the focus on *process*, and because it presents an alternative to a more managerial and purely instrumental understanding of knowledge and action in organizational settings.[55]

Though Cuff's study of architectural practice primarily employs ethnography, her study also employs aspects of ethnomethodology. One facet of this is her insistence on the significant role of interpretation both on the part of the respondents and on the part of the researcher. More important, her extensive analysis of crucial meetings within each firm, and with clients, demonstrates her intention to elucidate the processes by which knowledge is negotiated and decisions are made.

With its focus on the process of intersubjective co-construction of meaning and action, ethnomethodology seems to occupy an interstitial conceptual space between ethnography's tendency to emphasize the relative stability of group or organizational culture and much of architectural phenomenology's tendency to foreground the essential meaning of individual subjective experience.

7.3.3   *Grounded Theory*

Similar to the ethnographic and phenomenological traditions, grounded theory seeks to investigate a setting holistically and without preset opinions or notions.

A defining characteristic of the grounded theory approach is its stated aim to identify an explanatory theory as it emerges from the analytical process. Once the theory is proposed, other similar contexts can be studied to see if the emergent theory has explanatory power.

The term *grounded theory* has been particularly associated with the work of sociologists Barney Glaser and Anselm Strauss, who first articulated this approach in the late 1960s and the 1970s.[56] Their aim was to move the then prevailing norms of qualitative research from purely descriptive studies toward explanatory theoretical frameworks.[57] The underlying epistemological assumptions of grounded theory reflect the differing backgrounds of these two authors. While Glaser's background in quantitative empiricism led to codified methods and terminologies, Strauss's background in the more interpretive traditions in sociology led to a focus on the dynamic processes by which people interpret meaning and enact change.[58]

In later refinements of this approach, Strauss and Corbin offered this definition:

> In this method, data collection, analysis, and eventual theory stand in close relationship to one another. A researcher does not begin a project with a preconceived theory in mind (unless his or her purpose is to elaborate and extend existing theory). Rather, the researcher begins with an area of study and allows the theory to emerge from the data. . . . Grounded theories, because they are drawn from data, are likely to offer insight, enhance understanding, and provide a meaningful guide to action.[59]

Grounded theory can be further described in the following ways. First, it depends on an intensive, open-ended, and iterative process that simultaneously involves data collection, coding (data analysis), and memoing (theory building). The diagram in Figure 7.10, developed by Kathy Charmaz, suggests all combinations of iterative sequencing of these three tasks throughout the research process.[60] In explaining this process, Strauss draws a distinction between "grounded theory" research and other qualitative research: "This reexamination of all data throughout the life of the research project is a procedure probably engaged in by most qualitative researchers. But they do not usually double back-and-forth between collecting data, coding them, memoing."[61] In other words, in grounded theory research, it is assumed that the object of study is not fully explained "on the first take"; rather, repeated observation, data collection, and structuring the data into a working explanatory framework are all part of an iterative process that leads to an emergence of a theory.

The significant role of the in-depth coding process entailed in grounded theory is clearly reflected in Donna Wheatley's research on stakeholders' experiential

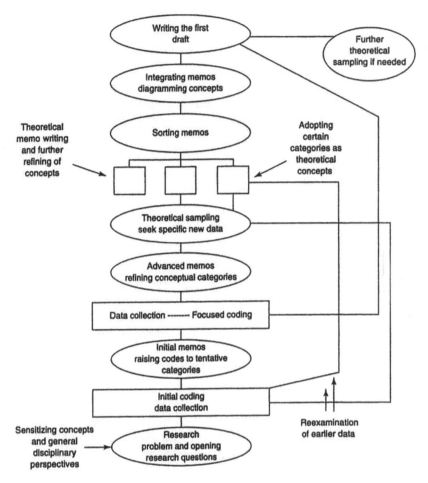

Figure 7.10 The Grounded Theory Process, Charmaz, 2006. Courtesy of SAGE Publications.

interpretations of workplace design. In coding the interview transcripts, Wheatley sought to identify key words that were linked as either environment-response pairs, response-response pairs, and less frequently environment-environment pairs. As the coding process progressed, care was taken to gradually refine the labeling of the underlying constructs inherent in each wording pair (see Figure 7.11). As conceived by Glaser, this analytical process is termed the "constant comparative method of analysis," and is also a defining feature of grounded theory. Wheatley elaborates on her coding process as follows:

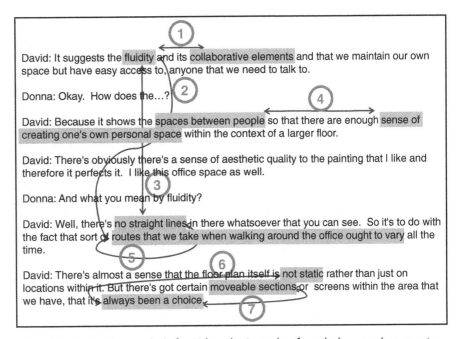

Figure 7.11   Coding analysis for Wheatley's study of workplace environments. Courtesy of Donna Wheatley.

This technique calls upon the researcher to take one piece of data (such as one statement or theme) and compare it to other pieces of data that are either similar or different. During this process, what makes this piece of data different and/or similar to other pieces of data becomes clearer. Due to the data base entry process, the transcripts on which a construct was based could be easily reviewed to check the appropriateness of the construct label refinement.[62]

Another defining feature of grounded theory is the ongoing role of memoing in theory building. As Strauss describes it:

Theoretical ideas are kept track of, and continuously linked and built up by means of *theoretical memos* [author's emphasis]. From time to time they are taken out of the file and examined and sorted, which results in new ideas, thus new memos. . . . *Sorting* [author's emphasis] of memos (and codes) may occur at any phase of the research. Both examination and sorting produce memos of greater scope and conceptual density.[63]

Groat and Ahrentzen's study of women faculty (described in the beginning of this chapter) entailed a substantial and ongoing memoing process as they were interviewing the faculty women participants. The authors routinely wrote and exchanged memos on their preliminary interpretations of the interviews, both to initiate the process of analysis and to guide the development of the remaining interviews (see Figure 7.12).

Finally, the process by which theory emerges within the iterative cycles of data collection, coding, and memoing has led a number of authors to characterize "grounded research" as an *exclusively* inductive process. Strauss, however, disputes this characterization; indeed, he argues that there is essential agreement that all scientific theories "require first of all that they be conceived, then elaborated, then checked out."[64] The terms he applies to this process are *induction* (theory conception), *deduction* (elaboration), and *verification* (checking out). He acknowledges that because he and Glaser attacked the application of speculative (ungrounded)

Perception that Architectural Education Reflects a Narrowing of the Mind. A number of women discuss the narrow focus, perspective, or intellectual inquiry in architectural education. Could these complaints stem from women whose educational background (or part of) was outside standard architectural education, hence they were exposed to other fields (e.g., Urban Studies, Music) that were more multidisciplinary and inclusive? I also wonder if this complaint may be a particular issue for those women whose own education/training was more "transformational," as discussed in the Aisenberg/ Harrington book and also discussed in Belenky et al.'s *Women's Ways of Knowing.* — SA to LG 10/14/92

Attractions, Realities, and Myths of Architecture. The meaning for architecture for women. This is a version of the hypothesis I outlined earlier: whether women architecture students tend to be motivated by more idealistic, socially oriented goals than their male counterparts. If this is the case, the actual realities of architectural education and practice might lead to higher frustration and disappointment, and ultimately to more attrition. Within the context of this study, this hypothesis cannot actually be tested, but it is possible at least to determine the extent to which our sample actually holds idealistically, socially oriented goals for architecture; the extreme frustration and attrition phenomena can not be measured without an extensive sample of deflected women.

In Sherry's discussion of the "narrowing of the field" concern expressed by many women, she speculated that this complaint might be more common among "women whose own education was more transformational." I think this is a good line to follow up. I suspect it may be true and also related to the tendency for women to come to architecture when they are older, i.e. after a broader range of life experiences.—LG to SA 11/2/92

Figure 7.12 Memoing from Groat and Ahrentzen, 1997. Courtesy of Linda N. Groat and Sherry Ahrentzen.

theory, people mistakenly interpreted the work as exclusively inductive. In truth, he suggests that deduction and verification are equally essential.

Over the years since Glaser and Strauss developed the principles of grounded theory, and scholars in a variety of disciplines have adopted this approach, an ironic confluence of trends has emerged. On the one hand, grounded theory has been influential in the development of qualitative research, while on the other, it has since the early 1990s been criticized for its positivistic assumptions. More specifically, in their classic grounded theory research, Glaser and Strauss appear to assume that there is a reality "out there," that theory can be discovered "from data that is separate from the scientific observer."[65] Moreover, grounded theory has frequently been employed by established researchers working from a postpositivist perspective in mixed methods studies[66] (see Chapter 12).

BOX 7.2

A Grounded Theory Approach to Understanding the Culture, Identity, and Teaching Environment of Graduate Design Programs

Deborah Littlejohn's dissertation explores academic culture in the context of great social, technological, and professional change in the practice of graphic and interaction design. It results in a new substantive grounded theory. In essence, her research question is: How do graduate-level design programs anticipate, define, and meet the demands of preparing students for change in the professional and social conditions of practice?

Using grounded theory as the conceptual framework for her inquiry, Littlejohn specifically employed analytic procedures outlined by Charmaz's constructivist perspective on grounded theory, supplemented by a visual mapping procedure known as "situational analysis."[a]

To investigate this question, Littlejohn conducted in-depth, semistructured interviews with 31 key faculty, at 4 leading U.S. graduate design programs, over a 5-month period. Programs were chosen to represent a range of organizational structures common to design schools in the United

[a] A. E. Clarke, *Situational Analysis: Grounded Theory after the Postmodern Turn* (Thousand Oaks, CA: SAGE, 2005); K. Charmaz, *Constructing Grounded Theory: A Practical Guide through Qualitative Analysis* (Thousand Oaks, CA: SAGE, 2006); J. Corbin and A. Strauss, *Basics of Qualitative Research*, 2nd ed. (Thousand Oaks, CA: SAGE, 2008).

(Continued)

States. Supplementary data included extensive on-site observations and a detailed analysis of existing curricular documents. Reflective field notes and situation maps helped Littlejohn unify concepts across the different data sources, enabling a thick, rich depiction of the properties, conditions, and dimensions that emerged in the final grounded theory.

The first step in the analytic process involves initial, open, and focused coding, whereby important ideas and events are identified in the data sources as concrete concepts, and the most significant codes are then used to sort, synthesize, and organize data into more abstract categories. The next step, axial coding, entails exploring the interactions among the developing categories (i.e., the possible conditions that give rise to them, the context in which they are embedded, the strategies that participants employ to manage or carry them out, and the consequences of these strategies). An example of axial coding in this study is external engagement, which ranges along the axis of "pushing out" to "pulling in" (see Figure 7.13). Consequences included "teaching differently," "new kinds of designers," and an "expanded/elevated field." Selective coding is the phase of analysis whereby the core category (transactive integration) is identified and the other major categories (external engagement, mediating meanings, and transparency) are oriented around the core to produce the grounded theory.

The final step of grounded theory entails consulting the literature to support the new theory. In this study, connections are made to extant theories in the areas of geographic pragmatism, affordance theory, situated learning, and activity theory. These domains share a concern with how

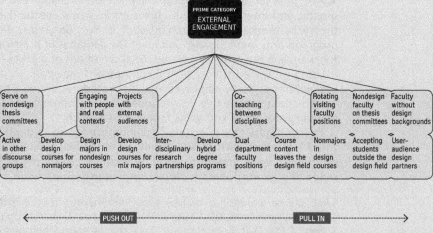

Figure 7.13   Process diagram for "external engagement." Diagram courtesy of Deborah Littlejohn.

individuals and groups learn through social interactions with others and their environment.

The theory that emerged from Littlejohn's research suggests a holistic view of the teaching environment and provides insight into how its design may enable effective responses to the changing conditions in design practice by promoting sense making, engagement, and transformation. The picture of program culture that emerged from the data was that of an interconnected network of social and spatial processes.

Perhaps the most striking finding is the degree to which programs are looking outside of the design field for innovative pedagogic ideas, evidenced by administrative policies that permit hiring faculty and accepting students without design backgrounds and that encourage a wide range of opportunities for both faculty and students to collaborate with peers outside of their program and discipline. The understanding of approaches to teaching new design competencies this study provides can be used to support other programs in the development of guidelines for designing effective instructional settings.

At the same time, many researchers using the qualitative research strategy have moved grounded theory away from its more postpositivist origins. These researchers have taken the prescribed tactics of ground theory (coding, memoing, etc.) and deployed them within constructivist or transformative schools of thought. Charmaz explicitly articulates the more intersubjectivist epistemology typical of many contemporary qualitative researchers:

> I assume that neither data nor theories are discovered. Rather, we are part of the world we study and the data we collect. . . . Research participants' implicit meanings, experiential views—and researchers' finished grounded theories— are constructions of reality.[67]

7.3.4   *Integrative Approaches to Qualitative Research*

The previous discussions of three schools of thoughts—ethnography, phenomenology, and grounded theory—have been presented in their historically situated disciplinary contexts as three relatively distinct research traditions. This perspective is useful in highlighting the defining principles and assumptions of each approach in its own terms.

Taken together, however, these three schools of thought evidence some significant intersections and commonalities. First, *within* each of the three qualitative traditions, noted research studies have been framed within each of the three previously noted systems of inquiry: postpositivist, naturalistic, and transformative. For example, phenomenological studies that seek to understand phenomena "as made up of essences and essential structures which can be identified and described if studied carefully and rigorously enough" could be interpreted as representing "a belief in a knowable world with universal properties," and hence a realist perspective consistent with postpositivism.[68] Similarly, early ethnographic studies aimed to provide "objective" descriptions and analyses of observed, often "native" cultures; and mention has already been made of the more postpositivist background and orientation of one of the originators of grounded theory.

Most recent examples of qualitative research, both across disciplines and within architecture, tend to be framed within either the intersubjective or subjectivist paradigms. For example, O'Neill's phenomenological study of ranch families' experience of place over time is more consistent with an intersubjective approach. Indeed, Finlay argues that many phenomenological studies implicitly accept both the validity of "essential structures" and the multiplicity of different appearances or voices, a position she argues is consistent with Lincoln and Guba's early definition of the naturalist paradigmatic framework (see Chapter 3).[69] Likewise, Cuff's ethnographic study of architectural practice within three firms, and Wheatley's grounded theory approach to understanding the experiential qualities of workplace environments from different stakeholder perspectives are consistent with an intersubjective orientation.

However, Keddy's phenomenologically based study of a hospital surgical unit from the perspective of nursing staff was conceived within an explicitly transformative school of thought. She argues that in order to go beyond the limitations of existing approaches and assumptions in research, she has adopted a poststructuralist feminist perspective. Within this paradigmatic framework, she has proposed the concept of embodied professionalism "as a socio-spatial experience that has definite time, body, people, and spatial components that are interconnected."[70] In essence, Keddy's research is consistent with what Finlay has described as "postphenomenology," which takes into account the "multidimensionality, multistability, and the multiple 'voices'" of phenomena, a perspective that seems to straddle the intersubjective and subjectivist paradigms.[71]

Keddy's study is also representative of a number of research studies that make use of elements from multiple schools of thought. So while Keddy's study is primarily phenomenological, she also integrates ethnography into her work in the form of "institutional ethnography," which was devised by a feminist sociologist, Dorothy Smith, as a way of studying marginalized groups. Smith advocates for beginning with each participant's "working knowledge of her everyday world."[72] From that foundational understanding, the researcher can then knit together the diverse standpoints of women.

Indeed, several noted qualitative researchers have described the tendency in recent research to integrate multiple methodological approaches. For example, Gobo lists an array of recent developments that have emerged from the critical re-evaluation of ethnography's origins, many of which are consistent with the transformative school of thought: feminist ethnography, interpretive ethnography, postmodern ethnography, constitutive ethnography, institutional ethnography, performance ethnography, and global ethnography.[73] Similarly, Charmaz described the emergence of "grounded theory ethnography." She distinguished this line of inquiry as an ethnography that focuses less on the stable structures of a setting (typical of the ethnographic tradition), and more on phenomena, or processes.[74]

7.4   TACTICS: AN OVERVIEW OF DATA COLLECTION, ANALYSIS, AND INTERPRETATION

Taken together, the exemplar studies described in the previous discussions of ethnographic research, phenomenology, and grounded theory represent a diverse range of processes and tactics typical of qualitative research.

7.4.1   *The Process*

In their classic book, *Qualitative Data Analysis*, Miles and Huberman describe the interactive relationship between data collection, data reduction, data display, and conclusion drawing/verifying this way:

> In this view the three types of analysis activity and the activity of data collection itself form an interactive, cyclical process. The researcher moves among these four "nodes" during information gathering/data collection and then shuttles among reduction, display, and conclusion drawing/verifying for the remainder of the study.[75]

Although the vocabulary that Miles and Huberman employ is not typically used by some qualitative approaches—particularly phenomenological studies of the hermeneutical or first-person type—the underlying procedures involved can still be understood loosely in the categories of analysis that Miles and Huberman identify. In the following subsections, we will review the range of possibilities available to qualitative researchers within each of these phases or categories of research processes.

7.4.2   Data Collection

Among the various descriptors of data collection tactics, Creswell offers a particularly handy framework. He identifies four basic types of information: interviews, observations, documents, and audio visual information.[76] Figure 7.14 presents a variation and elaboration of this framework, of course with the assumption that many design and architectural studies will entail objects, buildings, urban environments, and landscapes. In addition, a distinction can be made between interactive versus noninteractive engagement.

For our purposes, the four main categories might be better identified as Interviews and Open-Ended Response Formats, Observations, Artifacts and

Tactics	Interactive	Noninteractive

Interviews & Open-Ended Response Formats	face-to-face or phone in-depth interviews
	
	focus groups
	
	task-oriented formats, e.g.:
	  mapping exercises
	  multiple sorting task
	  projective surveys (games)
		online response to open-ended questions
		
		prompted journaling
		activity logs
		photo logs

Observations	participant observation
	  (research role concealed)
	
	participant observation
	  (research role known)
		nonparticipant observation

Artifacts and Sites	*in situ* observation & analysis of artifacts/ buildings/urban context/ landscape sites	photos, drawings, or virtual representations of artifacts and sites
Archival Documents		public documents audio visual material artifactual or site documentation personal journals, diaries, letters, sketches

Figure 7.14   The variety of data sources for qualitative research. Linda Groat and David Wang, *Architectural Research Methods* (New York, NY: Wiley & Sons, Inc. 2002); and John W. Creswell, *Research Design: Qualitative, Quantitative, and Mixed Methods Approaches* (Thousand Oaks, CA: SAGE, 2009).

Sites, and Archival Documents. Within each of these categories, there is a variety of formats, some of which can also be incorporated within other research designs. Indeed, data collection formats are the subject of entire books. For example, Barbara Czarniawska has written extensively about the increasing use of the narrative format in the social sciences, including oral histories, autobiographical journals, and so on.[77] Similarly, John Zeisel has written an insightful chapter on the observation of physical traces of use and behavior in various environments.[78]

Several of the exemplar studies already discussed in this chapter nicely represent a diverse range of data collection processes. The Wheatley study on stakeholders' experiential interpretations of workplace design made use primarily of in-depth interviews of up to one and a half hours' duration; within the interview format, participants were asked to sort and select images evocative of their experiences of their workplace. Other qualitative studies, such as the Nanta study of rural Thai houses, involved many months of research using multiple data collection tactics, including participant observation, multiple forms of documentation of the house, in-depth videotaped interviews, and interpretation of historical artifacts in the form of temple murals. Keddy's study of nurses' experiential understanding of a surgery unit also employed multiple tactics, including in-depth interviews, behavioral mapping, and observations. Her use of the "experiential collage" to get at participants' deeply held feelings echoes Cooper Marcus' use of role-playing and graphic sketches to uncover people's sense of attachment—or lack thereof—to their houses.[79]

7.4.3 *Data Reduction/Coding*

For readers not already familiar with the qualitative research strategy, the idea that transcripts of in-depth interviews or visual documentation of artifacts must be "reduced" to "data" may seem counterintuitive, or perhaps even an oxymoron. However, in order for research to eventually yield conclusions or theory, at least some categorization of the examined phenomena must be identified or screened out from the rest of the environment being studied. What distinguishes the qualitative strategy from other strategies (e.g., correlational or experimental) is the intention to capture the multifaceted and holistic qualities of the phenomena to the extent possible.

As author Zina O'Leary puts it: "[R]ichness is important, but qualitative analysis involves more than just preserving richness. Good qualitative analysis actually requires you to build it. Put it this way: raw data may be rich, but it is also messy and not publishable."[80] To move from messy data to theoretical interpretations,

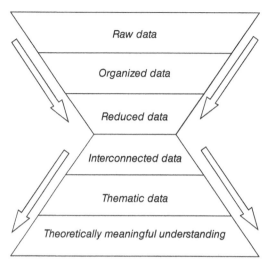

Figure 7.15   Working with qualitative data: drilling in and abstracting out. Courtesy SAGE Publications. Zina O'Leary, *The Essential Guide to Doing Your Research Project* (Thousand Oaks, CA: SAGE, 2010). p. 263, Figure 14.3.

O'Leary identifies the following six steps: (1) raw data; (2) organized data; (3) reduced data; (4) interconnected data; (5) thematic data; and (6) theoretically meaningful understanding. The first three of these entail "drilling in," whereas the latter three involve "abstracting out" (see Figure 7.15). Although this sequence reflects the overall arch of the analysis of qualitative data, this is typically not a linear process, but an iterative one.

In most qualitative research, there are likely to be extensive, sometimes voluminous, verbal or visual materials, in the form of interview transcripts, observational notes, or artifactual documentation. Particularly in the situation of coding interview transcripts, the sheer volume of verbal material can make the coding an arduous task. There is no one way to begin coding and reducing data; however, in order to retain mindfulness in coding, it is often useful not only to make use of a coding scheme, but also to include reflective marginal remarks. As Miles and Huberman put it: "[I]f you are being alert about what you are doing, ideas and reactions to the meaning of what you are seeing will well up steadily."[81]

An excellent example of the coding process is represented in Wheatley's study of office environments, and was described in detail earlier in this chapter's section on grounded theory. A further level of data reduction in Wheatley's study is represented in Figure 7.16. Here, as Wheatley describes it, the database from the

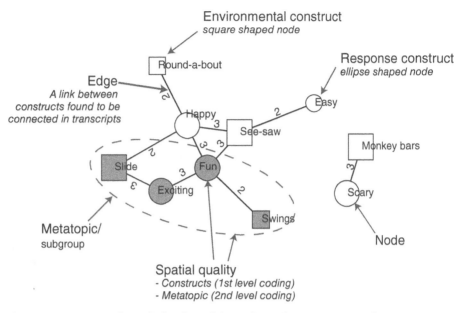

Figure 7.16 Network analysis of participant interviews. Courtesy of Donna Wheatley.

transcript coding for each participant group "was processed into a file that could be read by network analysis applications and visualization software."[82]

However, many researchers employing the qualitative research strategy choose to employ interview coding tactics that do not depend on computer software. For example, O'Neill chose to represent the coding structure of each interview with what is essentially a comparative bar chart (see Figure 7.17). In this case, the predominance of haptic experience for the interviewees is evident, whereas there is a clear difference among the participants with respect to significance of family stories and history.

For research studies in which the detailed documentation of built form and environments is essential, the visual representation of these environments may be extensive. For instance, in Nanta's study of the transformation of vernacular houses, she combined interview data from family members, photography, and floor-plan drawings to produce both an historical reconstruction and contemporary drawing.

Not surprisingly, there are a number of computer programs available for use with qualitative data that can facilitate data storage and management, coding,

248

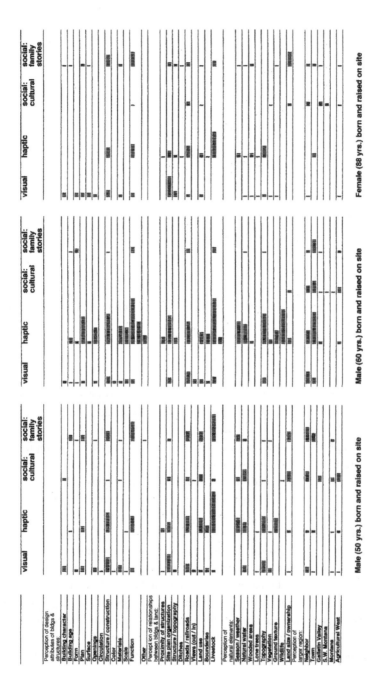

Figure 7.17 Thematic analysis of rancher interviews. Illustration courtesy of Maire O'Neill. Permission courtesy of Wiley.

interpretation, and display. Because these programs are so frequently updated, we have not attempted to identify specific programs and their capabilities.

7.4.4   Data Display

Although most empirical research studies involve some sort of displays, in the form of charts, tables, exemplar visual images, and so on, the qualitative research strategy is likely to include particularly complex textual and visual displays that aim to convey the multifaceted nature of the analysis and conclusions.

Among the studies already mentioned in this chapter, Wheatley's use of network analysis software is both innovative and appropriate to the overall purposes of the research. As Figure 7.18 illustrates, there is a significant contrast in the relative prominence of particular qualities perceived by users at Case 1 as compared to those at Case 2. Even without the color-coding used in the original document, the network diagram of Case 1 reveals that the experience of the social dimension is virtually nonexistent as compared to the aesthetic and physical. In contrast, the users' experience at Case 2 is represented by the prominence of "encouraging interaction" within a balanced constellation of aesthetic and physical attributes. Wheatley's interpretation of the network analyses is further supported by her comparative analysis of the clients' stated aspirational goals for each project as compared to users' interpretations. Whereas the aspirational goals were achieved in the users' experience at Case 2, this was not the case at Case 1.

Another effective data display is Nanta's concluding diagram representing the variety of transformations in the experience of the Thai house. Using a model of place experience that incorporates the intersection of physical attributes, activities, and meanings, Nanta demonstrates how each dimension of experience has shifted over time. In this one diagram, Nanta has integrated and compressed all the data derived from the many diverse sources she employed throughout the course of her research (see Figure 7.19).

7.4.5   Drawing Conclusions and Verifying

Once the data have been coded/reduced and displayed, the researcher gradually moves towards clarifying patterns, providing explanations, and evaluating these findings. This is no small task, and a full discussion of the tactics involved would

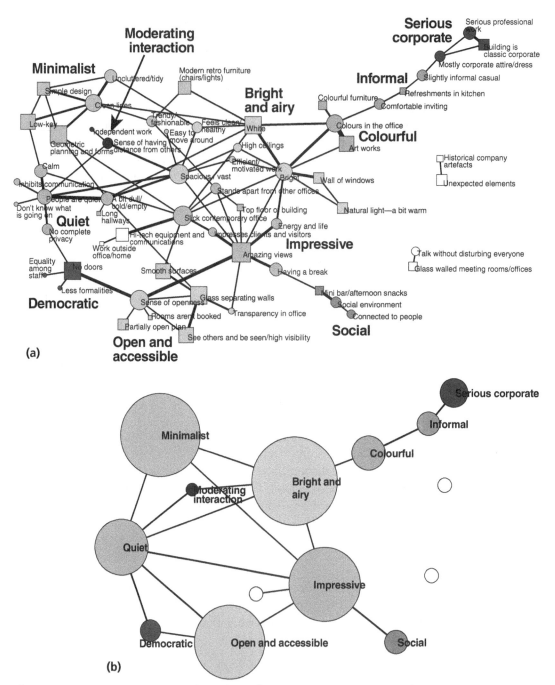

Figure 7.18 Comparative network analysis of users' interviews at Case 1 (7.18a and b) and Case 2 (7.18c and d). Courtesy of Donna Wheatley.

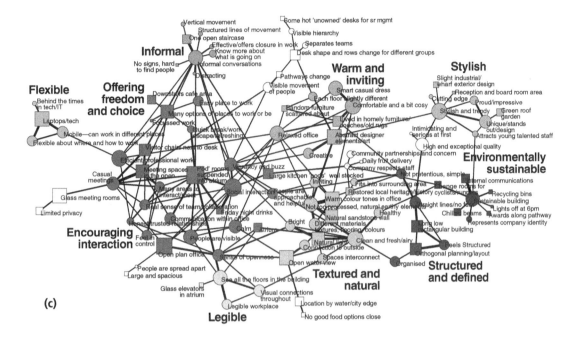

(c)

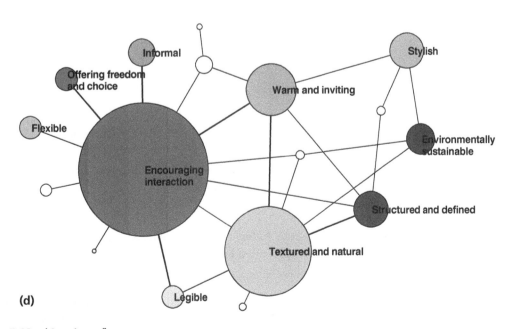

(d)

Figure 7.18 (*Continued*)

Figure 7.19   Model of place experience in the transformation of Thai vernacular dwellings. Courtesy of Piyarat Nanta.

entail too broad a scope to include in this chapter. Figure 7.20 summarizes the major considerations presented by Miles and Huberman in their chapter on the topic.[83] They remind us that:

> We keep the world consistent and predictable by organizing it and interpreting it. The critical question is whether the meanings you find in qualitative data are valid, repeatable, and right.[84]

Data quality	Checking for representativeness
	Checking for researcher effects
	Triangulation
	Weighting the evidence
Looking at unpatterns	Checking the meanings of outliers
	Using extreme cases
	Following up surprises
	Looking for negative evidence
Testing explanations	Making if-then tests
	Ruling out spurious relations
	Replicating a finding
	Checking out rival explanations
Testing with feedback	Getting feedback from informants

Figure 7.20   Testing or confirming findings; Miles and Huberman, 1994. Courtesy of SAGE Publications.

BOX 7.3

Qualitative Tactics for Practice: A Pre-/Post-Occupancy Evaluation

Faced with the need to update its Atlanta office, the architecture firm Perkins + Will came to the decision to move out of an early-20th-century residence that, along with incremental additions, had housed approximately 200 staff (see Figure 7.21). The firm chose to take on the challenge of rehabbing a vacant office building in the same Peachtree St. area where the firm had been located for nearly 30 years (see Figure 7.22). Conceiving of the project as a "living lab" and educational tool, the firm sought to emphasize its commitments to environmental values and sustainability through its LEED (Leadership in Energy and Environmental Design) Platinum status, design excellence, collaborative working strategies, and local community institutions, sharing the ground floor of the building with two civic organizations.

(Continued)

Figure 7.21   Original 1382 Peachtree St. house. Image courtesy of Perkins + Will.

With these purposes in mind, Perkins + Will initiated a Pre-/Post-occupancy Evaluation of the project in 2009, which was concluded in 2012 (see Figure 7.23).[a] The specific goals for the P/POE were identified as:

- Clarification of project parameters to inform performance objectives.
- Evaluation of the performance of the built project in relation to performance objectives.
- Calibration of the design response to increase satisfaction and engagement.
- Compilation of data to establish a knowledge base for future projects.

The P/POE document, published in 2012, describes in explicit detail the methodology employed to measure the impact of the design. To quote from the report:

Six research tactics inform the P/POE: building performance analysis, plan analysis, interviews, web survey, site observations and focus

---

[a] J. Barnes and R. Born, *Perkins+Will 1315 Peachtree Street Pre/Post Occupancy* (Atlanta: Perkins+Will, 2012).

Figure 7.22 New 1315 Peachtree St. office building. Image courtesy of Perkins + Will. © Eduard Hueber/archphoto.

(Continued)

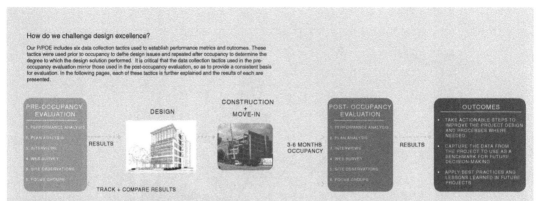

Figure 7.23   Pre-/Postevaluation phases for Peachtree St. office building. Image courtesy of Perkins + Will, 2012.

groups. Each tactic builds on the preceding, resulting in a cumulative understanding of the key issues that the . . . team had to solve. Each tactic is analyzed, a comparison between the pre- and post-occupancy is formed and a final synthesis . . . informs the research conclusions including best practices and actions to take.[b]

Among the several tactics mentioned are three (interviews, observations, and focus groups) that were deployed in a predominantly qualitative manner. For example, the one-on-one interviews covered themes from sustainability, to thought leadership, to celebration. Most interview themes revealed that pre-occupancy goals were successfully achieved in the new building. One area that suggested a need for ongoing attention concerned strategies for "retaining project memory once the moment of collaboration ends."[c]

The site observations were employed to "document and evaluate the actual use and feel of the space, and consider how actual use aligns with planned use."[d] The findings were documented with photography and field notes, revealing the following spatial attributes: sense of place, brand identity, individual work zones, and shared support. Among these, the one attribute that seemed to require fine-tuning was the individual work zones; recommended actions include the development of guidelines for working in an open environment and procedures to reduce the amount of paper storage.

In both the pre- and postevaluation phases, focus groups provided "a relaxed, interactive platform for individuals to share their unique

[b] Ibid., 12.
[c] Ibid., 97.
[d] Ibid., 141.

perspectives and goals. . . .[e] The group conversations produced a number of insights, particularly with respect to the following topics: aesthetics, brand, client focus, collaboration, flexibility, and location. One area that emerged as fruitful to explore is how better to seat project teams to increase interdisciplinary collaboration.

In sum, the combination of the several assessment tactics led to the identification of five major themes: transformative design; sustainable systems, brand experience, high-performance workplace, and interdisciplinary collaboration. This integrative "meta-analysis" underscores the robust and multifaceted nature of the P/POE process in this context.

---

[e] Ibid., 157.

7.5   CONCLUSION: STRENGTHS AND WEAKNESSES

Although there are certainly subtle, but important, differences between the several qualitative schools of thought, their overall strengths and weaknesses are substantially comparable (see Figure 7.24). The major strengths of qualitative research flow from its capacity to take in the rich and holistic qualities of real-life circumstances or settings. It is also inherently more flexible in its design and procedures, allowing adjustments to be made as the research proceeds. As such it is especially appropriate understanding the meanings and processes of people's activities and artifacts.

However, these very significant advantages come with some costs. Not least, researchers wishing to employ a qualitative research design will find relatively few "road maps" or step-by-step guidelines in the literature; the researcher is thus obliged to exercise great care and thoughtfulness throughout the research study.

Strengths	Weaknesses
Capacity to take in rich and holistic qualities of real-life circumstances	Challenge of dealing with vast quantities of data
Flexibility in design and procedures allowing adjustments in process	Few guidelines or step-by-step procedures established
Sensitivity to meanings and processes of artifacts and people's activities	The credibility of qualitative data can be seen as suspect with the postpositivist paradigm

Figure 7.24 Qualitative research strengths and weaknesses.

The second major challenge concerns the vast amount of unstructured data that must be coded or analyzed in some way, a task that is enormously time consuming. It is no exaggeration to say that many researchers spend literally years working through the many facets of their qualitative data. And thirdly, for researchers working in fields where a more rationalistic paradigm holds sway, the "trustworthiness" of qualitative data may remain suspect, despite the efforts of qualitative methodologists to provide systematic alternatives.

In the end, however, the apparent tendency, in fields such as architecture, to give credence to qualitative research through the peer review processes of scholarly journals and conference groups suggests that the role of the qualitative strategy will continue to grow as an important line of research.

NOTES

1. Dana Cuff, *Architecture: The Story of Practice* (Cambridge, MA: MIT Press, 1991).
2. Ibid., 7.
3. Ibid., 6.
4. Donna Wheatley, *Branded Spaces: Mental Mapping of Architectural Design and Experience.* PhD dissertation, University of Sydney, Sydney, Australia, 2010.
5. Ibid., 1.1.
6. Ibid., 3.11–3.14.
7. Ibid., 3.17.
8. Norman Denzin and Yvonna Lincoln, *Strategies for Qualitative Inquiry* (Thousand Oaks, CA: SAGE, 1998), 3.
9. John W. Creswell, *Qualitative Inquiry & Research Design: Choosing among Five Approaches* (Thousand Oaks, CA: SAGE, 2007), 43.
10. Wheatley, 3.4.
11. Linda N. Groat and Sherry Ahrentzen, "Voices for Change in Architectural Education: Seven Facets of Transformation from the Perspectives of Faculty Women," *Journal of Architectural Education* (1997): 273.
12. Denzin and Lincoln, 3.
13. Karen Keddy, *Embodied Professionalism: The Relationship between the Physical Nature of Nursing Work and Nursing Spaces.* PhD dissertation, University of Wisconsin-Milwaukee, Milwaukee, WI, 2006.
14. Karen Keddy, *New Methods of Researching Healthcare Facility Users: The Nursing Workspace.* Paper presented at the Architectural Research Centers Consortium (May 2009), 3.
15. Ibid., 4.
16. Ibid., 7.
17. Cuff, 9.

18. Groat and Ahrentzen, 273.

19. Creswell, 43.

20. Ernest Boyer and Lee Mitgang, *Building Community: A New Future for Architecture Education and Practice* (Princeton, NJ: Carnegie Foundation for the Advancement of Teaching, 1996).

21. Groat and Ahrentzen, 273.

22. Anselm Strauss, *Qualitative Analysis for Social Scientists* (New York: Cambridge University Press, 1987), 11.

23. Gaye Tuchman, "Historical Social Sciences: Methodologies, Methods, and Meanings," in N. Denzin and Y. Lincoln (eds.), *Strategies of Qualitative Inquiry* (Thousand Oaks, CA: SAGE, 1998), 225–260.

24. Ibid., 249.

25. Paul Atkinson and Martyn Hammersley, "Ethnography and Participant Observation," in N. Denzin and Y. Lincoln (eds.), *Strategies of Qualitative Inquiry* (Thousand Oaks, CA: SAGE, 1998), 110–136.

26. Alfred Radcliffe-Brown, as quoted in Giampietro Gobo, "Ethnography," in D. Silverman (ed.), *Qualitative Research: Issues of Theory, Method and Practice*, 3rd ed. (Los Angeles: SAGE, 2011), 18.

27. Atkinson and Hammersley, 111.

28. Gobo, 17.

29. Cuff, 5.

30. Piyarat Nanta, *Social Change and the Thai House: A Study of Transformation in the Traditional Dwelling of Central Thailand.* PhD dissertation, University of Michigan, Ann Arbor, MI, 2009.

31. Ibid., 71–72.

32. Ibid., 78–86.

33. Gobo, 17.

34. Timothy Auburn and Rebecca Barnes, "Producing Place: A Neo-Schutzian Perspective on the 'Psychology of Place,'" *Journal of Environmental Psychology* (2006): 39.

35. Creswell, 59.

36. Thomas Schwandt, *Qualitative Inquiry: A Dictionary of Terms* (Thousand Oaks, CA: SAGE, 1998): 221.

37. Zina O'Leary, *The Essential Guide to Doing Your Research Project* (Thousand Oaks, CA: SAGE, 2010), 120.

38. David Seamon, "A Way of Seeing People and Place: Phenomenology in Environment-Behavior Research," in S. Wapner, J. Demick, T. Yamamoto, and H. Minami (eds.), *Theoretical Perspectives in Environment-Behavior Research* (New York: Plenum, 2000), 157–178.

39. Gaston Bachelard, *The Poetics of Space* (New York: Orion Press, 1964); Edward Relph, *Place and Placelessness* (London: Pion, 1976); Christian Norberg-Schulz, *Genius Loci: Towards a Phenomenology of Architecture* (New York: Rizzoli, 1980); and Thomas Thiis-Evensen, *Archetypes in Architecture* (Oslo: Norwegian University Press, 1990).

40. Seamon, 7.

41. Francis Violich, "Towards Revealing a Sense of Place," in D. Seamon and R. Mugerauer (eds.), *Dwelling, Place and Environment* (Dordrecht, Netherlands: Martinus Nijhoff, 1985), 113–136.
42. Ingrid Stefanovic, "Phenomenological Encounters with Place: Cavtat to Square One," *Journal of Environmental Psychology* (1998): 42.
43. Ibid., 42–43.
44. Schwandt, 223.
45. Linda Groat, "Place, Aesthetic Evaluation and Home," in Linda Groat (ed.), *Giving Places Meaning* (London: Academic Press, 1995), 1–26.
46. David Canter, "Understanding, Assessing and Acting in Places: Is an Integrative Framework Possible?" *Proceedings of the Conference on Environmental Cognition and Assessment* (Umea, Sweden: University of Umea, 1988).
47. Seamon, 9.
48. R. von Eckartsberg, as quoted in Seamon, ibid., 9.
49. Maire O'Neill, "Corporeal Experience: A Haptic Way of Knowing," *Journal of Architectural Education* (2001): 3–12.
50. Ibid., 5.
51. Ibid., 10.
52. Ibid., 11.
53. John Creswell, *Qualitative Inquiry & Research Design: Choosing among Five Approaches* (Thousand Oaks, CA: SAGE, 1998 ed.), 53.
54. Auburn and Barnes, 38–50.
55. Lynn Butler-Kisber, *Qualitative Inquiry: Thematic, Narrative and Arts-Informed Perspectives* (Thousand Oaks, CA: SAGE, 2010), 52.
56. Barney Glaser and Anselm Strauss, *The Discovery of Grounded Theory: Strategies for Qualitative Research* (Chicago: Aldine, 1967); Barney Glaser and Anselm Strauss, *Time for Dying* (Chicago: Aldine, 1968).
57. Kathy Charmaz, *Constructing Grounded Theory: A Practical Guide through Qualitative Analysis* (Thousand Oaks, CA: SAGE, 2006), 6.
58. Ibid., 7.
59. Anselm Strauss and Juliette Corbin, *Basics of Qualitative Research* (Thousand Oaks, CA: SAGE, 1998), 12.
60. Charmaz, 11.
61. Strauss, 19.
62. Wheatley, 3.16.
63. Strauss, 18.
64. Ibid., 11.
65. Charmaz, 10.
66. Ibid., 9.
67. Ibid., 10.
68. Linda Finlay, "Debating Phenomenological Research Methods," *Phenomenology & Practice* (2009): 6–25.

69. Ibid., 16.
70. Keddy, 1.
71. Finlay, 17.
72. Keddy, 55.
73. Gobo, 24.
74. Charmaz, 2.
75. Matthew B. Miles and A. Michael Huberman, *Qualitative Data Analysis*, 2nd ed. (Thousand Oaks, CA: SAGE, 1994).
76. Creswell, 43.
77. Barbara Czarniawska, *A Narrative Approach to Organization Studies* (Thousand Oaks, CA: SAGE, 1998).
78. John Zeisel, "Observing Physical Traces," in *Inquiry by Design* (New York: W. W. Norton, 2006), 159–190.
79. Clare Cooper Marcus, *House as Mirror of Self* (Berkeley, CA: Conari Press, 1995).
80. O'Leary, 263.
81. Miles and Huberman, 67.
82. Wheatley, 3.18.
83. Miles and Huberman, 245–246, 263.
84. Ibid., 245.

Chapter 8

Correlational Research

8.1 INTRODUCTION

During the 1970s William Whyte's study of urban plazas in New York City became a driving force in the development of revised zoning codes regarding commercial high-rises.[1] At the time Whyte and his Street Life Project team began their research, New York City maintained a zoning ordinance by which developers could build more floor space into their buildings if they provided public plaza spaces. Yet many of these plazas were remarkably underutilized, while others seemed to be crowded with workers taking their lunch breaks in seasonable weather.

Whyte wanted to understand why and to suggest guidelines for the design of successful plazas. So, he and his team conducted six months of intensive observations of nearly 20 representative plazas, much of it with the aid of video film and basic people-counting at specified time intervals. Eventually, their charting of plaza use as a function of various plausible physical variables led them to identify the significance of several key design elements (see Figures 8.1, 8.2, 8.3, and 8.4). Chief among them is sitting space, a conclusion that Whyte acknowledges in hindsight should have been obvious, but was not when they first began the study. To support his analysis, Whyte presents charts that compare plaza use (numbers of people at the lunch hour) with the amount of open space available across all 18 plazas; there is no obvious relationship (see Figures 8.1 and 8.2). However, a similar chart comparing plaza use with the amount of sittable space demonstrates a much closer relationship between these two variables (see Figures 8.3 and 8.4).

Although Whyte and his team completed most of their data collection and analysis within about six months, their efforts to influence and modify New York

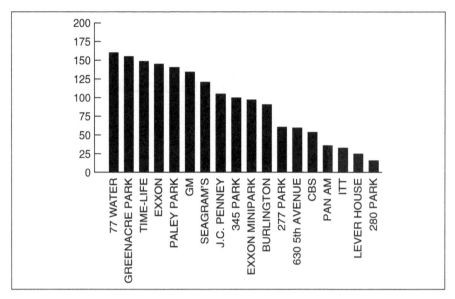

Figure 8.1   Plaza use: average number of people sitting at lunchtime in good weather. Courtesy of Project for Public Spaces, New York, New York.

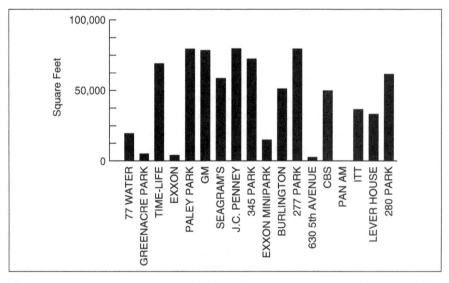

Figure 8.2   Amount of open space by lineal feet. Courtesy of Project for Public Spaces, New York, New York.

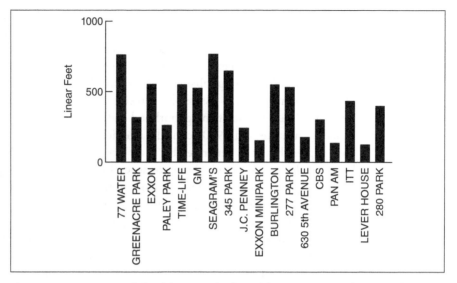

Figure 8.3   Amount of sittable space by lineal feet. Courtesy of Project for Public Spaces, New York, New York.

Figure 8.4   Sittable space at 345 Park Avenue. Courtesy of Project for Public Spaces, New York, New York.

City zoning ordinances took another two or more years. Happily, their proposed guidelines were eventually incorporated into a revised zoning code, with the result that new plazas were built to these guidelines and, just as important, many existing plazas were modified to meet the new zoning code.

In a notable study published in both scholarly and professional journals, Joongsub Kim sought to assess the perceived sense of community among residents of a "New Urbanist" neighborhood and a typical suburban development.[2] Indeed, since the mid-1980s considerable debate within both the professional and lay press has been generated by "New Urbanist" or "Neo-Traditional" neighborhood design. Although there are several variants to this approach, author Todd Bressi offers a general definition of this trend.[3] According to him, an underlying premise of New Urbanism is that "community planning and design must assert the importance of public over private values,"[4] or in other words, an enhanced sense of community. Among the several specific goals that New Urbanists seek to foster through design are social interaction and a greater sense of neighborhood attachment and identity, achieved in part through a more pedestrian-friendly layout.

To assess the extent to which these civic qualities are experienced in a New Urbanist community, Kim studied residents' reactions to their neighborhood both in Kentlands (a recently developed New Urbanist community in Gaithersburg, Maryland) and in a typical suburban neighborhood, comparable in demographic characteristics and located in the same town (see Figures 8.5, 8.6, 8.7, and 8.8).[5]

The principal tactic he employed was an extensive survey questionnaire that was distributed to every household in the two neighborhoods. In addition to some demographic and overview questions, Kim asked each resident to assess the extent to which specific physical features of the design facilitated their experience of the four key components of community identified in the literature: community attachment, pedestrianism, social interaction, and community identity. A 5-point scale from "not at all" to "very much" was used to measure residents' responses.

The results of Kim's research indicate that the Kentlands' residents consistently rated their community as promoting higher degrees of all four measures of sense of community. And within Kentlands, there was a relatively higher rating of these four components of community among the single-family house and townhomes residents. But even Kentlands apartment dwellers expressed a slightly greater sense of community than the suburban group's single-family house residents. Kim thus concludes that the relative success of the Kentlands community suggests that New Urbanist theory and practice deserve continued development and refinement.

Figure 8.5   A Kentlands street and park. Courtesy of Joongsub Kim.

Figure 8.6   A Kentlands street with no visible edges. Courtesy of Joongsub Kim.

Figure 8.7   Orchard Village housing. Courtesy of Joongsub Kim.

Figure 8.8   Orchard Village with typical street-access garages. Courtesy of Joongsub Kim.

8.2   THE STRATEGY OF CORRELATIONAL RESEARCH:
        GENERAL CHARACTERISTICS

The research strategy common to both the Whyte and the Kim studies is that of correlational research. Broadly speaking, each study sought to clarify patterns of relationships between two or more variables, that is, factors involved in the circumstances under study. Although details of two subtypes of the correlational strategy will be discussed in detail in section 8.3, it is useful first to clarify the overall characteristics of this research design. In the following subsections, we will review the following general characteristics: a focus on naturally occurring patterns; the measurement of specific variables; and the use of statistics to clarify patterns of relationships.

8.2.1   A Focus on Naturally Occurring Patterns

Both the Whyte and Kim studies sought to understand naturally occurring patterns of socio-physical relationships. For example, Whyte sought to understand the behavioral dynamics of plaza use, and in particular what physical features would encourage their use. Similarly, Kim sought to understand the patterns of relationship between the distinctly different physical attributes of two residential neighborhoods and the residents' behavior (pedestrianism, social interaction) and perceived meanings (attachment, identity).

In both cases, the researchers wanted to clarify the relationship among a complex set of real-world variables. By *variables* we mean the range of characteristics (of physical features, of people, of activities, or of meanings) that vary within the circumstance being studied and are also likely to affect the dynamics of socio-physical interaction. In its focus on real-world circumstances, correlational design is distinct from experimental design, the research strategy that will be discussed in Chapter 9. Whereas correlational design assumes that the researcher simply measures the variables of interest and analyzes the relations among them, experimental design depends on the researcher's active intervention in the form of a "treatment." (See Chapter 9 for details.)

8.2.2   The Measurement of Specific Variables

Second, both the Whyte and Kim studies focus on specific variables of interest that can be measured and quantified in some way. In this, correlational design is distinct from qualitative design. Although both strategies focus on naturally occurring patterns, qualitative research is more attentive to the holistic qualities of phenomena (see Chapter 7). As is typical for a correlational design, the researchers in Whyte's study employed a number of observational tactics whereby the sheer numbers of people or their specific behaviors could be counted. Thus, Whyte's data documented exactly how many people were using a given plaza at particular times throughout the lunch hour. And once he identified "sittable space" as a key physical feature, he and his team could measure such attributes as the total lineal feet of sitting space, and its various dimensions.

In other instances of correlational research, however, the focus may be less on observable behaviors but on people's attitudes, ascribed meanings, or even their perceptions of others' behavior. Such is the case with Kim's use of a survey questionnaire in the New Urbanist and typical suburban neighborhoods.[6] Kim sought to measure the extent to which the patterns of residents' perceived sense of community might differ between the two neighborhoods.

Although on a superficial level the notion of measurement may seem to be a rather straightforward proposition, this is not necessarily the case. Researchers using the correlational research design must decide on and understand the implications of using different levels of measurement precision, including categorical, ordinal, interval, and ratio. (Although we will define these terms briefly here, readers who seek a more detailed discussion should refer to some of the works cited in the chapter endnotes.)

Categorical Measurement. This term simply indicates that the variable of interest is sorted into discrete categories, based on verbal or nominal terms. In Kim's study many of the demographic questions are based on nominal or categorical measurement. For example, one survey question asked residents what mode of transportation they used to get to work, and the categories provided for the answers were walk, car, metrobus, metrotrain, other, and not applicable (for those who worked in the home). Similarly, in Whyte's study, if he were concerned with specifying the kind of activities people were engaged in, the researchers' observations might include the categories sitting, standing, and walking.

Ordinal Scales. Ordinal measurement provides a greater degree of measurement precision than nominal classification in that the variable in question can be *ordered* on some basis. In Kim's survey, for instance, other demographic questions provide a set of ordered categories. This is the case with a question about household income; six separate income categories from (1) under $40,000 to (6) $150,000 or more are provided. Similarly, in a study of architects and nonarchitects' responses to a stylistic variety of buildings, Groat asked respondents to rank-order the 24 building photographs according to their personal preference.[7] In this case, although the results reveal an order of preference, no assumptions about the interval of difference between one building and another can be made. Indeed, it is possible that the top two or three buildings might be highly preferred, while the next building in order might be much less liked.

Interval and Ratio Scales. A more precise measure still is one that specifies the exact distances (or intervals) between one measurement and another. Any system that relies on an established and consistent unit of measurement—whether it is dollars, feet, or degrees of temperature—satisfies the criterion of an interval scale.

However, the validity of measuring attitudes and feelings on an interval scale is a topic of much discussion and some disagreement.[8] In the case of Kim's questionnaire, we might ask if it is legitimate to assume that respondents using the 5-point scale—from very important (5) to not at all (1)—are employing a consistent increment of difference between responses of 4 versus 5 or 3 versus 4. If we assume that they are not employing a consistent interval of difference, then the attitudinal scale is, in fact, functioning as an ordinal measurement.

A further level of measurement precision is achieved with a ratio scale, whereby an absolute zero point on the scale can be established. This means that something that measures 20 on a ratio scale is legitimately understood as constituting twice the quantity of 10. In practical terms, there are few interval scales that are not also ratio scales, but one exception is that of temperature. Indeed, we cannot claim that 72 degrees is twice as hot as 36 degrees. However, we can assume consistent measuring intervals; the difference between 5 and 10 degrees is the same as the difference between 20 and 25 degrees.[9]

These distinctions among types of measurement precision frequently come into play in correlational research because so many variables—from demographic characteristics, to attitudes and behaviors, to physical properties—must be measured. And because different variables lend themselves to varying levels of measurement precision, great attention is paid to establishing legitimate data collection instruments and appropriate modes of quantitative analysis.

8.2.3 *The Use of Statistics to Clarify Patterns of Relationships*

Another characteristic common to both the Whyte and Kim studies is their use of statistical measures to describe the relationships among variables. In his book, *The Social Life of Small Urban Spaces*, Whyte relies primarily on graphic charts to represent visually the use patterns of the plazas he studied. For example, Figure 8.1 shows the average number of people using each of 18 plazas in good weather; and we can see, for example, that the most used plaza averages around eight times more people than the least used. This use of statistics is called *descriptive* statistics because it simply presents, or describes, important relationships among variables.

Kim's study of residential developments employs, in addition to basic descriptive statistics, what are called correlational statistics. These statistical measures are used to describe "the magnitude of the relationship between two variables."[10] For example, Kim presents the calculated correlations among all four of the measures of community, both for Kentlands and for Orchard Village (a pseudonym for the typical suburban development) (see Figure 8.9). As it turns out, all four measures of community are highly and positively correlated with each other, for each neighborhood development. So, for example, the Kentlands' ratings of the effect of various physical features on their sense of attachment have a similar pattern to their ratings for social interaction, and so on. In other words, in the perception of the residents, the role of the various physical features in achieving a sense of attachment, pedestrianism, social interaction, and sense of identity are quite similar. However, if the pattern of ratings on any two measures had been quite different, it would have been described as a negative correlation. All calculated correlation coefficients are indicated within a range of –1.00 (a negative correlation) to +1.00 (a positive correlation); and a correlation coefficient close to 0 indicates virtually no consistent relationship between variables.

8.3   STRATEGY: TWO TYPES OF CORRELATIONAL RESEARCH

Within the general framework of correlational research, as described in the previous section, two major subtypes can be identified: (1) relationship and (2) causal comparative.[11] While a number of research studies can be characterized as representing just one subtype, other correlational studies are multifaceted,

Relationship among Q1, Q2, Q4, Q7
(Orchard Village in parentheses)

Four Major Elements (K: based on 17 items only)
Q1: Community attachments
Q2: Pedestrianism
Q4: Social interaction
Q7: Community identity

	Q1 mean	Q2 mean	Q4 mean	Q7 mean
Q1 mean	1.000	.605 (.579)	.481 (.517)	.594 (.654)
Q2 mean	.605 (.579)	1.000	.639 (.662)	.514 (.530)
Q4 mean	.481 (.517)	.639 (.662)	1.000	.419 (.575)
Q7 mean	.594 (.654)	.514 (.530)	.491 (.575)	1.000

Findings:
Kentlands: Correlation is significant at the 0.01 level
Orchard Village: Correlation is significant at the 0.01 level

Figure 8.9 Relationship among questionnaire components. Courtesy of Joongsub Kim.

and as a consequence incorporate both of these subtypes. In the following paragraphs, we will describe and analyze examples of both relationship and causal comparative research.

8.3.1   Relationship Studies

Although all correlational studies, by definition, seek to describe the relationship between or among key variables, the term *relationship* study is meant to distinguish those studies—or components of larger studies—that focus specifically on both the nature and the potentially predictive power of those relationships.

A good example of an influential research study that sought to clarify relationships and predict outcomes is Oscar Newman's study of public housing in New York City, mentioned in Chapter 4.[12] To arrive at specific design guidelines for such housing, Newman's research team conducted an exhaustive investigation of the complex relationships between user demographics (including income and other socioeconomic factors), the physical variables of the housing/site design, and the incidence of crime. Newman's team examined the extensive existing records of the 169 public housing projects managed by the New York City Housing Authority. As Newman explains, this vast amount of data, combined with the immense variety of building types and site plans, made it possible to "determine exactly where the most dangerous areas of buildings are, as well as to compare crime rates in different building types and project layouts."[13]

As a consequence of this extensive analysis of these multiple variables, Newman and his team were able to identify consistent relationships and ultimately to propose a theory of "defensible space." Newman has defined the concept of defensible space as

> a model for residential environments which inhibits crime by creating the physical expression of a social fabric that defends itself.... [It] is a surrogate term for the range of mechanisms—real and symbolic barriers, strongly defined areas of influence, and improved opportunities for surveillance—that combine to bring an environment under the control of its residents.[14]

Not only does this theory of defensible space define a relationship between environmental variables and behavioral consequences (a decrease in crime), but it also offers a predictive capacity that can be articulated as design guidelines, specifically low-income housing that incorporates "real and symbolic barriers, defined areas of influence, and opportunities for surveillance" will be more likely to have lower crime rates (see Figure 8.10).

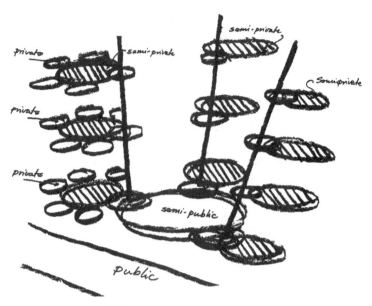

Figure 8.10 Newman's defensible space hierarchy in multilevel dwelling.
Courtesy of Oscar Newman.

Similarly, in the case of Whyte's study, he concludes that higher levels of plaza utilization are associated with the combined presence of several variables, including sittable space, proximity to street life, sun, water/fountains, trees, and availability of food from street vendors or cafes. Notice that Whyte (like other researchers employing correlational research) stops short of saying that sittable space causes plaza utilization. Indeed, there may well be hidden or intervening third factors (such the experience of sociability) that explain the correlations Whyte found. Indeed, many high correlations—for example, between the number of ice cream cones consumed and deaths by drowning—can be explained by hidden third factors, in this case hot weather.[15]

However, although Whyte does not attribute direct cause, his research does enable him to *predict* the association of certain key variables (i.e., sittable space, proximity to street life) with higher levels of plaza use. Despite the lack of causal attribution, the predictive accuracy of Whyte's work is the foundation for providing design guidelines that were eventually embedded in new zoning codes and used by many architects and landscape architects.

Likewise, Kim seeks to understand and predict the relationship among the various component measures of community. As the correlations described in section 8.2 indicate, the patterns of ratings for each of the four measures of community are predictive of each other. With a similar goal in mind, Kim also asked residents of each neighborhood development two overall questions about their sense of community. He first asked respondents to give their rating for "Living in Kentlands (or Orchard Village) gives me a sense of community." The second sought their rating for "The physical characteristics of Kentlands (or OV) give me a sense of community." Kim found that the answers to these two global questions were highly correlated with the ratings for each of the four component measures of community. In other words, the respondents' overall assessment of sense of community is predictive of their assessment of physical features for each separate component of community, and vice versa.

Finally, Kim assessed the strength of the correlations he found by using a test of statistical significance. Without going into great detail at this point, it is important to explain simply that such statistical tests—known by the general term *inferential statistics*—enable a researcher to determine how likely it is that the results are a consequence of a chance occurrence. In Kim's case, the correlations were found to be significant at the .01 level, meaning that there is only a 1 in 100 chance that the overall assessment of community is unrelated to the component measures.

8.3.2   *Causal Comparative Studies*

Causal comparative studies represent a type of correlational research that stakes out an intermediate position between the predictive orientation of relationship studies and the focus on causality that characterizes experimental research. In causal comparative studies, the researcher selects comparable groups of people or comparable physical environments and then collects data on a variety of relevant variables. The purpose of selecting comparable examples is to isolate the plausible relevant factor(s) that could reveal a "cause" for significant differences in the levels of measured variables.

Kim's study of Kentlands and Orchard Village serves as a good example of a causal comparative study. Although he was certainly interested in studying the relationships among variables (such as the predictive relationship between overall and component measures of sense of community), his primary purpose was to determine the extent to which the differences in the physical characteristics of Kentlands vs. Orchard Village might contribute to differences in the residents' perception of sense of community. Kim is, in effect, conceptualizing the multiple physical features of each neighborhood as independent variables and the residents' perceived sense of community as a dependent variable. In this regard, the research design has much in common with the experimental research strategy, in that the researcher is seeking to ascribe causal power to a variable (or set of variables) for the measured outcome.

However—and this is crucial—the causal comparative design can only ascribe cause in a provisional or hypothetical way. This is because causal comparative research (such as Kim's study) relies on studying naturally occurring variables (see section 8.2), as do all correlational studies. This is in direct contrast to experimental research (see Chapter 9), which characteristically involves a "treatment," which is an independent variable that is manipulated by the researcher. As a consequence, the causal comparative design depends on establishing the essential comparability between two examples that differ only in terms of the variable(s) to which cause can be ascribed. Unfortunately, there are many possible shortcomings in establishing the equivalence of the comparable examples/groups.

In the case of Kim's study of two housing developments, it is difficult to establish beyond doubt that the Kentlands and Orchard Village residents moved into their neighborhoods with equivalent attitudes towards sense of community. Indeed, a case could be made that future Kentlands residents were enticed to move there precisely because they already had a greater disposition toward community-oriented living; if that were the case, the higher levels of sense of community measured in Kentlands, as compared to Orchard Village, are simply a consequence of those initial attitudes. To counter such an argument, Kim can point to data gained from qualitative in-depth interviews and activity logs that suggest at least some residents either (1) changed their transportation patterns by walking more once they moved to Kentlands, and/or (2) became more socially interactive after living in Kentlands for some time. Even so, such a causal comparative study can only point to possible causation; it cannot establish cause with the same degree of rigor associated with experimental designs.

Similarly, Oscar Newman sought to bolster his study of New York City public housing by including a causal comparative component in his overall research design. Thus, Newman's team conducted in-depth analyses of housing project pairs, comparable in virtually every respect except the physical design variables. Newman's rationale for this is quite clear (see Figures 8.11 through 8.13).

A fair test of hypotheses concerning the impact of the physical environment on crime therefore requires comparison of communities in which the social characteristics of the population are as constant as possible—where the only variation is the physical form of the buildings.[16]

Although Newman argues as a consequence of the causal comparison study that the physical design unmistakably contributes to measured differences in crime rate between the two projects, he also acknowledges that his data cannot provide "final and definitive proof" of the effects of physical design.[17] In fact, Newman suggests that the negative image of criminal behavior in Van Dyke Houses (the design *without* defensible space) contributed to the police department's pessimism about the value of their presence, a factor which in and of itself could contribute to the

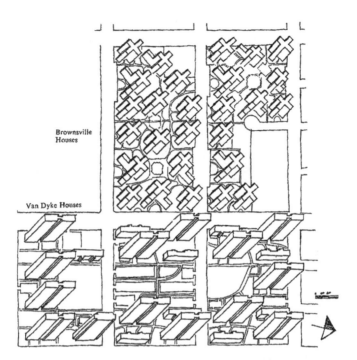

Figure 8.11 Plans of Brownsville and Van Dyke houses. Courtesy of Oscar Newman.

Figure 8.12 Van Dyke houses. Courtesy of Oscar Newman.

Figure 8.13   Brownsville houses. Courtesy of Oscar Newman.

recorded higher crime levels there. Thus, like Kim, Newman can point to cause in the form of physical variables (a strength of the research design), but cannot establish it beyond doubt (a weakness of the design).

8.4   TACTICS: COLLECTING DATA

Our intent in this discussion of tactics is to present a wide range of examples of data collection and analyses commonly used within a correlational research design. Four important issues relevant to this discussion are essential to acknowledge at the outset. First, because the range of both data collection and analyses is vast, we can only cite a few of the most common examples in the context of a single chapter. Second, a number of data collection tactics are frequently employed in other research designs as well; for example, observational techniques are common to qualitative research as well as to correlational research. And third, virtually every one of the tactics discussed here is likely to be the subject of entire chapters or even books. To provide readers with an entry point to these more focused sources, we will provide key excerpts and the relevant citations, so that interested readers can pursue whichever of these topics seem particularly relevant to their work.

The fourth issue signals a vitally important consideration that must be addressed prior to any data collection for correlational research: sampling. On what basis does the researcher decide how many and which residents to interview about their satisfaction with a new building project in their city? Or how many and which museum visitors should be observed for their choice of route through a new exhibit area? Although sampling is also a significant issue in other research strategies, it is often a more significant issue for correlational research because the goal of many correlational studies is to predict as accurately as possible the response or behavior of a large group of people, based on the patterns established among a smaller subset (i.e., sample) of that group.

This principle of prediction from a sample of respondents is particularly familiar to most of us during election campaign seasons, or in discussion of commercial product development. During election season, poll results that predict election outcomes are based on surveys of a sample of likely voters, numbering perhaps a few hundred or several thousand. Similarly, manufacturers test out their products—whether vacuum cleaners or toothpaste—on a small sample of consumers with the hope that they can predict the ultimate success of their product. In architecture, a designer might be interested in sampling users of a new workstation configuration before recommending that the same configuration be introduced on the other floors about to be renovated.

Within the vast literature on sampling, the most important distinction of concern to the researcher is that between a *probabilistic* and *nonprobabilistic* sample. The goal of probabilistic sampling is to achieve a sample that is truly representative of the larger population. In practical terms, this usually means some form of *random* sampling (that can be achieved through a variety of procedural mechanisms), whereby each item or member of the population has an equal chance of being observed or interviewed. As a consequence, it is then possible to use inferential statistics to determine how likely it is that the results are a function of chance. Typically, researchers consider the .05 level of significance (i.e., a 5% likelihood of a chance occurrence) to be the minimum standard for generalization to a larger population. (See section 8.3.1 for additional discussion of inferential statistics.) Readers who wish to make use of a probabilistic sampling procedure and to use inferential statistics to gauge their results should refer to some of the vast number of texts on this topic; several are listed among the notes at the end of this chapter.

In a nonprobabilistic, or *purposive* sample, the researcher is less concerned about generalizing to the larger population and more concerned about discovering useful patterns of information about particular groups or subsets of the population. For example, the architect of the office building renovation (described earler) might find it more valuable to interview only those workers who had previously registered complaints about the new workstation. In this case, the architect is making a choice to discover the particular sources of dissatisfaction in the workstation design rather than to simply seek an overall level of satisfaction that fulfills the owner's general requirements for employee satisfaction. (Again, there are a variety of procedural mechanisms for deriving such samples; interested readers should review some of the focused texts on the subject.)

With the previous discussion of sampling as a prelude, we can now turn to the variety of ways in which a researcher might collect data for a correlational study. The range of data collection tactics discussed in this section is intended to introduce the beginning researcher to a broad range of techniques. In addition, architectural practitioners will also find this discussion of great value for deriving critical information from clients, users, and other individuals involved in and affected by the design process.

8.4.1 Surveys

Among the variety of data collection tactics for correlational research, the survey questionnaire is perhaps the most frequently employed. Indeed, it is so ubiquitous and well established that the term *survey research* is sometimes regarded as essentially equivalent to the term *correlational research*. Our position, however, is that the survey questionnaire is just one (although perhaps the most popular) of many possible data collection devices available for the correlational research design.

The great advantage of survey questionnaires is that they enable the researcher to cover an extensive amount of information—from demographic characteristics, to behavioral habits, to opinions or attitudes on a variety of topics—across a large number of people in a limited amount of time. The consequent disadvantage, however, is that achieving this breadth of information usually comes at the cost of in-depth understanding of the issues surveyed. For instance, depth of understanding is more likely to be achieved through a qualitative research strategy. (See Chapter 7 for more on qualitative research.) Nevertheless, the long-standing popularity of the survey tactic stands as a testimony to its usefulness in many circumstances.

Joongsub Kim's study of New Urbanism (to which we referred earlier in the chapter) represents a good example of the use of the survey as a tool to gather broad—rather than in-depth—information.[18] Kim selected the survey as a tactic precisely because he wanted to compare the residents' *overall* assessments of the "sense of community," as achieved in a New Urbanist development and a typical suburban development. Within this overall goal, Kim also wanted to find out the extent to which a variety of specific design features contributed to this sense of community. As a consequence of his extensive literature review (see Chapter 5 for more on literature reviews), Kim determined that the notion of sense of community could be understood as having four relatively distinct components: sense of attachment, social interaction, pedestrianism, and sense of identity. Thus the bulk of his questionnaire asked the residents to rate the extent to which a set of design features (1–17) affected each of the four components of community (see Figure 8.14).

Additionally, Kim posed a number of demographic questions to each of the neighborhood's residents. The set of demographic questions achieved at least two purposes. First, it helped Kim establish the extent to which the populations of the neighborhoods were essentially equivalent; and, in fact, the two communities are quite similar in almost all demographic measures. Second, Kim sought to assess the extent to which key subgroups (i.e., residents of different housing types) responded differently to the four measures of community. As it turns out, single-family home and town-home residents indicate a higher level of sense of community than apartment and condominium residents. (See Figure 8.15 for a list of key issues a researcher must address in developing a survey questionnaire.)

Orchard Village Study

1. How important are these features to your feeling of attachment to Orchard Village

FEATURES of Orchard Village	very important	moderately important	some-what	minimally important	not at all
Residential density	(5)	(4)	(3)	(2)	(1)
Wetlands, public greens, tot lots, footpaths	(5)	(4)	(3)	(2)	(1)
Distance between sidewalks and houses	(5)	(4)	(3)	(2)	(1)
Architectural style	(5)	(4)	(3)	(2)	(1)
Block size	(5)	(4)	(3)	(2)	(1)
Club House-Recreation Complex	(5)	(4)	(3)	(2)	(1)
Overall layout of Washingtonian Woods	(5)	(4)	(3)	(2)	(1)
Street trees and other street landscaping	(5)	(4)	(3)	(2)	(1)
Overall size of Washingtonian Woods	(5)	(4)	(3)	(2)	(1)
Arrangement of houses on the block	(5)	(4)	(3)	(2)	(1)
Street width	(5)	(4)	(3)	(2)	(1)
Garage location	(5)	(4)	(3)	(2)	(1)
Onstreet parking	(5)	(4)	(3)	(2)	(1)
Lot size	(5)	(4)	(3)	(2)	(1)
Mixture of housing types	(5)	(4)	(3)	(2)	(1)
Overall design quality of housing	(5)	(4)	(3)	(2)	(1)
Street layout	(5)	(4)	(3)	(2)	(1)

Figure 8.14 Questionnaire segment of sense of community. Courtesy of Joongsub Kim.

General Considerations	Examples of New Urbanist Research

1. <u>Goals</u>
Determine main topics to be covered
 	
Clarify the purpose of each question
	Kim's topics were:
	    overall sense of community
	    4 components of community
	    demographic characteristics

2. <u>Response Formats</u>
Evaluate advantages of closed vs.
    open-ended format
	Sense of community questions used
	    5-pt. closed scale
	Demographic questions used combination
	    of closed and open formats

3. <u>Clarity in Phrasing the Questions</u>
Use short sentences
Avoid making 2 queries in a single question
Avoid framing questions in the negative (not, never)
Avoid using ambiguous wording
Employ non-threatening language
	Reviewed question design with others
	    knowledgeable in research and the
	    respondent sample
	
	Piloted questionnaire with respondents

4. <u>Question Order</u> Use logical sequence of topics Start with interesting, nonchallenging issues Don't place important items at end of long survey	Survey starts with sense of community questions Full page demographic questions last
5. <u>Format</u> Use appealing, but simple graphics Avoid prominent or flashy design	Simple, understated graphics Though long, did not appear dense
6. <u>Instructions</u> Explain reason, context for survey Provide description(s) of what respondents expected to do Explain where respondents turn in survey	Introductory explanation provided Surveys were hand-delivered Provision for return mailing

7. <u>Ethics</u>
State provisions for keeping individual
    responses confidential
	Statement of confidentiality provided
	Survey submitted to university human
	    subjects review board

Figure 8.15 Considerations in the design of a survey questionnaire. First column adapted from D. Mertens, *Research Methods in Education and Psychology,* SAGE Publications, 1998, pp. 115-117. Reprinted by permission of SAGE Publications.

BOX 8.1
Survey Tactics for Practice

As described in Chapter 7 (see Box. 7.3), the architecture firm Perkins + Will conducted a three-year pre-/post-occupancy evaluation on their move from their existing office space to a 1986 derelict office building which they rehabbed. In Box 7.3, we discussed their extensive use of various qualitative tactics within the P/POE. Here we focus on their use of a Web survey, a tactic that enabled the firm to solicit opinions from a large cross-section of perspectives around focused questions.[a] The particulars of the survey are described as follows in the P/POE report:

In both the pre- and post-occupancy evaluation, an electronic survey was delivered to each of the employees in the Atlanta office. The questions in each survey were parallel to allow for comparative analysis, and the format of the questions included scales, ranking, and space for free-form responses. The questions addressed a range of topics, including the following:

- Overall Workstation Comfort
- Meeting Rooms
- Supporting Clients
- Brand Communication
- General Experience
- Change Management

Among these several topics, there was general appreciation of the improvements in supporting clients and brand communication. One post-occupancy outcome that prompted organizational learning is the importance of structured change management even when the users are experts in the area. This insight has now been incorporated into the firm's larger workplace strategy because it's a common issue among most clients. An area of primary concern for many respondents had to do with particular features of the individual workstation environments. Features that achieved increased and decreased levels of satisfaction are presented in Figure 8.16.

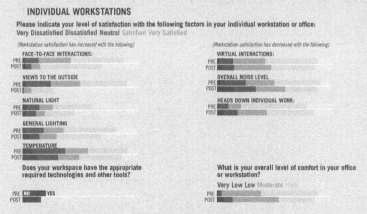

Figure 8.16 Web survey results of pre-/post-occupancy evaluation. Image courtesy of Perkins + Will, 2012.

[a] J. Barnes and R. Burn, *Perkins + Will 1315 Peachtree Street Pre/Post-Occupancy* (Atlanta: Perkins + Will, 2012).

8.4.2   *Observations*

Various forms of observation represent another frequently used set of tactics for data collection. As the earlier discussion of William Whyte's study of urban plazas indicated, Whyte's primary tactic was time-lapse film.[19] At each plaza a camera was placed in a location that enabled filming of the pedestrian areas, usually from a second- or third-story window, or terrace perch. In an extensive appendix section to his book, Whyte describes, in much and useful detail, the equipment and procedures used in the plaza study. Perhaps the most insightful section deals with the question of figuring out what to look for. Indeed, the process of establishing the appropriate coding categories for activities recorded on film can be a painstaking task. However, the great advantage of observation tactics is that even a "simple" numbers count, such as represented in a day in the life of the ledge at Seagram's (see Figure 8.17), can provide a detailed and powerful view of the human ecology of a particular setting. Combined with other similar graphic and pictorial analyses, Whyte's research led directly to numerous design modifications and the revision of New York City's zoning regulations.

Whyte's study represents a common application of observational tactics in architectural and design research in two respects: (1) the observed behavior is in a relatively accessible public environment; and (2) the size of each plaza is largely visible from a

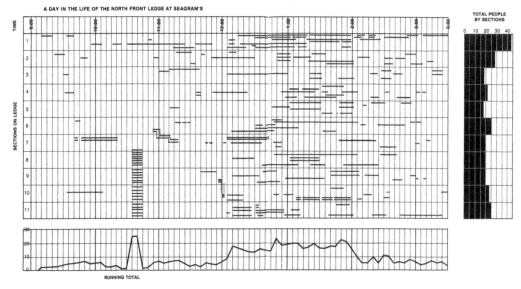

Figure 8.17   A day in the life of the north front edge at Seagram's. Courtesy of Project for Public Spaces, New York, New York.

BOX 8.2

Tactics for Correlational Research: Using Observations in Practice

In the realm of architectural practice, Harrigan and Neel in their book *The Executive Architect* clearly make the case for incorporating systematic observation techniques:

> [M]any design decisions . . . will be influenced by observation results, which makes it essential to devise a thorough observation program. The observer cannot simply follow his or her eye, for any observer may be overwhelmed by the complexity of the situation to such a degree that the approach becomes random and loses its representativeness. . . . A program of systematic observation is undertaken because it is possible to establish justified design objectives for a new facility by observing existing facilities and the activities of users. The time spent is . . . justified when one is confronted with a situation that is new, or one that is complex or highly variable.[a]

The authors go on to describe the range of variables that might be observed (including demographic characteristics, specific activities, and user reactions) and how they might be structured. In this regard, they address some of the issues of sampling and coding already discussed in this chapter. Figure 8.18 summarizes Harrigan and Neel's assessment steps for the preparation of systematic observation in architectural practice.

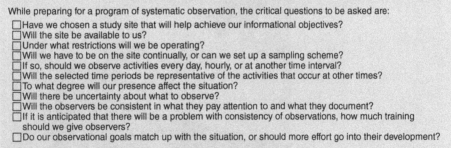

While preparing for a program of systematic observation, the critical questions to be asked are:
- ☐ Have we chosen a study site that will help achieve our informational objectives?
- ☐ Will the site be available to us?
- ☐ Under what restrictions will we be operating?
- ☐ Will we have to be on the site continually, or can we set up a sampling scheme?
- ☐ If so, should we observe activities every day, hourly, or at another time interval?
- ☐ Will the selected time periods be representative of the activities that occur at other times?
- ☐ To what degree will our presence affect the situation?
- ☐ Will there be uncertainty about what to observe?
- ☐ Will the observers be consistent in what they pay attention to and what they document?
- ☐ If it is anticipated that there will be a problem with consistency of observations, how much training should we give observers?
- ☐ Do our observational goals match up with the situation, or should more effort go into their development?

Figure 8.18 Assessment steps for systematic observation.
Courtesy of John Wiley & Sons.

---

[a] John Harrigan and Paul Neel, *The Executive Architect: Transforming Designers into Leaders* (New York: John Wiley & Sons, 1996), 311–312.

strategic vantage point. In comparison, Frederickson's study of design juries is notable because the observations entail: (1) categorization not only of actions but also of discourse; and (2) access to the juries requires the agreement of the participants involved.[20]

His goal was to study jury and student interactions, with a special focus on the possibility of gender and/or minority bias. To study these interactions, he videotaped a total of 112 juries at 3 architecture schools around the country (see Figure 8.19). Like Whyte, Frederickson should specify explicitly what activities and interactions of the jury process should be specified, coded, and measured. The variables identified by Frederickson included both time/frequency measures

Figure 8.19   Gender and ethnic dynamics in juries were the subject of Fredrickson's research. Courtesy of Taubman College of Architecture and Urban Design. Photo by Christopher Campbell.

(such as length of each student's presentation, length of jury comments, etc.) and content/process categories (such as collaborative idea building, use of rhetorical questions, and interruptions).

One of Frederickson's key findings is that women students are more likely than male students to be put at a disadvantage during their juries. As Figure 8.20 indicates, women students are more likely to be interrupted during their initial presentations to juries, and they are also more likely to receives shorter jury sessions overall. These differences are statistically significant at the .05 level, meaning that there are only 5 chances out of 100 (or 1 out of 20) that these results are due to chance. In other words, shorter jury time is strongly correlated, overall, with female gender.

Another way that Frederickson analyzed the data can provide important, potentially useful feedback to the schools he studied. Figure 8.21 shows Frederickson's analysis of the content of jury comments at each of the three schools studied. In this regard, the contrast between schools #1 and #3 is particularly strong. At school #3, there is a much stronger student-centered focus, evidenced by the greater emphasis

Verbal Participation and Interruptions of Female and Male Students

	Interruptions to Student Introduction (Isp)	Total Duration of Each Jury (Tottime)
All Students	**0.61**	**19.60**
(N = 112)	(p < .05)	
Female	**0.76**	**17.50**
(N =34)	(p < .05)	(p < .05)
Male	**0.54**	**20.61**
(N =78)	(p < .05)	(p < .05)

Figure 8.20 Verbal participation and interruptions of female and male students. © ACSA Press. Washington, D.C., 1993.

Content Varibales

	Mean	School 1	School 2	School 3
Collaborative Idea Building per Min. (Ib)	.14	.08	.10	.25
Nonrhetorical Questions per Min. (Real)	19	.10	.14	.32
Rhetorical Questions per Min. (Rhet)	.05	.08	.02	.03

Figure 8.21 Content variables analyzed by school. © ACSA Press. Washington, D.C., 1993.

on collaborative idea building and associated questions; at school #1 there is a much higher incidence of rhetorical questions, suggesting that the jurors are relatively more inclined to ask questions to make a point rather than to initiate dialogue.

These and similar analyses form the basis for a variety of recommendations to architectural educators, including an overall suggestion that design educators and administrators participate in faculty seminars that focus on the development of leadership, interpersonal communications, educational goals, and research skills.

Finally, compared to the previous two examples, Diaan van der Westhuizen's study of pedestrian behavior in three Detroit neighborhoods represents a much larger scale of observations.[21] The larger purpose of the study was to investigate the extent to which either destinations and/or spatial properties of the neighborhood street systems are more predictive of pedestrian movement than commonly used urban planning measures. To answer this question, it was absolutely essential to systematically track pedestrian activity at the neighborhood scale, which is clearly not possible from a single or limited number of vantage points. The following passage recounts the logistical arrangement entailed in doing such large-scale observations:

> Arrangements were made with the . . . research team . . . and the police were alerted that data would be collected within their precincts. Three measurement days were taken for each of the three neighborhoods—two weekdays and one weekend per area. Each day consisted of 3 time segments (9:00–12:00; 12:30–3:30; 4:00–7:00). . . . The same 50 miles of each neighborhood street space was observed during each time segment; overall, a total of 1,350 miles of street space was covered across the area.[22]

Needless to say, these arrangements also required that a research colleague serve as driver for van der Westhuizen to accomplish this rigorous regimen of observations. Figure 8.22 is an exemplar summary map of the observations for one neighborhood.

8.4.3   Mapping

Probably the most well-known example of using a mapping technique is Kevin Lynch's study, *The Image of the City*.[23] In an effort to assess the way the physical characteristics of cities were experienced and understood by ordinary people, Lynch conducted interviews with study respondents of three U.S. cities—Boston, Jersey City, and Los Angeles—and asked them to draw sketch maps of their city. Figure 8.23 represents the composite maps derived from the interviews with Boston residents, while Figure 8.24 represents the composite map derived from the

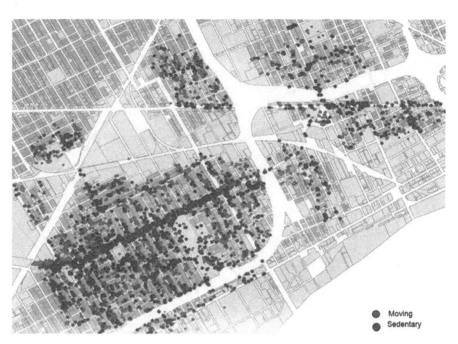

Figure 8.22   People counts for moving and sedentary behavior in the neighborhood in southwest Detroit. Courtesy of Diaan van der Westhuizen.

residents' sketch maps. Lynch concludes that overall there is a very high correlation between the two sets of maps for all three cities.

Based on these sets of mappings from the three cities, Lynch was able to derive his now famous five general categories of urban features: path, edge, node, landmark, and district. In other words, all five types of features were delineated in each of the three cities. However, the density of these imageable features varied from city to city. Figure 8.25 shows the relative impoverishment of the composite Jersey City sketch map, compared to that of Boston.

Over the years since Lynch's study, researchers have effectively adapted mapping to a variety of research purposes and contexts. Anne Lusk's study of greenway bicycle paths demonstrates particularly innovative adaption of mapping.[24] A longtime volunteer and activist in the greenway movement, Lusk's goal was to discover the frequency of and distance between "destination" places along the greenway path. Recognizing that there might be important differences between different types of bikeways, she selected for study a total of six greenways that were nationally recognized for their aesthetic qualities.

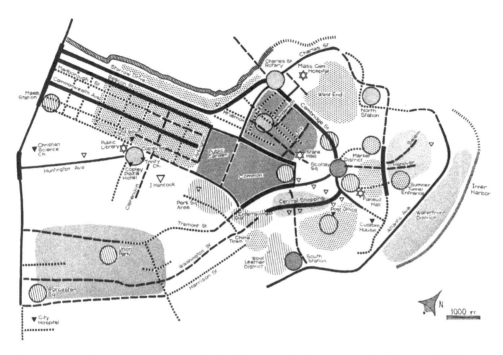

Figure 8.23 The Boston image as derived from verbal interviews. Courtesy of MIT Press.

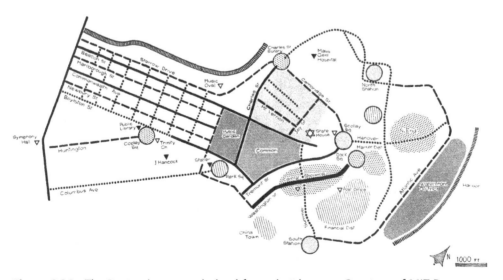

Figure 8.24 The Boston image as derived from sketch maps. Courtesy of MIT Press.

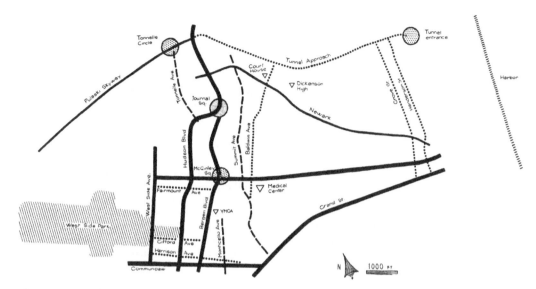

Figure 8.25 The Jersey City image as derived from sketch maps. Courtesy of MIT Press.

At each site, Lusk asked greenway users to apply stickers representing different qualities of physical features to greenway maps she provided to them. Figure 8.26 provides the mapping instructions, and Figure 8.27 represents a composite map for one of the greenways. Lusk was then able to measure distances between collectively established destination points using an odometer. Distances for each greenway were established and then general patterns for each greenway type were identified. Figure 8.28 represents a typical destination along the Stowe VT greenway; it is a place where multiple features converge, including cows (animals or people) to watch, a shady glen as a place to rest, a picturesque view of the mountains, and a lay-by large enough for people to interact with each other. Lusk was also able to determine that major destination points along the greenway occur about every two miles. These findings are comparable (i.e., correlated) to those of destination points on the other greenways studied.

More recently, Kush Patel adapted the sticker mapping technique developed by Lusk for his study of two iconic European projects: Bernard Tschumi's Parc de La Villette in Paris, and Lucien Kroll's medical student residence for L'Université Catholique de Louvain in Woluwé-Saint-Lambert, on the outskirts of Brussels.[25] As described in Chapter 4, Patel's purpose was to investigate the material implications of Henri Lefebvre's seminal work, *The Production of Space* (1974), and examine connections between Lefebvre's critical formulations of space and the built works

Bicycle Path/Greenway Survey

This voluntary survey is being conducted through the University of Michigan for a Ph.D. dissertation on the determination of attractive destinations and their features on a multi-use path. We would like you to help us identify the locations of these destinations and to also list the elements that make that destination preferred. Please use the attached stickers on the survey. Out of a trial of 6 survey techniques, use of the stickers emerged as the most effective technique.

First, use the following code for the stickers, placing them as appropriate, on the map. You do not have to use all of the categories of stickers and you can use as many or as few stickers as you like.

Second, beside the spangley star sticker for the destination or destinations, please describe the area or features so that the destinations can be located. Also, please assign a number in order of preference to the destinations with #1 being the most preferred destination. You can have as many or as few destinations as you like.

Third, on the additional sheet of paper, please list the destinations located by you on the map according to the rank order with #1 being listed first. Below each destination, please list the preferred features at this destination and identify with a check, the top three or four features at each destination.

 1. Put a plain star by one or more areas that serve as the place or places you start on the path.

 2. Put a spangley star by one or more areas that serve as destinations or places, which even though you may pass by, you feel you have "arrived."

 3. Put a smiley face circle by the places which you particularly enjoy and/or look forward to.

 4. Put squares by places that serve primarily as way-finders (visible cues about your location) that might be attractive or unattractive.

 5. Put a line of small dots by stretches that you find appealing.

 6. Put a long bar or many bars at the places or stretches where you are bored.

 7. Put bugs/ants by individual places or things that you find unappealing.

 8. Put an arrow/pointer indicating the direction where you enjoy a view.

Figure 8.26   Mapping instructions for Lusk's greenway study. Courtesy of Anne Lusk.

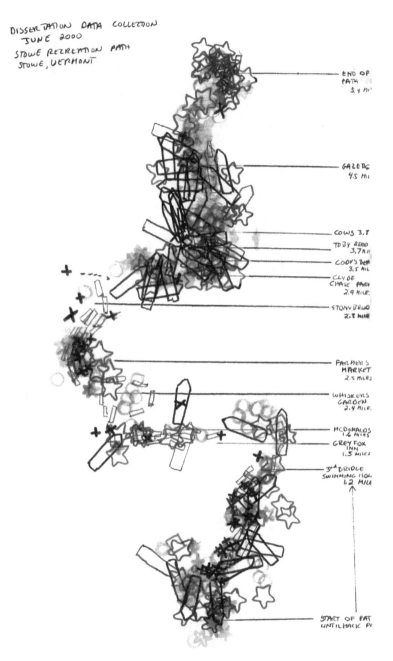

Figure 8.27 Composite map of Stowe, Vermont, greenway. Courtesy of Anne Lusk.

Figure 8.28 Typical greenway destination. Courtesy of Anne Lusk; photo by Jeff Turnaw.

of Kroll and Tschumi. Lefebvre's theoretical project offered a rethinking of the relationship between space and society, arguing for the presence of lived experience in spatial discourse. Within this theoretical framework, mapping spatial practices and symbolic associations specific to the two projects represents an essential tactic for the study.

8.4.4   *Sorting*

Another tactic that can be highly effective in both research and practice situations is the sorting task. This typically involves asking a respondent to sort a set of cards (usually between 20 and 30) with either words or pictures represented on them (see Figure 8.29).[26] In a directed sort, the researcher specifies a set of categories into which the cards must be sorted, such as a 5- or 7-point rating scale from highly preferred to least preferred. In an open sort, the respondent can establish whatever categories make sense to him or her; so, for example, the respondent might choose to sort a set of buildings into functional types, including houses, commercial buildings, churches, and so on. Or the respondent might choose to sort a set of houses by categories of traditional versus modern styles.

In a seminar/workshop class for architectural students, Groat has used the sorting task to clarify the design dialogue between the architect-student and a

Figure 8.29   A respondent beginning the sorting task.

friend who serves as the client. The student is asked first to do several sortings of the 20 photos of houses both to familiarize herself or himself with the sorting process and to elicit his/her own categorizations of the houses. Next, the student conducts an interview with the "client" who does his/her sortings of the houses. There is also a column at one edge of the sortings record sheet (see Figures 8.30 and 8.31) for both student and "client" to indicate a rank order of preference. Finally, the student is urged to discuss the similarities and differences in the sorting categories and the ranked preferences with the "client." So, for example, if both architect and client sort according to building materials, but the client prefers wood shingles while the architect prefers expansive glass with steel, there is a clear difference of approach to work out. Or perhaps, if both architect and client sort the houses on the degree of exposure to landscape and sunlight, it may be that this agreement can serve as a device for resolving the conflict over materials.

In a research context, both the preference rankings (an example of ordinal measurement as described in section 8.2) and the nominal sorting category designations can be subjected to statistical measures such that correlations between

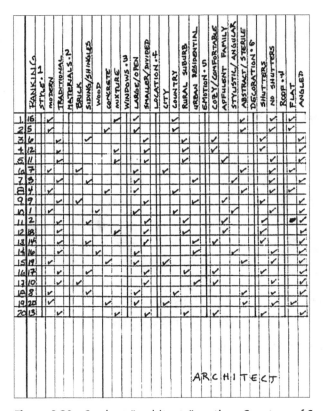

Figure 8.30 Student "architects" sorting. Courtesy of Sara Stucky.

rankings and sortings can be investigated. However, the use of the sorting task in a practice setting—between client and architect, or among a small number of client/ users—can often serve as an effective and creative foundation for dialogue at the outset of a project.

In the essays that students have written about this experience, it is clear that a visual exercise such as the sorting task can be a very effective alternative to simply asking clients to state their preferences in a conversation or verbally oriented interview. Indeed, it is through the process of actually sorting out alternative design elements, and articulating the categories that come to mind, that many non-architects can begin to articulate important ways of experiencing architecture—experiences that they might not otherwise be aware of or know how to express.

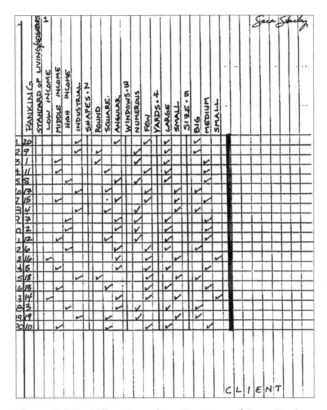

Figure 8.31 "Client" sorting. Courtesy of Sara Stucky.

BOX 8.3

Tactics for Correlational Research: The Sorting Task

Frances Downing has used the sorting task to great effect in uncovering architectural designers' use of image banks in their design process.[a] Downing was interested in finding out the extent to which beginning architectural students, graduating architectural students, and practicing architects differed in the way they thought about and used design imagery in their work. Her procedure involved asking her respondents a series

[a] Frances Downing, "Image Banks: Dialogs between the Past and the Future," *Environment and Behavior* 24(4) (July 1992): 441–470.

(*Continued*)

of evocative questions (e.g., As a child, what places did you live in that remain particularly memorable?) to elicit meaningful place images (see Figure 8.32). As respondents named these images, the name of each image was recorded on a small card for use in the sorting task. Once all the images evoked by the questions had been recorded, the respondents carried out as many *free* sorts as possible.

Figure 8.32   A memorable image that might be experienced in youth.

Figure 8.33   A memorable image that might be experienced during professional education.

Downing actually conducted her study at two different architecture schools, and included practicing professionals from the schools' respective regions. In this regard, Downing found some intriguing differences of emphases among the two groups of students and the professionals. Using a combination of inferential statistics for nominal data (see sections 8.3 and 8.4) and multivariate statistics (see section 8.5), Downing was able to discover that, in general, the more experienced architects (especially the practicing professionals) were more inclined to integrate or combine vernacular images from prearchitectural experiences with the more high-style images from their professional education and experience (see Figure 8.33). Entering students, by contrast, were less able to integrate the two types of images. Downing concludes that this is potentially problematic because architecture programs may be failing to help students make sense of their own experience of place in relation to the challenge of creating place in their professional roles.

Reflecting on the use of the sorting task tactic itself, Frances Downing found that her respondents—even the very busy professionals—quickly became captivated by the sorting process. (See Box 8.3 for an account of this award-winning study.) As Downing recounts:

> The memories that participants related were generally characterized by profound personal involvement. Soon it was evident that the information collected was central to the life of a designer: the reason why so many had made their career choices seemed bound up in the small white card with names of a history of places written on them.[27]

Taken together, Downing's experience with both students and practitioners, as well as Groat's experience with both designers and nondesigners, suggests that an interactive data collection device such as the sorting task can be a very effective tactic for both research and practice.

8.4.5   *Archives*

Yet another, though certainly less frequently used, tool for data collection is provided by archives. Newman's study of defensible space, in fact, put an existing database to extremely effective use. In this regard, Newman is quite explicit about how the precision and wealth of data kept by the New York Housing Authority contributed to the quality and successful outcome of his study. To be specific, Newman explains that the wealth of demographic variables measured by the Housing Authority included data on age, income, years of residence, previous backgrounds, and history of family pathology. Similarly, the Housing Authority's own police force maintained extensive records that included not only the nature of the crime and complaint, but also the precise location of the crime in the particular housing project.

These data on both demographic characteristics and the presence/location of criminal behavior could then be correlated with data on the physical properties of the various housing projects. Indeed, the physical quality of the housing projects was measured in terms of a great range of variables, including numbers of residents, size of housing site, population density, number of housing stories, plan type, and the like. As Newman explains: "With this data it has been possible to determine exactly where the most dangerous areas of buildings are, as well as to compare crime rates in different building types and project layouts."[28]

One particularly influential and notable correlation discovered by Newman is that of the relationship between crime rate and building height. As Newman concludes: "Crime rate has been found to increase almost proportionately with building height" for the projects administered by the New York Housing Authority.[29]

8.5   TACTICS: READING ABOUT AND UNDERSTANDING MULTIVARIATE ANALYSES

Up to this point in the chapter, our discussions have touched on some of the most typical descriptive and inferential statistical analyses entailed in doing correlational research. In this section, we will briefly describe a few examples of some of the more complex data analyses that can be deployed. We do *not* assume that either students or professionals at the beginning stages of learning about or doing research will employ these complex analytical techniques; rather, we do anticipate that both students and practitioners who choose *to read about* research findings during the conduct of a literature review may well find it useful to understand the intent of such procedures. To this end, we will describe in the chapter segments that follow four types of multivariate procedures: typological analyses, multiple regression, factor analysis, and multidimensional scaling. More experienced researchers who wish to actually employ such statistical tactics may want to refer to some of the detailed texts listed in the notes at the end of the chapter.

8.5.1   *Typological Analyses*

By the term *typological* we mean to include studies that incorporate analyses of multiple complex variables in order to illuminate broad categories of spatial relationships and formal attributes from the scale of building interiors to neighborhoods, and the like. In this case, rather than focusing on the analysis on each individual variable, the aim is to identify the presence and convergence of variables that, when taken together, define broad categories or types.

Fernando Lara and Youngchul Kim's study of modernist apartment buildings in Brazil and Korea is an example of this typological focus.[30] Broadly speaking, the authors' goal is to tease out the globalizing modernist influence on multifamily residential buildings in relation to the localizing influence of housing traditions in each country. Theoretically, this research purpose is informed by Kenneth Frampton's classic essay in which he proposes the concept of "critical regionalism," in response to hegemonic internationalization.[31] To address their research question, Lara and Kim reviewed a representative sample of 20 Brazilian and 20 Korean apartments, selected from a larger sample of about 100 apartments (see Figures 8.34 and 8.35). From a broadly qualitative perspective, the authors discovered that after reviewing 20 to 25 plans, the array of spatial variations had reached a saturation point, such that adding in more plans for analysis would provide no new information.

Having selected these sets of apartment plans, the authors undertook what is termed a "mean depth" analysis within the Space Syntax suite of computer programs. This measure calculates how many layers of space (or rooms) must be entered to move through the overall plan. Remarkably, as the authors note, the space syntax calculations provided numerical verification for what was already obvious from visual inspection: the Brazilian and Korean apartment plans represented two distinct spatial typologies. In general, the Korean apartment plans were characterized by greater spatial depth than the Brazilian plans.

One of the most important differences between the two apartments is revealed in the spatial arrangement of private versus social space:

> While Brazilian apartments show a striking differentiation between private areas and social/service areas . . . , the Korean apartments present a large social area as a middle ground with private areas split between two regular bedrooms on one side and one master bedroom on the opposite side.[32]

In light of the evident continuity of each culture's long-standing spatial traditions in housing, the authors conclude that global impact of modernist architecture is not so thoroughly "homogenizing" as it might first appear. Indeed, they find it remarkable "how flexible the modernist structural grammar has proven to be."[33]

A research study on the walkability of three Detroit neighborhoods represents the application of typological analyses at the neighborhood scale.[34] The research, funded by the National Institute of Environmental Health Sciences, sought to understand the design components that contribute to healthy neighborhoods, and more specifically to identify specific characteristics of the physical environment that contribute to localized physical activity. Although other more recent studies have identified several notable contributing physical features, the Wineman et al. study is important because it addresses walkability in less affluent neighborhoods that may lack the amenities that typically support walking, especially so in a classic exemplar of the "shrinking city" phenomenon.

As part of this larger study, the authors investigated the specific role of density and land use mix, both of which have been identified in previous studies as predictive of walking activity. However, rather than consider these two variables separately, the authors developed a typology of neighborhood types based on the *combination* of density and land use (see Figure 8.36). Their intent was "to identify a reasonable number (<10) of neighborhood types that shared readily observable differences that might be easily adopted by planners and designers."[35]

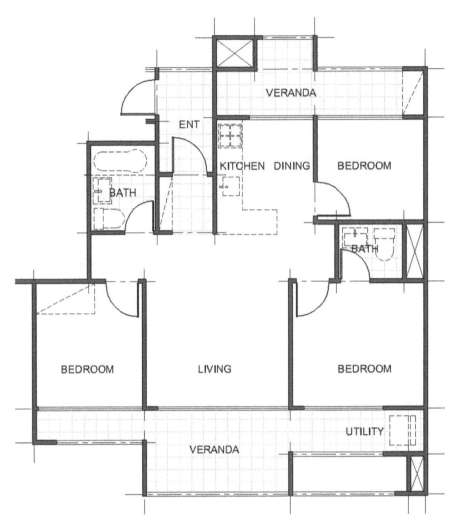

Figure 8.34   An example of Korean architecture with a social area as middle ground. Copyright Locke Science Publishing Co., Inc. Reproduced with permission. Lara F, Kim Y (2010) Built global, lived local: A study of how two diametrically opposed cultures reacted to similar modern housing solutions. *Journal of Architectural and Planning Research* 27(2): 91–106.

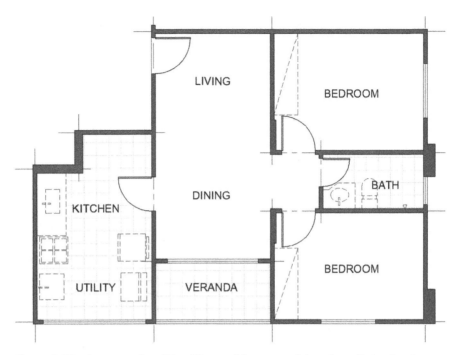

Figure 8.35 An example of Brazilian architecture with a clear distinction between social and private areas. Copyright Locke Science Publishing Co., Inc. Reproduced with permission. Lara F, Kim Y (2010) Built global, lived local: A study of how two diametrically opposed cultures reacted to similar modern housing solutions. *Journal of Architectural and Planning Research* 27(2): 91–106.

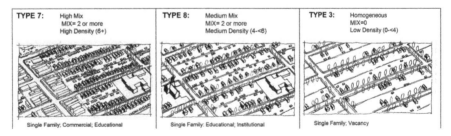

Figure 8.36 Examples of low-mix, medium-mix, and high-mix neighborhood types. Courtesy of Diaan van der Westhuizen.

The results of previous research had suggested that density and land use mix—when taken separately—were actually associated with lower levels of physical activity. However, the analyses from the Detroit study using the neighborhood typologies (based on categorical measures of density and land use) demonstrated an association with *more* physical activity. In this case, neighborhoods characterized by *both* higher density and higher land use mix report higher levels of localized physical activity. These results suggest that such typological analyses offer the potential for providing illuminating insights on the constellation of neighborhood design features that contribute to walkability.

8.5.2   *Multiple Regression*

In correlational research that seeks primarily to understand and predict relationships among several variables, multiple regression is frequently employed as an analytical tool. It is one of several devices that can be used to describe the strength and direction of relationships among two or more variables. More specifically, it is appropriate for interval or ratio data where the researcher has hypothesized several independent variables that can predict the value, or measured outcome, of another variable. In such cases multiple regression can provide a mathematical equation that indicates the amount of variance contributed by each of these independent (or predictor) variables.

An example of how multiple regression might work in environmental research is provided by Ewing and Handy's investigation of urban design qualities that promote walkability in urban communities.[36] One challenge in this area of urban design research is that many qualitatively understood qualities of urban design are very difficult to measure and operationalize in actual practice. Thus, the goal of this research was to test the extent to which over a hundred specific physical features could be predictive of the experience of five broadly defined urban qualities: imageability, enclosure, human scale, transparency, and complexity.

To measure the presence of specific physical features, the two researchers first analyzed the content of all 48 video clips of urban scenes used in the study. To assure the accuracy of the physical features ratings, commonly accepted procedures for assessing interrater reliability were employed. Next, a team of 10 panelists, experts in urban design and environmental research, rated each urban scene on each of the five broad urban design qualities. The conceptual framework for the study is represented in Figure 8.37. The physical features are conceptualized as independent variables that are hypothesized as being predictive of the expert panel's ratings (the dependent variables).

The purpose of the subsequent regression analyses is to identify the independent variables (the physical features) that are most predictive of the urban design

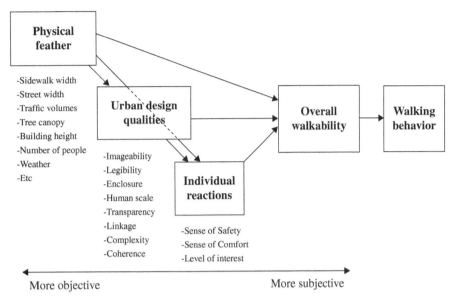

Figure 8.37 Conceptual framework for urban design qualities related to walkability. Courtesy of Reid Ewing.

qualities. For example, the quality of imageability is best predicted by the presence of people, proportion of historic buildings, courtyards/plazas/parks, outdoor dining, and major landscape features, among other physical properties. Regression also provides the researcher with measures of the overall predictive strength of the identified physical features variables, and the predictive strength of each variable individually. Many researchers find the use of regression useful because the apparent predictive precision is often interpreted as lending support to hypothesized causal links.

8.5.3   Factor Analysis

Like multiple regression, factor analysis also depends on interval or ratio data. But instead of multiple regression's focus on the relative salience of key variables for predicting the outcomes of other variables, factor analysis aims to articulate an overall structure or pattern among the variables. More particularly, factor analysis enables the researcher to identify thematic clusters of variables known as *factors*. Each factor is comprised of several variables that share similar patterns of responses or observations.

A good example of the use of factor analysis to uncover the underlying structure among a set of environmental design variables is provided by Kim's research on New Urbanist and conventional suburban developments.[37] As described in earlier segments of this chapter, Kim used a survey questionnaire to clarify the impact of a variety of physical features on residents' perceived sense of community in the two neighborhood developments.

What Kim discovered is that, even though the New Urbanist residents rated their perceived sense of community more highly than the residents of the conventional suburb, the underlying factors influencing the two groups' assessments were remarkably similar. For example, in the residents' evaluation of the community identity component of sense of community, the same three factors were identified for both neighborhood developments: community plan, community appearance, and amenities. In Figure 8.38, the relevant physical variables associated with each factor are indicated. However, the relative salience of the three factors and the specific variables associated with them are somewhat different. Whereas the community appearance factor was most salient for the Kentlands residents (see mean score in bold), the amenities factor was more salient to the Orchard Village residents' sense of community.

Q7: Distinctive Character

Q7	Physical features	Kentlands			Orchard Village		
		Com. Plan	Com App.	Ame.	Com. Plan	Com App.	Ame.
11	Street width	.77			.70		
14	Lot size	.76			.62		
5	Block size	.75			.62		
3	Distance between sidewalks and houses	.73			.65		
10	Arrangement of houses on the block	.71				.72	
12	Garage location	.69			.82		
1	Residential density	.66				.51	
17	Street layout	.59				.67	
16	Overall design quality of housing		.78			.86	
4	Architectural style		.71			.72	
15	Mixture of housing types		.70			.63	
7	Overall layout of Kentlands (or W.W)		.46			.67	
6	Club house-recreation complex			.75			.74
8	Street trees and other street landscaping			.63		.59	
9	Overall size of Kentlands (or W.W)					.59	
13	On street parking				.81		
2	Lakes (or Wetlands), public greens, tot lots, footpaths						.85
	Mean	4.20	**4.70**	4.27	3.45	4.02	**4.21**
	Alpha	.89	.77	.43	.89	.92	.62

Figure 8.38 Factor analysis of community identity. Courtesy of Joongsub Kim.

8.5.4   *Multidimensional Scaling*

The use of multidimensional scaling analysis offers relatively more flexibility than either factor analysis or multiple regression. Depending on the particular computer program used, it is possible to make use of nominal data as well as interval or ratio data. In addition, because the outcome of the analysis is a graphically represented spatial plot, it may also hold some inherent appeal for architectural researchers.

The overall goal of multidimensional scaling is similar to that of factor analysis in that it reveals an underlying pattern or structure among the variables analyzed. However, some multidimensional scaling programs allow a greater degree of interpretive flexibility than is the case with factor analysis. Whereas factor analysis typically results in numerical designations for the degree of salience of each variable within a factor, multidimensional scaling results in a graphic plot that locates spatially the relationship among all variables. In such a plot, two points (variables) in close proximity mean that these variables represent a similar pattern of responses; distant points (variables) on the plot represent a dissimilar pattern of responses or observations.

Linda Groat's research on architects' and laypeople's understanding of architectural style employs a form of multidimensional scaling that accepts the nominal data derived from a sorting task. Groat was interested in investigating the extent to which architects and laypeople (in this case a group of accountants) responded differently to modern versus postmodern styles.[38] Some architectural theorists and proponents of postmodernism had speculated that laypeople would find postmodern buildings more appealing and meaningful than modern buildings. So Groat asked her respondents to carry out a set of free sorts of building photographs that represented a range of modern to transitional to postmodern styles.

Figure 8.39 represents the multidimensional scalogram analysis plot of a typical architect's set of sortings. Groat's interpretation of the plot reveals that basis stylistic categorizations underlie the architect's sortings, regardless of whether the architect had consciously sorted according to materials, geometric form, preference, or any other criteria. Lines have been drawn to indicate that the plot can be understood in terms of three stylistic regions that, with minor exceptions, correspond to the designations employed by architectural critics of the time.

However, Figure 8.40 represents a typical accountant's set of sortings. In this case, it is not possible to find distinctive stylistic regions. Groat interprets this result to mean that the accountant's sortings do *not* reveal an underlying stylistic conceptualization in the way that the architect's plot does.

The sorting a of all 20 architects and 20 accountants were subjected to the same multidimensional analysis procedures. Groat was able to determine that while *no* accountant's plot revealed a postmodern stylistic region, the plots of 10 architects

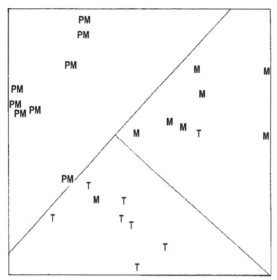

PM = Post Modern, T = Transitional, M= Modern

Figure 8.39   Underlying structure of an architect's sorting.

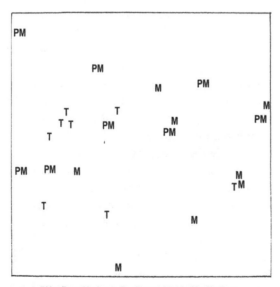

PM = Post Modern, T = Transitional, M= Modern

Figure 8.40   Underlying structure of an accountant's sorting.

did reveal a postmodern region. Further statistical analyses confirmed that this difference in response rate between the architects and accountants was significant at the .001 level, meaning that there is only one chance in a thousand that these results would be a chance occurrence.

As a result of this study, Groat concluded that the argument put forward by postmodern proponents at that time—that laypeople would respond more favorably to postmodern buildings, thereby distinguishing them from the modern buildings—was flawed.

8.6   CONCLUSIONS: STRENGTHS AND WEAKNESSES

As the many research examples described in this chapter demonstrate, the correlational strategy is well suited for exploring the relationship among two or more variables of interest. Unlike experimental research in which a variable is purposefully manipulated by the researcher, correlational research seeks to document the naturally occurring relationships among variables. This characteristic means that it is particularly appropriate in circumstances when variables either *can't* be manipulated for practical reasons or *shouldn't* be manipulated for ethical reasons (see Figure 8.41).

Second, because correlational research can accommodate the study of many variables measured in a variety of instances, the strategy is especially appropriate when the researcher seeks to understand a situation or circumstance *broadly*, rather than *in depth*.

In other words, one of the strategy's great advantages is its potential for studying the range and extent of multiple variables. However, its consequent disadvantage is that a robust and deep understanding of that circumstance may not be revealed.

Finally, researchers who choose to employ a correlational strategy will have to bear in mind the distinction between causality and prediction. By revealing

Strengths	Weaknesses
Can clarify the relationships among two or more naturally occuring variables	Researcher cannot control the levels or degrees of variables
Well suited to studying the breadth of a setting or a phenomenon	Less well suited to exploring the setting or phenomenon in depth
Can establish predictive relationships	Cannot establish causality

Figure 8.41   Strengths and weaknesses of correlational research.

consistent patterns of relationships among variables, correlational research can predict whether certain physical features may be associated with certain desired social outcomes. But that is not the same thing as establishing the physical variables as the cause of that outcome. Researchers who seek to establish direct causality between variables will need to turn to experimental and quasi-experimental strategies. And they are the subject of the next chapter.

NOTES

1. William Whyte, *The Social Life of Small Urban Spaces* (Washington, DC: The Conservation Foundation, 1980).
2. Joongsub Kim, "Creating Community: Does Kentlands Live Up to Its Goals?" *Places* 13(2) (2000): 48–55; Joongsub Kim, "Perceiving and Valuing Sense of Community in a New Urbanist Development: A Case Study of Kentlands," *Journal of Urban Design* 12(2) (2007): 203–230.
3. Todd Bressi, "Planning the American Dream," in Peter Katz (ed.), *The New Urbanism: Toward an Architecture of Community* (New York: McGraw-Hill, 1994).
4. Ibid., xxx.
5. Joongsub Kim, *Sense of Community in Neo-Traditional and Conventional Suburban Developments,* PhD dissertation, University of Michigan, Ann Arbor, MI, 2001.
6. Although the survey questionnaire may be the most common tactic for gaining an understanding of people's opinions and perceived meanings, a great many other response formats—such as mapping, the sorting task, and the like—are also possible. See section 8.4 later in this chapter for a more complete discussion of these tactics.
7. Linda N. Groat, "Meaning in Post-Modern Architecture: An Examination Using the Multiple Sorting Task," *Journal of Environmental Psychology* 2(1) (1982): 3–22.
8. H. Blalock, *Social Statistics* (New York: McGraw-Hill, 1960), 12–18.
9. Ibid., 15.
10. Donna M. Mertens, *Research and Evaluation in Education and Psychology,* 3rd ed. (Thousand Oaks, CA: Sage, 2010), 152.
11. Mertens presents a more hierarchically structured typology. She uses the terms *causal comparative* and *correlational* to designate two primary categories. Then, within correlational, she includes both relationship and prediction subtypes. We have chosen to simplify Mertens's hierarchy in part because pure "prediction" studies (which typically involve the study of a theorized outcome some months or years after the initial measurement of key variables) are relatively rare in architectural research. D. Mertens, *Research Methods in Education and Psychology* (Thousand Oaks, CA: Sage, 1998).
12. Oscar Newman, *Defensible Space: Crime Prevention through Urban Design* (New York: Macmillan, 1972).
13. Ibid., xiv.
14. Ibid., 3.
15. Mertens, 94.

16. Newman, xv.
17. Ibid., 48.
18. Kim, "Perceiving and Valuing Sense of Community."
19. Whyte, 102.
20. Mark Frederickson, "Gender and Racial Bias in Design Juries," *Journal of Architectural Education* 47(1) (1993): 38–48.
21. Diaan van der Westhuizen, *Concepts of Space and Place—Neighborhood Access, Pedestrian Movement, and Physical Activity in Detroit: Implications for Urban Design and Research*, PhD dissertation, University of Michigan, Ann Arbor, MI, 2010.
22. Ibid., 134.
23. Kevin Lynch, *The Image of the City* (Cambridge, MA: MIT Press, 1960).
24. Anne Lusk, *Greenways' Places of the Heart: Aesthetic Guidelines for Bicycle Paths*, PhD dissertation, University of Michigan, Ann Arbor, MI, 2001.
25. Kush Patel, *Practicing Lefebvre: How Ideas of Social Space Are Realized in the Works of Lucien Kroll and Bernard Tschumi*, PhD dissertation, University of Michigan, Ann Arbor, MI, 2013.
26. David Canter, J. Brown, and Linda Groat, "The Multiple Sorting Procedure," in Michael Brenner and David Canter (eds.), *The Research Interview* (London: Academic Press, 1985), 79–114.
27. Frances Downing, "Conversations in Imagery," *Design Studies* 13(3) (1992): 297. Downing's study was recognized by the 1992 Design Studies Award for the best paper published in the journal.
28. Newman, xiv.
29. Ibid., 27.
30. Fernando Lara and Youngchul Kim, "Built Global, Lived Local: A Study of How Two Diametrically Opposed Cultures Reacted to Similar Modern Housing Solutions," *Journal of Architectural and Planning Research* 27(2) (2010): 91–106.
31. Kenneth Frampton, "Towards a Critical Regionalism: Six Points for an Architecture of Resistance," in Hal Foster (ed.), *The Anti-Aesthetic Essays on Postmodern Culture* (Seattle: Bay Press, 1983).
32. Ibid., 100.
33. Ibid., 104.
34. Jean Wineman, Robert Marans, Amy Schulz, Diaan van der Westhuizen, Graciela Mentz, and Paul Max, "Designing Healthy Urban Environments: Neighborhood Design and Health-Related Outcomes for Residents of Detroit." Paper presentation, Environmental Design Research Association 43, Seattle, WA, 2012.
35. Ibid., 6.
36. Reid Ewing and Susan Handy, "Measuring the Unmeasurable: Urban Design Qualities Related to Walkability," *Journal of Urban Design* 14(1) (2009): 65–84.
37. Joongsub Kim and Rachel Kaplan, "Physical and Psychological Factors in Sense of Community: New Urbanist Kentlands and Nearby Orchard Village," *Environment & Behavior* 36(3) (2004): 313–340.
38. Groat, 3.

Chapter 9

Experimental and Quasi-Experimental Research

9.1   INTRODUCTION

Research on the performance of various building components has constituted a significant and long-standing domain within architectural research. Although much of this research has focused on improving various building technologies in the advanced industrialized world, a research study by Givoni, Gulich, Gomez, and Gomez focuses instead on radiant cooling by metal roofs, a significant issue for housing in developing countries.[1] Givoni et al. noted that, although corrugated metal roofs are effective for cooling in the evening, they are prone to overheating houses in the daylight hours. The researchers hypothesized that the installation of operable hinged interior insulating plates under the roof would reduce daytime heating while simultaneously not interfering with the nighttime cooling function of the metal roofs.

To test this hypothesis, the researchers built a small-scale mock-up of the typical house (termed a "test cell") whereby the heating/cooling effect of various test conditions could be measured (see Figure 9.1). To be specific, Givoni et al. tested three distinct conditions of insulation operation: (1) with the insulation panels closed both day and night; (2) with the insulation panels open at night and closed during the day; and (3) with the insulation positioned as in 2, but with the addition of a small ventilating fan from midnight to 5:00 a.m. In addition, two levels of thermal mass (as represented by water-filled bottles) were also tested.

Based on their testing of these conditions, the authors conclude that the combination of both insulating panels and fan venting (condition 3) provides better daytime cooling than without the fan ventilation. However, no appreciable

313

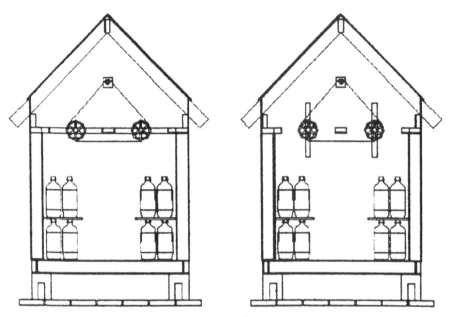

Figure 9.1 Test cell used by Givoni et al. Courtesy of American Solar Energy Society, Inc.

difference in cooling was noted as a consequence of the thermal mass condition. Finally, based on these data, the authors were able to develop predictive formulae for calculating the indoor maximum temperature as a function of the swing of the outdoor temperature.

Taking on a very different topic area, researcher Ann Sloan Devlin sought to discover the extent to which gender might have an effect on how job applicants are evaluated in architectural practice.[2] To be more specific, she hypothesized that "women architects would be less favorably rated than male architects," and more so at the more senior level.[3]

To test this hypothesis, Devlin created both a junior-level and senior-level résumé, the junior level with 4 years of architectural experience and the senior level with 13 years of experience. Half of each résumé type (junior or senior) was designated by a fictitious female name, and half by a fictitious male name. Each résumé included a career objective, professional experience, affiliation, registration, education, skills, and honors and awards. By using identical gender-designated résumés, Devlin is adapting a long-standing experimental design employed by researchers who have similarly tested out gender biases in other fields, including, for example, a study of faculty applicants to a psychology department.[4]

Respondents in Devlin's study were over 200 architects (156 men and 48 women) licensed in the state of Connecticut, but representing all regions of the country. Respondents were told that the study was about "the perception architects have of the characteristics possessed by those practicing architecture." These respondents then *randomly* received one of the four fictitious résumés and were asked to evaluate the candidates on a 7-point scale for the following qualities: technical aspects of the job, administrative aspects, interpersonal aspects, contribution to growth of firm's client base, creative contribution, advancement, and overall rating. Of particular significance, respondents were also asked whether they would accept or reject the candidate for hire.

The most salient result of Devlin's study was that the "male architect respondents were more likely to hire male applicants than female applicants as senior architects."[5] Devlin reaches this conclusion by comparing the hiring decisions of the respondents in relation to the four résumé conditions (male or female; intern or senior), using inferential statistical measures (see Chapter 8, section 8.3.1). She concludes that women in architecture may indeed "experience discrimination as they advance through the ranks."[6]

9.2 STRATEGY: GENERAL CHARACTERISTICS OF EXPERIMENTAL RESEARCH

In some very obvious respects, these two studies may seem to be worlds apart. On a thematic level, the Givoni et al. study tackles an aspect of environmental technology, while the Devlin study seeks to clarify the dynamics of gender discrimination in architectural practice. Second, the research contexts are very different. The former is conducted in a laboratory setting, while the latter makes use of a real-life or "field" setting. Third, the variables being investigated are quite different. The Givoni et al. study considers only physical variables, whereas the Devlin study focuses on behavioral or social conditions.

Despite this variety of notable differences, both the Givoni et al. and Devlin studies are nevertheless examples of experimental research design. Many readers are likely to read into that factual statement either a commendation of high praise or an invitation to disparage such research. This is because experimental research is so frequently portrayed as the standard against which all other research strategies should be judged. In general, readers who adhere to the postpositivist system of inquiry are likely to see the experimental strategy as the essence of credible "scientific" research. However, many researchers who adhere to the intersubjective or subjective paradigmatic positions have argued persuasively that the experimental design is often either inappropriate or insufficient for research about certain social and cultural dimensions of designed environments. We will address some of these concerns later in this chapter (see section 9.6). Nevertheless, we would argue that just as is the case with each of the several research strategies, experimental research can yield both outstanding or flawed research depending on how appropriately it is applied to a particular research question.

What, then, are the underlying commonalities that define the Givoni et al. and Devlin studies as experimental research? Briefly, the defining characteristics of an experimental research design include: the use of a treatment, or independent variable; the measurement of outcome, or dependent, variables; a clear unit of assignment (to the treatment); the use of a comparison (or control) group; and a focus on causality.[7] These five characteristics will be discussed in some detail in the following chapter segments.

9.2.1   *The Use of a Treatment, or Independent Variable*

In each of the two studies described earlier, the researchers are seeking to study the impact of one or more specific, identifiable variables on the phenomenon under study. In the case of the metal roof research, the researchers are seeking to test the thermal impact of several conditions, both in isolation and in combination, including *insulation, venting fan,* and *thermal mass.* Similarly, in her research on gender issues in professional practice, Ann Sloan Devlin is seeking to clarify the impact of *gender designations* on how architects evaluate job applicants. Although quite different in nature, these variables are *manipulated* or *controlled* by the researchers in some specified way, and as such these are considered to be *treatments* in the experimental strategy.

9.2.2   *The Measurement of One or More Outcome Variables*

In each of these studies, the researchers were able to specify the impact of the experimental treatment by carefully measuring certain outcome measures, or dependent variables. For Givoni et al.'s study of metal roofs, the dependent variables were the *temperature readings for indoor areas* of the test cell environments, including both the attic and the indoor living environment. More specifically, the researchers were able to ascertain how much the indoor temperatures were cooled by the several experimental conditions (see Figures 9.2 and 9.3). In a similar way, Devlin was able to assess the impact of gender designations through two measures: a questionnaire instrument whereby prospective employers could register their *evaluation* on a 1-to-7 rating scale, and a *hiring decision* to accept or reject. Again, although quite different in nature, both the temperature and evaluation measures are the outcome measures (or dependent variables) of these experiments.

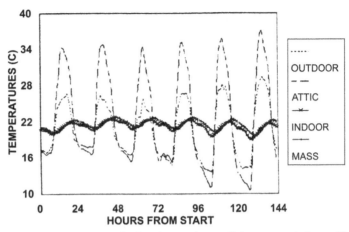

Figure 9.2 Temperature variation by each condition tested. From Givoni et al. Courtesy of American Solar Energy Society, Inc.

9.2.3 *The Designation of a Unit of Assignment*

In each of these studies, the researchers applied the experimental treatment to a specified *unit of assignment*. In the case of Givoni et al.'s research, the treatment conditions (various combinations of insulation, venting fans, and mass) are all applied to a *test cell*. This test cell was a small-scale mock-up of a metal-roofed residential unit in a hot climate, a 1-meter cube with metal-roofed gable (see Figure 9.1).

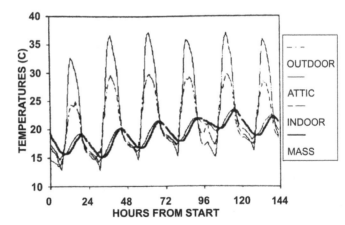

Figure 9.3 Temperature variation by each condition tested. From Givoni et al. Courtesy of American Solar Energy Society, Inc.

However, in Devlin's study the "unit of assignment" was not an inanimate object, but rather the *individual architects* who were asked to evaluate the fictitious job applicants. Each of these "units"—whether test cells or individual architects— received a treatment manipulated by the researcher.

9.2.4   *The Use of a Comparison or Control Group*

A fourth common feature of these two studies is their use of a comparison or control group. The control condition in Givoni et al.'s study is achieved with the insulation panels closed both day and night, such that no heating or cooling occurs. In all other conditions (i.e., treatment conditions), the insulation panels are closed during the day and opened at night to allow for cooling. In other words, the control condition is defined as one to which the treatment is *not* applied. However, in Devlin's study, it is more accurate to say that *comparison* groups received different treatments. This is because all architect respondents received some treatment, one of four combinations of male or female applicant, and junior or senior level. The purpose of using either a control or comparison groups is to allow measurement of the relative effect of the treatment, or independent variable, against the units that received either no treatment or a different treatment.

9.2.5   *A Focus on Causality*

The combined effect of these several defining features of the experimental research design (i.e., treatment, outcome measures, unit of assignment, and control or comparison groups) is to enable the researcher to credibly establish a cause-effect relationship. In general, the experimental researcher is seeking to ascertain and measure the extent to which one or more treatments cause a clearly measured outcome within a specified research setting, whether in a laboratory or in the field.

Although the underlying structure of the experimental research design is essentially consistent across diverse topic areas, there are nevertheless some differences in emphasis, specifically the extent to which the issue of "causality" can be taken for granted.[8] To be specific, experimental research in environmental technology (such as the metal roof study) is more likely to take causality for granted than research on sociocultural aspects of architecture (such as the gender designation research). This is because environmental technology, like much research in many fields of science and engineering, tends to incorporate the following characteristics: (1) the use of laboratory settings where relevant variables can be easily controlled; (2) variables that are in many instances inert, and therefore likely to remain consistent and amenable to accurate measurement; (3) explicit theories that enable researchers to specify the expected effects of a particular treatment; and (4) measurement instruments that are precisely calibrated to measure such effects. Given these more easily measurable conditions, then, causality in such research can often be assumed without much discussion or argument.

However, in research that involves people's reactions to physical and/or social variables (especially in field settings, as is the case in Devlin's research), researchers tend to be more explicit about how they have met the basic requirements of experimental design. For example, Devlin explicitly emphasizes the *random* assignment of résumé recipients to the four treatment conditions, random assignment being a significant hallmark of experimental design. Likewise, in drawing their conclusions, researchers who explore socio-physical dynamics in architecture tend to emphasize the conditions and limitations of a causal interpretation.

Similarly, this is exactly the case in the way Devlin qualifies her conclusion that male respondents tended to rate senior female applicants less positively than the senior male applicants. Devlin specifically mentions two limitations to a causal interpretation: (1) many respondents explained that they found it hard to rate the applicants because the résumé information was so limited; and (2) the response rate was only 30% and therefore the extent of generalizability to the larger population of architect employers is limited. Such problems and limitations in experimental research will be discussed in greater detail in segment 9.5 of this chapter.

BOX 9.1

The Effect of Intelligibility on Place Legibility

This study by Yixiang Long and Perver Baran aims to address the question: To what extent do certain objective physical features of cities, measured by Space Syntax analyses, affect people's subjective experience of the urban environment?[a] It is a notable undertaking in several respects. First, it builds on Kevin Lynch's classic and influential study, *The Image of the City*, and seeks to identify potentially causal objective measures that lead to people's experience of legibility encoded in Lynch's concepts of nodes, landmarks, districts, edges, and paths. Second, it employs Space Syntax, a school of thought and analytical framework developed by Bill Hillier and colleagues, to analyze how morphologies of space embody social and

[a] Yixiang Long and Perver K. Baran, "Does Intelligibility Affect Place Legibility? Understanding the Relationship between Objective and Subjective Evaluations of the Urban Environment," *Environment and Behavior*, in press.

(Continued)

cognitive logic. (See Chapters 8 and 11 for more discussion of Space Syntax.) By investigating the relationship between these two well-established conceptual frameworks, this study represents a innovative integration of two significant theoretical contributions. Third, although the correlational research strategy represents the most common methodology for investigating the relationship of spatial form to subjective cognitive responses, the authors have used a decisively experimental strategy to good effect.

The research design for this study entails a field experiment conducted in the city of Changsha, the capital city of Hunan Province in China. A space syntax analysis of the entire city was used to identify the two study areas for the experiment; a standard axial maps analysis was conducted for each neighborhood separately. A combination of measures (global integration, local integration, and connectivity) was used to differentiate the overall "intelligibility" of the two neighborhoods (see Figures 9.4 and 9.5). The first neighborhood, Dong-pai-lou, is characterized by a system of streets that is "highly permeable inward as well as outward . . . , indicating a clear relationship between global and local structure." However, the second neighborhood, Rong-wan-zhen, has a more treelike structure that "does not connect well with north and south sub-areas of the neighborhood . . . and there is an unclear relationship between the global and local structure."

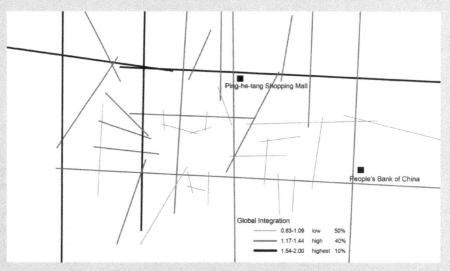

Figure 9.4   Dong-pai-lou system of highly permeable streets. Courtesy of SAGE Publications.

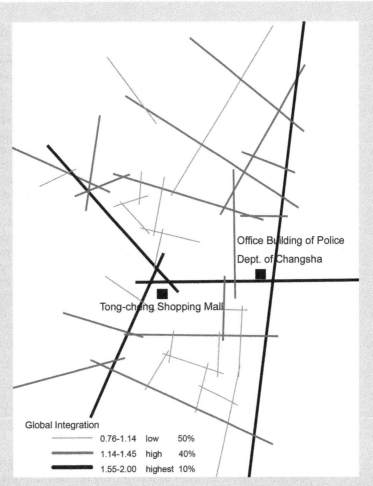

Figure 9.5   Rong-wan-zhen treelike structure of streets. Courtesy of SAGE Publications.

The stated hypothesis for the experiment is: "[T]his difference in intelligibility (our independent variable) will play an important role in individual's [sic] spatial cognition (i.e., place legibility)." To this end, the authors employed a "posttest-only two experimental group design," whereby university student volunteers unfamiliar with these neighborhoods were initially assessed on a spatial/visual-ability test and matched as comparable pairs. Students with the same gender and spatial ability

(Continued)

test scores were then randomly assigned to one of two groups of 24 participants.

Each of the two treatment groups met in the specific neighborhood location and was asked to "freely explore the neighborhood for an hour." Following the neighborhood exploration, they were asked to complete three tasks: (1) to draw a sketch map of the neighborhood they explored, (2) a scene-recognition test, and (3) a brief survey. In the brief survey, participants were asked to indicate their confidence regarding drawing the sketch map, the accuracy of their map and scene recognition, and giving directions. In a nutshell, the participants who explored the more intelligible neighborhood demonstrated more accurate path knowledge, recognized more scenes, and had more confidence in their spatial-cognitive abilities.

Over all, the hypothesis was generally supported: intelligibility (measured by space syntax analyses) does influence perceived legibility. The practical significance of this finding is that space syntax measures are easier and less time consuming to implement and compute than many other wayfinding performance measures taken with respondents either in real environments or simulated environments. In particular, space syntax measures can be taken during the design phase of an urban design or large architectural project such that the design can be modified for legibility before it is built.

9.3   STRATEGY: DISTINGUISHING BETWEEN EXPERIMENTAL AND QUASI-EXPERIMENTAL RESEARCH

So far in our discussion, we have discussed only the general requirements of experimental research, without recognizing the very important distinction between experimental and quasi-experimental designs. This distinction rests on the manner in which the units of assignment (whether test cells, people, etc.) are selected for either experimental or control treatments. Although the goal for both experimental and quasi-experimental research is to achieve comparability among the units in each treatment group, such comparability is more precisely established in experimental research through random assignment. In contrast, the quasi-experimental research design is often employed in field settings where people or physical variables cannot be randomly assigned because of either ethical or practical reasons. In such cases, the researcher seeks to ascertain or establish effective comparability across as many variables as possible. These considerations are discussed in greater detail in this chapter section.

9.3.1   *Random Assignment in Experimental Research*

Random assignment is an important criterion in experimental research where there is reason to believe that the units of assignment may not always be equivalent. In such instances, random assignment is considered the most effective way to ensure the essential comparability of treatment groups. If the "units" within treatment groups are truly equivalent, the observed differences in outcome measurements can then be credibly attributed to the treatment itself.

In the case of the gender discrimination study, Devlin was actually able to employ random assignment, even though the respondents were not conducting their evaluations in a laboratory setting. By choosing to manipulate the résumé conditions rather than depend on the real-life applicant resumes received by these architects, Devlin could assign résumé treatments *randomly* to the list of architects registered in Connecticut (Devlin's home state). This provides a greater level of assurance that the gender of the applicant actually had a measurable effect on the male architects' evaluations.

However, in experimental research based on inert materials (such as the Givoni et al study), the comparability of assigned "units" does not necessarily require the sort of randomization measures essential for studies about people's reactions to social or physical conditions. In most circumstances, the essential comparability of test cells or mock-ups can be assumed either because: (1) materials of the same physical specifications are used; or (2) the same physical unit can be reused in a different treatment condition. As a consequence, the authors of the metal roof study can claim that, given certain specified climatic conditions, the different measured cooling outcomes can be attributed to the differences in treatment conditions.

9.3.2   *Nonrandom Assignment in Quasi-Experimental Research*

As mentioned earlier, research studies conducted in the field frequently entail situations in which random assignments cannot be achieved because of either ethical or practical reasons. For example, if a researcher wanted to test the effect of four lighting systems on employee productivity in four separate office areas, it is unlikely that management would agree to assign the employees randomly to the four office areas such that important work group functions would be disrupted.

In this situation, researchers would likely adopt a quasi-experimental design in which they would identify four *existing* work groups, each of which would receive a different lighting treatment. In doing so, the researchers would attempt to find work groups comparable in as many respects as possible, including task or work objectives, mix of job types, gender mix, age range, level of education, and so on. If, for instance, the work groups' tasks were quite dissimilar, it would then be more difficult to attribute measured differences in productivity to the lighting treatment rather than differences in the tasks.

Another example of quasi-experimental design is a small research project conceived and conducted by students in one of Groat's research methods classes.[9] The students had raised in discussion the example of a small gallery area near the school offices that had been created to function as both an exhibit space and a lounge area for faculty and students. In the students' view, the space was seldom used as lounge. Discussion soon revolved around what sort of changes would have to be made for the space to function more as a lounge and social space. The students hypothesized that the gallery would be used more if the arrangement of furniture were more informal and if small screening elements were used to block the view through the glass wall along the doorway side of the space.

The students' research design involved two sets of observations of the space: the first observations recorded people's use of the space in its existing condition, and the second recorded its use under the experimental treatment. The observations were made on the Monday (studio day) and Tuesday (nonstudio day) of two successive weeks, starting at 8:30 in the morning and continuing to 7:30 at night. Each observation period was for 15 minutes duration starting on the half-hour and ending at 45 minutes after each hour.

The experimental treatment condition, used in the second two-day observation period, was designed to create a more "inviting" ambience; it entailed alteration of the furniture arrangement, lighting levels, and ambient sound (see Figures 9.6 and 9.7). More specifically, the following alterations were made: addition of screening elements to create more visual privacy from the hallway windows; relocation of some furniture elements for more privacy and to create groupings; lowering of fluorescent lighting levels; addition of incandescent table lamps; introduction of reading materials on the tables; use of soft background music; and introduction of plants.

Finally, the students also developed a one-page observation sheet that included the following information: a count of the number of people using the space during that observation period; a plan of the gallery including the furniture arrangement in which the people's movement and activities were mapped; and a coding system by which people's specific activities could be described (i.e., speaking, writing/reading, sleeping).

The general conclusion that the students were able to draw was that although the numbers of people using the space did not change substantially, the average amount of time each person spent in the gallery increased, and the nature of their activities changed as well (see Figures 9.8, 9.9, 9.10, 9.11, 9.12, and 9.13). Indeed, by the second day of the treatment condition, the proportion of staying activities was more than double that of the previous Tuesday in the control condition.

Figure 9.6   Existing and modified condition of the space observed. Courtesy of Barnes et al.

Figure 9.7   Existing and modified condition of the space observed. Courtesy of Barnes et al.

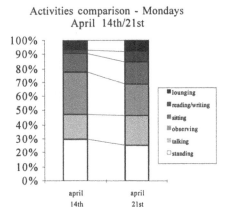

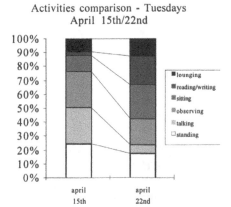

Figure 9.8 Comparison of the total observed activities. Courtesy of Barnes et al.

Figure 9.9 Comparison of the total observed activities. Courtesy of Barnes et al.

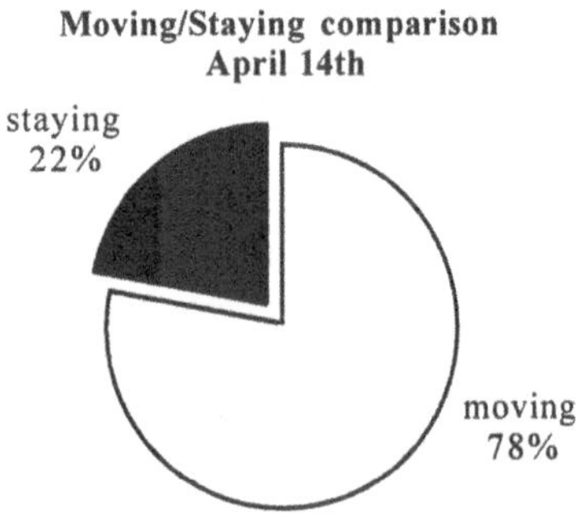

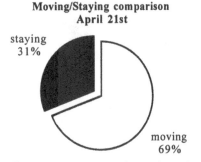

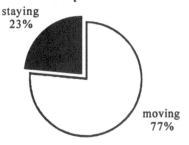

Figure 9.10 Comparison of moving/staying activities for each day of observation. Courtesy of Barnes et al.

Figure 9.11 Comparison of moving/staying activities for each day of observation. Courtesy of Barnes et al.

Figure 9.12 Comparison of moving/staying activities for each day of observation. Courtesy of Barnes et al.

Figure 9.13 Comparison of moving/staying activities for each day of observation. Courtesy of Barnes et al.

How much of this change can be attributed to the treatment effect? Due to the circumstances of the field setting, the students were unable to assign gallery users randomly to the two conditions, and so they adopted a quasi-experimental design. But since no specific measures of the gallery users were taken, it is not possible to gauge precisely how the users of the control condition compared with those in the treatment condition. Still, there were no obvious indicators that the groups were substantially nonequivalent. It is therefore likely, but not certain, that the "informal, inviting" condition did encourage and enable a change in the use patterns of the gallery space.[10]

9.4   DIAGRAMMING EXPERIMENTAL RESEARCH DESIGNS

From the experience of the architectural design process, we know that it is often helpful, sometimes even essential, to diagram the singular qualities of a design concept or parti. In a similar vein, experimental researchers have devised a way of diagramming the particular details of experimental research designs, using the following coding system:

{R = Random assignment}
{X = Experimental treatment}
{O = Observation of dependent variables (e.g., pretest or posttest)}

Although there are a great many typical or standard experimental research designs designated by an established nomenclature,[11] for our purposes it is a sufficient introduction to diagram the three exemplar studies that have been discussed thus far in the chapter.

Taking the Givoni et al. study of radiant cooling first, this research design can be represented as follows. Each row represents, from left to right, the sequence entailed in each treatment condition.

      O   {Observation only, with no prior treatment}
X1   O   {Treatment 1, and subsequent observation}
X2   O   {Treatment 2, and subsequent observation}
X3   O   {Treatment 3, and subsequent observation}

This notation system conveys the following essential points about the design of this study: (1) no explicit attention is paid to random assignment, as all the relevant procedures deal with standardized inert materials; (2) there are three different treatment conditions in addition to the control condition; and (3) only posttest (i.e., no pretest) observations are made.

Devlin's study of gender issues in architectural practice presents a slightly different research design in the following respects: (1) random assignment is an explicit and important consideration for establishing comparability across treatment groups; and (2) there is no explicit control condition. However, similar to Givoni et al.'s study, no pretest observations are made. Thus, the notation system for this study can be represented this way:

R X1 O {Random assignment, followed by treatment 1, observation}
R X2 O {Random assignment, followed by treatment 2, observation}
R X3 O {Random assignment, followed by treatment 3, observation}
R X4 O {Random assignment, followed by treatment 4, observation}

Finally, the Barnes et al. study of behavioral patterns in a gallery space presents a slightly more ambiguous research design. This is because the researchers were not able to determine the extent to which the people who experienced the original gallery arrangement were likewise the people who experienced the modified arrangement. (In retrospect, this might have been achieved by asking users if they had come into the gallery anytime during the previous Monday or Tuesday.) If the gallery users had been substantially the same group, then the notation of the research design would be as follows:

O O X O   O   {Two observations, treatment, followed by two observations}

This design is known as a "single-group interrupted time-series design," whereby two pretest observations were made, after which the treatment (physical modification) was applied, followed by two posttest observations.

However, if the two sets of users were substantially or completely different, then it would be more accurate to diagram the research design in the following way:

O O {No treatment, two observations only}
X O O {Treatment, followed by two observations}

This second diagram presumes that the group that experienced the original gallery arrangement constitutes the control group, whereas the group that experienced the new arrangement was the experimental treatment group. Both control and treatment groups were observed twice, the treatment group only as a posttest.

Finally, the Long and Baran study made use of a posttest-only two experimental group design. In other words, each of the two randomly assigned comparison groups received a different treatment condition (one of the two city neighborhoods explored), and there was no control group.

X   O   {Treatment, followed by one observation}
X   O   {Treatment, followed by one observation}

Readers who choose to make use of experimental research procedures are advised to consult some of the books cited in the chapter endnotes for further examples of specific experimental designs. These diagrammatic notations can be exceedingly useful to the researcher for clarifying the precise nature and assumptions of the experimental design he or she selects.

9.5   TACTICS: THE SETTINGS, TREATMENTS, AND MEASURES FOR EXPERIMENTAL RESEARCH

Thus far, our discussion of experimental and quasi-experimental research has focused on the defining characteristics of the research strategy itself. However, within the experimental design, there are numerous options regarding the tactics for achieving such an experimental strategy. For instance, the experimental setting can range from a highly controlled laboratory to less well-controlled field sites. Similarly, the treatment conditions can range from highly calibrated physical manipulations to categorical, nonphysical conditions, such as the gender designations in Devlin's study. Finally, measurement of the outcome variables can range from the instrumented measures of physical changes (such as air temperature measurement in the Givoni et al. research) to less finely measured indexes of a behavioral response (such as in Devlin's study).

In the examples that follow, the broad range and combinations of tactics available to experimental and quasi-experimental research will be discussed in the context of several specific research studies.

9.5.1   *Clarifying the Tactics of the Previously Discussed Studies*

Before considering additional examples of experimental research, we would like to characterize more explicitly the tactics selected by the researchers of the previously cited studies. For instance, Givoni et al.'s study of radiant cooling employs the sort of tactics typically associated with experimental research in environmental technology. The construction and treatment of the test cells was carefully monitored within a university lab setting. The physical treatment conditions of the test cells could be precisely specified and controlled by the experimenters; likewise, the outcome measures of air temperature could be exactly measured by laboratory instruments. (See Figure 9.14 for a complete summary of tactics used in the experimental studies cited in this chapter section.)

In contrast, the Devlin study represents a set of experimental procedures starkly different from the Givoni et al. study. Indeed, one could argue that the

Study	Setting	Treatment	Outcome Measures
1. Radiant cooling (Givoni et al.)	Lab	Environmental modifications insulation venting mass	Instrumented measures air temperature
2. Gender issues (Devlin)	Field	Résumés gender seniority	Attitudinal response applicant evaluation hiring decision
3. Gallery behavior (Barnes et al.)	Field	Environmental modifications furniture lighting ambient sound screens	Behavioral change staying/moving
4. Place legibility (Long and Baran)	Field	Neighborhood setting low vs. high intelligibility	Place legibility sketch maps recognition tests surveys

Figure 9.14 Summary of tactics in cited studies.

combination of the setting, treatments, and measures in Devlin's study represent virtually the opposite end of the spectrum. First, the research setting is not only a field setting, but one that is in effect dispersed across the country, to offices where the architects received the résumé conditions. Second, although the treatment conditions were conveyed physically in print through gendered names and stated levels of employment experience, the physical and interactive reality of a real-life applicant was absent. Finally, the outcome measures of evaluation and employment decision were rendered through scores on a questionnaire. In all of these ways, the focus of the study was on the social-cultural implications of nonphysical treatment conditions, measured through attitudinal responses.

Third, the Barnes et al. student study of the architecture gallery, though quasi-experimental in design, represents an intermediate range of tactics. First, although the study employs a field setting rather than a lab, the setting itself is relatively small and easily manipulated by the experimenters. Secondly, the treatment conditions are all physically based (i.e., arrangement of furniture, the type of lighting, etc.); as such, they can be clearly specified and measured in physical terms. Finally, although the outcome is behavioral and requires some interpretation, the standards for counting people and classifying behavior can be clearly standardized.

Lastly, the Long and Baran study on the effects of the qualities of urban form on people's experience of place legibility is likewise a field experiment. In this case the treatment condition entailed the exposure of two comparable groups of students to one of two neighborhood locations—one with a higher level of intelligibility, and the other with a much lower level. All subjects were instructed to "freely explore the neighborhood for an hour." To test the extent to which the individual students were able to perceive legibility in the neighborhood they explored, three outcome measures were used: (1) the drawn accuracy of a sketch map; (2) a scene recognition test; and (3) a survey questionnaire aimed to test the subjects' sense of confidence in their sketch map, scene recognition, and direction giving.

9.5.2   *Environmental Performance of Automated Blinds in Office Buildings: Using a Behavioral Survey Prior to Lab Experiment*

Research by Kim et al. focuses in particular on the use of blinds to conserve energy and improve comfort in modern office buildings.[12] Their study focuses on the potential efficacy of automated Venetian blind systems as compared to the use of manual or motorized systems. Considerable research on the use of the latter two options has previously demonstrated the limitations of both these systems, largely because office occupants rarely modify the position of the blinds in response to changing environmental conditions. Thus, the authors hypothesize that automated blinds may have relatively greater potential for energy savings and improved comfort.

To test this hypothesis, the researchers began first by conducting a survey of blind usage by the occupants of a 22-story office building in Seoul, Korea. The blinds in each office were operated either directly by the occupants themselves or through a central control center. Blind operations were monitored over two clear days and two cloudy days, at 10-minute intervals. The overall conclusion confirmed the general results of much previous research, that is, that most blinds were never or rarely operated (see Figure 9.15). Moreover, the pattern of operation varies by building facade exposure, with the fewest adjustments made by occupants of south-facing offices. Overall, this pattern of usage "is not sufficient to meet the energy savings requirements and environmental demands for comfort."[13] Based on the survey of blind operations, the authors selected for their experiment a south-facing office condition, with the blinds set at an occlusion index of 75%, the average reading for clear sky conditions.

To conduct their set of experiments, the authors built two full-size, side-by-side mock-up test rooms. The rooms were built to the same dimensions, and with identical heat loss and gain properties; test room 1 was fitted with the automated blinds, while test room 2 was fitted with manual or motorized blinds. To assess the thermal performance of the blinds, measurements were taken of both the difference between indoor and outdoor temperatures, and the rate at which the temperature

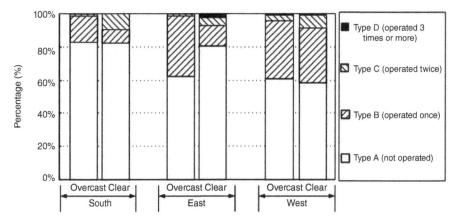

Figure 9.15   Blind operation frequency analysis. Courtesy of Elsevier.

decreased over time. Secondly, to assess the visual performance of the blinds, measurements were taken of both the interior and exterior illuminance.

Test conditions as indicated in Figure 9.16 were run on six days in August, and measurements for three performance criteria were taken: temperature difference between indoor and outdoor, energy consumption, and visual comfort. The authors conclude that given the conditions tested in the mock-up offices, the automated blinds system demonstrated both potential energy savings and comfort enhancement. In addition, the authors noted that the automation of the blinds in these experimental cases was based solely on changes in the outdoor conditions; however, a significant enhancement of the automated system could be achieved by modifying the algorithm to include indoor conditions.

9.5.3   *Occupant Comfort from Air Movement: Using a Lab Setting, Physical Treatments, Instrumentation, and Subjective Measures*

Although much environmental technology research relies on combining lab settings with exclusively instrumented measures of physical outcome variables, many other variations of lab setting research are possible. One such example is a study by Edward Arens et al. concerning the use of personally controlled air fans to achieve cooling and perceived comfort.[14] The goal of this study was to evaluate the effectiveness of using fans, instead of compressor-based air conditioning, as a means to achieve cooling comfort. In doing so, the study was conducted in an environmental chamber (i.e., lab setting) where individual subjects could be exposed to a controlled range of warm temperatures (see Figure 9.17). The environmental chamber was designed to "appear as a realistic residential or office space."[15]

Case	Date	Test Room 1	Test Room 2	Cooling	Remarks
1	8/12	Automated blind: Energy-saving mode	Manual (fully opened)	X	Evaluate temperature difference
2	8/16	(see Table 1)	Manual (fully closed)	X	Evaluate temperature difference
3	8/19		Manual (fully opened)	O	Evaluate energy consumption
4	8/20		Manual (fully closed)	O	Evaluate energy consumption
5	8/18	Automated blind: Comfort mode	Manual (fully opened)	O	Evaluate comfort
6	8/29	(see Table 2)	Motorized[a]	O	Evaluate comfort

[a]Occlusion index 75%, slat angle: 90°.

Figure 9.16 Summary of six experimental cases utilized to study the impact of the automated blind on environmental performance. Redrawn from *Building and Environment* 44, Kim, Ji-Hyun, Park, Young-Joon, Yeo, Myoung-Souk, & Kim, Kwang-Woo. "An experimental study on the environmental performance of the automated blind in summer," 1517–1527 (2009).With permission from Elsevier.

The 119 subjects (57 female, 62 male) were divided into two comparison groups. One group was asked to control the fan settings in a fluctuating mode; the second group used the fan's constant mode, "in which the inherent turbulence of the airstream was at higher frequencies than in the fluctuating mode."[16] During both experimental protocols, the subjects' time in the experimental chamber included two distinct activity segments generating two distinct metabolic rates: one which included both sitting and step-climbing (1.2 met), and another which was entirely sedentary (1.0 met). Throughout all sessions, the subjects experienced a range of temperatures from 25°C to 30°C. Thus, the treatments represented a combination of both lab-based controls and behavioral regimens.

The outcome measures included both instrumentation and subjective ratings of perceived comfort. The former was achieved by recording the subject's choice of fan speed, and the latter was measured by a 7-point scale from cold to hot indicating how the subject experienced the temperature of the environment. More than 80% of the subjects in the 1.2-met condition were able to maintain comfort up to 29°C. As a result, the researchers are able to conclude that within certain temperature zones, the use of personal air fans can serve as an effective alternative to mechanical air conditioning.

Figure 9.17   Temperature range versus fan speed level. Arens, 1998. Courtesy of Prof. Edward Arens.

BOX 9.2

Experiment: Energy Conservation in Housing

Malcolm Bell and Robert Lowe sought to test the impact of various energy saving techniques in housing administered by the Housing Authority of York, UK[a] (see Figure 9.18). As such, it therefore represents a field setting experiment.

As part of a larger three-stage program in energy conservation monitoring, the authors report on a 30-house scheme in which the impact of energy saving improvements were measured against a "control group of dwellings in the same modernization scheme but with no additional

Figure 9.18 Typical house type in Malcolm Bell and Robert Lowe's energy-efficient modernization study. Reprinted from *Energy and Buildings* 32 (2000), with permission from Elsevier Science.

---

[a] Malcolm Bell and Robert Lowe, "Energy Efficient Modernization of Housing: A UK Case Study," *Energy and Buildings* 32 (2000): 267–280.

(Continued)

energy efficiency works."[b] The 21 houses in the experimental group were modernized with a combination of clearly specified physical treatments: insulation, draft-proofing of doors and windows, central heating with gas condensing boiler, and a gas fire as a secondary heat source. The 11 houses in the control group, with no additional energy efficiency works, were well matched with the experimental houses in terms of the initial energy characteristics. As a consequence, any consistent differences in energy consumption could then be attributed to the experimental treatment.

Monitoring measures included internal temperatures and gross energy consumption for the entire period, both of which are based on instrumentation. Although the difference of 5,536 kWh between the experimental and control groups is statistically significant at the .03 level, the measured savings are about half of what was predicted by energy modeling. Further investigation, including interviews with residents, indicated that some residents used the secondary heat source, the gas fire, for so many hours on a daily basis that the energy efficiency of the gas boiler was compromised. In this regard, the monitoring of energy efficient modifications in a field, or real-world, housing setting, provided important insights about the limits of conservation hardware, when it is not accompanied by changes in human behavior.

_____

[b] Ibid., 272.

9.5.4   Experimental Monitoring of Thermal Comfort and Simulation of Energy Usage: Using a Purpose-Built Testing Prototype, Physical Treatments, Instrumented Measures, and Numerical Simulations

An increasingly common strategy in experimental research is to augment it, either iteratively or in distinct phases, with simulation modeling. Such is the case in a study of solar walls in residential buildings conducted by Stazi, Mastrucci, and di Perna, and briefly described earlier in Chapter 3.[17] The goal of the study was to test whether the use of a Trombe wall design (a solar wall with vents at the top and bottom for ventilation) combined with a shading device would result in improved thermal comfort and energy savings over a standard nonventilated solar wall. In particular, the authors aimed to develop potential modifications to solar wall and/or Trombe wall designs suitable for the Mediterranean climate, where the use of solar walls is advantageous in winter months but prone in summer months to increased cooling requirements and overheating. Three operating conditions (or treatments) were tested: (1) a nonventilated solar wall; (2) a Trombe wall in winter mode with air thermo-circulation; and (3) a Trombe wall in summer mode with cross-ventilation. (See Figure 3.1 for treatment of the solar wall and the Trombe wall in winter and summer conditions.)

Figure 9.19   View of the building. Courtesy of Elsevier.

These treatments were built into a prototype south-facing residential building, consisting of nine apartment units, in central Italy. The several treatment conditions were monitored for several years and over different seasons; measurements were taken of the thermal behavior of the solar walls, indoor thermal comfort conditions, and energy consumption (see Figures 9.19 and 9.20).

Figure 9.20   Exterior view of the Trombe wall. Courtesy of Elsevier.

Once the researchers had collected an extensive set of data from the case study experiments, numerical simulations were performed using an existing software program using an algorithm already validated for Trombe walls. Taking other modifications and calculations into account, the authors then compared the values obtained from the simulation model with the experimental data "in order to verify the reliability of the simulation tools in reproducing real situations. Once the model had been calibrated, it was possible to generalize the results running the calculation for the whole year."[18]

As a result of the combination of the case study experiments and simulation modeling, the authors then returned to the experimental mode with the goal of testing modifications of the Trombe wall design for summer conditions, including shading solar walls with overhangs, use of opaque shutters, activating the cross-ventilation of the Trombe wall, and improving natural ventilation. Although the monitoring of this treatment condition occurred during a period of extreme heat, the modified Trombe wall design nevertheless maintained operative temperature within the comfort range for the entire period. The authors conclude that the tested Trombe wall configuration in Mediterranean climate conditions can be an efficient system for both energy savings and thermal comfort.

See Figure 9.21 for a summary of the tactics used in the studies discussed in this chapter section.

Figure 9.21   Summary of tactics in cited studies.

Study	Setting	Treatment	Outcome Measures

1. Blind operation systems (Kim et al.)	Field	Blind systems
		    manual
		    motorized
		    automated
			Instrumented measures
			    Temperatures indoors
			    and outdoors
			    Illuminance indoors
			    and outdoors

2. Personally controlled air fans (Arens et al.)	Lab	Physical treatments
		    temperature
		    activity level
		    fan type
			Instrumented measures
			and behavioral response
			    fan speed choice
			    perceived comfort

3. Energy use in housing (Bell and Lowe)	Field	Environmental modifications
		    gas boiler
		    insulation
		    draft proofing
		    secondary heat
			Instrumented measures
			    internal temperature
			    gross energy
			    consumption

(Continued)

Figure 9.21 *(Continued)*

Study	Setting	Treatment	Outcome Measures
4. Solar walls (Stazi et al.)	Field/ Prototype	Solar/Trombe modifications glazing ventilation shading	Instrumented measures temperature readings energy use/savings simulation modeling
5. Perceptions of facades (Stamps)	Lab	Treatment of facade features visual area façade elements fenestration articulation	Perception of architectural mass

BOX 9.3

Experiment: A Case Study of Facade Treatments

Stamps's study of the effects of design features on people's perceptions of architectural mass is based on an experimental design, and in that regard it is unusual.[a] Many, probably most, studies of nonarchitects' or users' responses to building facades have employed a correlational design involving assessments of actual buildings. Stamps's research design involved the use of computer-generated sketches of building facades that systematically varied the architectural treatment of each facade. Four key variables, based on a previous pilot study, were identified as having a potential impact on respondent assessments: visual area, partitioning of facade elements, fenestration, and articulation (e.g., bays or notches) of the facade plane. Using an experimental design protocol that enables multiple treatments to be combined across a limited number of stimuli (i.e., the facades), Stamps generated the nine facade examples represented in Figure 9.22. To achieve a random selection of respondents, Stamps relied on a survey research firm to recruit a random selection of respondents from the local area. Each respondent was asked to view paired sets of the facades and indicate which facade appeared to be more massive.

---

[a] Arthur Stamps, "Measures of Architectural Mass: From Vague Impressions to Definite Design Features," *Environment and Planning B: Planning and Design* (1998): 825–836.

(Continued)

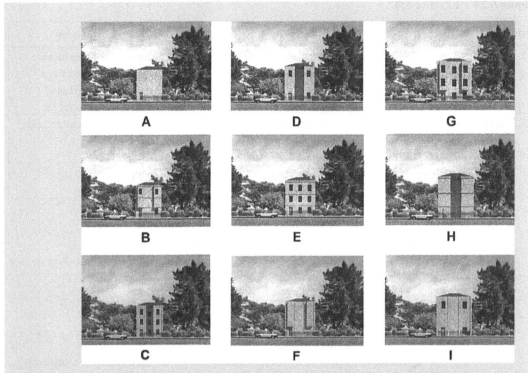

Figure 9.22 Computer-generated facade stimuli from Arthur Stamps. Courtesy of Pion Limited, London.

The results of Stamps's study indicate that the most influential variable by far was visual area, which can be modified *in situ* by setback requirements. Fenestration treatments had a much more modest impact on perception of mass, and both articulation of the facade plane and the partitioning of facade elements had minimal impact.

9.6   THE COMPLEMENTARY NATURE OF EXPERIMENTAL CULTURES IN DESIGN AND RESEARCH

In Chapter 2, we argued that the relationship between design and research is far more nuanced and multifaceted than a black-and-white statement of equivalence or difference. Here we want to address the application of the term *experimental* to design studio and practice endeavors in recent discourse with how we have discussed the notion of experimental research design in this chapter.

It should already be clear by this point that for the purposes of peer-reviewed scholarly research, the use of the term *experiment* (including *quasi-experiment*) is restricted to the relatively precise characteristics already discussed in sections 9.2 and 9.3. However, some proponents of the role of research in design studios and practice have pointed out the utility of understanding the comparably experimental culture of research and design.[19] This is true in a very general sense, and consistent with our discussion in Chapter 2 concerning the equivalence of logics in use, and so on. Still, many instances of the research enterprise in studio and practice contexts are experimental in a more generic or metaphorical sense. While many valuable insights are generated through inductive exploration (i.e., the logic of discovery), often the iterative sequence of testing and documentation through deductive logic is missing or less developed.

In this context, a *JAE* article by Stephen Kieran (of Kieran Timberlake) establishes a legitimate claim to design experimentation that meets the claim of experimental research.[20] He describes in some detail the increasing emphasis on research as the core of his practice. He then discusses how over recent years the firm has "introduced the process of monitoring what we have planned and built."[21] In this endeavor, their designs for technically innovative curtain walls have been built as prototypes at the University of Pennsylvania's research and teaching facility for the School of Engineering. And, in collaboration with Professor Ali Malkawi, a system of monitoring devices has been employed.

Finally, Kieran's description of the design for a residence in Maryland details a thoughtful process of integrating natural ventilation, adjustable solar shading, and a bifolding hanger door as a thermal pocket over the glazing layer. As he explains it, the monitoring data from this design proposal suggested further lines of development, including the introduction of thermal mass into the cavity to store heat for evening hours. He concludes by suggesting an experiment to draw heated air out of the top of the cavity, thus "using the facade as a type of Trombe wall"[22] (see Figure 9.23).

In sum, what Kieran describes is not too much different than the Trombe wall study by Stazi et al. Both "experiments" involved an iterative process of tinkering with and testing out empirically different modifications to a wall system; both also extensively used monitoring devices to collect data and evaluate the effectiveness of the wall treatments. In some contrast, Stazi and his colleagues, as established researchers, began with an intention to test out solar/ Trombe wall systems, and then developed a broader analysis through numerical simulations to thermal comfort and energy savings that might be generalized throughout the seasons and in similar climate conditions. Moreover, Stazi et al. systematically tested multiple treatment conditions, whereas Kieran Timberlake

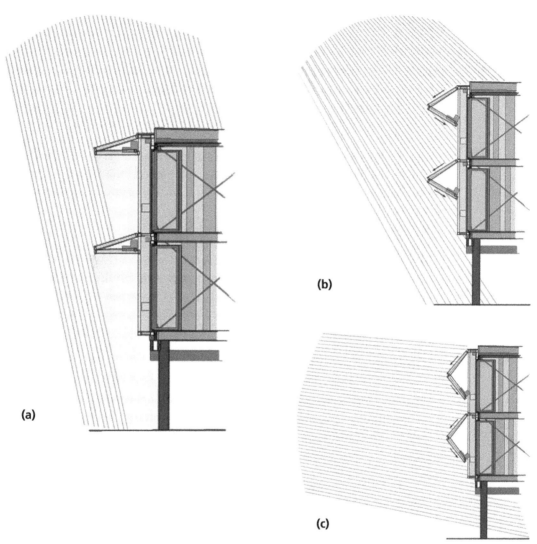

Figure 9.23 Varying positions of the accordion-style glass doors of the Loblolly House by Kieran-Timberlake Associates LLP. © Kieran Timberlake.

aimed to develop a design for a particular client that gradually evolved into considerations for the design of a Trombe wall system. Despite these differences, the distance between these examples of experimental design and experimental research is close indeed.

BOX 9.4

Applications of Experimental Research in Practice and Education

In the vast majority of practice and educational settings, design decision making in the most technical areas of architecture typically relies on a foundation of extensive experimental research. This is certainly the case with issues such as building skin design and materials development.

In a notable collaboration between a professional firm (Perkins + Will) and an architectural design studio (University of Cincinnati), the studio employed computational design techniques, analytical tools, and digital fabrication to achieve performance goals for the design of a building facade retrofit.[a] Prior experimental research is the basis for not only the various performance criteria but also the development of various simulation and analytical tools.

The particular building site was an actual project from the Perkins + Will office, and office personnel participated as resources to the studio. The task of the studio was to "reskin" the former cold storage facility near downtown Chicago that was being converted to a commercial office building. Figure 9.24 outlines the various stages and techniques that served as the framework for the studio work.

In this studio context, the integration of simulation techniques for parametric design and fabrication led to a variety of solution types. These included: (1) an adaptable building skin responsive to daily or seasonal changes; (2) a double skin with a kinetic shading system; (3) an external shading system; and (4) a tectonic building form. The development of this range of solution types demonstrates the integrative potential of experimentally developed analytical, visualization, and fabrication tools. Not only can such design processes lead to a much higher level of building performance criteria, but they can also offer a venue for effective collaboration and knowledge transfer between professional and academic settings.

---

[a] A. Aksamija, T. Snapp, M. Hodge, and M. Tang, "Re-skinning: Performance-Based Design and Fabrication of Building Facade Components: Design Computing, Analytics and Prototyping," *Perkins + Will Research Journal* 4(1) (2012): 15–28.

(Continued)

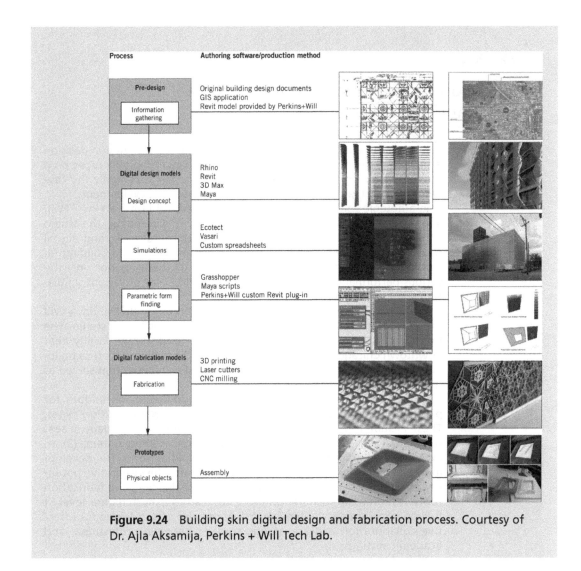

Figure 9.24   Building skin digital design and fabrication process. Courtesy of Dr. Ajla Aksamija, Perkins + Will Tech Lab.

9.7   CONCLUSIONS: STRENGTHS AND WEAKNESSES

Of all the research design strategies commonly employed by researchers, the experiment is, in all likelihood, the most controversial. On the one hand, experimental design is considered by postpositivist researchers to represent the highest standard of research.

The best method—indeed the only fully compelling method—of establishing causation is to conduct a carefully designed experiment in which the effects of possible lurking variables are controlled. To experiment means to actively change {x} and observe the response {y}.[23]

This quotation is revealing because it so crisply encapsulates the essence of what is seen as experimentalism's major strength: the most credible device for determination of causality, observed through a sequence of a specified treatment and its outcome.

On the other hand, the experimental design strategy is widely criticized, for a variety of reasons, by researchers representing both the intersubjective and subjectivist paradigms. Feminist scholars, in particular, have articulated a number of major concerns.[24] Most center around one of the following issues: (1) efficacy and accuracy, (2) misapplication of experimental procedure, or (3) ethical issues (see Figure 9.25).

Efficacy and Accuracy. The essence of the argument concerning the efficacy of experimental method is that most real-life settings or sociocultural phenomena are far too complex to be reduced to a small set of treatment and outcome variables. Moreover, the laboratory setting is seen not as a "neutral social environment" but rather as a "specific social environment that exerts its own effects."[25] Critics argue that instead, settings and phenomena must be studied in complex and messy natural settings. As Michelle Fine and Susan Gordon put it:

If you really want to know either of us, don't put us in the laboratory, or hand us a survey, or even interview us separately alone in our homes. Watch me (MF) with women friends, my son, his father, my niece or my mother and you will see what feels most authentic to me. These very moments, which construct who I am when I am most me, remain remote from psychological studies of individuals or even groups.[26]

Strengths	Weaknesses
Potential for establishing causality	Reduction of complex reality to identify "causal" or independent variables
Potential for generalizing results to other settings and phenomena	Misuse by overgeneralization to different ethnic, gender populations
Ability to control all aspects of experimental design enables attribution of causality	Overemphasis on control yields ethical problems, dehumanization

Figure 9.25 Strengths and weaknesses of experimental research.

Misapplication. Critics who cite the misuse or misapplication of experimental protocol frequently focus on the way biases or oversights can inadvertently influence the results of such research. This critique is articulated quite clearly by the well-known feminist researcher, Shulamit Reinharz. She argues:

> [P]ublication practices and experimental design highlight differences and hide similarities between groups. Overgeneralization that masks differences in race, age, education, and other factors is clearly inappropriate and possibly dangerous. Too often studies done on white populations are generalized to all groups, just as studies done on men are generalized to all people, thereby producing distorted results.[27]

However, a number of feminists and others affiliated with various schools of thought (including transformative, phenomenological, and others) have proposed a more nuanced and pragmatic perspective whereby the experimental research design is actually employed to reveal gendered and racist practices. Indeed, Devlin's study of gender discrimination in hiring is one such example. Implicit in this exploitation of the experimental method is the belief that, given the power and respect it commands in so many quarters, feminist and other emancipatory research will only be seen as credible if it is conveyed in the form of the influential experimental strategy.

Ethical Issues. The core of the ethical concerns that have been raised about experimental design is that the manipulative control exercised by the researcher puts research "subjects" in an essentially powerless position. Treatments are applied to subjects without their consultation. Or alternatively, a potentially advantageous treatment (i.e., better lighting or gender-neutral pedagogy) might be withheld from the "control" group of subjects. Indeed, even the objectified language of "subjects"—as opposed to people or individuals—tends to dehumanize the people who participate in such studies.

In the end, it would seem that the selection of the experimental design offers the potential to confer both profound benefits and potentially serious weaknesses. The former includes the attribution of causality, as well as prestige and credibility in some circles. Indeed, in some areas of research—notably in the more technical areas—the premises of experimental work remain unchallenged, although now frequently complemented by computer simulation models.

However, its shortcomings, as identified earlier, include: (1) inappropriate simplification of complex research issues; (2) potential for misapplication; and (3) the potential for serious ethical problems. Yet even feminist critic Shulamit Reinharz argues that despite its apparent weaknesses, researchers may do well to exploit its strengths:

Combining the strengths of the experimental method with the strengths of other methods is probably the best way to avoid its weaknesses while utilizing its power. Similarly, combining the strength of research with the power of other forms of persuasion is probably a useful approach for creating change.[28]

The notion of combining distinctly different research strategies is one that has become increasingly popular among researchers in diverse fields and disciplines. It is a topic to which we will return in Chapter 12.

NOTES

1. Baruch Givoni, Michael Gulich, Carlos Gomez, and Antulio Gomez, "Radiant Cooling by Metal Roofs in Developing Countries," *Proceedings of the 21st National Passive Solar Conference* (Boulder, CO: American Solar Energy Society, April 1996), 83–87.

2. Ann S. Devlin, "Architects: Gender-Role and Hiring Decisions," *Psychological Report* 81 (1997): 667–676.

3. Ibid., 670.

4. L. S. Fidell, "Empirical Verification of Sex Discrimination in Hiring Practices in Psychology," *American Psychologist* 25 (1970): 1094–1097.

5. Devlin, 667.

6. Ibid., 674.

7. William R. Standish, Thomas D. Cook, and Donald T. Campbell, *Experimental and Quasi-Experimental Designs for Generalized Causal Inference* (Boston: Houghton Mifflin, 2002).

8. Ibid.

9. Janice Barnes, Kaninika Bhatnagar, Fernando Lara, Satoshi Nakamura, Pirasri Povatong, Tien Chien Tsao, and Victoria Turkel, "Results of a Quasi-Experimental Treatment in the Architecture Gallery." Unpublished student paper, University of Michigan, Ann Arbor, MI, 1997.

10. Despite these conclusions, a major obstacle to changing the furniture arrangement on a permanent basis was that the intended lack of visibility meant the security of the exhibits could not be monitored from the offices across the hall. As a result of this quasi-experiment, then, the student group made a policy recommendation to the administration that a separate student/faculty lounge area should be provided. Several years later, a new lounge was built.

11. Standish et al.; John Creswell, *Research Design: Qualitative, Quantitative and Mixed Methods Approaches* (Thousand Oaks, CA: Sage, 2009); D. Mertens, *Research Methods in Education and Psychology*, 3rd ed. (Thousand Oaks, CA: Sage, 2010).

12. Ji-Hyun Kim, Young-Joon Park, Myooung-Souk Yeo, and Kwang-Woo Kim, "An Experimental Study on the Environmental Performance of the Automated Blind in Summer," *Building and Environment* (44) (2009): 1517–1527.

13. Ibid., 1521.

14. Edward Arens, Tengfang Xu, Katsuhiro Miura, Zhang Hui, Marc Fountain, and Fred Bauman, "A Study of Occupant Cooling by Personally Controlled Air Movement," *Energy and Building* 27 (1998): 45–59.

15. Ibid., 46–47.

16. Ibid., 47.

17. Francesca Stazi, Alessio Mastrucci, and Constanzo di Perna, "The Behaviour of Solar Walls in Residential Buildings with Different Insulation Levels: An Experimental and Numerical Study," *Energy and Buildings* 47 (2012): 217–229.

18. Ibid., 220.

19. David Salomon, "Experimental Cultures: On the 'End' of the Design Thesis and the Rise of the Research Studio," *Journal of Architectural Education* 65(1) (2011): 33–44.

20. Stephen Kieran, "Research in Design: Planning Doing Monitoring Learning," *Journal of Architectural Education* 61(1) (2007): 27–31.

21. Ibid., 29.

22. Ibid., 31.

23. D. Moore and D. McCabe, *Introduction to the Practice of Statistics* (New York: Freeman, 1993).

24. P. Lather, "This IS your Father's Paradigm," *Qualitative Inquiry* 10(1) (2004): 15–34; E. A. St. Pierre, "Scientifically Based Research in Education: Epistemology and Ethics," *Adult Education Quarterly* 56(4): 239–266.

25. Shulamit Reinharz, *Feminist Methods in Social Research* (New York: Oxford University Press, 1992): 100.

26. Michelle Fine and Susan M. Gordon, "Feminist Transformations of/Despite Psychology," in M. Crawford and M. Gentry (eds.), *Gender and Thought: Psychological Perspectives* (New York: Springer-Verlag, 1989), 106.

27. Reinharz, 107.

28. Ibid., 108.

Chapter 10

Simulation Research

10.1   INTRODUCTION

Simulation research comes out of a broader human fascination with the replication (*mimesis*, imitation) of real-world objects and settings. Very early in Western ideas, Plato warned of the deceptive nature of copies of reality, while Aristotle valued their therapeutic value (specifically the viewing of theatrical performances). Both these points of view relate to simulation research. Mirroring Plato's concerns, simulation's very goal is to create "copies" of reality. How accurate are the copies? What do copies of real things leave out about those real things?[1] For simulation researchers, these are basic questions. And then there is Aristotle. Aristotle taught that art's very nature (specifically poetry, which includes drama) is to represent how things *could* be, not how things actually are, and viewing enactments of these possibilities can be therapeutic. This is because we can experience emotions stirred by the representations without undergoing the dangers of the real things they represent. Applied to simulation research, this is one of its strengths: we can learn about earthquakes without loss of life; we can learn to fly airplanes without fear of crashing; we can simulate an entire bustling city without the expense of actually building it.

Simulation is a remarkably ubiquitous research design, which can be deployed across a broad range of topics, for purposes that span from highly targeted applications in design projects to theory building. Just as significantly, simulation frequently lends itself to many uses as a tactic within other research strategies, or as a full partner in combined strategies (see Chapter 12).

In particular, the combination of experiment and simulation in sequenced phasing is commonly deployed in environmental technology research (see Chapter 9 for some specific examples). Similarly, within the context of other research designs (for example, correlational or qualitative designs), people's reactions to various settings, simulated by photographs, full-scale mock-ups, and the like, can be effectively investigated. Likewise, simulation can also augment historical research to investigate the technical advances in notable building exemplars over time, as described in an example later in this chapter.

With this overview as a backdrop, we first focus on some of the most recent developments in simulation research enabled by advances in computer technology.

10.2   CURRENT EXAMPLES OF SIMULATION RESEARCH

The dictionary defines *simulation* as "the representation of the behavior or characteristics of one system through the use of another system, especially a computer program designed for the purpose."[2] This definition covers the general meaning of simulation, but it also recognizes the increasing dominance of the computer in this field. In the 10 years since the first edition of this book was released, this has become the case with regard to simulation as an architectural research strategy; computer technology has enormously expanded. "Building information modeling," understood in its generic sense, not only dynamically models buildings spatially and operationally in 3D, it can also model construction management sequences of a building project (called 4D), life-cycle factors projected over longer periods of time, and project costs in real time (called 5D). Here are some examples of how computers have revolutionized simulation studies.

10.2.1   *Simulation of Complex Human Factors*

Evacuation of Buildings during a Fire. The first edition of this book provided a simple example of computer modeling for evacuation of a building during a fire.[3] Advances in this technology can be seen in recent computer simulations of different evacuation scenarios in the World Trade Center North Tower during the September 11, 2001, attack:[4] What if one stair shaft remained intact above the impact zone in the initial hours after the tower was hit? What if the occupant load was at full capacity (about 25,000 persons); how many would have perished given the actual exiting configurations? What was the impact of firefighters *entering* the building on people trying to evacuate the building? What was the wait time for people exiting from the upper floors? "Five years ago," the authors say, "it would have been considered a challenge to perform an evacuation design analysis for a 110-story building with 25,000 people. With today's sophisticated modeling tools and high-end personal computers this is now possible."[5] For example, the authors found that, for a fully occupied building, all surviving occupants above the 91st floor (topmost floor of impact) could have exited the building prior to its collapse if at least one stair remained intact. Obviously, this calls for strategic dispersal of stairs in future designs. The researchers further postulated from their modeling that, while it is intuitive that higher floors result in longer wait times for exiting, there may come a point when wait times hold steady above a threshold height. This may raise questions as to why we need to build ever-taller buildings. This study is also significant in showing that simulation research is not only useful for projecting future conditions; it can perform analyses of a forensic nature for past events.

10.2.2   Simulation in Earlier Stages of Architectural Design Process

Virtual Reality in Schematic Design and Design Development; Rapid Prototyping. Earlier systems of computer-aided design were more properly called computer-aided drafting: the computer as a sophisticated pencil for producing construction documents. The second generation of computer-aided systems, such as the Revit software, is "smarter" in that the system responds to a change made by the user by updating all other conditions affected by that change. Now computers are beginning to assist design decisions in the earlier stages of schematic design and design development. For example, researchers at the University of Washington studied the use of virtual reality imaging technology in a student architectural studio.[6] Early design ideas were programmed so the spaces could be experienced virtually. Interestingly, one result was a return of interior design as a primary architectural task:

> The use of VR early in the design process forced the detailed development of the interior space as much as the exterior. By having the opportunity to "go inside" the design and see it from within, the designer was forced to solve complex connections and details which would not have been apparent with other media.

The technology brought to light "spatial implications . . . with and without furniture." All of this was not available by conventional means. Limitations still abound. The researchers show that early schematic design is still difficult to adapt to the computer; it is only after initial design concepts have been sketched by hand and programmed into the computer that the virtual modeling becomes helpful in design development. Nevertheless, what is significant here is the blurring of human with computer capacities in the earlier stages of architecture design, with the result that the conventional means of representing architectural design (plan, section, elevation) seems to be increasingly giving way to animation technology allowing for dynamic three-dimensional models. In actual professional practice, the architectural firm Perkins + Will is leading the way in understanding how building information modeling (BIM) simulation can inform each stage of the design process, including conceptual design and schematic design. At these earlier stages, simulation helps to understand climate information, shading scenarios, orientation, and passive strategies.[7]

This leads to another example of simulation in early design thinking: rapid prototyping technology. Michael Speaks has proposed that the rapidity with which this technology allows a designer to produce three-dimensional alternative solutions has blurred the distinction between thinking and doing. The prior order of things, Speaks argues, privileged thinking over doing in that design actions were guided by predetermined theoretical principles held to be true. But if thinking can be expressed almost simultaneously by three-dimensional rapid prototyping, design prototypes can be "tested, redesigned, retested quickly, cheaply, and under conditions that closely approximate reality."[8]

10.2.3   *Integration of Simulation Software*

UrbanSim, ESRI ArchGIS; Virtual City Template. Because it is the nature of simulation research to provide holistic representations of real-world venues or events, accuracy of representation requires inputting as much data about those venues and events as possible. Here again computers are the ideal platform for simulation research; computers can "simulate the tiny forces binding molecules . . . the support structures of huge skyscrapers . . . the behavior of the economy," and so on.[9] Computerized geographic information systems (GISs) construct models predicting urban growth, transportation networks, and other large-scale built phenomena. These computer models manage extremely complex databases. For example, CityEngine is a 3D modeling software specializing in detailed urban environment simulation, used by urban planners and architects. Supporting industry-standard formats such as ESRI shapefile, 3D models, and AutoCAD DXF files, it enables designers to easily import and export data to create detailed simulation of urban environments. Its interactive design tools facilitate quick editing and modification of urban street layouts and facades. ESRI's Virtual City Template is an example of this technology.[10]

Another example is a program developed at the University of Washington to model urban growth (UrbanSim). This software expanded the scope of traditional two-dimensional GIS modeling, usually covering large scales of spatial area, to fine levels of detail, with integration of three-dimensional modeling capability. The ability of geographic information systems tools to capture, store, and analyze mass data enables projections of urban design scenarios that can dynamically simulate outcomes if given a set of hypothetical inputs.[11] Households, businesses, developers, and governments all make decisions. "By treating urban development as the interaction between market behavior and governmental actions UrbanSim is designed to maximize reality, thereby increasing its utility for assessing the impacts of alternative governmental plans and policies related to land use and transportation."[12]

The notion of "maximizing reality" requires further study. Increasingly powerful computer simulation technology raises a concern over the difference between "reality," understood as everyday real-world contexts and events, and "hyper-reality." This latter term designates computer-generated images and environments that may be "more real" than what we can expect in actuality. And so, while a persistent tactical concern of simulation technology is its ability to accurately represent reality, there now emerges a concern of what we might call overrepresentation. At any rate, one question for powerful programs such as UrbanSim is to what extent they can strike the balance between underrepresenting the outcomes of large interactions of data, versus producing outcomes that are more idealized than real.

BOX 10.1

GeoDesign Suite Tool

We are at a juncture in computer technology where computer-aided design tools are being updated by the next stage, which are simulation tools. This enables computer technology to be more active at earlier stages of design thinking and process. The GeoDesign Suite tool, being developed at the School of Design and Construction at Washington State University, is an example. The GeoDesign Suite works with parametric modeling. The program has a concept function generator, with smart sketching technology, which not only receives the designer's own inputs, but immediately relates it to known images and patterns via Google Goggles.

The research shown (see Figure 10.1) also proposes a more advanced simulation modeling capability, called algorithmic tools. Here, a 3E Dashboard provides calculation gauges for the three significant aspects of sustainable design: equity, efficiency, and environment (the 3E). By providing sophisticated algorithms for each component of the 3E, this tool outputs detailed assessments for different design scenarios in real time, which tremendously enhances the decision-making process. With this simulation technology, designers can quickly adjust their designs for specific goals, making optimal decisions based on real-time feedback from the gauges.

(Continued)

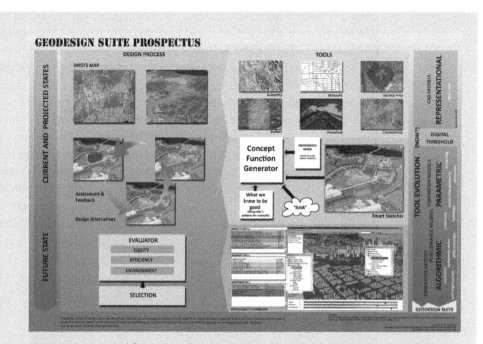

Figure 10.1 Panel featuring the GeoDesign Suite Tool, being developed at Washington State University School of Design and Construction. Courtesy of Brooks, K., A. Joplin, and M. Xu.

10.2.4   Real-Time Simulation

"Sentient Buildings." In the first edition of this book, we noted the trend toward "intelligent buildings." Jong-Jin Kim described a scenario using an "intelligent card":

> [W]hen an employee enters a main entrance lobby using an IC card, the central building administration system sends an elevator to the lobby. As the person proceeds and enters his/her office, the IC card sends instructions to turn on the lights and the air distribution unit. In the evening, IC cards help to determine whether a space is occupied and, if it is unoccupied, the environmental systems are turned off automatically.[13]

This research has of course progressed. Computer programs can tailor a building's mechanical and electrical systems to perform in response to user needs in real time. Patterns of user behavior are recorded by sensors distributed throughout a building. From this data, a computer program then internally simulates alternative scenarios of optimal configurations for energy savings in lighting or thermal levels for real-time occupant loads. In his "Self-Organizing Models for Sentient Buildings," Ardeshir Mahdavi designates four basic components to a sentient building system. First is the *controlled entity*, which can be a single space or spaces networked over an entire building. Second, sensors in the controlled entity (or impact zone) measure a range of inputs such as environmental factors, real-time occupancy loads, outdoor conditions, and the like. A *controller* is the decision-making agent, the computer program that simulates "representations" of possible scenarios. It can then make changes in the controlled entity by means of altering a *control device*.[14] There are now commercial products that can perform simple versions of these functions; the Nest Thermostat is an example.[15] This control device not only records patterns of energy use for easy review of costs, it also learns the behavior of the occupants. For instance, it automatically adjusts temperature settings based on patterns for when occupants leave the home or retire for the night. Godfried Augenbroe outlines an easily envisioned future development for this technology:

> Simulation may be part of an e-business service, such as the web-hosted electronic catalogue of a manufacturer of building components. Each product in the catalogue could be accompanied by a simulation component that allows users to inspect the product's response to user-specified conditions.[16]

With increasing miniaturization, a more radical idea for component simulation is smart cells, working as computerized components within our bodies. Upon inputs such as exposure to infection, these cells can "represent" various scenarios and trigger the most favorable responses within our bodies. An idea such as this underlines the fact that the computer revolution will probably redefine "architecture" as we know it much more than the Industrial Revolution ever did.

10.2.5   *Immersive Building Simulation*

CAVE. This is technology by which a user can be placed "into" a three-dimensional computer-generated environment, one that responds (ideally) to the user's real-time actions. The term *virtual reality* is often used in this sense. Virtual simulation can be immersive, in which the user experiences complete inclusion in the simulated setting; or augmented, in which a device allows the user to see into some sort of simulated context overlaid on real-world settings. The first edition of this book cited CAVE (Computer Assisted Virtual Environments), to illustrate this technology; a collection of research papers on this technology is still available online.[17] Ali

Malkawi's "Immersive Building Simulation"[18] outlines the progress of this research since that time. Malkawi notes that building simulation of this kind actually lags behind other uses of virtual or augmented reality simulation, such as flight simulator technology or military applications of simulated theater operations. Malkawi notes that this technology is still experimental, and costs are still high. But, again, it is quite easy to envision how totally immersive environments will be part of our lives in the not too distant future. This has implications not only for architecture, but also for medicine, conduct of business, entertainment, travel, and a host of other areas of life.

10.2.6   *Modeling Construction Sequences*

Building Information Modeling (BIM) enables dynamic simulation of at-one-point scenarios, but more significantly, the behavior of structures under construction over time. For instance, the program models initial concrete pours, but also follows the concrete as it cures; thus, it is able to guide when forms can be removed. The program calculates the loads on the building frame during pouring and during vibration of the concrete (which creates large loads), and calculates the new distributed loads while forms are removed. The BIM program manages basic information, which includes the 3D geometric data of the project; 4D information, which contain resource information, site information, and scheduling and processes data; and structural information (loading conditions, structural profiles, and the like). It generates integrated solutions from these data sources. One outcome is the ability to project (so as to avoid) collisions of machinery on construction sites. The authors claim their work is the first to establish a "4D space-time model" that helps managers "analyze and avoid possible collisions during the whole construction process."[19]

10.3   STRATEGY OF SIMULATION RESEARCH

Here we address the defining characteristics of simulation as a research strategy. Part of this task is to clarify some terms often found in the simulation literature. Because advances in computer technology occur so quickly, it is useful to consider some of these definitions. Following these clarifications, we outline some relationships simulation research has to other research strategies.

10.3.1   *Representation versus Simulation*

The word *representation* often occurs, with various shades of meaning, in the simulation literature. For our purposes, representation denotes a fixed image that stands for a real object because the image has measurable qualities that describe and depict the real thing. In this sense architectural drawings are representations. Photographs, the medium that much of architectural education has been dependent upon up to now, are also representations under this definition. To-scale three-dimensional architectural models are representations as well. It is only when data from various scenario inputs can be generated from representations that we can say simulation is taking place. This can be achieved with fixed representations.

An example is a study utilizing photographs (slides) and to-scale models of nursing homes. Rather than bringing elderly people to the actual buildings, seniors were shown models and a series of slides of the spaces. It was shown in this case that those experiencing the depicted environments had a better "working knowledge" of the buildings than those who actually visited them. The latter group experienced difficulty finding places out of sequence from their initial site exposure, but the group that was exposed to the fixed photographs and models did not experience similar difficulty (they in fact found places not included in the simulated visit).[20] Because data came out of these interactions with the still images, the research was included in a collection of examples of simulation research.

Computer technology has further blurred the distinction between representation and simulation. For example, the popular software Sketchup, freely downloadable from Google, offers almost infinite views of a building, in plans, sections, aerial views, and the like, after the dimensions have been input. Is this representation or simulation? Most would say it is a representational tool because the many views Sketchup generates are still themselves fixed and operated by the user. It is not until there is a "smart" capacity in a computer modeling program that allows for dynamic interactions yielding measurable data that we can say simulation modeling is taking place. Closer toward simulation is something like sun path scenarios. Autodesk's Revit program projects the sun's position relative to a building at any time and any location. These are fixed representations that nevertheless begin to offer dynamic information. Perhaps the salient point is that advancing computer technology may bring us to a point, as some of the preceding examples suggest, at which an infinite number of fixed representations in sequence achieve simulations of "real-time" behaviors. Because we are in this transitional time, the word *representation* may be used with differing shades of meaning by various commenters in the simulation arena.

10.3.2　*What Is a Model?*

This is another ubiquitous word used in simulation research. In simulation terms, a *model* is the overall system that simulates the reality being studied. A model can exist in a variety of forms: from a mathematical model comprised of abstract numerical expressions, to laboratory spaces outfitted (for instance) into conference rooms to test lighting,[21] to what architects still most often think about when the word *model* is used, small-scale three-dimensional representations of actual spaces (see Figure 10.2a). In the Netherlands, it was a practice for full-size mock-ups of entire residences to be tested before actual construction proceeded (see Figure 10.2b). The process is able to reveal under research conditions why, on subjective grounds, some people prefer certain environments and not others.[22] (This is another example of a "fixed representation," here a full-sized replica of a residence, yielding data through dynamic interactions with "residents"; therefore, it is simulation).

In a recent book on design research, Sally Augustin and Cindy Coleman discuss how simulation findings can be derived from fixed models. They call it *space simulation,* by which they mean fixed models that can range from "incredibly detailed and realistic" to three-dimensional boxes that roughly approximate a space. One point to take from their observations is that these space simulations ought to be able to "learn" over time: "As users interact with one simulation, it should be

Figure 10.2a A to-scale model of a proposed church interior. One can orient the model to the sun in such a way that would suggest how the actual space might look under the same conditions. But generally, fixed architectural models are representations more than simulations. Courtesy of Professor Matthew Melcher.

Figure 10.2b   Full-size mock-ups of residential spaces in Amsterdam: residents participated in these simulated environments prior to actual construction of the design. Courtesy of Plenum Press. From Marans/Stokols *Environmental Simulation* (1993).

reconfigurable" so that more information can be gained from multiple enactments.[23] This learning over time—or what we term *data generation* from a variety of input scenarios—is the simulational aspect of these fixed models. Note also that this use of fixed models can be a tactic for qualitative research; Augustin and Coleman's "users" imply live subjects, perhaps focus groups.

Colin Clipson classifies four types of simulation models: *iconic, analog, operational,* and *mathematical.*[24] The first two have more to do directly with physical contexts. *Iconic* models are used in the direct testing of materials or products under simulated conditions. For example, actual wall assemblies are tested for fire resistances; carpeting and other interior materials are tested under simulated conditions to determine their flame spread ratings. *Analog* denotes "dynamic simulation of an actual or proposed physical system." Flight simulators are of this variety. *Operational* models deal with people interacting within physical contexts; the data is generated by role-play. Hospital emergency room scenarios, or response to terrorist attacks, can be simulated in this way. *Mathematical* models are systems of numerical coding that capture real-world relationships in quantifiable abstract values; this is the domain of expanding computer technology vis-à-vis simulation. As noted earlier, increasingly the direction is toward computer models that integrate enormous amounts of information via databanks.

Again, when representations, whether two- or three-dimensional, are deployed such that they generate measurable data from dynamic interactions under various scenario inputs, simulation is taking place.

10.3.3   *Prediction versus Projection/Pattern*

Simulation gives us knowledge about possible real-world conditions without going through the ethical barriers, physical dangers, or financial expense of the actual conditions. Let's now consider further the kind of knowledge we can obtain. We have all taken part in fire drills to prepare for the likelihood of the real thing. But what do we learn? We don't learn anything that can accurately predict future behavior. But our experience in the simulation teaches us *patterns* of behavior, or *projections* of possible behavior, grounded in a realistically and hopefully rigorously prepared replica of the actual circumstances. In the World Trade Center simulation cited earlier, the authors ran through 50 computations each of 4 scenarios to obtain their results. In other words, it was the statistical composite of 50 sets of data that gave them confidence regarding patterns of behavior for the scenarios (e.g., with and without firefighters; with and without an intact stair from top to bottom; etc.). This is not to say that projection or pattern replaces prediction; it just increases the range—or perhaps the kinds—of predictive outcomes. Building Information Modeling (BIM), for example, can easily perform simulation studies of the predictive kind, such as modeling airflow, or the curing rate for concrete in a particular application.

10.3.4   *Simulation Research in Relation to Experimental and Correlational Research*

As previously described in Chapter 9, experimental research aims to test research hypotheses and identify the causal effects of key variables on outcome measurements. In this regard, a limitation of experimental research is that it is necessarily reductive; it isolates real-world variables in order to study the essential causal linkages within the phenomenon of study. In contrast, correlational research seeks to illuminate relationships among discretely measured variables in naturally occurring circumstances (see Chapter 8).

In contrast, simulation strategy aims to replicate in a holistic manner all the relevant variables in a setting or phenomenon. In other words, it can illuminate how a symphony (or perhaps a cacophony) of inputs all contribute to the holistic reality. When the behavior of that holism is simulated, we can then observe what significant variables are in play, and postulate further steps. William Crano and Marilynn Brewer put it this way: "A well-designed simulation has the potential to isolate the social phenomenon of interest without destroying its natural contextual meaning."[25] The holistic nature of simulation is both its attraction and its limitation. It is attractive because the simulated context promises a real-world view of a hypothetical situation. A corresponding limitation, however, is that the intentional "holism" of simulation cannot always be satisfactorily replicated (see section 10.4.1).

Nevertheless, the differing considerations of key variables of interest in the three research designs (experimental, correlational, and simulation) offer great potential for combining pairs of strategies in a mixed methods research design (see Chapter 12). Alternatively, as several examples in this chapter illustrate, simulation can be used as a very effective tactic within one of the other research strategies.

10.3.5   *Simulation Research in Relation to Qualitative and/or Historical Research*

For simulation research to be meaningful, accompanying research activities are required that are not strictly within the domain of simulation strategy. This is particularly true for analogue or operational types of simulation when human actors are involved. Often, data must be collected about the subjects before their participation in the simulation. This can involve interviews, checking records or documents, or other kinds of field work that have little to do with simulation strategy. Simulation can also be a tactic in historical research, that is, qualitative reenactments of past events or conditions. We provide an example of this in Chapter 6: Jean-Pierre Protzen's reenactment of how Inca masons might have dressed the stones for their large masonry constructions. This intermixing of other strategies for use as tactics in this one underlines just how fluid simulation research design can be. This leads to how simulation aids in theory building.

BOX 10.2

Computer Simulation for Historical Research

Computers aid research in historic structures. This study used computer modeling to show that the ornamental tracery on the hammerbeam trusses in London's Westminster Hall, built in 1395, actually plays a structural

(Continued)

role. The authors contend that the load-bearing behavior of these trusses had escaped thorough analysis through the years because of their complex configurations. Structural calculations by hand necessarily require "rounding off" to easier numbers. Computer calculations do not round off. What is more, computers can easily calculate "what if" scenarios.[a] In other words, it can simulate scenarios. In the study's truss diagrams reproduced in Figure 10.3, the lower one shows the much larger bending moments (dark areas) in a scenario in which the computer has deleted the ornamental tracery from the calculations.

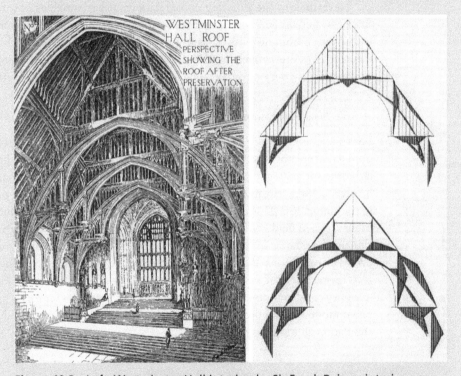

Figure 10.3   Left: Westminster Hall interior, by Sir Frank Baines, interior perspective (1914); Right: Computer models of the Westminster Hall truss using Finite Element Analysis. The lower diagram reveals larger bending moments when the ornamental tracery is deleted from the calculations. Courtesy of Stephen Tobriner.

---

[a] Toby E. Morris, Gary Black, and Stephen O. Tobriner, "Report on the Application of Finite Element Analysis to Historical Structures," *Journal of the Society of Architectural Historians* 54(3) (1995): 336–347.

10.3.6   Simulation Research and Theory Building

Simulation is useful both in developing theory and in testing theory. This is also a point made by Crano and Brewer.[26] They note that simulation research is often useful at an "intermediate" point of knowledge acquisition. That is, when a logical explanatory system has been framed (see Chapter 11), simulation research can help test, or at least enact, that conceptual system in an empirical venue. This is particularly true in theory-driven proposals for how physical environments can enhance (or otherwise alter or benefit) some aspect of life. For instance, full-size residential simulations provide data for affirming or disproving theoretical preconceptions; it can also provide material for new theory making.

One example of how simulation can be used at an "intermediate" point of knowledge acquisition is in the development of broadly conceived design guidelines (a form of theory that explains or describes a given object or setting, or how to realize such objects/settings). In the first edition of this book, we referenced Rohinton Emmanuel's research in urban heat islands: how orientation, size of windows, and paint colors can help in abating heat gain for residences in Sri Lanka.[27]

Advances in computer technology have pushed this kind of research further. In a study published in 2011, TRNSYS (a "transient simulation tool") calculated the impact of variations in street width, street orientation, and different roofing profiles on "urban canyon" heating. In other words, the authors researched both urban design and architectural design parameters in determining ideal guidelines for residential street sections vis-à-vis passive heating strategies. The authors found that street width significantly influenced the radiation yield of a residential street-to-building cross-section, while a street's orientation was less significant. They also found that single-pitched roofs on east-west-oriented streets produce higher radiation yields, and so on. These findings led to recommendations for future design guidelines.[28]

10.3.7   Simulation without Computers

As important as the computer has become for simulation research, it is important to remember that the computer itself is not integral to simulation as a strategy. Modeling scenarios to learn from them, as we suggested at the outset, is something humans were doing long before computers came along. Nothing about this changes with regard to simulation at the level of strategy. Even as this chapter is being written, the author was made aware of a simulated rhinoceros escape at a Japanese zoo. How can zoo workers prepare for such an eventuality? Two workers dressed up as the front and back ends of a rhinoceros on the loose, while other workers practiced setting up emergency fencing. One worker collapses to the ground, feigning injury by the rhino.[29] This is an elementary operational simulation, that is, role-playing by human actors. Of course, the accuracy of the simulation can be questioned. Humans have trouble simulating other humans (during terrorism scenarios, for instance, or as emergency room patients under duress); how can they know what a rhinoceros would do? But this is a critique of the simulation tactic, not a question about its strategy. Here is an example of simulation (without computers) used as a tactic in an experimental design. John E. Flynn and colleagues arranged a space in a lighting laboratory to look like a conference room. They then asked 12 groups (96 subjects total) to react to 6 different lighting combinations of overhead down-lighting and wall lighting. The authors sought to measure four factors: evaluative impression, perceptual clarity, spatial complexity, and spaciousness. Among other results, they found that overhead down-lighting scenarios, regardless of low or high footcandle intensity, were rated "hostile" and "monotonous" compared with options involving wall lighting.[30] This research used simulation: six lighting scenarios in a simulated conference room. Aside from not using computers, this example illustrates how simulation research can overlap experimental research. Box 10.3 and Figure 10.4 address another example of simulation without computers playing a direct role.

BOX 10.3
Operational Simulation with Actors

The following wording is supplied by Jacob Simons, NBBJ/rev: Simultaneously replacing a facility or undergoing an extensive remodel in order to integrate state-of-the-art technology and improved processes, all while managing excellent care delivery and costs, requires a departure from standard management and oversight practices. Without a doubt, every transition is an exciting opportunity to improve quality, safety, and performance, but for many, it is a "once-in–a-lifetime opportunity" that presents huge challenges and risks for the organization.

Simulations are conducted in the weeks before occupancy of a new facility. We fine-tune the environment (e.g., communication systems, equipment placement, faulty mechanical systems, etc.) and document all operational outcomes and design observations. This data is communicated to the firm to inform future projects. At Valley Medical Center, real-life scenarios were developed, with professional actors playing the roles of patients to test the entire system. Technology systems, staffing protocols, EMS staff, nurses and MDs, as well as the facility itself were put to the test—identifying critical environmental modifications as well as enhancing confidence among the staff before opening day.

Figure 10.4 Simulations with live actors at Valley Medical Center, Renton, Washington, a project by NBBJ, Seattle, Washington. Courtesy of Jacob Simons, Research & Design Lead, NBBJ/rev.

10.4 TACTICAL CONCERNS FOR SIMULATION RESEARCH

As we noted at the beginning of this chapter, replicating the real world is a difficult task, particularly if the goal is to obtain useful information from the simulated world to guide action in the real one. There are four general areas of concern: completeness of data input, accuracy of the replication, "programmed spontaneity," and cost/workability. These concerns also reveal the limitations of simulation research, and ways to overcome them are a large part of the tactics of this research strategy.

10.4.1   Accuracy of Replication

We return to the concerns noted at the outset of this chapter. Because simulation research seeks to replicate holistic real-world venues (in contrast, again, to experimental or correlational research), this implies embracing a potentially infinite number of variables. How can accuracy be achieved? Part of the answer depends on the type of simulation in question. In simulations of physical objects or materials, this is addressed by using the actual objects and/or materials in the scale that they would exist in the real world (e.g., full-size mock-ups). The simulation should take place with as many connections to the real-world setting as possible.

In iconic simulation, a product or material has to be tested in the very conditions (thermal, wind, geologic, etc.) in which the real object will be situated. Testing the color durability of window frames, for example, can be conducted by placing the full-size window in intense sunlight conditions for a prolonged period of time. The simulation might have to involve mechanical devices that can replicate the effect of sunlight. The same goes for a window's resistance to wind and rain: performance can be evaluated by mechanically replicating wind and rain impinging upon the full-sized window.

In analog or operational simulations, the actors involved should be individuals who are actually from the real setting. Sometimes professional actors are hired. But using actors and generating artificial climates obviously challenge the accuracy of replications. This concern increases when we deal in computer simulations, say, of complicated projections of urban growth, or how wildlife habitats would respond to alterations in urban infrastructure. In these instances, the need to "harmonize data" from a wide variety of databases is an increasingly demanding one; one resource is the Federal Geographic Data Committee (FGDC).[31]

There is probably no definitive answer to the question of how an artificially constructed scenario can be exhaustively accurate. Here, Herbert Simon's notion of "satisficing" is helpful. When Simon's *Sciences of the Artificial* first came out in 1996, the computer revolution was just getting started, but his insights are still relevant today for any kind of simulation research. Simon made the distinction between the inner world of the artifact (this can be a single object, such as a clock, or it can be society as a whole) and the outer world, the larger setting within which the artifact must function.[32] From this simple framework, Simon derived many insights. One is that we do not need to know everything about the inner environment of the artifact; the key question is whether it can fulfill its intended use in relation to the outer environment. Simon used economic forecasting and design of schedules for complex transportation networks as examples of large "inner" environments. He noted that computer models or models based in operations management are perforce simplifications of reality. But then he noted that these models usually forecast sufficiently well, or "good enough." That is, they satisfice.[33]

Simon's wisdom is that, when dealing with complicated systems, the best we can do is to understand the bounded domain of the system as much as we can, and then work along the lines of an agreed-upon set of assumptions to project its future trends. This does not exempt simulation researchers from care in defining the bounds of the domain they wish to simulate. But it does offer comfort in that "reality" itself may be more accommodating than a purely experimental approach may demand. Says Simon: "In facing uncertainty, standardization and coordination, achieved through agreed-upon assumptions and specifications, may be more effective than prediction."[34]

10.4.2   Limitations of Data Collection

Refer again to the first example we cited, the simulation of evacuations during the World Trade Center attack. Despite the computational power, the authors still underline the limitations that persist. For example, how do you model fatigue for both

BOX 10.4
Simulation for Friday Harbor Terminal, Washington State Ferries

Students at Washington State University's School of Design and Construction use Autodesk Revit and Autodesk Ecotect to simulate architectural and landscape conditions for a new design of the Friday Harbor ferry terminal in the Washington State Ferries system (Figure 10.5). Revit models topographical conditions of the land, while the Ecotect software inputs weather data from the region (this includes solar orientation and radiation levels, wind analysis, temperature, and rainfall patterns). Currently at this site, rain runoff goes directly into Puget Sound and inefficient queuing processes cause long loading times for getting cars on and off the ferry, especially during peak hours. Students can simulate scenarios for greenways and tidal parks, which treat the runoff before releasing it into the sound. The software also helps simulate alternatives for traffic routing to reduce the wait times. The Autodesk program can input massing configurations of the architectural form into the scenarios for more realistic studies.

(Continued)

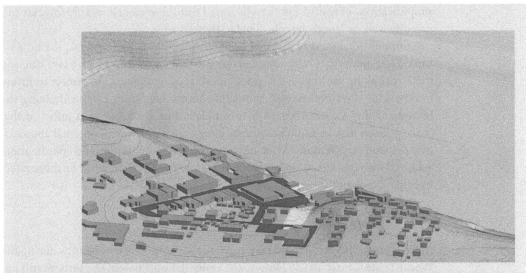

Figure 10.5 Students input preliminary designs of a greenbelt into a 3D site model, allowing them to see how the greenbelt will interact with the town and the topography. Using a model with all of this information allows designs to develop and progress while considering existing conditions. Courtesy of Allison Dunn and Jon Talbott.

exiting occupants and firefighters loaded down with equipment? How does the impact of group dynamics influence occupant response times?[35] Similarly, Robert Marans documents a study of hospital rooms that went through several mock-up iterations before the study was completed, each one made more "real" after assessing the simulated actions of the players (doctors and nurses) acting as themselves.[36]

These examples underline that simulated enactments themselves, whatever forms they take, are dependent on a variety of preenactment data collection. No matter how advanced simulation technology becomes, it is still dependent on the limitations of available data. These limitations take different forms.

First is simply that the data are *incomplete*. Consider evacuation of buildings during fire. In the first edition of this book, we cited Feliz Ozel's computer modeling of human behavior during fire emergencies (see Figure 10.6). To do this, she had to translate actual (reported) human actions into computer code. This required collection of data from the real event (where the fire started, the location of the 94 persons on the floor at the time, etc.). She concludes her paper by noting that relevant field notes from actual fire emergencies are so scarce that it is

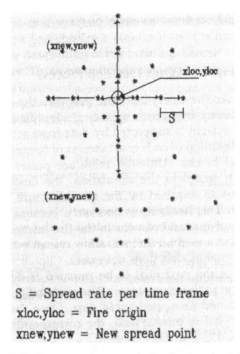

S = Spread rate per time frame
xloc,yloc = Fire origin
xnew,ynew = New spread point

Figure 10.6 This 1993 diagram of a spread of a fire in a building, coded in computer terms, may seem simple compared to today's coding of complicated human behaviors. But the limitations are the same: translating data on human behavior into code that the computer can understand necessarily entails a reduction of real-life factors. Courtesy of Plenum Press. From Marans/Stokols *Environmental Simulation (1993)*.

difficult to test the accuracy of the patterns of behavior derived from computer simulations—and so it is incumbent upon the researcher to go and collect her own field data.[37]

The evacuation of the World Trade Center's North Tower was modeled with much more advanced computer technology, but the data collection limitations remained the same. The authors had to rely on estimates of the evacuation population from *USA Today*. Even so, the distribution of where these people were at the time of attack is unknown, so the authors had to assume. Also, some of the layouts of the floors, which were designed as open plans to maximize office flexibility, were unknown at the time of the tragedy; assumptions also had to be made.[38] The upshot is this: Ozel had to translate the actions of 94 persons into code; but Galea et al. had to account for over 9,000 persons. So even with the increased computing power, in what way does a hundred-fold increase in uncertainty about people movement and location affect the accuracy of the outcomes?

Second, the data are also *not spontaneous*. For example, in enactments of hospital emergency room operations, even professional actors still cannot fully replicate the spontaneity of human free agency. And of course, the individual receiving care in these instances, for obvious ethical reasons, cannot be a real case. The preceding Marans example is one way to improve the certainty: conduct multiple enactments, with a view towards learning iteratively from each enactment. And as noted earlier, in the WTC evacuation simulations, there were multiple computer runs (50) for each scenario, so that the final projections were statistical composites. Another way to overcome lack of spontaneity is what Clipson calls the *empathic* model, in which a role is played for prolonged periods of time by the researcher. The example is offered of one 26-year-old individual who, with meticulous makeup and costuming, transformed herself into an 80-year-old woman—and lived in this role for three years, three to four days per week. Clipson also suggests that participants who can internalize their roles will be more successful in generating realistic outcomes.[39] Linkages between these practices and qualitative research (e.g., ethnography or grounded theory) should be obvious.

Another aspect of spontaneity is currency of the data. It is true that computer technology can now integrate many different databases into one dynamic model (see Figure 10.7). But how current is the information in each database? If the dates of the databases are not generally current relative to each other, accuracy of the model can also be compromised.

Third, simulation data *must be interpreted*. The full-scale residential simulations mentioned earlier are an example. It is one thing to enact human interactions in full-size mock-ups of house interiors; it is another thing to actually derive meaningful results from the activity. In short, data had to be available to interpret the *meanings* of the decisions made by participants as they arranged the spaces to their liking. Specifically, Lawrence wanted to find connections between participants' past and present housing experiences to their present choices in giving shape to their next home. To do this, he had to collect information via interviews, as well as develop space syntax diagrams of the participants' past and present home plans. This meant that Lawrence had to draw from logical frameworks developed by Hillier, along with ones by March and Steadman. The study illustrates the stakes in discerning what kind of data must be included in the research design before a simulated study can have meaning.

10.4.3   *Cost Limitations*

Simulation research can be expensive: equipment costs, professional actors, stage settings for enactments, the time it takes to track down numerous databases, and

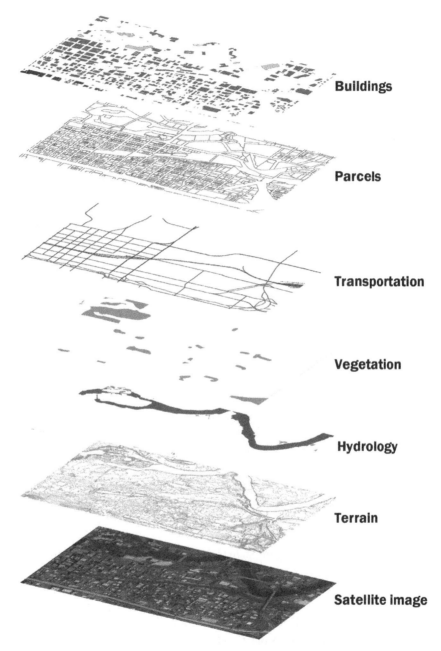

Buildings

Parcels

Transportation

Vegetation

Hydrology

Terrain

Satellite image

Figure 10.7 GIS layers. It is important for all of these databases to be synchronized in date for the resulting model to be dependable. Courtesy of Richard Xu.

then the permissions required to access them. Malkawi notes this explicitly with regard to immersive building simulation.[40] The hardware required is one form of cost. Another is the sheer technicality of the subject, which increases with computer sophistication; experts, as Malkawi notes, can be expensive. Earlier, in section 10.3.7, we noted that simulation does not have to be yoked to computer technology. One benefit of this is that simpler simulation studies, that do not use computers, can be less expensive as well. This helps simulation research in academic settings. Episodic (and hence less costly) efforts at simulation can have heuristic value while lowering expectations for strict data outcomes. We are referring to venues in which students can enact simulated experiences of design and/or practice, with the understanding that the "outcomes" can be viewed as having heuristic value aside from any "hard" data that might be produced. Full-size mock-ups of student designs are one example of what we mean. At Ball State University, Professor Wes Janz describes this third-year undergraduate studio assignment, along with its heuristic value:

> The project was the design of a pedestrian canopy for a public plaza on the Ball State campus. About halfway into the project, each student constructed a full-scale mock-up of a section of the canopy and hauled it across the campus in order to locate the mock-up in the exact place it was designed for .... The students interviewed passers-by regarding their designs, watched persons interacting with the mock-ups, and sketched a three-frame sequence that studied the pedestrian interaction with the canopy from a variety of distances. For the final presentation ten days later, each student selected a key detail of the canopy which he/she then mocked up at full-scale as well. This was in addition to plans, sections, small models, and perspective of the final canopy design. ... Among the benefits to the students are the realization that the small, important models they do become infinitely more complex (and interesting) as they approach ideas about material, connection, and a way of thinking for the project."[41]

At Washington State University, Professor Nancy Clark-Brown designed a studio project in which her students simulated the practice sequence of programming, design development, schematic design, working drawing, and construction phase submittals. Because the studio was an interdisciplinary mix of architecture, interior design, and landscape architecture students, each student played the role of his/her discipline. The project itself was fairly simple: an "intervention" into a transitional space such as a monumental stairway or a corridor (see Figure 10.8). A key thrust of the effort was the operational simulation of actual practice. Clark-Brown

Figure 10.8 Installation of translucent panels in a grand staircase. The exercise gave an interdisciplinary team of design students (architects, interior designers, landscape architects) the opportunity to simulate a process of design, documentation, and construction with real-world time and budget constraints. Courtesy of Professor Nancy Clark Brown.

programmed restrictions into the process that mirrored limitations faced by the practitioner in actual practice: time restraints, budget restraints, construction restraints, and so on:

> [The] design process model provided a structure representational of a model used by professional design teams to structure project deadlines. . . . After defining the project goals and designing the intervention students completed a working drawing set to construct the project from. The construction time allotted was two hours and they were given a budget of $100.00 maximum per team for the purchase of materials. Students were allowed to prefabricate pieces necessary to the construction process prior to the installation of the project.[42]

Clark-Brown reports one heuristic outcome as follows: "students expressed a greater appreciation for the orientations of the distinct disciplines and made connections between them in the design process."

10.5   CONCLUSION

It is helpful to remember that the very nature of the discipline and practice of architecture, because it intimately involves "representation," deals with replications of reality. The added caveat is that architects deal with replications of reality that do not (yet) exist. Architects project new realities onto existing contexts, and thereby change those existing contexts hopefully for the better. We therefore want to return to how we began this chapter: the conflict between Plato's and Aristotle's views of representation. Plato was concerned about the dangers of *mis*representations: they can lead to false understandings of life; ultimately they stir morally undesirable ways to live. Aristotle, however, taught that narration of realities that *can* be (as opposed to realities that are) can have a positive influence. Architecture should heed both these insights, recognizing that the stakes, arguably, are higher in what it does. This is because architecture's goal is to make envisioned realities real ones. Its productions are not "just" about artistic works that continue to be demarcated from "real" life. Architecture's productions become part of real life. So in this sense we ought to give extra heed to what the strategy and tactics of simulation research can teach us. See Figure 10.9 for a summary of the strengths and weaknesses of simulation research.

Strengths and Weakness

Strengths	Weaknesses
We considered simulation's relationship with neighboring strategies earlier in this chapter. We conclude by noting that simulation may be particularly amenable for use as a tactic in other research strategies. In conjunction with other tactics, the data from simulation can be triangulated with data yielded by other means for more robust results. This certainly was the case, for instance, in Protzen's reenactment of Inca masonry fitting (see Chapter 6): had he only used the reenactment, his claims would not have been as strong as its use supplemented by other tactical findings. Triangulation of data from various tactics is indeed another means by which some of the limitations noted in section 10.2 can be overcome.	We considered the inability of simulated environments to ever be exhaustive representations of their real-world counterparts. And so the challenge is always to determine what amount of input data will lead to outcomes that, at best, in Simon's terms, "satisfice." We also noted the cost limitations of simulation research. In many cases, the challenge is to design simulation frameworks that are reasonable in cost. To help in this, it might be good to set up a scale of expectations for the outcomes, between "heuristic" for teaching purposes, to "measured" for actual applications in marketing or planning.

Figure 10.9   Strengths and weaknesses of simulation research.

NOTES

1. To be more accurate, Plato was not concerned about copies of "reality," but rather about copies of ideals of reality. Everyday realities, for Plato, were already copies of their ideal forms. For those interested in this, refer to his *Republic*, the seventh and (particularly) the tenth books. But this point is more fine-grained than this present chapter requires.

2. Dictionary.com Unabridged (Random House, Inc.), s.v. *simulation*. http://dictionary.reference.com/browse/simulation. Accessed January 27, 2012.

3. Feliz Ozel, "Computer Simulation of Behavior in Spaces," in Robert W. Marans and Daniel Stokols (eds.), *Environmental Simulation* (New York: Plenum Press, 1993), 202– 211.

4. E. R. Galea, G. Sharp, P. J. Lawrence, and R. Holden, "Approximating the Evacuation of the World Trade Center North Tower Using Computer Simulation," *Journal of Fire Protection Engineering* 18 (May 2008): 85–115.

5. Ibid., 86.

6. Dace A. Campbell and Maxwell Wells, "A Critique of Virtual Reality in the Architectural Design Process," www.hitl.washington.edu/publications/r-94-3/. Accessed February 8, 2012.

7. Ajla Aksamija, "Building Simulations and Sustainability in Architectural Practice: Use of Building Information Modeling (BIM) for Integrated Design and Analysis," Perkins + Will, *Tech Lab Annual Report* (2011): 131.

8. Michael Speaks, "After Theory," *Architectural Record* 193(6) (2005): 72–75.

9. Clifford Pickover, *Computers and the Imagination* (New York: St. Martin's Press, 1991), 15.

10. "Virtual City Template Enables 3D City Modeling," *ArcNews Online,* ESRI. www.esri.com/news/arcnews/summer10articles/virtual-city.html. Accessed February 22, 2012.

11. Michael Noth and Paul Waddell, "An Extensible, Modular Architecture for Simulating Urban Development, Transportation, and Environmental Impacts," www.prism.washington.edu/lc/noth_et_al_architecture-journalversion.pdf. Accessed March 1, 2012. A note on this document says that a reprint of this paper was submitted to Elsevier Science on 5 September 2001.

12. UrbanSim, www.urbansim.org/Main/UrbanSim. Accessed February 13, 2012.

13. Jong-Jin Kim, "Intelligent Building Technologies: A Case of Japanese Buildings," *Journal of Architecture Science* 1 (Summer 1996): 124.

14. Ardeshir Mahdavi, "Self-Organizing Models for Sentient Buildings." in Ali M. Malkawi and Godfried Augenbroe (eds.), *Advanced Building Simulation* (New York and London: SPON Press, 2004), 164.

15. "Welcome Home: Meet the Nest Thermostat." Nest, www.nest.com/. Accessed March 1, 2012.

16. Godfried Augenbroe, "Trends in Building Simulation," in Ali M. Malkawi and Godfried Augenbroe (eds.), *Advanced Building Simulation* (New York and London: SPON Press, 2004), 18.

17. Cavern Papers, www.evl.uic.edu/cavern/cavernpapers/index.html. Accessed February 28, 2012.
18. Ali M. Malkawi, "Immersive Building ," in Ali M. Malkawi and Godfried Augenbroe (eds.), *Advanced Building Simulation* (New York and London: SPON Press, 2004), 217–246.
19. J. P. Zhang and Z. Z. Hu, "BIM- and 4D-based Integrated Solution of Analysis and Management for Conflicts and Structural Safety Problems during Construction: 1. Principles and Methodologies," *Automation in Construction* 20 (2011): 155–166.
20. Michael E. Hunt, "Research for an Aging Society.," in Robert W. Marans and Daniel Stokols (eds.), *Environmental Simulation* (New York: Plenum Press, 1993), 98.
21. John E. Flynn, Terry J. Spencer, Osyp Martyniuk, and Clyde Hendrick, "Interim Study of Procedures for Investigating the Effect of Light on Impression and Behavior," *Journal of the Illuminating Engineering Society* 3(1) (1973): 87–94.
22. Roderick J. Lawrence, "Simulation and Citizen Participation," in Robert W. Marans and Daniel Stokols (eds.), *Environmental Simulation* (New York: Plenum Press, 1993), 143–145.
23. Sally Augusin and Cindy Coleman, *The Designer's Guide to Doing Research* (Hoboken, NJ: John Wiley & Sons, 2012), 230.
24. Colin Clipson, "Simulation for Planning and Design," in Robert W. Marans and Daniel Stokols (eds.), *Environmental Simulation* (New York: Plenum Press, 1993), 30–34.
25. Willam Crano and Marilynn Brewer, *Principles and Methods of Social Research* (Mahwah, NJ: Lawrence Erlbaum, 2002), 87.
26. William Crano and Marilynn Brewer, *Principles of Research in Social Psychology* (New York: McGraw-Hill, 1973), 117–118.
27. Rohinton Emmanuel, "Urban Heat Island and Cooling Load: The Case of an Equatorial City," in *Architecture, Energy and Environment* (Lund, Sweden: Lund University, LTH, 1999), 16-1–16-10.
28. M. M. E. van Esch, R. H. J. Looman, and G. J. de Bruin-Hordijk, "The Effects of Urban and Building Design Parameters on Solar Access to the Urban Canyon and the Potential for Direct Passive Solar Heating Strategies," *Energy and Buildings* 47 (2012): 189–200.
29. "Zoo Simulates Rhino Escape: Tokyo Staff Holds Drill to Practice for Possible Emergency Situation," ABC News, News Videos, February 2, 2012, http://abcnews.go.com/International/video/zoo-japan-simulates-rhino-escape-15542500. Accessed February 9, 2012.
30. Flynn et al., 87–94.
31. The Federal Geographic Data Committee exists to coordinate databases, based on the Content Standard for Digital Geospatial Metadata (FGDC-STD-001-1998). See www.fgdc.gov/. Accessed March 5, 2012.
32. Herbert Simon, *Sciences of the Artificial* (Boston: MIT Press, 1996), 6. "An artifact can be thought of as the meeting point—an 'interface' in today's terms—between an 'inner' environment, the substance and organization of the artifact itself, and an 'outer'

environment, the surroundings in which it operates. If the inner environment is appropriate to the outer environment, or vice versa, the artifact will serve its intended purpose."

33. Simon, "Economic Rationality," in ibid., 25–49.

34. Ibid., 42.

35. Galea et al., 114.

36. Robert Marans, "A Multimodal Approach to Full-Scale Simulation," in Robert W. Marans and Daniel Stokols (eds.), *Environmental Simulation* (New York: Plenum Press, 1993), 113–131.

37. Filiz Ozel, "Computer Simulation of Behavior in Spaces," in Robert W. Marans and Daniel Stokols (eds.), *Environmental Simulation* (New York: Plenum Press, 1993), 202–211.

38. See Galea et al., 87, 90, 92.

39. Colin Clipson, "Simulation for Planning and Design," in Robert W. Marans and Daniel Stokols (eds.), *Environmental Simulation* (New York: Plenum Press, 1993), 45–49.

40. Malkawi, 217–246.

41. Statement by Professor Janz in an e-mail correspondence with the authors, October 2000.

42. Statement by Professor Nancy Clark-Brown given to authors, October 2000.

Chapter 11

Logical Argumentation

11.1 INTRODUCTION

Logical argumentation entails the framing of broad explanatory theories. Of course, theoretical thinking permeates any research design. But when a broad explanatory theory is itself the targeted outcome of a research endeavor, most likely the strategy used to get there is logical argumentation. This chapter describes and analyzes various manifestations of logical argumentation across a spectrum that includes alphanumerically expressible systems, explanatory models of cultural processes, and design-polemical treatises. Exemplars of these logical argumentation types will be presented in some detail, along with the strategies and tactics to frame them.

First, however, we want to emphasize the most basic trait that logical argumentation exhibits: the enumeration of first principles. A *first principle* is a fundamental proposition that is so self-evident that it need not be derived from even more elemental proofs. First principles are therefore logical building blocks by which, or upon which, broad explanatory theories can be constructed. One of the reasons we felt this chapter was needed in the first edition of this book—and our view remains the same—is that much of what passes today as architectural theorizing *ought to be* exercises in logical argumentation. But because first principles are not clearly derived or established, or because the large domain needing to be captured in a logical frame is not made clear, what results is muddled reasoning. Here is one simple example: Prince Charles—admittedly not a professional theorist—has proposed his "Ten Commandments of Architecture"; ostensibly, following these Ten Commandments would result in successful architectural design. But the commandments are far from clear. For example: what is the relationship between "Decoration" (7) and "Art" (8)? What does "Ugly" mean (in 9)? How does "Harmony" (4) relate to "Scale" (3)?[1]

A much clearer set of categories for the same problem was proposed some two thousand years ago: *firmitas, utilitas, venustas.*[2] After millennia, it remains difficult to add to, or take away from, the Vitruvian categories for successful building design.

For an example of clear first principles, as well as a clear large domain needing to be captured in a logical frame, take an early example from Aristotle's philosophy. In explaining cause, Aristotle proposed four categories: the material, the formal, the efficient, and the final causes.[3] Aristotle sometimes used house construction to illustrate his thinking:

1. A house requires *material* to build; in Aristotle's view the requisite material needed to build a house is itself a cause in the sense that, without material, a house could not result.

2. A house requires a *formal* cause. Unlike Plato before him, who held that an empirical object is always an imperfect imitation of its ideal immaterial form, Aristotle held that the material of an object is distinguished from how the material is arranged and/or distributed; this latter distribution is the form. Immaterial ideals play less of a role; Aristotle's conception of form is resident in the object. The beginnings of empirical science trace to this origin.

3. A house requires an *efficient* cause. This is the reasoning agent that manipulates the material in accordance with the form (the distribution) of the house. Perhaps the easiest of the causes to understand, architects and builders are obviously efficient causes of houses in this sense. Writ large, the Aristotelian notion of efficient cause enormously influenced medieval conceptions of God as the efficient cause of the world.

4. A house requires a *final* cause. Aristotle held that all things existed for ends: for example, the end of doctoring is health; the end of a house is habitation; and so on. The end of a thing is also a cause.

Our goal here is not to expound upon Aristotle, but rather to illustrate first principles as basic conceptual building blocks of broad explanatory theories. Note the logical irreducibility of Aristotle's four categories; there is no need to derive constructs even more basic than these. Note also that each category is clearly demarked from the others; the terms do not overlap conceptually. Finally, the categories form a logically complete explanatory structure of a large domain that can be expressed by the question "what is cause?"; it would be difficult to add a fifth category descriptive of cause to Aristotle's reasoning. (We might also add that Aristotle's four categories encompass a much larger scope than what we today think of as "cause." Our contemporary view has been largely reduced to the third of his categories, efficient cause, conceived through the lens of scientific method.)

Not all logical frameworks related to architecture are as broad as Aristotle's philosophical framework explaining cause; in fact very few are. Nevertheless, it is probably safe to say that, of all the research strategies covered in this book, logical argumentation comes closest in its ways of analysis, and hence in its tools and tactics, to philosophical construction. This point will become clearer as this chapter unfolds.

Consider efforts at logical argumentation in a rapidly evolving area of architectural research—Building Information Modeling (BIM):

> Information technology has the potential to transform current design processes into a network of design, manufacturing, and management organizations where multiple professions are involved and geographic locations are insignificant. Understanding the future of architectural practice is even more challenging, since currently available computational tools are starting to change design processes, communication and fabrication . . . . [A] paradigm shift in architecture and construction industry has been originated by BIM design and management technology.[4]

The authors of this statement, Ajla Aksamija and Ivanka Iordanova, sense this paradigm shift, and their article illustrates an attempt at constructing a logical frame for the new order of things. This is because BIM platforms take the traditional (2D) modes of representing buildings—with each representation as a separate document—and transform the entire architectural design process into a holistically interactive 3D representational modality. What is more, construction sequence through time (termed 4D), as well as real-time cost estimating and adjustments (termed 5D), are all programmable as representations within these BIM platforms. The challenge in this emerging technology remains how design knowledge in its nonpropositional (or "implicit") forms can be captured in rule-based computer language. Aksamija and Iordanova try to answer this question by deriving fundamental characteristics—first principles—of "implicit" knowledge such that it can interact with explicit alphanumerically expressible knowledge in BIM platforms. Most of this technical article is frankly beyond the ken of this author (Wang). But the strategy is clear: Working backwards from an established artifact, which they call a *referent* (say, a building), the authors itemize the "hidden" implicit knowledge inputs that went into its realization. They then propose several data structures that can represent this, whether it is by itemizing how the literature has generally tried to capture implicit knowledge in categories (physical, logical, and conceptual) or in "chunks of knowledge" (categorized as Issue, Concept, and Form); or whether it is by categorizing "ontologies." Once a referent library is set up, the hope is that implicit design knowledge can become integrated with the rule-based projections of the BIM platform. What matters for us here is the logical frameworks that the authors had to set up to "capture" the essential traits of nonpropositional implicit knowledge; they needed to describe this knowledge categorically such that no aspect of it is left out, and no category overlaps with another.

This BIM example highlights another characteristic aspect of logical argumentation: It organizes a large and disparate reality into a comprehensible framework so that others are freed to do work within the domain without having to define fundamental parameters *de novo*. We use the word *domain* loosely.[5] Domain here is simply the conceptual area that a logical framework defines—and that area can be of a significant scope. Explaining and describing an integration of alpha-numerically expressible knowledge with "design knowledge," which is more implicit, perhaps tacit: how to get a computer program to accommodate both in a single system? This is a large domain.

BOX 11.1

Finding First Principles in Designing a "Total Health Environment" (NBBJ)

The architectural firm NBBJ conducted a research-based, member-focused study to generate "21 Critical Experiences" that are factors for creating "a total health environment." The following chart was the result of an iterative process of participatory workshops, literature review, market research, brainstorming sessions, and other qualitatively based research tactics (see Figure 11.1). These 21 factors, in effect, are being proposed as the first principles in a logical framework for designing a successful total health environment. This is a workable heuristic for the realm of practice. Critical assessment of the list can be conducted with regard to: (1) the uniqueness of each principle (do principles overlap?); (2) sorting the factors for principles of quantity, quality, origin; and (3) testing the list, that is, gathering evidence as it accrues from project to project for evaluations of whether the list is complete, or can be simplified.

Figure 11.1 "21 Critical Experiences" in designing a total health environment. Courtesy NBBJ, Jacob Simons.

Consider a more established example: Stewart Brand's *How Buildings Learn*. Brand's insight is that any building can be conceived of as an assemblage of six layers (site, structure, skin, services, space plan, and stuff; see Figure 11.2).[6] For each layer, the rate of change over time increases from the immobile site, which never changes, to the stuff in the interior that shifts almost daily: chairs, phones, pictures, hairbrushes, and so on. Brand built his framework on an earlier model of building-as-layers proposed by Frank Duffy.[7] But these are sometimes cited in tandem as one explanatory theory.[8] Like Aristotle's logical framework explaining cause, here we have clear conceptual categories that do not overlap, and there is no need for additional categories. Note also that the six-layer model is not a stepping stone towards new knowledge; the model itself is the new knowledge of Brand's research efforts. In turn, the model is useful for those in facilities management, in historic preservation, or simply as a tool for architects to guide clients through projections of future alterations or additions.

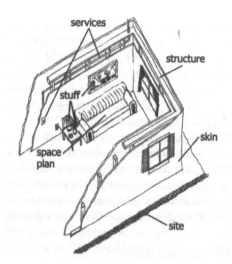

Figure 11.2 Student drawing illustrating the six "S" categories of Stewart Brand's theory for the rate at which building layers change. The site hardly ever changes; as we go up (or into) the hierarchy, the rate of change increases. A building's "stuff" changes every day. Courtesy of Angela Feser.

Our task in this chapter is to outline how works like Brand's and Aksamija and Iordanova's can be recognized as research using logical argumentation. There are two challenges to this task. First, admittedly, "logical argumentation" is a moniker not as well recognized as other research strategies, say, correlational research or history research. This is because, when logical argumentation is being framed, its framers often do not call it logical argumentation—as a researcher conducting correlational research, for instance, would typically say, "I am doing correlational research." At the strategic level, when broad explanatory theories are being framed, the *implicit* aim is the creation of a logical framework. Through it all, the researcher may not explicitly say it is an exercise in logical framing. But if the outcome is a broad explanatory theory, the chances are high that logical argumentation is precisely what was used. At the tactical level, when masses of data from any research strategy are being organized into a coherent summary, logical argumentation often is at work in determining the categories. Again, this framing is often not explicitly called logical argumentation.

The second challenge is addressed in the next section: there exists a range—we call it a *spectrum*—of logical argumentation typologies. This chapter aims to cover examples from this overall spectrum, from formal/mathematical examples (such as BIM research) to what we call cultural/discursive examples. Design-polemical architectural theories tend to reside at the cultural/discursive end of the logical spectrum. Part of our aim for this book on *architectural* research methods is to include these kinds of polemical theorizing as examples of research inquiry, and we propose that logical argumentation is where they can fit.

11.2   A SPECTRUM OF LOGICAL ARGUMENTATION TYPOLOGIES

In human experience, things "make sense" in different ways. When Aksamija, Iordanova, and other researchers in the BIM field can finally capture tacit design knowledge in alphanumerical terms, they will have accomplished a task in logical argumentation. But when Mies van der Rohe utters, "Less is more," and influences two generations of design, there is an undeniable way in which the slogan *made sense* (e.g., it was logical) to numerous architects who committed their lives to Modernist design. For heuristic convenience, then, we propose the spectrum shown in Figure 11.3.

At the left pole are formal/mathematical frameworks. The first edition of this book noted the ability of computer software to "analyze extant designs for their basic syntactic rationale, or those that generate new figurative schemas based upon a formal-syntactic rationale." One example given was research in shape grammar, in which rule-based computer programs can analyze the figural grammar, for instance, of Palladio's Villa Macontenta; or generate design configurations that resemble Wright's prairie houses. These examples now look very tame. In just 10 years, we have computer-aided design (CAD) programs with intelligent 3D objects (Revit) that aid programs such as BIM. Geographic information systems (GISs), just emerging a decade ago, are now *de rigueur* for architectural departments, many design offices, and public planning agencies. Chapter 10 addresses these developments. Suffice it to say here that we categorize all these software programs as formal/mathematical frameworks of logical argumentation.

At the other pole of the spectrum are systems that have persuasive force because they capture some aspect of a large cultural worldview distilled into a "logical" argument with both theoretical clarity and rhetorical power. Again, examples of what we called design-polemical theory in Chapter 4 reside at this end of the logical spectrum.

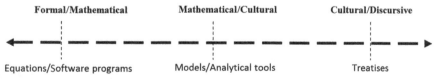

Figure 11.3 Spectrum of logical argumentation.

In between these two poles are logical frameworks that share characteristics of both formal/mathematical systems and cultural/discursive ones. Like formal/mathematical systems, they may use numerical factors or rule-based constructs in their analyses of space and form. But they do so with the view that the resulting data can shed light upon social/cultural values. An example is Bill Hillier and Julienne Hanson's *The Social Logic of Space*. This work frames a system in which an architectural plan is reduced to an abstract "map" (called a gamma map) along with a variety of numerical quantities that unveil how patterns of social behavior relate to space adjacencies (see Figure 11.4). In one of their own studies, for instance, the authors found that a great variety of English homes nevertheless all have the same hierarchy of space adjacencies, a hierarchy linked to the values expressed in the social etiquette regulating contact between family and community.[9]

Hillier's research is significant in that it integrates what can be regarded as the qualitative with the quantitative dimensions of environmental design. For instance, in a more recent work, *Space Is the Machine*, city fabrics are reduced to maps of

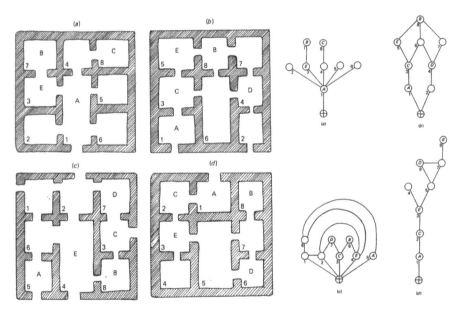

Figure 11.4 From Hillier and Hanson, *The Social Logic of Space:* The floor plans on the left are reduced to the gamma maps on the right. These maps are able to reveal patterns of spatial adjacencies. When the function of each space is factored in, along with how many spaces removed each space is from the entry, patterns of adjacencies, reflecting social values, can be defined over a large sample of plans. By permission of Cambridge University Press.

linear relationships indexed to a subject's possible visual fields as he or she moves through urban space. Composites of all possible visual volumes (called *isovists*) for any person's location in space yield empirical patterns that can be useful, for instance, in assessing the vitality of urban open spaces.[10] We now summarize some strategic traits of logical argumentation.

11.3   THE STRATEGIC TRAITS OF LOGICAL ARGUMENTATION

11.3.1   *Paradigmatic Innovation*

Logical argumentation tends to take a set of previously disparate factors, or previously unknown and/or unappreciated factors, and interconnect them into unified frameworks that have significant and sometimes novel explanatory power. In other words, systems of logical argumentation tend to be innovative ones. If the explanatory system is successful, it provides a new way of looking at old facts or existing phenomena, and may well shape discourse at a paradigmatic level. Before Brand, no one thought of buildings, especially as they evolve through the years, in six categories starting with "S." Of course, all of them starting with "S" is an added bit of alliteration for clarity (itself perhaps a tactic). The key is mapping six categories of things that, together, comprise the whole object being described and explained; nothing seems left out, and no category overlaps with another.

Two examples, one very broad and very established, and the other just emerging, come to mind. Thomas Kuhn's *Structure of Scientific Revolutions*—which made the word *paradigm* and the phrase *paradigm shift* into everyday coinage—is in essence one of the most significant examples of logical argumentation in the philosophy of science in the 20th century. The idea is that scientists work within a paradigmatic worldview that determines how they "see" data, thereby linking scientific research with cultural realities (Kuhn's classic example is the earth-centered Ptolemaic view of the solar system versus the one we have today; Galileo, for example, almost lost his life for suggesting that it is the earth that revolves around the sun and not vice versa), and this idea has enormously influenced fields outside of the natural sciences (see section 11.3.3).

Miwon Kwon's book *One Place After Another* attempts to define "site-specificity as a problem idea" vis-à-vis public sculpture in contemporary postmodernist culture.[11] Since Rosalind Krauss's "Sculpture in an Expanded Field" in 1985,[12] Kwon's book is probably the most systematic in tackling the question of the status of sculpture as public art in which "site" and "sculptural object" no longer enjoy a fixed relationship. Each of the six chapters of the book—exemplified by the chapter headings themselves—is an exercise in logical argumentation, as Kwon tries to frame different pieces of an overall domain in which sculpture is no longer fixed and object-centered, but is part of "spatial-political" cultural systems. Though not nearly as influential as Kuhn, Kwon is nevertheless innovating an explanatory paradigm, and she uses logical argumentation to do so.

11.3.2   *A Priori Argumentation*

First principles denote the enabling conditions for a given explanatory framework; they are logically *a priori* in relation to the subject at hand. If an *a priori* first principle can be identified, then *necessary* consequences ensue from it. Antony Flew defines necessity as follows: "A proposition is said to be necessarily true, or to express a logically necessary truth if and only if the denial of that proposition would involve a self-contradiction."[13] For formal/mathematical systems that are rule based and computer driven, necessary first principles often amount to the variables that comprise equations, and the like. At the cultural/discursive end of the logical argumentation spectrum, theorists often depend on the force of rhetoric to demonstrate necessity. Chaim Perelman and L. Obrechts-Tyteca, in their important work *The New Rhetoric*, argue that in our everyday modes of thinking we must deliberate on a multitude of factors that ultimately shape, not so much our grasp of abstract truth, but our adherence to one point of view over another.[14] Cultural/discursive treatises often identify first principles of this nature upon which design explanations are based. Coming to mind are Gottfried Semper's "four elements" of architecture, in which he proposes that all architecture can be reduced to hearth, roof, enclosure, and "mound."[15] Or Marc Antoine Laugier's "general principles of architecture": column, entablature, pediment, stories of a building, windows, and doors.[16] There is also Le Corbusier's *Five Points of a New Architecture*: supports, roof-gardens, free plan, the long window, the free facade.[17] Once *a priori* first principles are identified, any empirical instance is only ratification of those principles.

11.3.3   *Logical Argumentation Frameworks Tend to Be Interdisciplinary*

The broad applicability of many logical argumentation systems renders them interdisciplinary in scope. One reason is that *a priori* principles of logical argumentation are often so basic that they transcend disciplinary boundaries. Kuhn's theory of paradigms and paradigm shifts have been adapted to work in anthropology,[18] comparative literature,[19] criminal justice,[20] art history,[21] education,[22] and feminist studies,[23] to name a few. Wang himself has published an article positing parallels between scientific paradigms and how they change with architectural stylistic periods and how *they* change.[24] More specifically in design, logical frameworks, once made clear, can apply at different scales. For example, in *Space Is the Machine*, Hillier deals with locations of persons in space, and the visual fields seen from those locations.[25] This logic can be applied to cities as well as to residential interiors; there is no reason why visual fields, *qua* visual fields, couldn't be applied to landscape design. Also, Brand's categories (again: site, structure, skin, services, space plan, stuff), already applicable to all buildings, need not be limited to buildings; they can be used at the scale of city morphology, as was attempted in a 2000 master's thesis: Figures 11.5a, b, c applied Brand's theory to the formal evolution of Riverside Avenue, in Spokane, Washington, over 100 years.

11.3.4　*Primary and Secondary Logical Frameworks*

It is easy to see that Aristotle's four causes frame an explanatory system so broad that it has applicability in almost any mode of inquiry. Kuhn's theory of paradigm shift is also primary in this sense. Primary logical systems define first principles and relationships that sustain the system, but because of this, they spawn subsequent frameworks having smaller, but more focused, ranges of application. These secondary studies usually do not expand the primary system with any new material. Rather, they tend to go deeper into the domain mapped by the primary system.

Brand's six categories (site, structure, skin, services, space plan, and stuff) frame a primary system that other, more focused studies make use of. For example, the *Open Building* concept is a direct application of Brand's system. Here, building components are constructed "off site in an environment where efficiency, cost, and climate can be controlled," and then brought to the site to be easily connected together.[26] (See Box 11.2.)

March and Stiny's early work in shape grammar can be considered a primary system. They describe the general logical foundations of the approach:

> [A]rchitecture requires the delineation of one part of space from another. Such delineation, a configuration of lines, characterizes *shape*. The organization of a system of shapes gives space an *architecture*. Architecture in this sense may be applied to natural as well as to cultural phenomena, to works of nature and to works of man.[27]

The system posits that both natural and human-made forms are reducible to discrete rules regulating line-to-space relationships. Together these rules form a grammar that can describe the composition of extant works at an elementary level (perhaps uncovering traits unknown to the designer). It can also provide the basis for the design of new structures.

Figure 11.5 Zhenyu Wang's 2000 master's of science in architecture thesis analyzed Spokane, Washington's Riverside Avenue as it changed morphologically over
100 years. The top two photos of appeared in the first edition of this book in 2002.
Below them, we add an additional photo of the same location now, in 2012. Of the
buildings, some "stuff" has changed (awnings, mural on side wall is gone, parking
lot at left is new) but the structures remain. But at urban scale, what is not seen is
that the "structure" of Riverside has changed significantly: It is now a throughway
to Martin Luther King Way two blocks to the east, linking this main downtown
avenue with the University District. Courtesy of (a) Spokane Public Library;
(b) Zhenyu Wang; and (c) David Wang.

Because March and Stiny's work is rule-based, enormous strides in this arena have
taken place since the last edition of this book, given the ever-increasing powers of computer technology. "Procedural Modeling of Buildings," a paper published by Muller et
al. in 2006, describes CGA Shape, a modeling technology that can "generate massive
urban models with unprecedented level of detail." Using shape grammar rules, CGA

Shape generates a model of Pompeii using 190 design rules, or an aerial model of Beverly Hills using 150 rules. Say the authors: "We believe that our work is a powerful adaptation of Stiny's seminal shape grammar idea for computer graphics."[28]

BOX 11.2
Open Building at Bensonwood Homes

The Open Building concept was developed by Tedd Benson of Bensonwood Homes (see Figure 11.6):

> Under the Open Building concept, a building is viewed as a series of systems—from the mainframe exterior structure to the walls that divide

Figure 11.6 Bensonwood Homes separates different components of a building, prefabricating many assemblies in controlled environments. This also controls waste. Courtesy of Bensonwood Homes.

(Continued)

kitchen from living room to the plumbing and electrical systems to the dresser in your bedroom.[a]

This of course echoes Stewart Brand's theory of Structure: structure, services, stuff, etc. Advantages are the interchangeability of the systems; prefabrication of the systems off site also increases control over waste and predictability of time and cost. Bensonwood Homes has collaborated with the MIT Department of Architecture in developing the Open Prototype Initiative. One project was a transitional residence for brain injured patients and their families. As a resident's needs change, the residence adapts to him/her.

---

[a] Tim O'Sullivan, "Open Houses," in *Smart Home Owner*, January/February, 2007. See www.smart-homeowner.com/September-2007/Open-Houses/. Accessed June 18, 2012.

11.4   HOW DOES ONE FIRST CONCEIVE OF THE IDEA FOR A LOGICAL FRAMEWORK?

Before outlining the tactics of logical argumentation research, the question can be asked: Given that logical argumentation frameworks are paradigmatically innovative, how does one conceive of a logical framework in the first place? It is not an easy question to answer, other than that it comes with practice in a particular way of seeing connections between disparate elements in a field of information, with a desire to frame them into large but succinct explanatory networks. Designers tend to forget that research is itself a creative activity; perhaps this is one reason research agendas are often called research *designs*. "Creative researchers invent and discover," says John Zeisel. Furthermore:

> In the beginning of a project, emerging concepts are visions defining what data to gather. In the middle, information clarifies the concepts. At the end of a successful research project, clearly stated concepts summarize increased insight and define areas where further research can increase precision.[29]

Zeisel goes on to cite this extremely interesting point made by Michael Polanyi (the italics are in the text):

> How can we concentrate our attention on something we don't know? Yet this is precisely what we are told to do: "Look at the unknown!"—says Polya (1945)— "Look at the ends . . . *Look at the unknown.* Look at the conclusion!" No advice could be more emphatic. The seeming paradox is resolved by the fact that even though we have never met the solution, we have a conception of it in the same

sense as we have a conception of a forgotten name . . . *we should look at the known data, but not in themselves, rather as clues to the unknown, as pointers to it and parts of it*. We should strive persistently to feel our way towards an understanding of the manner in which these known particulars hang together, both mutually and with the unknown.[30]

A term coined by Charles Sanders Peirce is helpful here: *abduction*. (We also addressed abduction in Chapter 2, particularly in Box 2.3.) Abduction is a logical operation that is different from deduction and induction, to be addressed shortly. Abductive thinking involves the "educated guess," which is the stuff of all hypothesis making. We see a condition which we take to be a representative case of a larger rule, without (yet) the hard evidence to make that larger assumption.[31] Specifically in logical argumentation, the goal is to look beyond the specific case of anything toward general patterns of relationships within which the specific case can find a conceptual home. Put another way, the researcher asks the question: What larger system is this case an instance of? For those so inclined, questions of this sort can come any time. For instance, you are in a narrow alley in Rome, and it opens onto a small piazza. The question comes: Can all city morphologies be reduced to a discrete set of forms—a vocabulary? Or one day the thought comes to you that changing your kitchen cutlery is easier than changing your kitchen, which is again much easier than moving your entire house. The question arises: Can a theory be developed to explain how buildings change based on the rates of change of building components? (We are not suggesting this is how Kevin Lynch or Brand came upon their ideas; we are simply saying this is how ideas for logical argumentation emerge.) In a case of Wang's work with a doctoral student regarding collaborative design, the question arose: What exactly *is* collaborative design? Two years later, that question resulted in *A Heuristic Structure for Collaborative Design*, which enumerated five basic components that typify collaborative design: multiple epistemological domains, distinct threads of conceptual exchange, knowledge brokering, iterative process, and documentable (externally valid) new knowledge.[32] These may well be taken to be the first principles of collaborative design, and the first inklings about them were abductive in nature.

11.5 THE TACTICS OF LOGICAL ARGUMENTATION: DEFINING FIRST PRINCIPLES AND LOGICAL RELATIONS

11.5.1 *Defining First Principles*

The first principles of logical systems are almost always expressed by *technical terms* that, together, make up the conceptual chassis upon which the system is framed. If the system is influential, these terms are used and/or elaborated upon by subsequent secondary systems. It is impossible to grasp the intent of a logical system without a thorough grasp of its technical terms. Here are a few examples of first principles expressed as technical terms:

> The basic marketing functions that must be performed by one or several individuals are the following: closer, counter, lead finder, coordinator, marketing manager/director . . . (Weld Coxe).[33]
>
> [T]he whole matter of building is composed of lineaments and structure . . . lineaments have [nothing] to do with material . . . lineaments [are] the precise and correct outline, conceived in the mind, made up of lines and angles, and perfected in the learned intellect and imagination (Alberti).[34]
>
> We define the shape of a building plan as a set of wall surfaces and a set of discontinuities. We define discontinuities to include the edges of freestanding walls and the corners formed at the intersection of two wall surfaces . . . (Peponis et al.).[35]
>
> [W]e require of any building . . . that it act well; that it speak well; that it look well . . . (Ruskin).[36]
>
> [I]t is useful to distinguish between *positive* and *normative* theory and between *substantive* and *procedural* theory . . . (Lang).[37]

These disparate sentences all have one thing in common: they state technical terms that amount to the chassis upon which a logical system is built. How does one arrive at technical terms that amount to the structural foundations of logical systems? Are there any general characteristics of technical definitions that can be identified? The following lists different kinds of first principles.

First Principles of Quantity   First principles of quantity[38] are common features of logical argumentation. In the *Metaphysics*, Aristotle says this about the sciences: "those with fewer principles are more exact than those which involve additional principles."[39] He suggests that the simpler system is always closer to the essence of something than a more complex one. It is in this vein that Coxe captures "basic marketing functions" by listing five headings: closer, counter, lead finder, coordinator, marketing manager/director. For Vitruvius, there are five "fundamental principles of architecture": arrangement, eurythmy, symmetry, propriety, economy.[40] (It is then a question how these five fit his other three: *firmitas, utilitas, venustas*.)

First Principles of Quality   Intimately related to principles of quantity are principles of quality: it is often implicit that a determination of essential quantity is necessarily a determination of essential quality. For instance, the Greek quest for "the good" (*eudaimonia*) is not only *the* primary virtue (a question of quantity), but also the *highest* aim of life (a question of quality). Hence Aristotle, in requiring that good science is one that defines essential quantities, notes also that the highest science is the study of the Good.[41]

The simultaneity of quantity and quality can be seen in today's systems of logical argumentation, in two senses, both of which flow from Aristotle's point of view. In some systems, the argument for quality is implied in essential *elements* of quantity; once the quantity has been determined, the quality is determined as well. For example, in Marc Antoine Laugier's theory of the primitive hut, the components of the hut (column, entablature, pediment, etc.), which are elements of quantity, also guarantee quality: "The parts that are essential are the cause of beauty."[42] And here is Dana Cuff's theoretical statement about what constitutes excellent buildings: "I maintain that there are three principal evaluators of any building's quality and these are the consumers or the public at large, the participants in the design process, and the architectural profession."[43] This is immediately a statement of essential quantity as well as of essential quality.

First Principles of Origin   Origins provide another kind of first principle. There are two senses in which an argument from origin can work: the *genetic* sense and the *enabling* sense. Certainly, the "hut theories" (Vitruvius,[44] Laugier, R. D. Dripps,[45] to name three) emphasize genetic origins. Such theories assume that, because something originated in such and such a fashion, the present condition can be explained in that light. Or consider Heidegger's treatment of "dwelling" in *Building Dwelling Thinking*. In this work, Heidegger explores a host of old German words related to *bauen* (to build),[46] implying that uncovering the original meanings of the words is equal to uncovering the meaning of dwelling itself. The *enabling* sense of an argument from origin can be illustrated, again, by Cuff's theory of excellent buildings. The complete title of her chapter is "Excellent Practice: The *Origins* of Good Building" (our italics).[47] Aside from positing that if the three ingredients (quantity) are in place, the building will be excellent (quality), Cuff's title also holds that these three quantities are the enabling conditions from which quality springs.

11.5.2   Defining Relationships

After the technical definitions have been made clear, a logical framework must demonstrate certain *relational* linkages that make the system coherent.

Relation between Terms: Necessity   *Necessity* is that which is explicitly embedded in a proposition. For instance, given Mr. Jones, it is necessary that he is a man. Given that Mr. Jones is a bachelor, it is necessary that he is unmarried. Necessary relationships between the various terms of a logical system ensure the explanatory dependability of that system. Contrarily, if the relationships between terms are *contingent* rather than necessary—that is, if one proposition can lead to a variety of results—then the explanatory certainty of a system may be reduced. Necessity in formal systems, such as in rule-based computer programs, is based upon the logic of numerical relations. Necessity in cultural/discursive systems is of another kind, what the *Oxford Dictionary of Philosophy* calls *nomic* necessity, by which is largely meant the dependable patterns of nature's behavior. For instance, cultural/discursive systems often ground their arguments in a larger frame of reference such as nature, culture, or the machine. Embedded in this is an argument from nomic necessity: Because the larger domain is thus and so, therefore architectural action must be thus and so. For example, Vitruvius argued that buildings must be "symmetrical" because nature had made the human body "duly proportioned."[48] This is arguing from nomic necessity. When Le Corbusier bemoaned "eyes which do not see" in his *Vers une architecture*, he was chiding his fellow architects for not seeing a necessary connection, that being the logic of the machine in informing how the new architecture should be realized (see Figure 11.7).[49]

Relation between Terms: Deduction/Induction   Related to necessity are deduction and induction. Deduction draws conclusions explicitly contained in a set of facts: given Mr. Jones, we deduce that he is a man. That is, deduction involves *necessary* connections. In contrast, induction draws generalizations from given facts beyond what is embedded in just those facts. If Mr. Jones comes to his office every day at 8:00 a.m. for a week, we read into this a possible *general* pattern: he will always show up at this time. This is an inductive operation. Induction involves contingency, and contingent propositions are never as strong as

Figure 11.7   Le Corbusier's superimposition of various buildings over the ship *Aquitania*. Images such as this fill his *Vers une architecture*, with the aim of supporting the author's view that the machine age is the larger realm from which principles for architectural design must be derived. By permission of Dover Publications.

necessary ones. But then, induction can *do* more, in the sense that it promises explanatory power for a larger reality than the observed instances. A system framed only on deduction has a tendency to restate the obvious, and so may not be of much use. A system framed only by contingent (induced) connections is not a strong one, because the more contingency, the less the expectation that it can actually explain or predict.[50]

BOX 11.3
Defining Relationships: Syllogistic Frameworks for Relations between Terms

A syllogism is constructed of a primary and a secondary premise leading to a necessary conclusion. The typical construction is as follows: A = B; C = A; therefore C = B. The typical example: all men (A) are mortal (B); Socrates (C) is a man (A); therefore Socrates (C) is mortal (B). In formal/mathematical systems, syllogistic relationships are taken up in the transitive nature of the logic (A = B; B = C; A = C). At the cultural/discursive end of the spectrum, it is not uncommon to have syllogistic *frameworks* embedded in logical systems. Because they are cultural/discursive, and because they encompass so many contingent assumptions, these frameworks cannot be considered pure syllogisms in any formal sense of the word. But they are framed in such a way that two related premises are given, out of which a deductive operation drives the theorist's point of view as an assumed *necessary* conclusion. For instance, throughout the centuries architectural theories have appealed to nature as the basis for good architecture. For Vitruvius, it was nature as expressed in natural proportions most exemplified in the idealized human body (see Figure 11.8a). Framed syllogistically, we have this:

A	Nature informs	B	architectural beauty
C	Human proportions	A	are idealized nature
THEREFORE			
C	Human proportions	B	inform architectural beauty

Figure 11.8a   Vitruvius syllogism (nature and architectural beauty).

(Continued)

By the advent of the machine, theorists sought to include the machine as a natural production—also through the human being (see Figure 11.8b). Here is Frank Lloyd Wright in *The Art and Craft of the Machine* (1901): "the essence of this thing we call the Machine, [is] no more or less than the principle of organic growth working irresistibly the Will of Life through the medium of Man . . . ."[a]

A	Nature informs	B	architectural beauty
C	The machine	A	exemplifies organic (natural) growth
THEREFORE			
C	The machine	B	informs architectural beauty

Figure 11.8b   F. L. Wright syllogism (machine and architectural beauty).

More recently, Greg Lynn appealed to nature in his theory of "versioning," in which computer technology has now made it possible to conceive of a building as a *series*, rather than as a fixed object—just as nature itself is not static; it is rather "a continuous evolution of form."[b] Hence, designed environments should follow suit. Thus (Figure 11.8c):

A	Nature informs	B	architecture
C	Versioning (via computers)	A	exemplifies natural evolution of form
THEREFORE			
C	Versioning	B	informs architecture

Figure 11.8c   Syllogism based on Lynn's versioning rationale.

[a] Frank Lloyd Wright, "Art and Craft of the Machine," cited in Harry Francis Mallgrave and Christina Contandriopoulos (eds.), *Architecture Theory*, vol. 2 (Blackwell, 2008), 132.
[b] Ingeborg M. Rocker, "Versioning: Architecture as Series?" Graduate School of Design, Harvard University, www.gsd.harvard.edu/people/faculty/rocker /versioning.pdf. Accessed May 18, 2011.

Relation between Terms: *A Priori/A Posteriori*   The concept of *a priori* (which means "previous to experience") also comes out of necessity. In contrast, *a posteriori* refers to facts or truths that are established as a result of experience. Logical systems identify *a priori* conditions so that those conditions can in turn be the bases for explaining particular instances of experience. In our previous BIM example, Aksamija and Iordanova posit *a priori* data structures (categorized as Issue, Concept, and Form) that capture implicit "chunks" of knowledge. Or consider Louis Sullivan's cultural/discursive statement "form follows function."[51] For Sullivan, the inner essence of nature in things is the necessary *a priori* for their subsequent expressions as matter. Nature is also the *a priori* for the Vitruvius argument already cited.

11.6   THE TACTICS OF LOGICAL ARGUMENTATION: RHETORICAL TACTICS IN CULTURAL/DISCURSIVE SYSTEMS

For formal/mathematical systems, alphanumerical logic is less dependent upon cultural contingencies. But cultural/discursive systems depend upon rhetorical tactics to convey their arguments. Thus they use the logic of persuasion: an audience will not come around to a particular point of view unless that view *makes sense.* For cultural audiences, Perelman and Obrechts-Tyteca speak of the need to "gain the adherence of minds," which is a deliberative matter.[52] The very need to deliberate implies the lack of absolute necessity in these matters; something "makes sense" because of other factors rooted in the logic of persuasion and rhetoric. We examine some of these elements here as they relate to logical argumentation in cultural/discursive systems.

11.6.1   *Rhetorical Tactics: Naming*

"One of the essential techniques of quasi-logical argumentation is the identifying of various elements which are the object of discourse: We consider this identification of entities, events, or concepts as neither arbitrary nor obvious, that is . . . it is justifiable by argument."[53] In this statement, Perelman and Olbrechts-Tyteca point out that definition in itself can be a persuasive enterprise, or at least can have a persuasive component to it. The goal is to achieve a sense in the hearer that what is being defined has something to do with him or her not only at the level of cognitive reason, but also at the level of emotional or psychological identity. The tendency of cultural/discursive treatises to root their arguments in a larger transcendental realm (nature, morals, history, the machine, etc.) arises just because of their need to establish identification.

One tactic toward this end is simply *naming*. For instance, Ruskin's first principles of quality, that buildings must "act well . . . speak well . . . look well," makes a connection between architecture and moral considerations. How can one argue with morals? Or consider Semper's four elements of dwelling: Hearth, roof, enclosure, and mound are culled out of the mythical past by Semper simply by naming them. Of course, not any name is acceptable. In both Ruskin's and Semper's cases, the terms are categorically distinct from one another; they seem to capture a complete representation of their domains (etiquette for buildings; the basic components of the dwelling house); and they seem to be descriptive of all instances of their domains.

11.6.2   *Rhetorical Tactics: Association or Disassociation*

Another way to "make sense" to an audience is by *association*, by which, again, cultural/discursive treatises connect to larger realms. Consider the Greek orders in their connection to anthropomorphic ideas. The Doric is masculine; the Ionic matronly; the Corinthian maidenly. These are essential factors for their appeal and durability, because they not only give physical forms numerical guidelines for their composition but also associate them with issues of character and human identity. Early Modernist treatises often associate architecture with the machine to justify design. Here is Moisei Ginzburg in *Style and Epoch* (see also Figure 11.9):

> It is precisely the machine, the main occupant and the master of the modern factory, which, having already exceeded its bounds and gradually filling all the corners of our way of life and transforming our psyche and our aesthetic, constitutes the most important factor influencing our conception of form.[54]

Related to association is *disassociation*. Dissent is its own rhetorical tool. To disagree with an established norm often demands a hearing, provided that the one who dissents is acceptable to the audience on other grounds. J. N. L. Durand, for instance, argued forcefully against the Vitruvian position that classical proportions are derived from measurements of the human body. He measured a human foot, and claimed he was not able to derive from it the building proportions that this venerated argument prescribes.[55] Durand's authority, apart from his professional and academic standing, draws from the cultural ideas of his day, namely, the gradual substitution of an anthropomorphic understanding of nature with a machine-based functional/utilitarian view. So, for the cultural/discursive end of the spectrum, an active question is always this: Are there factors in contemporary culture that can be used as the bases by which to mount a dissenting point of view against precepts already accepted, but perhaps based on outmoded cultural factors?

Figure 11.9 Image of a crane from Ginzburg's *Style and Epoch*. Like Le Corbusier, Ginzburg looked to the machine as the larger paradigm from which to derive the design principles for modern architecture. Courtesy of MIT Press.

11.6.3 *Rhetorical Tactics: Analogy*

Cultural/discursive logical systems often depend on analogy. A new system is predicated upon a likeness between the attributes of its contents and the attributes of some other domain. Consider the parallel between biology and architecture. D'Arcy Thompson's *On Growth and Form* is a seminal example of this approach.[56]

Philip Steadman's *The Evolution of Designs: Biological Analogy in Architecture and the Applied Arts*, draws from Thompson's earlier work[57]; Steadman frames a systematic assessment of architecture with a series of analogies all having to do with the biological premise. These include morphology and structure (the anatomical analogy), trial and error in design progress (the "Darwinian" analogy), tools as extensions of the physical body, and design process as a kind of biological growth. Michael Pawlyn's *Biomimicry and Architecture* represents more recent developments in analogously connecting architecture with nature.[58]

11.6.4   *Rhetorical Tactics: Story*

Along with association comes *story*, in which something that is named is amplified by an account that is in fact not provable, but perhaps takes on the power of myth. The origin of the Corinthian capital is a case in point: a "freeborn maiden" takes ill and passes away; her nurse places some of her belongings in a basket over her grave with a roof-tile on top to keep it in place. An acanthus plant eventually surrounds the basket with its leaves.[59] John Summerson suggests that Vitruvius' "personalization" of the orders in this fashion opened the way for many such anthropomorphisms in the Renaissance; the Corinthian came to be associated with notions such as "virginal," "lascivious," and so on.[60] Another example is the enduring story of the primordial hut: from Vitruvius to Laugier to Le Corbusier to Joseph Rykwert[61] (among others), the primitive hut as the source of all architecture is itself a distinct line of architectural theory through the centuries.

11.6.5   *Rhetorical Tactics: Graphic Images*

Sometimes a picture is indeed worth a thousand words. This is because it acts to coalesce into one graphic image complex propositions with elements of feeling, story, and subjective identity. Laugier's memorable image of that venerable structure in his *Essay on Architecture* has come to be *the* emblem not only of his argument, but of the entire hut tradition. Robert Venturi's *Learning from Las Vegas*,[62] one of the early treatises that influenced the Postmodern movement in architectural design, is a work that illustrates how the graphic image can give focus to a way of life not possible to describe merely in words (see Figure 11.10). Perelman and Olbrechts-Tyteca recount the story of the king who sees an ox on its way to sacrifice; he orders a sheep to take its place and later confesses that his decision was based upon having seen the ox and not having seen the sheep. They follow Piaget by positing that "the thing on which the eye dwells, that which is best or most often seen, is, by that very circumstance, overestimated."[63]

Figure 11.10   Tanya billboard in Las Vegas. Courtesy of Venturi Scott Brown and Associates, Inc.

11.6.6   *Rhetorical Tactics: Appeals to Group Identity*

A cultural/discursive system emerges out of group experience, and it is to that group that it makes its primary appeal. For instance, the English architect and theorist A. W. Pugin (1812–1852) argued along lines of national identity in championing a return to Gothic architecture as the style that rightly characterized his country: "[W]hat does an Italian house do in England? Is there any similarity between our climate and that of Italy? Not the least . . . we are not Italians, we are Englishmen."[64] Here is Daniel Liebeskind subtly invoking group identity to explain his choice of materials on his Jewish Museum (see Figure 11.11):

> I got the idea of using zinc from Schinkel. Before his very early death, he recommended that any young architect in Berlin should use as much zinc as possible. . . . In Berlin, untreated zinc turns to a beautiful blue-gray. Many of Schinkel's Berlin buildings . . . are built of zinc . . . . When you knock them, you can tell that they are just covers. That is very Berlin-like.[65]

At a more problematic level, Robin Wagner-Pacifici and Barry Schwartz explore the implications of designing a commemorative structure that is necessarily laden with *conflicting* public points of view: the Vietnam Veterans Memorial. Does the design commemorate a lost war? Or does it commemorate the bravery of soldiers apart from the war? When there are competing interest groups with opposing rhetorical positions, it is very difficult to achieve a coherent design. Wagner-Pacifici and Schwartz point out the subsequent addition of a flag and a more conventional representational sculpture of three soldiers to the original design, due to the lack of consensus.[66]

Figure 11.11   Liebeskind's Jewish Museum, Berlin. Courtesy of Henry C. Matthews.

11.6.7   Rhetorical Tactics: Dividing or Integrating

Related to group identity, but also to disassociation, is *dividing*.

Identification is stirred in the audience by presenting two or more opposed groupings. "Making sense" is then dependent on certain choices the audience makes, either for one group and against another, or about how choices should be arranged in some sequence. For example, with John Ruskin and William Morris, the division was clearly between the machine and its by-products (mass production, iron and steel, for instance), as inferior, to handcraft, as superior. For Ruskin, if iron or steel is used to substitute for wood or stone as a load-bearing material, the project "ceases . . . to be true architecture."[67] In contrast, on the other side of the Atlantic, Frank Lloyd Wright's approach to this question used *integration*. In "The Art and Craft of the Machine," originally a speech given to the Chicago Arts and Crafts Society in 1901, Wright argued for the integration of the machine as another tool in the production of Art.[68] These two different positions over the same issue illustrate how "logical argumentation" of this kind is dependent upon how the argument is situated within larger factors. For the European tradition, the larger realms of historical truth (Ruskin), nationalism (Pugin), and handcraft (Morris) led to a rejection of the machine. For Wright, "nature" and "Art" are the larger venues that, in his argument, included the machine as a tool towards the greater end of Art.

11.6.8   *Rhetorical Tactics: Authority*

Aside from internal logic, a system gains authority (1) if it is spoken by an established voice, (2) if it is connected to a larger body of voices saying related things, or (3) if it can harness the energy of an emerging trend. We see instances of the first approach commonly in everyday life: manufacturers spend large sums linking their products to celebrities who are paid to endorse those products. In cultural/discursive systems, endorsements occur as well. It did not hurt, for instance, that Venturi's *Complexity and Contradiction in Architecture,* written relatively early in the architect's career, appeared with an introduction by Vincent Scully, hailing it as "probably the most important writing on the making of architecture since Le Corbusier's *Vers une Architecture.*"[69]

As for the second approach, it is not unusual for cultural/discursive arguments to emerge in topical collections. Ulrich Conrads' *Programs and Manifestoes of 20th Century Architecture*[70] includes short works that by themselves may not attain the level of "treatise." But as a collection, the whole gives each more of a sense of logical coherence. So arranged, the whole is also revealed to be the production of a particular trend in the worldview of a particular period. Indeed, the value of edited works in general is that they suggest a systemic character for a collection of separate voices.

In an instance of the third approach, the writing that accompanied the 1988 Johnson/Wrigley Museum of Modern Art (MoMA) exhibit on "Deconstructivist Architecture" came at the emergence of a trend, and perhaps helped to legitimize "deconstruction" in architecture.[71] Here, aside from the authority of a Johnson and the authority of a MoMA, the success of the show was also thanks to the *zeitgeist* of the day. It was fashionable to associate with Jacques Derrida and the developments in deconstruction in the realm of linguistics. In short, it was just the right time and place to promote a "deconstructivist architecture."

11.7   THE TACTICS OF LOGICAL ARGUMENTATION: CATEGORIES AND WAYS TO ARRANGE THEM

We have repeatedly addressed categories as a basic feature of logical frameworks; here we review more specifically some ways categories are used.

11.7.1   *Simple Categories*

Again, the goal of categorization is to enumerate the first principles of a logical system such that the entire domain is captured, with no conceptual overlaps in the categories, and nothing left out. The task is anything but simple because, usually, masses of input—often apparently disparate—must be sorted, and then described/ explained by these categories. On these measures, we noted at the outset, for

BOX 11.4

Categories as a Tactic in Logical Argumentation: The Four Stages of the Experience Economy

Joseph Pine and James Gilmore's article "Welcome to the Experience Economy"[a] can serve as a small reference manual on different ways to use categories in framing a logical domain. Perhaps the most memorable is their argument that economic progress can be conceived in four stages (see Figure 11.12). These stages comprise four simple categories that

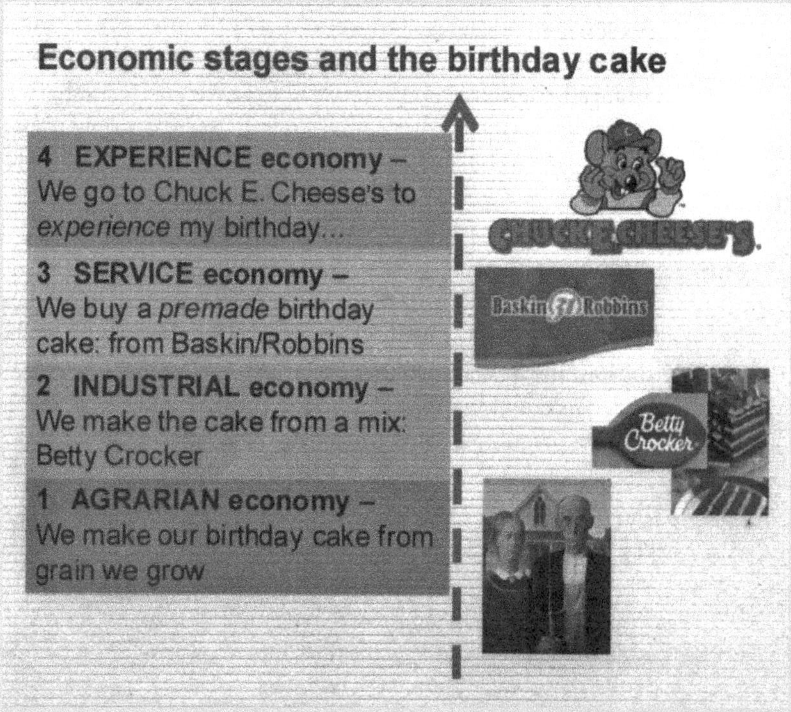

Figure 11.12   Pine and Gilmore's four stages of the economy: categories and stories used in service of logical argumentation. Artwork by David Wang.

---

[a] Pine and Gilmore, "Welcome to the Experience Economy," *Harvard Business Review* (July/August 1998): 97–105.

innovatively cover their overall domain, with no overlap and nothing left out. In the agrarian economy, a family made a birthday cake from wheat it grew and harvested. In the industrial economy, the cake was made from prepackaged cake mixes (e.g., Betty Crocker). In the service economy, the entire cake was premade, and can be picked up at the Baskin-Robbins ice cream store. Finally, in the experience economy, the entire birthday *experience*—cake, all of the party trappings and games that go along with the event—can be had at Chuck E. Cheese's. (Note how these categories also involve the story element as a tactic.)

Published in 1998, Pine and Gilmore's logical frame is now outdated: the Internet and cyber technology force the question: can't we call the new stage we are in now something like "the dematerialized economy"? Or simply: "the E-conomy"? We can now send e-birthday cards; even e-birthday cakes (see www.theoworlds.com/birthday/).

The Pine and Gilmore article endures as a reference for other ways categories are used in logical argumentation; we highly recommend it.

instance, that Prince Charles's "Ten Commandments of Architecture" do not work nearly as well as the Vitruvian Three: *firmitas, utilitas,* and *venustas* endures as a logical frame to describe and explain good architecture.

Other examples of simple categories: The chapter headings of Venturi's *Complexity and Contradiction* amount to categories of Postmodern design ("Ambiguity," "Both-And," "Double-Functioning," etc.); these categories form the logical framework of his treatise. Categorization is also the tactic Christian Norberg-Schulz uses to tackle the notion of "dwelling." In *The Concept of Dwelling,* he holds that "when dwelling is accomplished, our wish for belonging and participation is fulfilled."[72] But this fulfillment is accomplished when architecture facilitates (1) the enabling of meetings for the exchange of ideas, products, and feelings; (2) the ability to come to agreement with a common set of values; and (3) the creation of a sense of "having a small chosen world of our own."[73] These are further categorized into "modes" of dwelling: the collective, the public, and the private. Finally, the three modes are assigned architectural form-equivalents of urban space (the collective, or the settlement), institution (public buildings), and house (the private retreat). One can argue whether or not Norberg-Schulz captures "dwelling" with these categories. But this takes nothing away from the fact that it is logical argumentation.

11.7.2 Cross-Categories

In Lisa Heschong's *Thermal Delight in Architecture,* four technical terms (her first principles) are posited: *necessity, delight, affection,* and *sacredness.* [74] These then

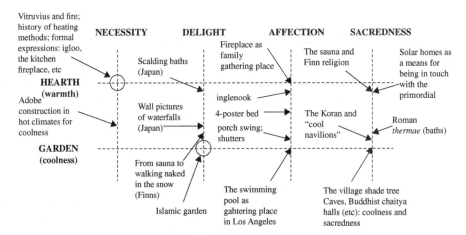

Figure 11.13   Diagrammatic of Heschong's logical structure for *Thermal Delight in Architecture*. Diagram by David Wang.

"intersect" with another pair of categories: *hearth* and *garden*. The latter two point to the internal domicile (*hearth*), on the one hand and, on the other, external nature that has been incorporated into the realm of human dwelling (*garden*). These six terms form an orthogonal grid, at a conceptual level, upon which she then places a range of examples (see Figure 11.13).

J. B. Jackson's *Westward Moving House* is also a fine example of using cross-categories for a logical frame. [75] Jackson uses three generations of the Tinkham family (horizontal in Figure 11.14) and documents their relationship to a large sampling of the *same* material/cultural categories: the house, the land, nature, church, tools, family relations, road networks, money, moral outlook, and relation to community (vertical in Figure 11.14). These categories crossed with the three families together paint a compelling picture of cultural change in relation to the American landscape.

11.7.3   *By Spectrum or Spectra*

Some data resist clear categorization; they are better arranged along a spectrum. At focus are still first principles expressed as categories. But in cases of spectra, to insist on clear boundaries between each category would involve an uncomfortable Procrustean bed operation. Our own spectrum for logical argumentation typologies in Figure 11.3 is of this kind. Wang's *Prediction in Theoria: Towards an Interdisciplinary Range of Theories Related to Architecture*[76] arranges extant theories in architecture on a spectrum from "strict prediction" through "thick description," from "thick description to polemics," and finally from "polemics to fictional constructions."

	Reason for settling	The House	Relation to LAND	Relation to NATURE and envirom't	Religion/ Church	Tools and Labor	Animals and Livestock	Relation to FOOD	Education & Knowledge
Nehemiah and Submit, Jerusha, New England. 300 years ago	Settler from Old World 10	Cut own trees, house not functional, bleak 14-15, built to last/inflexible/labor intensive/15unadorned	Given it 60 acres 10	Lawless 17-18 fearful of nature 18, dreaded nature 29	Church was center 16-18 superfamily 14 hierarchical 13-14, stem God 14, Israel 18, strove for holiness 18, preaching on horseback 19	No nails 10 Broadaxe By hand 12, owned one piece of farm machinery 27	None to start 12	For survival 11-12	Catalogue of needful things 10, the bible
Pliny and Matilda, Illium, Illinois, 100 years ago, Pliny died in 1892 (29)	To farm on larger scale 20; escape domestic tyranny 22, left NE for a different society, econ, landscape 22-3, flight from OT 23	1860 (24), Larger 21 House designed for resale 24 away from neighbors 24 revolutionary features 24, flexible 25, functional 26, balloon 25, with nails 25, fam rm	Bargain/bought it 20, twenty acres of wheat 21 Cash crop 27, bought other farms to expand holdings 27, leased/sold land 27, functional 26	No "hostiles" 21 fertile 21 Loved nature 21, loved unspoiled nature 29, nature as expanding organism 37	Three churches in Illium 22, minister visited but didn't come back 22, house took place of church 26, Worship God in nature 28,	Nails 25, wagons, plows, cultivators, harrows, buggy 27, wooden fencing changed his fields at will ie, flexible 27	Horses, oxen, milch cow, 20	Beginning years were harsh 21-22	Handbook 20, Matilda made candles, soap, sugar from corn-done by specialists in Jerusha 21, Practical knowledge 22
Ray and Shirley, Bonniview, TX, assume modern	Move out from home of Old Man 31	Not finished 30 cement blk 31 nothing permanent 34, labor saving devices 33, save $$: no fireplace 33, separate rooms 35, no books 35, like motel 35, house a transformer 36	Land is functional 36, large crops of wheat/cotton/ sorghum/ caster beans, depending on market 31,	Economic energy transfer 38, geography as pattern 31, doubtful of nature 37-38	Did not go to church 35, no scientific evidence for religion 42 wisdom of the east, 41	Bulldozers Earthmovers 31 Pickup truck 32	Steers 31, paint pony (for enjoyment) 37	Supermarket 32	Went to an agricultural college 32, no books in home 35

	Family relations	Road network	$$$	Moral outlook/ personal character	Relation to Community	View of the cosmos	Social standing	Politics	Provision for family
Nehemiah and Submit, Jerusha, New England. 300 years ago	Never dreamt grandchildren would desert the place .. 30	Poor communications with outside world 12	Jerusha pioneer economic conditions 18, Indifferent to money 23	Fearful 18, exiles 18	Family/village interchangeable terms13, house designed for social self-sufficiency 26	Part of order 17, going to next world 17, yeoman 41, fragment of creation 37	3 sorts - gentleman, handicraftsman, husbandman 13	Nothing really democratic 12-13	Nehemiah's responsibility 27
Pliny and Matilda, Illium, Illinois, 100 years ago	Free individuals 29	Got a buggy after road improvement 27	Wanted wealth 23 Cash crop 27, house easy to be sold 24	Optimistic and adventurous 21	Neighbors remote 22, felt like outsider 22, no village at all 24, chief artificer an individual 24	Nature as expanding organism 37	Social self sufficiency (house) 24		Railroad brought goods from the east 27
Ray and Shirley, Bonniview, TX, assume modern	Children spend lots of time away from home: go to public schools 33-34, discipline left to teachers 34, impatient with old ways 35	Very developed 33, good roads and efficient transportation 38	Operates on credit 31 Land spec. 31-32 uses accountant 33, work=time=money 37, the farm as part of outside world 38	Wife chose different looks cosmetically 41, mobile identity 41, not a child of God,or Nature, but an efficient transformer 42	Committed to nothing	energy trans-formation 36	Depends on organizations they belong to, car they drive, clothes they wear, furnishings 34		

Figure 11.14 Diagram of Jackson's Westward Moving House.

11.7.4 By Adjacency Matrices

Sometimes the fluid boundaries between groupings of data work better situated in a loop rather than on a line. That is to say, the groupings are arranged adjacent to each other, more as conceptual regions with multiple borders, rather than sequentially from pole to pole. Examples can be found in Pine and Gilmore's article mentioned earlier. Rosalind Krauss uses an adjacency matrix in her essay "Sculpture in the Expanded Field."[77] The problem confronted by Krauss is how contemporary sculpture is no longer a clearly "bounded category." Instead, earthworks, tunnels, rock arrangements in the landscape, and other forms and constructions are all now accepted examples of sculpture that do not fit the conventional definition. Krauss captures her logic for an "expanded field" of sculpture by using what is called a Klein group diagram (we were not able to obtain permission to use Krauss's diagram, but it is in the article we reference). The diagram is constructed of a landscape/architecture binary along a "complex" axis; the opposites of these categories (not-landscape/not-architecture) form another "neuter" axis parallel to it. Thus, four nodes are created that interact with each other vertically. The diagonal links (called *diexes*) further enrich adjacent oppositions (e.g., landscape/not-architecture). This complex diagram becomes a logical frame for expanding the field of sculpture. For example, Robert Smithson's Spiral Jetty can be understood as an example of sculpture as "marked site," which lies in between landscape and not-landscape; his Partially Buried Woodshed is a "site construction," in between architecture and landscape.

11.8   CONCLUSION

As noted earlier, logical argumentation is often *implicit* in various modes of research and writing. Many of the examples we cited in this chapter do not explicitly identify "logical argumentation" as their research strategy. (See Figure 11.15 for a summary of strengths and weaknesses of logical argumentation research.) But we noted that this strategy comes closest to philosophical inquiry. Of all the disciplines, it is noteworthy that works of philosophy themselves often do not state a "research method." Why? Because the task of philosophy is to identify *fundamental* principles that frame a domain; in one sense philosophical inquiry encompasses any method to get to these principles. (One way to reflect on this is to recall what "PhD" means. When any

Strengths	Weaknesses
Logical argumentation identifies first principles as the common denominator(s) for a wide variety of seemingly disparate factors and provides an underlying (or overarching) framework that ties them together into a conceptual system that can describe, explain, and predict within its area of concern. First principles are part of any research design; hence the principles of logical argumentation can help identify them and organize them in an understandable manner. In other research designs, logical argumentation is therefore useful as a tactic for arranging fundamental principles coherently.	As with the Prince Charles example, it is not easy to identify fundamental categories; examples abound in the literature of unclear categories. It is also easy to fall into the trap of wishing for well-accepted numbers of categories: for example, three, or seven, while six tends to "feel" incomplete. Prince Charles was obviously thinking of precedent when he termed his list "the Ten Commandments." But there is no internal reason why the *substance* of his system had to be comprised of *10* items. A logical system may in fact not be an accurate representation of the reality it purports to explain and yet still be internally consistent from a logical point of view. For this reason, logical systems must be tested (and they should be amenable to testing).

Figure 11.15   Strengths and weaknesses of logical argumentation research.

discipline awards its highest degree, it awards "the doctorte of philosophy *in*" . . . the discipline. Insofar as a doctoral curriculum captures the fundamental principles of its discipline, it is a logical framework; mastery of it earns the PhD, regardless of which discipline.) A final example: Consider the difference between these two questions: (1) What is this piece of art? and (2) What is art? The first question might require a specific research method. The second question requires logical argumentation.

NOTES

1. Prince Charles, "Ten Commandments of Architecture," in Harry Francis Mallgrave and Christina Contandriopoulos (eds.), *Architectural Theory, Volume II: An Anthology from 1871 to 2005* (Malden, MA: Blackwell), 527. Prince Charles's entire list: Place, Hierarchy, Scale, Harmony, Enclosure, Materials, Decoration, Art, Signs, and Lights.
2. Vitruvius, *The Ten Books on Architecture* (New York: Dover Publications, 1960), I.3.2.
3. Aristotle, *Physics*, Book II, section 3.
4. Ajla Aksamija and Ivanka Iordanova, "Computational Environments with Multimodal Representations of Architectural Design Knowledge," *International Journal of Architectural Computing* 8(4) (2010): 442–460.
5. It is not exactly domain as Howard Gardner would have it, that is, a kind of cultural field of endeavor that matches one of his intelligence categories (music, for instance, or mathematics). Howard Gardner, *Frames of Mind* (New York: Basic Books, 1983), 25–27.
6. Stewart Brand, *How Buildings Learn* (New York: Viking, 1994), 2–23.
7. See Stewart Brand, "Shearing," in William W. Braham, Jonathan A. Hale, and John Stanislav Sadar (eds.), *Rethinking Technology: A Reader in Architectural Theory* (New York: Routledge, 2007), 335–336.
8. For instance, see Andrew Dey, "Reinventing the House," *Fine Homebuilding* (October/ November 2006): 58–63.
9. Bill Hillier and Julienne Hanson, *The Social Logic of Space* (Cambridge, UK: Cambridge University Press, 1984), 155–163.
10. Bob Hillier, "Cities as Movement Economies," in *Space Is the Machine: A Configurational Theory of Architecture* (Cambridge, UK: Cambridge University Press, 1996), 149–181.
11. Miwon Kwon, *One Place After Another: Site Specific Art and Locational Identity* (Cambridge, MA: MIT Press, 2002).
12. Rosalind Krauss, "Sculpture in the Expanded Field," in Hal Foster (ed.), *Postmodern Culture* (London: Pluto Press, 1985), 31–42.
13. Antony Flew, *Philosophical Dictionary*, rev. 2nd ed. (New York: St. Martin's Press, 1979), 242.
14. Chaim Perelman and L. Olbrechts-Tyteca, *The New Rhetoric: A Treatise on Argumentation* (Notre Dame and London: University of Notre Dame Press, 1969), 13–17.

15. Gottfried Semper, *The Four Elements of Architecture and Other Writings,* trans. J. F. Mallegrave and W. Hermann (Cambridge, UK: Cambridge University Press, 1989), 101–102.

16. Marc-Antoinne Laugier, *Essay on Architecture* (1752), trans. Wolfgang and Anni Hermann (Los Angeles: Hennessey and Ingalls, 1977), 11–38.

17. Le Corbusier, "Five Points of a New Architecture," in Tim Benton and Charlotte Benton (eds.), *Architecture and Design: 1890–1939* (New York: Whitney Library, 1975), 153–155.

18. John Tresch, "On Going Native: Thomas Kuhn and Anthropological Method," *Philosophy of the Social Sciences* 31(3) (2001): 302–322.

19. Robert Weninger, "Comparative Literature at a Crossroads? An Introduction," *Comparative Critical Studies* 3(1–2) (1981): xi–xix.

20. Alexander W. Pisciotta, "Theoretical Perspectives for Historical Analyses: A Selective Review of the Juvenile Justice Literature," *Criminology* 19(1) (1981): 115–130.

21. Caroline Jones, "The Modernist Paradigm: The Artworld and Thomas Kuhn," *Critical Inquiry* 26(3) (2000); "Response," 27(4) (2001): 489–528.

22. For example, see "Science and Education," http://ihpst.arts.unsw.edu.au/journal.html.

23. Helen E. Longino, "Does the Structure of Scientific Revolutions Permit a Feminist Revolution in Science?" in Thomas Nickles (ed.), *Thomas Kuhn* (Cambridge and New York: Cambridge University Press, 2003), 261–281.

24. David Wang, "Kuhn on Architectural Style," *Architectural Research Quarterly* 13 (2009): 49–58.

25. Hillier, *Space Is the Machine.*

26. Dey, 59.

27. L. March and G. Stiny, "Spatial Systems in Architecture and Design: Some History and Logic," *Environment and Planning B: Planning and Design* 12 (1985): 31. Italics in text.

28. Pascal Muller, Peter Wonka, Simon Haegler, Andreas Ulmer, and Luc Van Gool, "Procedural Modeling of Buildings," Association for Computing Machinery, Inc., 2006, 0730–0301/06/0700–0614, 614–622.

29. John Zeisel, *Inquiry by Design* (New York: W.W. Norton, 2006), 34.

30. Ibid., 35. The quote comes from Michael Polanyi, *Personal Knowledge: Towards a Postcritical Philosophy* (Chicago: University of Chicago Press, 1958), 127–128. The citation within the quote is to G. Polya, *How to Solve It: A New Aspect of Mathematical Method* (Princeton, NJ: Princeton University Press, 1945).

31. For a readable explanation of abduction, see "Charles Sanders Peirce" in the online *Stanford Encyclopedia of Philosophy,* http://plato.stanford.edu/entries/peirce/. Accessed September 9, 2011.

32. David Wang and Isil Oygur, "A Heuristic Structure for Collaborative Design," *Design Journal* 13(3) (2010): 355–371.

33. Weld Coxe, *Managing Architectural and Engineering Practice* (New York: John Wiley & Sons, 1980), 58–64.

34. Leon Battista Alberti, *On the Art of Building in Ten Books* (1453), bk. 1, sec. 1, trans. Joseph Rykwert, Neil Leach, and Robert Tavernor (Cambridge: MIT Press, 1994), 7.

35. John Peponis, J. Wineman, M. Rashid, S. Hong Kim, and S. Bafna, "On the Description of Shape and Spatial Configuration Inside Buildings: Convex Partitions and Their Local Properties," *Environment and Planning B* 24 (1997): 762.

36. John Ruskin, *The Stones of Venice*, vol. 1 (New York: E. P. Dutton & Co., n.d.), 33.

37. Jon Lang, *Creating Architectural Theory* (New York: Van Nostrand Reinhold, 1987), viii.

38. For this discussion on quantity and the following subsection on quality, we are indebted to material from Perelman and Olbrechts-Tyteca. Perelman and Olbrechts-Tyteca treat these two terms under their general heading of "loci." Here, we have used these terms in another manner, but we recommend *The New Rhetoric* as an important work from which readers interested in logical argumentation can benefit.

39. Aristotle., *Metaphysics*, 982a.

40. Vitruvius, book I, ch. 2, 13–16.

41. Aristotle, *Metaphysics*, 982b. "And that science is supreme, and superior to the subsidiary, which knows for what end each action is to be done; i.e., the Good in each particular case, and in general the highest Good in the whole of nature. . . ."

42. Laugier, 12.

43. Dana Cuff, *Architecture: The Story of Practice* (Cambridge, MA: MIT Press, 1993), 196.

44. Vitruvius, book 2, ch. 1, Sections 1–2, 38–39.

45. R. D. Dripps, *The First House* (Cambridge, MA: MIT Press, 1997).

46. Martin Heidegger, "Building Dwelling Thinking," in David Krell (ed.), *Basic Writings* (San Francisco: Harper Torchbooks, 1993), 347–363.

47. Cuff, 195.

48. Vitruvius, 3.1.4.

49. Le Corbusier, 89–103.

50. Any deduction involves a tacit inductive step, which is the assumption that nature is uniform in its behavior. This is the position of David Hume: "For all inferences from experience suppose, as their foundation, that the future will resemble the past, and that similar powers will be conjoined with similar sensible qualities. If there be any suspicion, that the course of nature may change, and that the past may be no rule for the future, all experience becomes useless, and can give rise to no inference or conclusion." *An Enquiry Concerning Human Understanding* (Indianapolis and Cambridge: Hackett Publishing, 1993), 24. (Originally published in 1748.)

51. Louis Sullivan, "The Tall Office Building Artistically Considered," in *Kindergarten Chats and Other Writings* (New York: Wittenborn, Schultz, 1947), 207–208.

52. Perelman and Olbrechts-Tyteca, 13–17.

53. Ibid., 13–17.

54. Moisei Ginzburg, *Style and Epoch*, trans., A. Senkevitch (Cambridge MA: MIT Press, 1982), 80–81.

55. J. N. L. Durand, "Summary of the Lectures on Architecture," in E. Holt (ed.), *A Documentary History of Art*, vol. 3 (Garden City, NY: Anchor, 1966), 206–207.

56. D'Arcy Thompson, *On Growth and Form* (London: Cambridge University Press, 1971).

57. Philip Steadman, *The Evolution of Designs: Biological Analogy in Architecture and the Applied Arts* (London: Cambridge University Press, 1979).

58. Michael Pawlyn, *Biomimicry and Architecture* (London: RIBA Publishing, 2011).

59. Vitruvius, 4.1.9–10.

60. John Summerson, *The Classical Language of Architecture* (London: Thames and Hudson, 1980), 14–15.

61. Joseph Rykwert, *On Adam's House in Paradise* (Cambridge, MA: MIT Press, 1981).

62. Robert Venturi, Denise Scott Brown, and Steven Izenour, *Learning from Las Vegas* (Cambridge, MA: MIT Press, [1977] 1996).

63. Perelman and Olbrechts-Tyteca, 116–117. It should be noted that the authors here mean verbal images: "... make present, by verbal magic alone ..."

64. A. W. Pugin, *True Principles of Pointed Christian Architecture* (New York and London: St. Martin's Press, 1973), 64–65. (Originally published in 1841.)

65. Daniel Liebeskind, *1995 Raoul Wallenberg Lecture* (Ann Arbor: University of Michigan, 1995), 40.

66. Robin Wagner-Pacifici and Barry Schwartz, "The Vietnam Veterans Memorial: Commemorating a Difficult Past," *American Journal of Sociology* 97(2) (1991): 376–420.

67. John Ruskin, "The Lamp of Truth," in *The Seven Lamps of Architecture* (New York: John Wiley & Sons, 1865), 34. (Originally published in 1849.)

68. Frank Lloyd Wright, "The Art and Craft of the Machine," in Edgar Kaufman and Beb Raeburn (eds.), *Frank Lloyd Wright: Writings and Buildings* (Cleveland OH: World, 1960), 55–73.

69. Vincent Scully, "Introduction," in Robert Venturi, *Complexity and Contradiction in Architecture* (New York: Museum of Modern Art, 1985), 9. (Originally published in 1966.)

70. Ulrich Conrads (ed.), *Programs and Manifestoes of 20th Century Architecture* (Cambridge, MA: MIT Press, 1970).

71. Philip Johnson and Mark Wigley, *Deconstructivist Architecture* (New York: Museum of Modern Art, Distributed by New York Graphic Society Books, and Boston: Little Brown, 1988), 10–20.

72. Christian Norberg-Schulz, *The Concept of Dwelling: On the Way to a Figurative Architecture* (New York: Rizzoli, 1985), 7.

73. Ibid., 13.

74. Lisa Heschong, *Thermal Delight in Architecture* (Cambridge, Mass.: MIT Press, 1999).

75. J. B. Jackson, *Westward Moving House* in Ervin H. Zube, ed., *Landscapes: Selected Writings of J. B. Jackson* (Cambridge, Mass.: University of Massachusetts Press, 1970), 10–42.

76. David Wang, "Prediction in Theoria: Towards an Interdisciplinary Range of Theories Related to Architecture," *Architectural Research Quarterly* 10(3/4) (2006): 263–274.

77. Krauss, 31–42.

Chapter 1 2

Case Studies and Combined Strategies

12.1   INTRODUCTION

In 1961, Jane Jacobs wrote her classic book, *The Death and Life of Great American Cities*. Jacobs's book challenged the conventional wisdom of Modernist-inspired urban renewal popular at that time. Her insights about how to maintain and foster the vitality of cities are derived almost entirely from vignettes of life in New York City (see Figure 12.1).

However, the richness and depth of her many examples of the socio-physical dynamics of life in New York were powerfully persuasive; as a consequence, the book had an enormous impact on the planning and architecture professions. Moreover, the themes she identified were observed and documented in other cities in subsequent analyses. In her introduction, she presents an articulate rationale for the strategy of her investigation:

> In setting forth different principles, I shall mainly be writing about common, ordinary things.... The way to get at what goes on in the seemingly mysterious and perverse behavior of cities is, I think, to look closely, and with as little expectation as is possible, at the most ordinary scenes and events, and attempt to see what they mean and whether any threads of principle emerge among them.... I use a preponderance of examples from New York because that is where I live. But most of the basic ideas in this book come from things I first noticed or was told in other cities.... I hope any reader of this book will constantly and skeptically test what I say against his own knowledge of cities and their behavior.[1]

415

Figure 12.1 Cityscape in Brooklyn Heights, New York. Photograph courtesy of Linda Groat.

In a study of popular Modernism in Brazil, Fernando Lara poses the questions: Why was Modernist architecture better received in Brazil than in Europe or the United States? How were the attributes of Modernism promulgated such that many working and middle-class houses of the 1950s were built with visible attributes of Modernism? And to what extent were these houses truly Modernist?[2]

To explore these questions, Lara identified the Brazilian city Belo Horizonte as the focus of his study. Belo Horizonte was selected for at least two reasons: (1) the great number of 1950s popular Modernist houses in major sections of the city; and (2) the presence of one of the first and most significant ensembles of Modernist public buildings, the Pampulha complex built in the early 1940s (see Figures 12.2 and 12.3). In this regard, Pampulha represents an officially sanctioned and close-at-hand example of Modernism, known to the entire city's population.

In framing the contours of the study, Lara identified three types of data sources: (1) archival research to ascertain the influence of various social, economic, cultural,

Figure 12.2　A typical popular Modernist house, Belo Horizonte, Brazil. Photograph courtesy of Fernando Lara.

and media transmissions; (2) formal analyses (of facade design and interior layouts) in a sample of 300 houses in two sections of the city; and (3) in-depth interviews with 20–30 residents of popular Modernist houses, many of whom—though elderly—were original owners. In this way, Lara has combined multiple data sources that address the broad cultural influences, the physical extent of Modernist adoption and/or adaptation, and the residents' own understanding of their homes in relation to the larger cultural context.

Figure 12.3　Part of the Pampulha complex, Belo Horizonte, Brazil. Photograph courtesy of Fernando Lara.

From this rich array of data sources, Lara is able to explain in very detailed and nuanced ways how and why Modernism came to infuse the building of middle-class residential areas of Belo Horizonte. Indeed, some of his analyses uncover unexpected patterns and relationships. For example, although popular magazines were full of both advertisements and stories about the artifacts of modernization, many of the families who built Modernist-style homes were most influenced through personal connections and/or direct exposure to the homes of more well-to-do families (see Figure 12.4).

Moreover, the application of Modernist principles was often inconsistent or piecemeal. For example, Modernist features were applied to the facade of houses, while the interior layouts reflected the social traditions of pre-Modernist houses (see Figure 12.5).

These two studies illustrate two powerful, and sometimes overlapping, approaches to research design. Jacobs's study is a preeminent and well-respected example of the *case study* strategy; she uses the example of New York City—as a particular case—to explore the multiple socio-physical dynamics that contribute to the vitality of urban life. Although she may have gained insights from her experience in other cities, and others may have studied other cities in light of her conclusions, the heart and soul of her study, is about the particular case of New York City.

Lara's research is also a case study, in that he focuses on the multifaceted dynamics that led to adoption and adaptation of Modernism in one city: Belo Horizonte, Brazil. But his study also represents quite emphatically the power of *combined strategies,* in this instance the historical and the qualitative strategies.

In the remainder of this chapter, we will examine in detail both the case study strategy and models for achieving effective *combined strategies.*

12.2   STRATEGY: GENERAL CHARACTERISTICS OF THE CASE STUDY

In the one of the most frequently cited books on case study research, Robert Yin provides the following definition: "A case study is an empirical inquiry that investigates a contemporary phenomenon within its real-life context, especially when the boundaries between phenomenon and context are not clearly evident."[3] To make the definition more clearly applicable to architectural research, we would amend Yin's definition to read: an empirical inquiry that investigates a phenomenon or setting. By deleting the word *contemporary* and adding the word *setting,* this definition would specifically accommodate the explicit inclusion of historic phenomena and both historic and contemporary settings as potential foci of case studies.

What, then, are the primary identifying characteristics of the case study? Briefly, the five particularly salient characteristics are: (1) a focus on either single or

Figure 12.4 A typical product advertisement, Brazil, 1950s. Courtesy of Fernando Lara.

multiple cases, studied in their real-life contexts; (2) the capacity to explain causal links; (3) the importance of theory development in the research design phase; (4) a reliance on multiple sources of evidence, with data converging in a triangular fashion; and (5) the power to generalize to theory. These five characteristics will be discussed in detail in the following chapter segments.

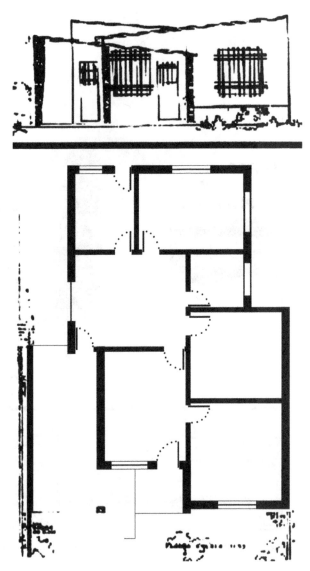

Figure 12.5   Typical facade and floor plan from Lara, 2008. Courtesy of Fernando Lara.

12.2.1 *A Focus on Cases in Their Contexts*

The essence of the case study strategy is its focus on studying a setting or phenomenon embedded in its real-life context. As Yin describes it, the case study strategy implies much more than simply studying a phenomenon in the "field." Rather, the case study involves studying a case in relation to the complex dynamics with which it intersects and from which the case itself is inseparable. This definition of the "case" is clearly evident in both the Jacobs and the Lara studies. For instance, Jacobs's investigation of urban vitality in the case of New York City is substantially linked to a multitude of contextual factors and phenomena—from the rise of the automobile culture, to federal funding policies, to trends in planning theory. Similarly, Lara's study of Modernist houses in the case of Belo Horizonte entails a wide range of issues from the role of modernization in Brazil, to the economic prosperity of the 1950s, to the influence of local political leaders. As both of these examples demonstrate, the context of the case becomes virtually inseparable from the definition of the case itself.

BOX 12.1
Case Study: A 100% Flexible Workspace

A combination of recent trends—including the globalization of markets, rapid growth of telecommuting and telecommunications, the shift toward collaborative work or project teams, and the increasingly flexible assignment of office space, such as hot desks—has led many organizations to reconsider how they plan for and use their office environments. In some organizations, the changes have been so profound that it is unclear how, or if, ongoing work practices are being supported by the design of the physical environment. In particular, Janice Barnes wanted to investigate this question: How does the design of the physical environment support the way project teams share knowledge in a 100% flexible workplace?

The focus of this case study research was one office site within a major global consulting organization of over 130,000 employees, with operations in over 50 countries. The particular site was chosen because it had recently been designed by a local architectural firm to meet the new workplace standards established by the organization in 2000. The design intention was to provide a 100% flexible workplace in which no person, even at the partner level, claims a dedicated office. All office assignments are temporary, and extensive telecommuting is accommodated.[a] In addition to site

[a] Janice Barnes, *Situated Cognition in Flexible Work Arrangements*. PhD dissertation, University of Michigan, Ann Arbor, 2001.

(Continued)

visits for observations, Barnes conducted open-ended interviews with approximately 25 people, including members of various project teams, office support staff, facilities department staff members, human resources staff, a national facilities staff member, and several members of the architectural firm that had designed the site.

Barnes concludes that in this new environment, project teams most frequently share knowledge via an array of artifacts displayed in the team work room (see Figure 12.6). These artifacts may include reference documents from clients, workflow diagrams pinned to wall surfaces, diagrams from brainstorming sessions, and so on. Few, if any, representations of knowledge are located or displayed in individual offices or cubicles. And since these offices are constantly reassigned, virtually no personalization of offices occurs. This new design standard for the workplace seems to serve the short-term interests of the project teams reasonably well, but interviews revealed that employees felt little, if any, attachment to the workplace and invested no energy in getting to know other employees within it. Much as artifacts exhibit short life spans in the organization (duration of the project), so too do many working relationships.

Figure 12.6 Typical project team work room, with the artifacts representing the project team's shared knowledge. Drawn by Fernando Lara.

12.2.2   The Capacity to Explain Causal Links

One of the most frequently discussed issues in research design is that of causality. As we discussed in Chapter 9, for instance, the experimental research design is fundamentally orchestrated so as to ascertain the causal capacity of the independent or treatment variable. By contrast, correlational design can identify patterns of relationships, but stops short of attributing cause (see Chapter 8). Yet we have also seen that both interpretive-historical and qualitative strategies can also address the issue of causality, albeit in quite a different way than experimental research; both of these strategies offer the potential to uncover the multiple, complex, and sometimes overlapping factors that eventually lead to particular outcomes. It is in this latter sense that case studies can also identify causal links among an array of socio-physical factors and events.

In arguing that case studies can, like experiments, be *explanatory*, Yin suggests that case studies can also be either *descriptive* or *exploratory* in purpose.[4] Whether a particular case study is explanatory, descriptive, exploratory, or some combination of these is a function of the researcher's purpose—or more precisely the nature of the research question—rather than any limitation inherent in the case study strategy. To clarify his point, Yin develops a case study typology that distinguishes among both research goals and design structure.

Type of Structure	Purpose of Case Study		
	Explanatory	Descriptive	Exploratory
1. Linear-Analytic Typical article format: problem statement literature review methods results	X	X	X
2. Chronological (narrative sequence)	X	X	X
3. Theory-Building Sequence of chapters depends on logic of theory development	X		X
4. Unsequenced Sequence of chapters interchangeable		X	

Figure 12.7 Typology of case study designs. Adapted from Robert K. Yin, *Case Study Research: Design and Methods* (Thousand Oaks, CA: Sage, 1994), 138. (Yin includes two other types not commonly employed in architectural research.) Courtesy of Robert K. Yin and SAGE Publications.

Using Yin's typology, we can classify Jacobs's study as a theory-building study that has both exploratory and explanatory purposes. The exploratory nature of her investigation is reflected in the following sentiment, quoted earlier in greater length: "The way to get at what goes on in the . . . behavior of cities is, I think, to look closely . . . and attempt to see what they mean and whether any threads of principle emerge among them."[5] But Jacobs also clearly intends to do more than just find out; she also wants "to *explain* [emphasis ours] the underlying order of cities."[6] To this end, she identifies what she calls the most "ubiquitous principle" right off the bat in her introduction: "[T]he need of cities for a most intricate and close-grained diversity of uses that give each other constant mutual support, both economically and socially."[7] This combination of exploratory and explanatory goals is clearly articulated in the four-part structure of her book. In Part One, the exploratory component is represented in her observations on the nature of cities. In Part Two, Jacobs lays out the heart of her explanatory argument by identifying four key conditions for city diversity. Finally, the next two sections discuss the implications of the diversity principle for the regeneration of cities, including specific tactics for achieving such regeneration.

Similarly, Lara's study of Brazilian Modernism is driven primarily by an explanatory purpose. His basic research questions are these: Why and how was Modernism so much more enthusiastically embraced by the Brazilian middle class than it was in the United States and most of Europe? Secondarily, Lara's research also reveals both exploratory and descriptive purposes. With respect to the former, he seeks to explore the complex dynamics of Modernism's infusion into Brazilian culture through multiple—and previously unexamined—materials, including archives, documentation of the physical artifacts, and oral histories. With respect to the latter, Lara's exhaustive mapping of Modernist houses in two multiblock neighborhoods of Belo Horizonte is a descriptive feat of major proportions. In the light of Yin's typology, Lara's study clearly represents the *linear-analytic* type of case study, a structure that follows the traditional outline for an academic research study: identification of a research question, literature review, methods, findings, discussion, and conclusions (see Figure 12.7). Not only does this organizing structure accommodate Lara's multiple purposes, but it is also the most conventionally suitable for a scholarly book.

12.2.3   *The Role of Theory Development*

Despite the relatively open-ended and broad qualities of the case study focus, described in the previous section, Yin recommends that the case study research design

BOX 12.2

Case Study: The Public Design Process for the Seattle Public Library

The Seattle Public Library, designed by world-renowned architect Rem Koolhaas, is considered by many in the architectural and design communities to be one of the most notable built projects in recent years (see Figures 12.8 and 12.9). While most architectural critics and scholars have lavished considerable praise on the building's innovative design concept, Sharon Mattern's case study of the project focuses instead on the lengthy and complex process of public input over the years both preceding and during Koolhaas's role in the project.[a]

Figure 12.8 Exterior of Seattle Public Library by Rem Koolhaas. Photograph courtesy of David Wang.

---

[a] Sharon Mattern, "Just How Public Is the Seattle Public Library?" *Journal of Architectural Education* 57(1) (2003): 5–18.

(Continued)

Figure 12.9 Interior of Seattle Public Library atrium by Rem Koolhaas. Photograph courtesy of David Wang.

To illuminate the role that the various stakeholders played in the funding, planning, and debate on the project, Mattern relies on a broad array of source material, including public documents, memos, newspaper articles and opinion pieces, presentation materials, and personal interviews. On one level Mattern's article clearly follows the historical narrative of how the library administrators and the architect sought to engage the public throughout the process. Simultaneously, Mattern illuminates the frustration that arose among the key actors concerning the role they envisioned for themselves in the design process.

Mattern concludes that right from the start the public was given the impression that they would play a major role in the physical planning and design of the building by virtue of both their financial support (through their vote for funding) and the grassroots public meetings held by the city librarian. But, as Mattern argues: "[R]ight from the beginning of the process, the library and design team delimited the field of imaginable ideas and framed the discourse surrounding the project."

Mattern also extends her analysis beyond the confines of the project it-self, and the particular personalities involved, to suggest the implications for a broader understanding of engagement in the public realm: "The communications within and around a public design project serve not only in deliberating over the design itself but also in negotiating just how "public" a public space will be. . . . [A]rchitects are in the business of build-ing not only buildings, but also consensus—and, in the process, values, identities, and ideologies."

be guided by theoretical development. As he puts it: "[T]heory development as part of the [research] design phase is essential, whether the case study's purpose is to develop or to test theory. . . . The complete research design [should embody] a 'theory' of what is being studied."[8] He then goes on to explain that by *theory*, he does not mean a "grand" theory; rather, the goal is to have "a sufficient blueprint for your study"[9] that will suggest what data must be collected and what criteria should be used for analyzing it. Perhaps it is fair to say that the role of theory development Yin proposes has some equivalent to the notion of "hypothesis" in much postpositivist research.

In both Jacobs's and Lara's studies, the role of theory development in the research design is evident. As Jacobs reveals in her introduction:

[M]ost of the basic ideas in this book come from things I first noticed or was told in other cities. For example, my first inkling about the powerful effects of certain kinds of functional mixtures in the city came from Pittsburgh, my first speculations about street safety from Philadelphia and Baltimore, my first notions about the meanderings of downtown from Boston, my first clues to the unmaking of slums from Chicago.[10]

These observations from other similar cities prompted the theoretical propositions underpinning her case study research in New York, as she put it, "at my own front door."[11]

However, it was Lara's observations of *dissimilarity* between 1950s middle-class housing in Brazil and the United States that prompted the theory development underlying his case of Belo Horizonte. Thus, Lara's research design was guided by his intention to *explain how* and *why* popular acceptance of Modernism was so much more pervasive in Brazil than in more developed industrialized countries in Europe or in the United States.[12]

12.2.4   *Using Multiple Sources of Evidence*

Another key feature of the case study is its incorporation of multiple sources of evidence. Thus, while Jacobs, as a resident and participant observer of her Greenwich Village neighborhood, focuses her attention and analytical insights on the case of New York City, she also draws heavily and freely on her observations of other cities, as well as from commentaries of officials and community leaders in various cities.

Lara's case study is particularly notable for the range and variety of data sources, which included archives, oral history, and artifactual inventories, as well as formal and spatial analyses. To be specific, the archival work included (1) an examination of all issues of popular housing magazines from 1950 through 1959, which yielded hundreds of pages of articles about, and advertisements of, Modernist housing and building products; and (2) a review of 25 house plans filed with the Buildings Office of Belo Horizonte (see Figure 12.10). In addition, Lara conducted 21 interviews with family members, most often elderly widows, still living in their Modernist-inspired houses of the 1950s. These interviews were particularly

Figure 12.10   House plan diagrams. Courtesy of Fernando Lara.

important in uncovering the informal relationships and experiences that influenced the residents' choice of housing style. Third, Lara and his research team conducted a thorough artifactual survey of all houses within two multiblock neighborhoods to ascertain the proportion of Modernist-inspired housing. Finally, Lara analyzed: (1) a sample of houses in order to classify these houses along a continuum of traditional to Modernist, based on their use of specific facade design features; and (2) conducted both a visual and computer-based analysis of the spatial qualities of the floor plans (see Figures 12.11 and 12.12).[13]

12.2.5 *Generalizability to Theory*

Although a conventional criticism of case study research is that there is no basis for generalizing from one case to other cases, Yin contests this argument very vigorously. In effect, he argues that the premise of much correlational research—that one can

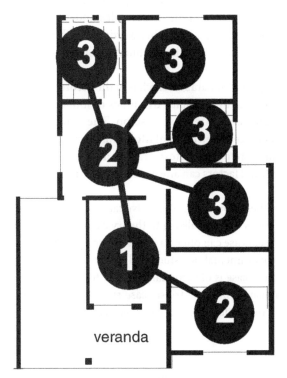

Figure 12.11 Depth analysis of a traditional house. Courtesy of Fernando Lara.

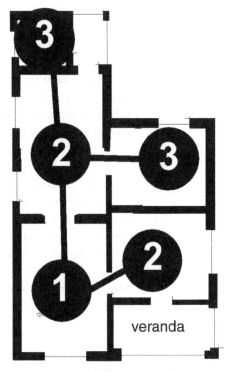

Figure 12.12 Depth analysis of a Modernist house. Courtesy of Fernando Lara.

only generalize from a representative sample to a larger population—is beside the point. Instead, he maintains, the case study's strength is its capacity to generalize to theory, much the way a single "experiment" can be generalized to theory, which can in turn be tested through other experiments. To substantiate his point about generalizability, Yin actually cites Jacobs's study. His insights are worth quoting in some detail:

> The book is based mostly on her experiences from New York City. However, the chapter topics, rather than reflecting the single experience of New York, cover broader theoretical issues in urban planning, such as the role of sidewalks, the role of neighborhood parks, the need for primary mixed uses, the need for small blocks, and the processes of slumming and unslumming. In the aggregate, these issues in fact represent the building of a theory of urban planning.

Jacobs's book created heated controversy in the planning profession. The result, in part, was that new empirical inquiries were made in other locales to examine one or another facet of her rich and provocative ideas. Her *theory*, in essence, became the vehicle for examining other cases, and the theory still stands as a significant contribution to the field of urban planning.[14] In other words, the influence and power of Jacobs's case study lies in the robust theory building she was able to achieve.

In a similar vein, the potential power of Lara's research is in the theoretical principles he is able to identify concerning the complex dynamics of modernization, political influence, indigenous architectural trends, and so on. The implication of his case study is not that the acceptance or rejection of Modernist architecture can be predicted and thereby generalized to other contexts; rather, its power will be to clarify how and why particular cultural factors can affect middle-class receptivity to architectural trends.

In contrast to Yin's stance on theory building, some advocates of the case study warn researchers that too great a focus on generalizing to theory can obscure the intrinsic value and uniqueness that each case can offer on its own terms.[15] Stake distinguishes between what he calls the instrumental case study and the intrinsic case study. For researchers using the former, the case is of secondary interest to the generalizations or theory that can be established. In the intrinsic case study, the research is "undertaken because one wants better understanding of this particular case."[16]

12.2.6   *Distinguishing the Case Study*

The case study, as we have described it here, is a distinct research design. Although the research literature may sometimes employ the term "qualitative case study," this does not mean that the case study research design is equivalent to or necessarily associated with the qualitative research design. Indeed, there is no necessity for qualitative research to adopt a case study design. And by the same token, case studies can be based almost exclusively on quantitative data (see section 12.3.2 in this chapter), or they may entail a theory-driven focus rather than the more inductively oriented approach frequently favored in much, though not all, qualitative research.

Similarly, the case study as a research design should also not be confused with case study *teaching*. True, both practices are defined by their focus on the case. But in the pedagogical context, the case materials can be deliberately altered to serve particular instructional purposes.[17] Such a practice is obviously antithetical to the principles and purposes of research. Nevertheless, case study research and case study teaching do both benefit from the compelling power of the robust and multifaceted character of the case focus.

12.3   STRATEGY: SINGLE OR MULTIPLE CASES?

Up to this point, we have focused on research examples of the single-case variety: urban vitality through the case of New York City, and popular Modernism through the case of Belo Horizonte, Brazil. Indeed, the single-case study can be highly compelling and—as with Jacobs's study—very influential. However, there are times when a researcher may want to consider a multiple-case design. On what basis does one make such a choice? And if one does choose a multiple-case design, how many cases are needed?

There is no quick and easy formula for making the choice *between* single- and multiple-case design, or about the *number* of cases necessary for a multiple-case design. But two principles are paramount, and both of them build on the special characteristics of the case study strategy identified in the previous chapter section: (1) the nature of the theoretical questions, or research questions, involved; and (2) the role of replication in testing or confirming the study's outcomes.

As single-case studies, both Jacobs's and Lara's work sought to investigate socio-physical phenomena involving multiple and highly complex factors. Each study dealt with issues from the scale of very broad cultural trends to the more intimate moments of sidewalk interaction and supervision of children (in Jacobs's case) or familial relationships represented in house plans (in Lara's study). From a theoretical point of view, it was more important for each of these researchers to uncover the very complex dynamics of one setting of interest than to limit the theoretical scope of the research by looking less deeply at more settings. From a practical point of view, the level of complexity involved also suggested the virtue of a single-case design.

In other instances, a researcher may frame a theoretical question that is relatively narrower in scope, and in which identifiable factors of importance may vary from one case to another. In these circumstances, the multiple-case design might be advantageous. This raises the question: How many cases are enough? Here the answer is essentially the same as with the single-case design: the power of generalizability comes from the concept of replication, rather than the concept of sampling. Yin explains this quite well:

> [T]he decision to undertake multiple-case studies cannot be taken lightly. Here, *a major insight is to consider multiple cases as one would consider multiple experiments*—that is, to follow a "replication" logic. This is far different from a mistaken analogy in the past, which incorrectly considered multiple cases to be similar to the multiple respondents in a survey (or to multiple subjects *within* an experiment)—that is, to follow a "sampling" design.[18] (Emphases the author's)

This quotation highlights not only Yin's insistence on the significance of the replication logic, but also another important principle, namely that every case should serve a specific purpose within the overall scope of inquiry. To clarify what he means by this, Yin describes the distinction between *literal* and *theoretical* replication. A *literal* replication is a case study (or studies) that tests precisely the same outcomes, principles, or predictions established by the initial case study. In contrast, a *theoretical* replication is a case study that produces contrasting results but for predictable reasons.[19]

For example, if in the future Lara seeks to replicate his findings of the popular acceptance of Modernism in Belo Horizonte, he might seek to do so by conducting both literal and theoretical replications. In general, any other Brazilian case would be subject to the broad sociocultural trends of modernization, political history, and economy. However, a literal replication would also include conditions similar to those found in Belo Horizonte, specifically the building of an iconic exemplar of Modernism in that city, with the enthusiastic support of the city's political leadership. Without comparable conditions, another Brazilian case study city would constitute a theoretical replication. Similarly, if Lara were to study the popular acceptance of Modernism in another developing country, but without the overt support of Modernism by the nation's president, this would also constitute a theoretical replication.

With these considerations in mind, we will now consider two examples of multiple-case study designs.

12.3.1   *A Multiple-Case Study: The Public Realm in College Towns*

The goal of Anirban Adhya's research was to explore the nature of the public realm in everyday urban experience, specifically in terms of how public places are physically manifested, how they are understood, and how they are actually used. In doing so, Adhya sought to go beyond the formulations of contemporary theories and practices of urban design that conceive of publicness as "an undifferentiated and universally accessible place."[20]

To investigate this issue, Adhya chose to focus on the public realm in college towns, in part because they represent a distinct urban condition that features many of the qualities to which other cities aspire. Yet college towns face many of the same challenges in sustaining a viable public realm in the face of economic downturns, privatization, and competition from exurban developments.

Within this broad conceptual framework, Adhya concluded that he would study a limited set of case study towns in order to compare and contrast potentially similar and different conditions among them. Since there are no hard and fast rules about the number of cases to select, each researcher must assess the degree of depth versus comparative breadth that best suits the research question(s) he or she has posed. In this instance, Adhya chose to select two smaller university towns with campuses developed initially in the 19th century, and two state capital cities with campuses developed primarily in the mid-20th century. The four towns are: Ann Arbor, Michigan; Athens, Georgia; Tallahassee, Florida; and Lansing, Michigan. As indicated in Figure 12.13, Adhya decided to combine a *literal* and *theoretical* replication design. Thus, in theory the Ann Arbor/Athens and Tallahassee/Lansing pairs represented two *literal* replication pairs; in addition, he was able to test the outcomes of each replication pair against a pair of *theoretical* replications.

Another important feature of Adhya's research design is the elaboration of his primary research question about the nature of everyday experience of the public realm into a set of three subquestions concerning the experience of physical form,

College Town Types

Small—19th-Century Development	Capital Cities—Mid-20th-Century Development
1. Ann Arbor, Michigan	1. Tallahassee, Florida
2. Athens, Georgia	2. Lansing, Michigan

Figure 12.13   Multiple-case study design by Anirban Adhya. Courtesy of Anirban Adhya.

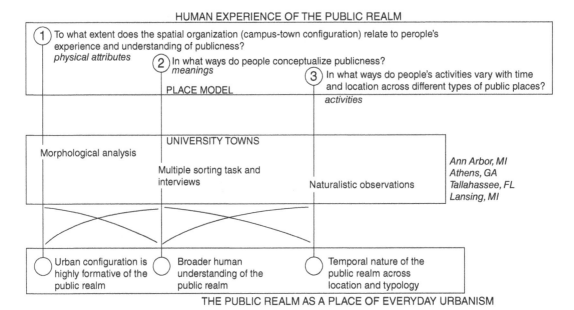

Figure 12.14   Research design for everyday experience of the public realm. Courtesy of Anirban Adhya.

qualities of meaning, and range of activities. For each of the three questions, he devised a distinctly appropriate tactic for data collection and analysis. This overall research design is represented in Figure 12.14.

In sum, this is an exceedingly robust study yielding many complementary and interrelated conclusions about the comparative experience of the public realm across the four cities. As it turns out, the initial categorization of the two literal and replication pairs was only partially confirmed. Although Ann Arbor and Athens are experienced in relatively similar ways (as are Tallahassee and Lansing), the four cities form more of a continuum of urban experience. This result was confirmed through multiple measures and analyses. Representative findings are presented in Figures 12.15 and 12.16.

12.3.2   *A Multiple Case Study: Life-Cycle Assessment (LCA) of Low-Rise Office Buildings*

Since one of the significant advantages of case study research is its capacity to investigate a setting or phenomenon embedded in its real-life context (see section 12.2.1), it is most commonly used in disciplines or specialty areas associated with

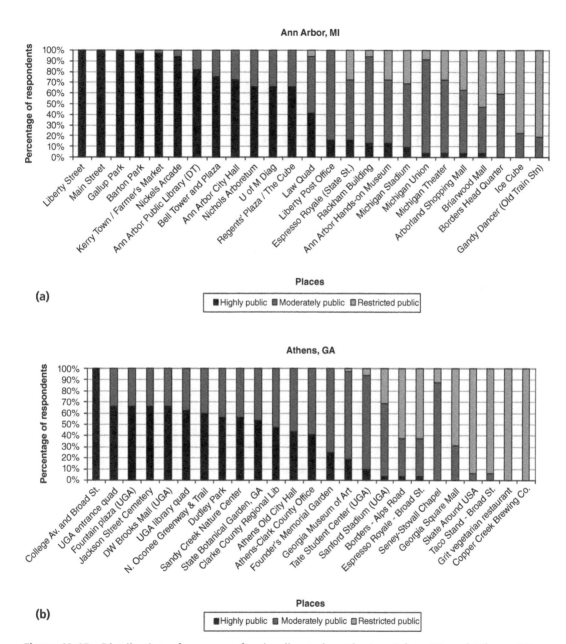

(a)

(b)

Figure 12.15 Distribution of responses for the directed sort in Ann Arbor, MI, and Athens, GA. Both Ann Arbor and to a lesser extent Athens have many places that are interpreted as highly or moderately public. Courtesy of Anirban Adhya.

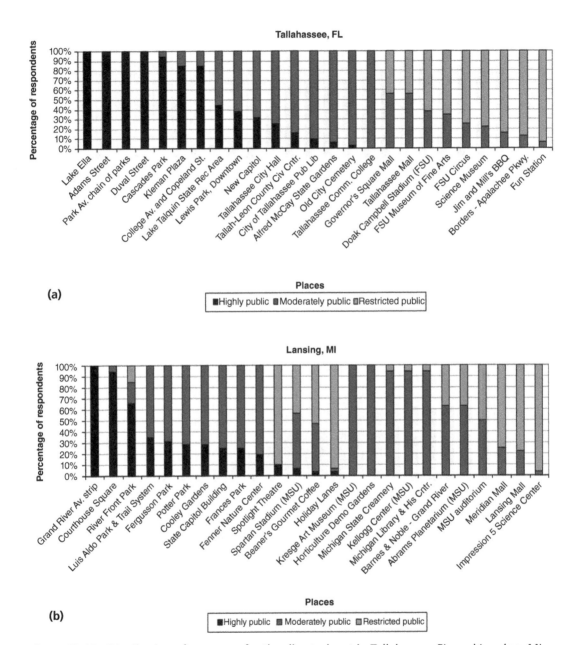

Figure 12.16 Distribution of responses for the directed sort in Tallahassee, FL, and Lansing, MI. Both Tallahassee and Lansing have relatively fewer places that are interpreted as highly public. Courtesy of Anirban Adhya.

sociocultural phenomena. And, although it is quite common for case study research to make use of both qualitative and quantitative data, it is relatively rare to find case studies that employ exclusively quantitative data.

Nevertheless, at least one relatively technical area of research that increasingly lends itself to case study research is that of sustainability. In this regard, Ashraf Ragheb's research using a life-cycle assessment (LCA) of low-rise office buildings suggests the potential for increased use of the case study strategy for more technical areas of environmental research. Ideally, LCA measures all inputs to a building and all outputs released to the environment.[21] Although earlier studies have employed LCA to assess individual buildings, they have tended to use fewer assessment criteria or limited life-cycle phases. Also, among the studies that have employed a more comprehensive focus, they have tended to apply LCA to residential buildings.

In this light, Ragheb's goal was to develop a fully comprehensive model that could be applied to the multiple case study of a set of commercial buildings. Ragheb chose three low-rise commercial office buildings as a set of literal replications. All three buildings share the following features: location in southeast Michigan, and therefore the same climatic conditions; relatively new construction, typical of a metropolitan suburban area; and low-rise configuration of one to four stories. In addition, for the purpose of actually accomplishing the research goal and measurement requirements, the owners and designers of each building were willing to participate in the study.

Because the range of LCA criteria were so comprehensive, it is beyond the context of this text to summarize the findings adequately. Although numerous comparative differences in impact were found among the three buildings, some overall generalizations could be derived. For example, the study found that the use phase of all buildings has the highest impact (over 90%) in the categories of energy consumption, global warming potential, and respiratory effects, whereas the manufacturing phase has the highest impact in the category of ozone depletion (87%).

BOX 12.3
Case Study: The Origins of Vancouverism

Robert Walsh's study of the emergence of "Vancouverism" critically examines the incremental process by which the distinctive urban architecture of Vancouver, British Columbia, developed through the combined contributions of several generations of local architects and planners. In

(Continued)

essence, Walsh's purpose was to answer the question: How did the development of urban form in Vancouver actually become "Vancouverism"?[a]

A term that first became popularized in 2004, "Vancouverism" is characterized by several critical features: separated residential point towers, a continuous street frontage of townhouses and low-rise buildings, a pedestrian streetscape with excellent street trees, a well-developed network of public waterfront parks, and a comprehensive system of protected natural views (see Figures 12.17 and 12.18). The net result is an environment in which a pedestrian-oriented planning ethos has been combined with moderately high development densities, producing a dynamic, commercially viable yet visually appealing urban environment.

Walsh's in-depth and multifaceted case study of Vancouverism draws on historical and archival material, interviews with key participants, extensive

Figure 12.17   Marina Crescent neighborhood at the Concord Pacific Place project, overlooking False Creek. Photograph by Robert Walsh.

---

[a] Robert Walsh, *The Origins of Vancouverism*. PhD dissertation, University of Michigan, Ann Arbor, MI, 2012.

Figure 12.18   Coal Harbor Mega Project, overlooking the Burrard Inlet and Vancouver Harbor. Photograph by Robert Walsh.

in situ observation, and detailed analysis of building designs and planning regulations. In particular, to illuminate the gradual evolution of Vancouver's urban architecture, Walsh undertook a critical assessment of many generally accepted but mistaken notions about how Vancouverism came to be, such as the popular misconception that it was recently imported from Asia. Although there has been a recent influx of immigration and capital from Asia that has helped to fuel the rapid development of Vancouver, the building forms themselves were not imported from Asia. In the process of unraveling the Asian import myth and other popular myths, a new picture began to emerge.

Indeed, Walsh discovered that the development of Vancouverism can be traced through the work of local architects and planners, struggling over an extended period of time to find solutions that made sense within the particular context of Vancouver. This context includes a combination of influential local factors: economic, climactic, geographic, cultural, political,

(Continued)

and historical. In choosing to focus on these local factors instead of relying upon established standard solutions, the planners and architects working in Vancouver gradually developed a different form of urbanism better adapted to the unique needs and conditions found in their city.

Perhaps the most significant outcome is that Walsh's research effectively challenges the widely held view that Vancouverism represents a general typology useful in other urban contexts. Instead, as a locally developed response to an exceptional context, Vancouverism should probably not be expected to work well elsewhere. Instead of continuing to copy Vancouverism in foreign cities, planners and designers might actually learn more from the example of Vancouver by appreciating more fully the importance of cultivating their own local urban ideals, and relying upon the local knowledge base. In this way the example of Vancouverism has the potential to point the way to a vast new range of unique local urbanisms each well suited to its setting, each relying upon local creativity, and each a reflection of local values of the community.

12.4   CASE STUDIES: STRENGTHS AND WEAKNESSES

Many of the strengths of the case study research design flow naturally from the defining characteristics already identified in section 12.2. To be specific, the first four items listed in Figure 12.19 directly mirror those earlier section headings. However, those acknowledged advantages also give rise to the potential for corresponding weaknesses. For instance, the embeddedness of the case study in its context can lead to such an expansion of scope that the study itself becomes unwieldy. And although the case study can uncover and explain causal links, this understanding of causality is likely to be more variegated and multifaceted than the attribution of causality to a "treatment" in an experimental design. Similarly, while the incorporation of multiple data sources can provide confirmation of findings across different data sources, establishing the coherence of the study as a whole becomes more challenging. Not least, although meeting the standard of generalizing to theory—rather than from sample to population—represents an important strength of the case study, confirmation of the theory still requires replication in other case studies.

Taken together, these strengths and weaknesses lead to the more general assessment listed under item 5 in Figure 12.19. Indeed, the depth, complexity, and multifaceted quality of the case study contribute to its robust capacity as a research design. Examples such as Jacobs's study of city life reinforce the point that a case

Strengths	Weaknesses
1. Focus on the embeddedness of the case in its context	1. Potential for overcomplication
2. Capacity to explain causal links	2. "Causality" likely to be multi-faceted and complex
3. Richness of multiple data sources	3. Challenge of integrating many data sources in coherent way
4. Ability to generalize to theory	4. Replication required in other cases
5. Compelling and convincing when done well	5. Difficult to do well; fewer established rules and procedures than other research designs

Figure 12.19   Case study strengths and weaknesses.

study, when done well, can be a particularly compelling form of research. However, there are fewer established rules and procedures for designing and conducting case study research. Almost by definition, the case study is conceived in terms of case-particular considerations, and great latitude is afforded the researcher in devising the overall research design and selecting a particular combination of tactics. This contrasts quite sharply with the much more prescribed components of the experimental strategy, or the measurement of clearly specified variables in correlation research. Although just "following procedures" in experimental or correlational designs by no means guarantees quality, it is even more true that the case study requires the researcher to carefully think through both the overall framework and the details of the research design.

12.5   COMBINED STRATEGIES: INTEGRATING MULTIPLE RESEARCH DESIGNS

Increasingly, researchers in many fields, including architecture, are advocating a more integrative approach to research whereby multiple methods from diverse traditions are incorporated in one study. Because each typical research strategy brings with it particular strengths and weaknesses (as we have noted in the previous chapters), many researchers believe that combining methods provides appropriate checks against the weak points in each, while simultaneously enabling the benefits to complement each other.

Indeed, over the past two decades, there has been an explosion of interest and active development of the mixed methods concept in a variety of disciplines. In an article in the newly initiated *Journal of Mixed Methods Research*, author Jennifer Greene argues that mixed methods advocates are particularly active in fields that involve "a dynamic interplay with creative practice in highly practical fields."[22] Greene and the founding editors of the journal identify a number of fields as active areas of mixed methods research, including architecture, educational psychology, nursing and health care, management, sustainability, anthropological demography, and development economics.[23] Although readers with design backgrounds might question the extent to which "creative practice" is embodied in some of these fields, Greene's argument is that each of these fields depends upon a dynamic relationship between "thinking/knowing and acting/doing."[24]

A potentially confusing aspect of the discussion, however, is that the many authors writing on mixed methods often do so at very different levels of the research process, such as specialty topic areas, paradigms, schools of thought, research design, or the level of tactics in data collection. For example, in discussing the apparent paradigmatic dichotomy in architectural research (framed as myth vs. science), Robinson[25] offers a number of examples of integrative research described primarily in terms of specialty areas. (See Chapter 3 for a detailed discussion of this article.) In particular, she describes Geoffrey Broadbent's work as combining design methods and human behavior;[26] Susan Ubbelohde's work as an integration of technology, history, and human behavior;[27] and Juan Paul Bonta's research as linking mathematics, art, and social science.[28]

More recently, some authors have claimed that the mixed methods perspective constitutes its own "paradigm." For example, Tashakkori and Teddlie (editors of the *Handbook of Mixed Methods*) argue that mixed methods research is best conceived under the rubric of pragmatism.[29] (In Chapter 3 we defined pragmatism not as a distinct system of inquiry, but as a school of thought.) However, even among authors who situate mixed methods within the framework of pragmatism, there is some disagreement as to whether to emphasize pragmatism as deeply rooted in the philosophical tradition of Dewey or as a more generically pragmatic sensibility. In contrast, educational psychologist Donna Mertens has situated mixed methods as more appropriately framed by the transformative-emancipatory tradition derived from critical theory—another tradition earlier identified as a school of thought in Chapter 3.[30]

Yet other authors have argued that, rather than conceiving mixed methods as a distinct paradigm or school of thought, it is more appropriate to recognize the diversity of paradigms *within* mixed methods. To that end, author Gitte Harrits analyzes two mixed methods studies: one in the field of comparative politics by E. S. Lieberman, in which the goal was to strengthen causal inference; the second, a study by French sociologist Pierre Bourdieu on the concept of "habitus" (defined as systematic patterns in actions and events), in which he employed survey data in combination with "interpretive analysis of texts, pictures, and interviews."[31] As a result of her in-depth analyses, Harrits identifies two distinct sets of underlying epistemological and ontological positions. Whereas Lieberman's study embodies a critical realist stance using both quantitative and qualitative data to confirm causal mechanisms within the "same" understanding of "reality," Bourdieu's study assumes that society is understood as both a "system" and a "lifeworld," thereby representing two realities that are necessarily not "translatable."

Despite the competing arguments about the predominance, or lack thereof, of a particular paradigm or school of thought within mixed methods research, most authors tend to describe the actual mixing of methods within a given study as a combination of quantitative and qualitative data techniques.[32] Indeed, over the past decade, many advocates of mixed methods research have developed complex typologies of research designs specifying options for sequencing QUAN and QUAL components of a research project. Readers of this book who choose to adopt a mixed methods approach will certainly benefit from clarifying how they might employ both quantitative and qualitative sources and analyses; we recommend the sources referenced above as useful guides.

Nevertheless, we would argue that emphasizing the level of tactics (quantitative or qualitative) in mixed methods research may obscure the broader issues of research design that may be central to the complex fields of architecture and design research. Given that environmental design research necessarily addresses the complicated dynamics of physical form/settings, purposive actions, and interpretations of meaning over time, many studies are likely to encompass a broader range of research designs than in other fields or disciplines. Indeed, the research design types presented in the previous six chapters of this book are testament to this range and diversity in our fields.

For this reason, we will focus the following discussion of mixed methods primarily at the level of strategy, or research design. For instance, how might a researcher go about combining the historical strategy with simulation, or the correlational with the qualitative? Although there are no quick formulas for developing a research design in the first place, much less a combined strategy, Creswell does offer three general models that are suitable for our consideration: (1) the two-phase approach; (2) the dominant–less dominant design; and (3) the mixed methodology design.[33] In the following chapter sections we will discuss each model in turn, along with appropriate examples of actual research studies.

12.5.1 *A Combined Strategy: A Two-Phase Design*

As the term itself suggests, a two-phase research design involves combining two or more strategies in a sequence of distinct phases. The advantage of such an approach is that the particular procedures and standards associated with each strategy can be presented fully and distinctly. A possible disadvantage is the potential for a perceived lack of connection or coherence if the strategies are not conceptually well linked.

One example that well represents the potential advantages of a two-phase mixed method design is Wall et al.'s study of commuting mode choice among staff and students at a university in England's midland region.[34] The research design was conceived by the authors such that phase 1 focused on respondents' intentions, while phase 2 focused on actual behavior; in that sense, the two phases were complementary. In phase 1, a quantitatively based survey questionnaire was employed; and based on the data analyses for phase 1, a purposive sample of participants (representing typological responses) was selected for in-depth interviews. For this second phase, the authors' goal was to enable participants to explain the various influences on their travel behavior in their own terms.

Overall, the authors found that although respondents' intentions for limiting car use were strongly influenced by personal-normative motives (phase 1 results), their actual behavior was significantly influenced by their perceived behavioral control, that is, the lack of practical options for avoiding the use of a car. On a policy level, this study led to the implementation of many environmental interventions that could lead to increasing perceived control over choice of travel mode.

In methodological terms, the authors conclude that since the study aimed to contribute to the development of theory (explaining how participants' mental constructs interacted), the mixed methods design demonstrated that the interview results were consistent with the statistical results of phase 1. Moreover, the authors note that the research design embodies the description of abductive reasoning "that moves back and forth between induction and deduction—first converting observations into theories and then assessing those theories through action." This, the authors claim, demonstrates the value of a research design that is both "theory-led and data-led."[35]

In contrast to the travel mode study, it is also possible to employ a two-phase research design without adopting an overall case study design. For example, Ahrentzen and Groat conducted an extensive study of the status and viewpoints of women faculty in architecture that utilized a correlational design as the first phase and a qualitative design for the second phase. In the first phase of the research,[36] the authors employed a survey questionnaire that was sent to all faculty women in architecture, as well as a shorter survey that was sent to architecture program chairs. Although the bulk of their report from this phase utilized descriptive statistics, they also highlighted the relationships between the faculty women's and the chairs' perceptions of women's status in their schools.

In the second phase of the research, Groat and Ahrentzen[37] adopted a qualitative research strategy. They made use of the faculty women's perceptions, especially their responses to two open-ended questions, as a basis for developing the interview protocol for in-depth phone interviews with approximately 40 faculty women respondents. In this phase, in contrast to the survey phase, there was no intention to achieve a random sample of respondents; rather, "the goal was to maximize the variety and range of perspectives."[38] As a consequence, the sample of respondents was more heavily weighted to tenured women, precisely the group of women who are more likely to exert some influence within the academy. The interviews themselves entailed three broad themes: attractions to architecture as a career, career experiences, and visions of architectural education. The outcome of this second phase was an analysis of the extent to which the faculty women's perspectives mirrored aspects of the recommendations of the Carnegie Foundation study of architectural education.[39]

12.5.2   *A Combined Strategy: A Dominant–Less Dominant Design*

As its name suggests, the dominant–less dominant design entails the insertion of one type of research design within the framework of a distinctly different research design. The advantage of this design is that it offers the potential of maintaining the overall coherence of the study as it is vested in the dominant research design. The less dominant design is then used to provide greater depth and/or validity concerning a particular aspect of the study. The consequent disadvantage is that the full and potentially complementary strengths of the less dominant design will not be fully realized.

A useful example of this dominant–less dominant design is Joongsub Kim's study of New Urbanism in Kentlands[40] and a comparable conventional suburban design, described in considerable detail in Chapter 8. Earlier, we characterized Kim's study as a causal comparative design, under the more general category of the correlational strategy. This indeed is the dominant strategy of the study. The primary means of data collection was a detailed survey questionnaire designed to elicit from residents of the two neighborhoods their perceived sense of community. The questionnaire asked the respondents to evaluate the extent to which they believed that various physical features affected their responses to four different indicators of community: sense of attachment, pedestrianism, social interaction, and sense of place identity. As is typical of the correlational strategy, various statistical calculations were used to assess the relationships among multifaceted variables measured in the study.

However, included in Kim's study is a secondary element: in-depth interviews with over 100 residents, which generally conform to a qualitative research strategy.

Kim had several reasons to incorporate such interviews as a less dominant component in his study. First, he wished to explore in a more open-ended fashion and in greater depth some of the themes from the survey questionnaire: for instance, narrative vignettes of the kind of social interactions they had with their neighbors, and how such interactions affected their sense of community. A second reason Kim chose to include the qualitative interviews is that he has no way to establish the comparability of the two different neighborhood groups (a weakness of his causal comparative design). Is the reason that Kentlands residents evaluate their sense of community more highly because the people who chose to move there are more community-minded in the first place? Through the interviews, Kim was able to establish that many—though not all—residents had moved to Kentlands without any particular intention about social interaction, pedestrianism, or community sensibilities, but once in residence their habits and inclinations had changed.[41] Thus, as a consequence of these interviews Kim was able to address directly a potential threat to the validity and interpretation of his study.

12.5.3   *A Combined Strategy: Mixed-Methodology Design*

The mixed-methodology design represents the most complete level of integration among two or more research designs. In this model, the researcher would conduct aspects of both strategies in roughly comparable sequences, and with approximately equal degrees of emphasis. The advantage of such an approach is that presumably the strengths of each research design will complement each other, while the weaknesses of each design will be substantially offset. However, the mixed methodology may well require a level of sophistication in multiple research designs that is not always common for people trained in a very specific research tradition. Moreover, some "purists" may find the combination of research designs too unconventional and therefore suspect.

A good example of a mixed-methodology design is Lara's study of popular Modernism in Brazil, a study we have already described in considerable detail as a case study.[42] In fact, it is clearly both, as we noted earlier in this chapter; because the case study strategy typically makes use of multiple sources of evidence, it may frequently entail the combination of not just data collection tactics but also distinct research designs. Indeed, in Lara's study the combination of historical and qualitative designs is virtually seamless (see Figure 12.20). Within the historical design, he has included extensive archival research on the portrayal of Modernism in popular media, archival documentation of Modernist house plans in the city offices of Belo Horizonte, an artifactual inventory of all the houses in two multiblock areas of the city, and a detailed stylistic analysis of each house facade within the neighborhood

Strategies	Tactics: Data Sources
Interpretive-Historical	Housing inventory of 2 neighborhoods Stylistic analysis of all houses Archival documentation of houses in city records Verbal / visual analyses of media representations
Qualitative	In-depth, open-ended interviews with original residents Configurational analyses of representative house plans Computer-based spatial analyses of house plans

Figure 12.20   Diagram of combined strategies of Fernando Lara.

inventories. Also note that Lara has, even within this historical strategy, incorporated not only verbal and visual data (e.g., the media analyses) but also more quantitative data (e.g., the housing inventories).

Second, Lara simultaneously interweaves a qualitative research design within his study. Included within this component are open-ended interviews with 21 original residents of popular Modernist homes in Belo Horizonte; and detailed spatial analyses of the house plans, linked with the residents' commentaries on the social dynamics of their family life. Just as Lara incorporates both quantitative and qualitative data and analyses in the historical component, he also incorporates both quantitative and qualitative elements in this segment of his study. For example, the floor plan analyses depend on quantitative measurements as well as social history provided by the residents; also, verbal, qualitative analyses of the floor plans are complemented by computer analyses of "spatial depth." In sum, Lara's deft and complementary use of two research strategies, as well as both quantitative and qualitative tactics within each, makes this study a very telling example of the mixed-methodology design.

12.6   COMBINED STRATEGIES: STRENGTHS AND WEAKNESSES

Figure 12.21 briefly summarizes the relative strengths and weaknesses of the three models of combined strategies that were presented in each of the separate chapter segments. Taken together, the chart suggests that while there is much to be gained by integrating different research designs, the researcher may also find that combining strategies requires a higher level of sophistication in research methodology than would be expected if he or she were to use a more conventional approach. It is still the case that in many academic disciplines, and certainly in architecture, particular research designs are often taken for granted as the preferred method for research in

Model of Combination	Strengths	Weaknesses
1. Two-phase	Each strategy can be presented fully and distinctly	Potential lack of connection and coherence
2. Dominant – less dominant	Potential for maintaining coherence through emphasis on dominant design Less dominant design can provide depth and validity	Complementary strengths of less dominant design not fully realized
3. Mixed methodology	Potential to maximize strengths and minimize weaknesses of each design	Need for level of sophistication in multiple research design Mixed methodology too unconventional for some purists

Figure 12.21 Strengths and weaknesses of combined strategies. Adapted from J. Creswell, *Research Design: Qualitative & Quantitative Approaches* (Thousand Oaks, CA: Sage, 1994), 177–178. Reprinted by permission of SAGE Publications.

particular topic areas. This means that many researchers have been exposed to and trained primarily in one or perhaps two research strategies; as a consequence, it may require considerable effort to go beyond and augment the preferred strategy with a suitably complementary strategy.

Even if the researcher is knowledgeable about multiple research strategies, there still remains the challenge of how to combine strategies in an effective and coherent way. To be specific, the two-phase design may put the overall coherence of the study at risk in the effort to highlight the distinctly different qualities of separate research strategies. However, the dominant–less dominant design tends to privilege the coherence of the study by placing the less dominant strategy in a secondary role, thus compromising the potential strengths of that less dominant strategy. Finally, the mixed-methodology model tends to present the greatest challenge for the researcher in reconciling and integrating two (or more) disparate strategies. Yet, if done well, it may yield the greatest payoff, as the complementary strengths of the combined strategies may be most fully realized.

Despite the assorted pitfalls and challenges, it is nevertheless our contention that combined strategies research represents an enormous opportunity for architectural research. By definition, architecture is a multidisciplinary professional field.

Yet, to date, much architectural research has continued to be conducted within the confines of subdisciplinary topic areas, such as environmental technology or architectural history.

Certainly, there will always be a valuable role for research efforts in these and other traditionally defined areas, but likewise there are many other important topic areas that defy easy categorization. Should research on environmental comfort or on energy conservation habits of building users be considered environmental technology research or behavioral research? If it is both, then shouldn't some combination of the research designs typically used in each research tradition be combined so as to investigate the phenomenon or setting in a more effective and multifaceted way?

Because there are, at this point, fewer established rules and procedures for designing combined research strategies, the researcher must exercise more care and build on a greater range of knowledge in research methodologies. But, despite this higher level of challenge, we believe that architectural research that combines strategies represents an important and necessary frontier in our field.

NOTES

1. Jane Jacobs, *The Life and Death of Great American Cities* (New York: Random House, 1961), 13, 23, 25–26.
2. Fernando Lara, *The Rise of Popular Modernist Architecture in Brazil* (Gainesville: University Press of Florida, 2008).
3. Robert K. Yin, *Case Study Research: Design and Methods*, 4th ed. (Thousand Oaks, CA: Sage, 2009), 18.
4. Ibid., 176.
5. Jacobs, 23.
6. Ibid., 25.
7. Ibid., 23–24.
8. Yin, 35–36.
9. Ibid., 36.
10. Jacobs, 25.
11. Ibid., 25.
12. Lara, 1–2.
13. Ibid.
14. Yin, 44.
15. Robert E. Stake, "Case Studies," in Norman Denzin and Yvonna Lincoln (eds.), *Strategies of Qualitative Inquiry* (Thousand Oaks, CA: Sage, 1998), 86–109.
16. Ibid., 88.
17. Yin, 14.

18. Ibid., 53–54.

19. Ibid., 54.

20. Anirban Adhya, *The Public Realm as a Place of Everyday Urbanism: Learning from Four College Towns.* PhD dissertation, University of Michigan, Ann Arbor, MI, 2008.

21. Ashraf Ragheb, *Towards Environmental Profiling for Office Buildings Using Life Cycle Assessment (LCA).* PhD dissertation, University of Michigan, Ann Arbor, MI, 2011.

22. Jennifer Greene, "Is Mixed Methods Social Inquiry a Distinctive Methodology?" *Journal of Mixed Methods Research* 2(1) (2008): 8.

23. Abbas Tashakkori and John W. Creswell, "Mixed Methodology across Disciplines," *Journal of Mixed Methods Research* 2(1) (2008): 5.

24. Greene, 8.

25. Julia Robinson, "Architectural Research: Incorporating Myth and Science," *Journal of Architectural Education* 44(1) (1990): 20–32.

26. Geoffrey Broadbent, *Design in Architecture* (Chichester, UK: John Wiley & Sons, 1973).

27. Susan Ubbelohde, "Oak Alley: The Heavy Mass Plantation House," *Eleventh Annual Passive Solar Conference Proceedings,* American Solar Energy Society, 1986.

28. Juan Paul Bonta, *Architecture and Its Interpretation: A Study of Expressive Systems in Architecture* (New York: Rizzoli, 1979).

29. Abbas Tashakkori and Charles Teddlie, "Major Issues and Controversies in the Use of Mixed Methods in the Social and Behavioral Sciences," in Abbas Tashakkori and Charles Teddlie (eds.), *The Handbook of Mixed Methods in Social & Behavioral Research* (Thousand Oaks, CA: Sage, 2003), 20.

30. Donna Mertens, "Mixed Methods and the Politics of Human Research: The Transformative-Emancipatory Perspective," in Abbas Tashakkori and Charles Teddlie (eds.), *The Handbook of Mixed Methods in Social & Behavioral Research* (Thousand Oaks, CA: Sage, 2003), 159.

31. Gitte Harrits, "More than Method? A Discussion of Paradigm Differences within Mixed Methods Research," *Journal of Mixed Methods Research* 5(2) (2011): 150–166; Evan Lieberman, "Nested Analysis as a Mixed-Method Strategy for Comparative Research," *American Political Science Review* 99(3) (2005): 435–452; Pierre Bourdieu, *Distinction: A Social Critique of the Judgement of Taste* (London: Routledge, 1984).

32. Abbas Tashakkori and Charles Teddlie (eds.), *The Handbook of Mixed Methods in Social & Behavioral Research* (Thousand Oaks, CA: Sage, 2003); John W. Creswell, *Research Design: Qualitative & Quantitative Approaches,* 3rd ed. (Thousand Oaks, CA: Sage, 2009); Charles Teddlie and Abbas Tashakkori, *Foundations of Mixed Methods Research: Integrating Quantitative and Qualitative Approaches in the Social and Behavioral Sciences* (Los Angeles: Sage, 2009).

33. Creswell, 206–207.

34. Rob Wall, Patrick Devine-Wright, and Greig Mill, "Interactions between Perceived Behavioral Control and Personal-Normative Motives: Qualitative and Quantitative Evidence from a Study of Commuting-Mode Choice," *Journal of Mixed Methods Research* 2(1) (2008): 64.

35. Ibid., 83.

36. Sherry Ahrentzen and Linda Groat, *Status of Faculty Women in Architecture Schools* (Washington, DC: Association of Collegiate Schools of Architecture, 1990); Sherry Ahrentzen and Linda Groat, "Rethinking Architectural Education: Patriarchal Conventions & Alternative Vision from the Perspectives of Women Faculty," *Journal of Architecture and Planning Research* 9(2) (1992): 95–111.

37. Linda Groat and Sherry Ahrentzen, "Voices for Change in Architectural Education: Seven Facets of Transformation from the Perspectives of Faculty Women," *Journal of Architectural Education*, 50(4) (1997): 271–285.

38. Ibid., 273.

39. Ernest Boyer and Lee Mitgang, *Building Community: A New Future for Architecture Education and Practice* (Princeton, NJ: Carnegie Foundation for the Advancement of Teaching, 1996).

40. Joongsub Kim, "Perceiving and Valuing Sense of Community in a New Urbanist Development: A Case Study of Kentlands," *Journal of Urban Design*, 12(2) (2007): 203–230.

41. Ibid.

42. Lara.

Author Index

Subject Index

Survey(s), 11, 13, 32, 69, 83, 192, 220, 223, 226, 244, 256, 266, 270, 279–283, 306, 310, 322, 330–331, 339, 345, 429, 432, 442, 444–446. *See also* Questionnaires
Systems of inquiry, 9–10, 14, 26–27, 63–99, 112, 141, 155, 242

T

Tactics, 10–11, 13, 15, 18–19, 23, 32, 37, 45, 66, 68, 71–75, 88, 97, 101, 112, 126, 141, 148, 160, 162–163, 168, 182, 424, 434, 441–443, 446–447
in correlational research, 278–309
in experimental research, 329–339
in historical research, 194–207
in logical argumentation, 393–410
in qualitative research, 243–257
in simulation research, 366–373
Theory:
applying theory, 123, 141
applied theory in consultancy work, 132–136
big/middle/small, 27, 41–43
design/polemical, 111, 116–122, 131, 136, 379, 384–385
in education, 136
explanatory, 111–114
extant theory informing building design, 128–131
literature, role in 143–151
meta-theory, 159
normative, 68, 92, 111, 115–120, 394
new theory from extant theory, 125, 128–131, 240, 385, 389

praxis, relation to 110, 115, 123, 125
social, 75, 110, 168
Triangulation, 81, 84, 86, 253, 374

U

Unit of assignment, 316–318
User(s), 29, 44, 48–49, 95, 105, 113–114, 123, 125, 133–136, 139, 159, 163, 216, 249–251, 258, 273, 279–280, 283, 285, 291, 295, 327–328, 339, 351, 354–355, 357–359, 449

V

Validity, 6, 52, 82, 125, 136, 201, 207, 242, 271, 446, 448. *See also* Quality standards
External, 81, 82, 393
Internal, 81
Variables:
dependent, 275, 304, 316, 327
independent, 275–276, 304, 316, 318, 321, 345
measurement, 316, 330, 339
treatment, 17, 269, 276, 316–319, 322–324, 327–333, 336–341, 345–347, 423, 440
Virtual reality, 351, 355–356, 375

W

Wayfinding, 110, 132–135, 140, 322
Window(s), 17, 82–83, 162, 167, 169, 202, 284, 324, 336, 363, 366, 388
Workplace, 60, 133, 140, 173–174, 216–219, 236–237, 242, 245, 257, 283, 421–422

ARCHITECTURAL
RESEARCH METHODS